English Drama of the Early Modern Period, 1890–1940

English Drama of the Early Modern Period, 1890–1940

Jean Chothia

Longman
London and New York

Longman Group Limited
Longman House, Burnt Mill,
Harlow, Essex CM20 2JE, England
and associated Companies throughout the world.

*Published in the United States of America
by Longman Publishing, New York.*

© Longman Group Limited 1996

First published 1996

ISBN 0 582 067383 CSD
ISBN 0 582 067391 PPR

British Library Cataloguing-in-Publication Data

A catalogue record for this book is
available from the British Library

Library of Congress Cataloging-in-Publication Data

Also available

Set by 20 in 10/11 Bembo
Produced by Longman Singapore Publishers (Pte) Ltd.
Printed in Singapore

Contents

Editors' Preface

The multi-volume Longman Literature in English Series provides students of literature with a critical introduction to the major genres in their historical and cultural context. Each volume gives a coherent account of a clearly defined area, and the series, when complete, will offer a practical and comprehensive guide to literature written in English from Anglo-Saxon times to the present. The aim of the series as a whole is to show that the most valuable and stimulating approach to literature is that based upon an awareness of the relations between literary forms and their historical context. Thus the areas covered by most of the separate volumes are defined by period and genre. Each volume offers new and informed ways of reading literary works, and provides guidance to further reading in an extensive reference section.

As well as studies on all periods of English and American literature, the series includes books on criticism and literary theory, and on the intellectual and cultural context. A comprehensive series of this kind must of course include other literatures written in English, and therefore a group of volumes deals with Irish and Scottish literature, and the literatures of India, Africa, the Caribbean, Australia and Canada. The forty-seven volumes of the series cover the following areas: Pre-Renaissance English Literature, English Poetry, English Drama, English Fiction, English Prose, Criticism and Literary Theory, Intellectual and Cultural Context, American Literature, Other Literatures in English.

David Carroll
Michael Wheeler

Author's Preface

What at first sight seemed somewhat barren, has proved to be a period rich in theatrical activity. The plays of Shaw, Synge and O'Casey have entered the international as well as the national repertoire. So has Wilde's *Importance of Being Ernest*. But the work of numerous other dramatists is of more than local interest. These include Pinero, Granville Barker, Elizabeth Robins, Githa Sowerby, Noel Coward and J. B. Priestley, as well as D. H. Lawrence, Henry James and T. S. Eliot in new guise. There are also areas of dramatic activity, notably in the suffrage and workers' theatre movements and the new broadcasting medium, radio, that have rarely got into histories of drama. Important in their own time, these also threw up a number of plays worthy of attention beyond the immediate historical context.

In the years between 1890 and the outbreak of the Second World War theatre consumed plays voraciously. They came and went in quick succession, the majority never finding their way into print. William Archer's claim that some hundred new plays were produced annually in the 1890s, may be an underestimate. The Lord Chancellor's Chief Examiner for Plays read 297 in 1890, 466 in 1900 and 604 in 1910. Many that were produced opened and closed within days, and six weeks was considered a decent run. Given this plethora of plays, any account of the drama of the period must necessarily be selective. The claims to attention of works which, self-evidently, have survived their time and still speak to audiences, are obvious. But what of the rest? How to establish the context in which the major dramatists wrote? And are there, perhaps, neglected masterpieces or, at least, still-viable and stimulating plays among the multitude of rarely performed or scarcely available works of fifty to a hundred years ago? These have been constant questions in my investigation of the wider out-reaches of dramatic writing.

A dogged trawl through the Examiner's records can unearth evidence to support almost any thesis. Slippage into idiosyncracy and special pleading occurs all too easily. In extending my discussion beyond the most obvious works, I have concentrated on those which informed subsequent dramatic writing, or seemed to reflect attitudes and conflicts of the time with notable clarity. Helpful indicators here have been unusually long runs or lively discussion in the press, whether approving or, as more often in this period, scandalised. My own judgement of a play's intrinsic value and stage-worthiness has also played its part. Numbers of dramatists whose work has consequently been skimped in my main text are included in the Author Biographies at the end of this book and these should be consulted for a fuller picture. I am conscious that many other minor figures might have been included even there. In deciding between one and another, I went for those who seemed to me to be the most interesting of their kind.

In the three big chronologically ordered chapters that make up Part One, I offer an overview of plays in the historical and theatrical context of the years between 1890 and 1940. In Part Two, I explore areas of particular interest that have emerged from study of drama and theatre in the period, and engage in close-reading of individual plays. The work of certain dramatists inevitably occurs in both Parts – each of them, however distinct, was also part of the theatrical and cultural scene – but detailed discussion of any particular play has been included only in that Part where it best seemed to fit. Dates throughout refer to first British production unless otherwise noted and quotations from plays are immediately followed by Act – and, where appropriate, scene – divisions.

Although a separate volume of this series will be concerned with Irish Literature, Irish dramatists contributed so much of what was vital to the British drama of the period that to omit them from discussion would have been perverse. At least until Independence was achieved in 1921, these writers are, anyway, legitimately included here. Although Sean O'Casey's plays were the first major works to emerge after Independence, he lived more than half his adult life in England, where all his later plays were first produced. He is simply too big a figure and too influential on subsequent British drama, to be ignored.

An account such as this necessarily draws on the efforts of numerous other scholars whose work is gratefully acknowledged in the Notes and Bibliographies. But I am indebted to many people for more direct assistance. My parents' searches of second-hand bookshops unearthed many now-neglected play-texts. Specific support, ideas and/or the loan of difficult-to-obtain texts, has come from my husband and from friends and colleagues including Penny Wilson, Wil Sanders, Tamsin Palmer, Andrew Kennedy, Margot Heinemann, Peter Holland, Eric Griffiths and Nicky Grene. The expertise and generosity with time and equipment of Tom Chothia, Olly Betts and the Matthewman family extended the life of my crumbling computer system to enable completion of the book. David Carroll has been a valuably meticulous and encouraging editor. My personal debt is greatest, as always, to Lucy, Tom and Cyrus Chothia.

Jean Chothia
Cambridge, 1995

Longman Literature in English Series
General Editors: David Carroll and Michael Wheeler
University of Lancaster

Acknowledgements

We are grateful to the following for permission to reproduce copyright material:

Faber & Faber Ltd for an extract from *The Aims of Poetic Drama* (1949) by T. S. Eliot (published by The Poet's Theatre Guild); Faber & Faber Ltd/ Harcourt Brace & Company for extracts from 'Poetry and Drama' from *Selected Prose of T. S. Eliot* edited with an introduction by Frank Kermode, Copyright © 1975 by Valerie Eliot, 'Choruses from "The Rock" ', from *Collected Poems 1909–1962* by T. S. Eliot, Copyright © 1936 by Harcourt Brace & Company, Copyright © 1964, 1963 by T. S. Eliot, and *Murder in the Cathedral* by T. S. Eliot, Copyright © 1935 by Harcourt Brace & Company and renewed 1963 by T. S. Eliot; Faber & Faber Ltd/Harvard University Press for an extract from *The Use of Poetry and the Use of Criticism* by T. S. Eliot, Copyright © 1933 by the President and Fellows of Harvard College, © 1961 by T. S. Eliot.

A version of Chapter 8 appeared in D. Margolies and M. Joannou, eds, *Heart of the Heartless World: Essays in Cultural Resistance in Memory of Margot Heinemann* (Pluto Press, London, 1995).

For Mary, Gil and James
and in memory of
Gordon

Chapter 1
Introduction

In 1890 George Moore, stirred by the French première of Ibsen's *Ghosts* at the Théâtre Libre in Paris, asked:

> Why have we not a Théâtre Libre? Surely there should be
> no difficulty in finding a thousand persons interested in art
> and letters willing to subscribe five pounds a year for twelve
> representations of twelve interesting plays? I think such a
> number of enthusiasts exists in London. The innumerable
> articles which appear in the daily, the weekly and monthly
> press on the London stage prove the existence of much vague
> discontent, and that this discontent will take definite shape
> sooner or later seems more than possible.[1]

The question could be asked repeatedly of the years from 1890 to 1940. Why have we not a Théâtre Libre? – an Ibsen, a Strindberg, a Chekhov, a Pirandello, a Lorca? Where is British theatrical naturalism, symbolism, expressionism, futurism to be found? What are the dramatic equivalents of the innovations in prose fiction of late James and Conrad, Lawrence and Joyce? Where the theatrical counterparts of the poetic modernism initiated by Ezra Pound and T. S. Eliot in the second decade of the new century? of the radical political commitment of 1930s poets and novelists? It is my purpose to address such questions in this book as well as to consider how it was that, in a period in which cinema came to replace theatre as the major popular form, the discontent did take such definite shape that the existence of drama as one of the lively arts, which had seemed lost in the nineteenth century, was reasserted.

The period was an astonishingly creative one in the history of Western drama. Although dominated by the plays of Ibsen, Strindberg and Chekhov, works by writers as distinct as Tolstoi, Hauptmann, Shaw, Synge, Brecht, Pirandello and O'Neill also joined the international repertoire. What such a list immediately makes apparent, however, is that in contrast with earlier golden ages – fifth-century Athens, Renaissance London, seventeenth-century Paris – this was an *inter*national resurgence. If the new movement began with Ibsen in Northern Europe, it did not remain localised in any one country. Plays, ideas and theatrical methods crossed national barriers: in some cases directly, in others in so modified a form as to be barely recognisable. The English drama, like other national dramas of the time, is a component of the scene – an idiosyncratic combination of influence, inspiration and insularity.

The availability and the style of the theatres in which plays are performed, as George Moore's plea implied, affect not just the reception but the very existence of the drama and, throughout this period, a close interconnection is evident between new writing and the existence of particular theatrical ventures. Notably, as numbers of writers, actors and directors laid claim to a drama of greater significance than the light entertainment that characterised current commercial theatre, the idea of avant-garde, independent, alternative theatre (the labels change but the organising principles remain remarkably similar through to the present day) was created and this, rather than commercial or mainstream theatre, became the source of serious new drama.

André Antoine's Théâtre Libre, founded in Paris in 1887, was the first of a succession of independent theatres which sprang up throughout Europe to provide an outlet for new writing that had been rejected as uncommercial or in some way morally offensive or that, as with work by Ibsen and Tolstoi, had fallen foul of censorship regulations. Small, initially amateur, operations underwritten by a subscription list of supporters, they acted as magnets to the literary and social avant-garde and, with an impact far beyond their modest means, provided the basis for the division into avant-garde and commercial theatre which has become common in the twentieth century. Shaftesbury Avenue, the Boulevard and Broadway, against whose values these independent theatres have been pitted, have tended eventually to absorb the method, ideas and even, often, the plays of the avant-garde. Mainstream practice has thus been altered by a process that might be thought of as permeation rather than revolution, even as a new avant-garde has begun experimenting with a different style and a new seriousness. It is hard to identify a single major dramatist of the period whose work did not first find an audience through one or another of the independent theatres, Tolstoi (Théâtre Libre); Hauptmann (Freie Bühne); Maeterlinck (Théâtre d'Oeuvre); Strindberg (Stockholm Intimate Theatre); Chekhov, Gorki (Moscow Art Theatre); Shaw (Independent Theatre, Court Theatre); Granville Barker (Court Theatre); Yeats, Synge and O'Casey (Abbey Theatre); O'Neill and Susan Glaspell (Provincetown Players) and Clifford Odets (Group Theatre).

Jacob Grein, who had witnessed Antoine's opening productions in Paris in 1887, asked in an article the year before George Moore's much publicised piece whether 'a British Théâtre Libre, a theatre free from the shackles of the censor, free from the fetters of convention, unhampered by financial consideration' was possible, and offered a practical answer when, in March 1891, he gave a closed house performance of Ibsen's *Ghosts* as the opening production of the Independent Theatre.[2] Shaw commented:

> Everything followed from that: the production of *Arms and the Man* by Miss Horniman and Florence Farr at the Avenue Theatre, Miss Horniman's establishment of repertory theatres in Dublin and Manchester, the Stage Society, H. Granville Barker's tentative matinées of *Candida* at the Court Theatre, the full-blown management of Vedrenne and Barker, Edy Craig's Pioneers, and the final relegation of the nineteenth-century London theatre to the dustbin by Barrie.[3]

But the truth is that in England, by comparison with most of the rest of Europe, these things took a considerable time to follow for reasons rooted in late nineteenth-century British culture.

Public life was notably conservative and paternalistic. The daily press assumed the role of guardian of public morality. *The Times*, which denounced the Théâtre Libre as 'the happy hunting ground of the ultra realistic or *fin de siècle* dramatist who specially affects the horrible and revolting' (5.2.1889). did not protest when Tolstoi's *Power of Darkness*, the work that had put Antoine's venture on to the international map and the play into the international avant-garde repertoire, was forbidden performance in London. Whereas the French critics had attacked *Ghosts* as morbid or even tedious, much of the English press, led by Clement Scott's notorious denunciation of the play as 'a dirty act done publicly,'[4] registered deep offence and moral shock on behalf of their readers and engaged in debate about what was and was not fit for the *public* stage.

Various commentators have noted the provincialism and insularity of English culture in the 1890s. According to one of the most acute, Samuel Hynes:

> What England was splendidly isolated *from* was the great intellectual ferment on the continent. In Europe those were the years [1870s–90s] of the new realism in French fiction, of the great Russian novels, of Ibsen, of French Symbolism and Impressionism – the years when the foundations of twentieth-century art and thought were laid. In England they were the years of the laureateship of Tennyson, who wrote of the 'poisonous honey spread from France' and 'the thoughts of Zolaism'. In the last decade of Victoria's reign you couldn't buy a translation of *La Terre, The Idiot, The Possessed, The Brothers Karamazov* in London or see *Ghosts* or

> look at any French Impressionist picture in any public
> or private gallery.[5]

But numerous literary figures including Yeats, Synge and Wilde whose subsequent writing would be germane to the renewal of the English theatre, did visit the continent to taste the poisonous honey, while growing discontent with the social and political system in Britain is evinced in the successive foundation of such groups as the Fabian Society (1884), the Independent Labour Party (1893) and the National Union of Women's Suffrage Societies (1897). The plays of Ibsen, even more than the writings of Zola and the French Naturalists, seemed to speak to and for each of these groups and, despite the personal puritanism of such leading Fabians as Shaw and the Webbs, the attack on stage censorship figured strongly among their proposed social and political reforms.

The matter of Britain

The fifty years covered by this book coincide with the hesitant arrival of modernity to Britain in the form of more fully democratic government, recognition of the idea of female emancipation and, by the end of the period, a technologically based society which, it was believed, could and, as importantly, should improve the living standards of the whole society. Internationally, the period is punctuated and concluded by two horrific European wars and the establishment of totalitarian regimes in Germany and Russia which slaughtered millions of their own population in concentration camps in the name of ideologies. Positioned at the outer edge, Britain was both a part of and apart from the experience of the rest of Europe. Although not itself invaded, it nevertheless suffered terrible losses and millions of its citizens found themselves on alien territory for the first time. The British Empire, seemingly wholly secure in the 1890s, came under increasing pressure, while America and Russia slowly emerged as dominant world powers. The impression of British invincibility, dented by the Boer War (1899–1902), was further undermined by the Easter Rising in Dublin (1916) and the ceding of Irish Independence (1921). Its title to rule the colonies, source of raw materials and secure markets for manufactures, was increasingly questioned and, in India, the cornerstone of colonial power, horror at the 1919 Amritsar shootings helped establish Ghandhi's independence movement.

Change was already apparent in many spheres in late Edwardian Britain.

Received ideas were increasingly questioned. The great nineteenth-century debates about religion were over. Although church-going continued, it was in decline throughout the period and for many was more of a social than a spiritual activity. In philosophy there was a retreat from metaphysics into linguistic analysis. Ongoing urbanisation meant that by 1911, 80 per cent of the inhabitants of England and Wales lived in towns and the development of public transport, the underground railway and then the motor bus made populations within those towns much more mobile. Quasi-scientific social surveys in the last decade of the nineteenth century, beginning with Charles Booth's massive *Life and Labour of the People of London* (1891–1903) and successive investigations and occasional papers published by the Fabian Society, had exposed the extent of poverty in Britain and helped create a climate in which ideas of social justice could be discussed and changes in social organisation could at least be contemplated. Such anthropological works as Frazer's massive study of ritual and religions *The Golden Bough* (1890–1915), introduced a new sense of cultural relativism while the psychological sciences undermined clear-cut notions of good and evil in human behaviour. The writings of Freud and Jung directed attention, in ways that would be directly relevant to the stage, to biological instincts and the workings of the subconscious and to the tendency of these to reveal themselves in dreams, in slips of the tongue and in implications to be read into every-day talk.

Agitation had led to debate, to an Irish Home Rule Bill (1893), a Divorce Bill (1902), a Female Enfranchisement Bill (1907) and to Parliamentary Select Committees on Censorship (1892; 1909), a Royal Commission on Labour (1891) and on Divorce (1909), if not yet to changes in the law. The First World War, with its accompanying upheaval in the young male population, its need for a female labour force and its huge and horrifying slaughter and rumbling questioning of decisions made by government and military establishment, has rightly been taken as marking the watershed in a period in which old certainties were questioned.

In the immediate post-First World War period, there was an identifiable shift in the composition of the British ruling class. While the king, unlike the Kaiser, the Tsar and the Austro-Hungarian Emperor, had kept his throne, he had had to act to secure it in 1917 by changing his House's name to Windsor from Saxe-Coburg and Gotha in response to anti-German sentiment and by distancing himself from his friend and cousin, Tsar Nicholas, following the Bolshevik Revolution in Russia. The image George V presented of bourgeois rectitude, with none of Edward VII's inclination to high living and womanising, seemed appropriate to his time and, although he gave up none of his personal wealth, he notably summoned a commoner, Stanley Baldwin, to form the government in 1923 instead of the aristocrat, Lord Curzon. Indeed, although most Members of Parliament were still primarily drawn from the moneyed and privately educated classes, there were now very few titled figures in the Cabinet.

Although poverty was widespread among the working classes and working conditions were still terrible, for example in the mines, the idea that government should play its part in providing for its people and creating a more equitable distribution of wealth was acknowledged in Lloyd George's 'People's Budget' (1909). The London County Council had improved organisation of services in the capital since its foundation in 1888, and national expenditure on social services doubled between 1905, when the Liberals took office, and the outbreak of the First World War. That the working classes were increasingly politicised and unionised is demonstrated by the scale of its involvement in the 1926 General Strike and by the progress of the Labour Party which, while continuing to collaborate with them, replaced the middle-class Fabians as the major voice of the left; it also overtook the Liberal Party for the first time in the 1922 election and formed a minority government, albeit short-lived, following the 1924 and 1929 elections under the leadership of the Board School-educated Ramsay MacDonald. Responding to and feeding the need for intellectual stimulation, Penguin began publishing its sixpenny paperbacks in 1935 and, the following year, Victor Gollancz's Left Book Club began operating. The growing politicisation registered in some unexpected and some very direct ways in the theatre.

Investigations of sexuality by the likes of Edward Carpenter and Havelock Ellis in the 1890s, although much denounced – Ellis's *Studies in the Psychology of Sex* being suppressed shortly after publication in 1897 – fed a widening concern with issues of gender. If working people in the later nineteenth century were developing a more confident sense of self and of individual rights, so were women, strengthened by new educational possibilities and changes in property rights. Women began to write and speak out publicly, despite attacks on them as unfeminine 'platform women'. Voices declaring the right of unmarried girls to be treated as individuals and insisting on woman's duty to herself faced ridicule to pit themselves against a culture that promoted female self-effacement and self-sacrifice as an ideal.[6] And, just as working-class demands found a voice through Trade Unionism and the Labour Party, so demands for female emancipation found a focus in the suffrage movement.

Various disparate groups having united in 1897, the movement developed teeth with the founding of the more fiercely activist Women's Social and Political Union (1903) led by Emmeline Pankhurst. The Women Writers' Suffrage League and the Actresses' Franchise League, founded in 1908, played a leading role in promoting arguments for electoral reform through their productions at meetings, in theatres hired for the occasion and under the auspices of such independent groups as Edy Craig's Pioneer Players which had a specifically feminist agenda. The scale of suffrage support was famously demonstrated in the seven-mile long Women's Coronation Procession to mark George V's accession (1911). The message of the suffragists having finally infiltrated, women with an age or property qualification gained the vote in 1918 and all women in 1928, although the number of women elected into parliament remained tiny.

Real changes in the situation of women, particularly middle-class women, did follow the agitation although they were vulnerable to vagaries of the economic situation. War work took many women out of the home and into relative independence for the first time during the First World War but many were obliged to cede their jobs to the returning forces at its end. Low-paid domestic service, shop and factory work continued to be the lot of working-class women but, particularly in the factories, pay and conditions improved somewhat. Opportunities for middle-class women in clerical and secretarial work were taken up to fill the time before marriage, but also as necessary support for the surplus of widows and spinsters created by the death or devastating injury in war of a generation of men. Single women with the persistence and the family background to reach higher education emerged as feature writers, civil servants, doctors or teachers, although the top jobs remained elusive and teachers, at least, in the years before the Second World War, were compelled to give up work on marriage. Women's work outside the home was directly affected by the 1929 stock market collapse but other advances were maintained, the single most significant one being the increasing availability of more effective birth control, through the pioneering work of Marie Stopes and others.

The impact of these changes and fracturings is registered very directly in the literature of the period. The major sources of significant writing proved to be America, Ireland or non-ascendancy Britain: exciting new work in fiction and poetry was overwhelmingly foreign, female or working-class in origin. If commercial interests made this less obviously the case in the theatre, the representation of working people on the stage changed markedly in the course of the period, and the dramatists whose work most evidently survives its time were predominantly Irish in origin. As for the role and representation of women in drama, I had intended to devote a single chapter to discussion of this but it quickly became apparent that discussion could not reasonably be partitioned in this way. The debate about women's rights, the extension of education and the divorce laws reverberated in the theatre where, throughout the period, the role and condition of women was the predominant subject of drama whatever the sex of the author. While none of the women dramatists of the period achieved the fame of Shaw, Galsworthy or Barker, the work of all three shows the shaping influence of works by Elizabeth Robins, Githa Sowerby and numerous suffrage plays which, neglected by theatre historians until very recently, were written by women.[7]

Two specific demands for change in the theatre, the assault on censorship and the campaign for a National Theatre and the subsidising of serious drama, already signalled in Grein's 1887 appeal for a theatre 'free from the shackles of the censor . . . unhampered by financial consideration', recurred throughout the period. Although not fully met until after the Second World War, the war of words they stimulated contributed to the cultural centrality theatre claimed and laid the foundations of later twentieth-century theatre.

The censorship question

Shaw's 1890 lecture on Ibsen, subsequently developed for publication as *The Quintessence of Ibsenism* (1891) is a satisfying starting point for a study of modern English drama but the period might equally be said to begin in 1886 with the refusal of a licence for a centenary production of Shelley's *The Cenci*. In 1889 a three-month jail sentence was imposed on Henry Vizetelly for his publication of English translations of French Naturalist novels and Antoine's production of Tolstoi's *Power of Darkness* was banned. In 1892 Oscar Wilde's *Salomé* and, in 1893, Bernard Shaw's second play, *Mrs Warren's Profession* were denied licences. Censorship, the institutional face of the insularity identified by Hynes, had consequences for the development of English theatre.

Recurrent acts of censorship in the twentieth century affected both drama and prose fiction but novels, of which Joyce's *Ulysses* and Lawrence's *Lady Chatterly's Lover* are notorious examples, completed in private, need only a bold, probably foreign, publisher and printer to gain a footing. Plays, on the other hand, need the whole rigmarole of producers, actors and performance spaces before they can be fully realised. Under the 1843 Theatres Act, a licence for public performance of a play had to be obtained before production from the Office of the Lord Chamberlain whose Chief Examiner of Plays determined which changes or prohibitions were necessary 'for the preservation of good manners or decorum or of the public peace'.[8] Any attempt to represent biblical or royal figures on stage and any use of the Scriptures was subject to an automatic ban. With the advent of new kinds of drama, in the late Victorian period, the formula was used to prevent the serious questioning or analysis of political, religious, historical and sexual matters.

The argument against stage censorship, pursued notably by Frank Harris, William Archer and George Bernard Shaw in the 1890s and by an increasing number of writers and critics thereafter, was that the ignorant and arbitrary judgements of the Examiner led to the suppression of work essential to the life and growth of the English theatre while trivial, vulgar writing was condoned as harmless. Incompetence and vulgarity are the charges Shaw levelled at the late Examiner, E. F. Smyth Pigott in his 1895 obituary:

> The late Mr Pigott is declared on all hands to have been the
> best reader of plays we have ever had; and yet he was a
> walking compendium of vulgar insular prejudice, who, after
> wallowing all his life in the cheapest theatrical sentiment
> (he was a confirmed playgoer), had at last brought himself
> to a pitch of incompetence . . . It is a frightful thing to see
> the greatest thinkers, poets, and authors of modern Europe
> – men like Ibsen, Wagner, Tolstoi, and the leaders of our own
> literature – delivered helpless into the vulgar hands of such
> a noodle as this aimiable old gentleman – this despised and
> incapable old official – most notoriously was.[9]

Shaw's opinion might well seem to be confirmed by the gross generalis-ation Pigott offered, in evidence to the 1892 Royal Commission on Censorship, that Ibsen's characters were 'all morally deranged'. Certainly, although only 103 of the 19,304 plays applying for licences between 1852 and 1912 were disallowed they, and particularly the thirty denied licences between 1895 and 1912, included a number of significant works which became *causes célèbres* and subsequently entered the international rep-ertory.[10]

But Shaw's recognition that those 'on all hands' had declared in favour of Pigott coupled with Wilde's observation that no leading actor had protested against the banning of his play,[11] acknowledge that the Examiner's role was widely approved; an approval endorsed by the Royal Commission's conclusion that censorship, having worked satisfactorily, should continue in its present form. In appointing G. A. Redford, a bank manager, to succeed Pigott, the authorities signalled their determination to uphold middle-brow values in the theatre. Zola, whose own fiction had been heavily censored in Britain, recognising that the Examiner spoke for the received ideas of his class, observed that 'the English will not endure upon their stage any human study which is in the least degree serious. They turn everything to romance; they regard everything with a certain conventional propriety.'[12] And William Archer, too, ceded the point when he wrote of *Salomé*:

> Its suppression by the Censor was perfectly ridiculous and
> absolutely inevitable. The Censor is the official mouthpiece

of Philistinism, and Philistinism would doubtless have been
outraged had *Salomé* been represented on the stage. There
is not a word in it which can reasonably give pain to the
most sensitive Christian; but Philistinism has not yet got
rid of the superstition that art is profane, especially the art
of acting, and that even to name certain names – and much
more to present certain persons – in the theatre, is necessarily
to desecrate them.[13]

The battle was fought fiercely on both sides. When the Shelley Society
circumvented the ban on *The Cenci* by leasing the Grand Theatre for a
private performance, the Chamberlain's Office countered by demanding
the inclusion of a clause forbidding future private productions of unlicenced plays as a condition of renewal of the Grand's licence. Following
the furore over *Ghosts*, the Independent Theatre's plans for a production
of *Thérèse Racquin*, were similarly quashed, leading the *Saturday Review* to
report that the Chamberlain:

has simply let it be known that, if unauthorized plays were
produced in any theatre over which he had control, it was
exceedingly probable that when the lessee came for renewal
of the licence the request would not be granted and the
Independent Theatre Society had consequently to provide a
programme of a sort very different indeed from that which
it must be assumed, from the precedent of *Ghosts*, it was
intended to purvey.[14]

The use of the word 'purvey', made the paper's own attitude clear. After
the turn of the century, however, public opinion spurred no doubt by the
agitation of Shaw and his colleagues, began to move ahead of the censorship.

The Stage Society, more resilient than its 1890s counterparts, gave
closed-house performances of such unlicenced plays as Shaw's *Mrs Warren's
Profession* (1901), *The Power of Darkness* (1904), Brieux' *Maternity* (1906)
and Barker's *Waste* (1907). The fact that venues could now be found, even
if with difficulty, suggests some movement in public feeling, as does the
response of *The Times* to a letter of protest against the banning of Maeterlinck's *Monna Vanna* (30.6.1903). Echoing the arguments of the 1890s
avant-garde, the newspaper commented on the absurdity of Redford's
willingness to licence the 'gross indecency' of *The Girl from Maxim's* when
'any tinge of literary merit seems at once to excite his worst suspicions'.
The letter was signed by Swinburne, Meredith and Hardy among others;
another, four years later (29.10.1907), included signatures of seventy-one
writers, again including Hardy and the other great living men of letters,

Henry James, W. B. Yeats and Joseph Conrad, as well as the new generation of dramatists. The following year, a deputation to meet the Home Secretary was led by J. M. Barrie.

Some acts of censorship, such as the banning of Gilbert and Sullivan's comic opera, *The Mikado*, during the visit of the Japanese Crown Prince Fushimi in 1907, caused widespread mirth. Shaw's suffragette farce, *Press Cuttings*, allowed to proceed on condition that the names Mr Balsquith and General Mitchener be altered, resulted in an explosion of derisive cheers at the first mention of 'Prime Minister Johnson'. Others assumed a more significant role. Shaw's deliberately provocative *The Shewing Up of Blanco Posnet*, refused a licence on the grounds of blasphemy, was produced in Dublin by the Abbey Company despite attempts to suppress it by Dublin Castle. The demonstration that the Chamberlain's remit did not extend to Ireland became an assertion of Irish independence as well as a gesture against censorship. As James Joyce recorded, 'all over Dublin they are talking about the clash between Bernard Shaw and the Viceroy . . . while Dubliners who care nothing for art but love an argument passionately, rubbed their hands with joy'.[15]

A second Commons Select Committee heard the case for and against theatrical censorship in 1909. Against the claims of the Lord Chamberlain's Office and the theatre managers, an astonishing collection of luminaries of the literary and dramatic worlds gave evidence for abolition. Shaw's 11,000 word deposition having been refused on grounds of excessive length, was published as the preface to *Blanco Posnet*. Barker, personally hurt by the banning of *Waste*, repeated the claim that frivolously indecent works were regularly allowed while serious plays were cut or banned altogether. A letter from Henry James read to the Committee noted the disparity between treatment of stage plays and other literary works arguing that the censorship had had the effect of relegating the theatre to a minor art form and expressing the astonishment writers accustomed to freedom in other genres felt at the 'ignoble dependency' of the drama.[16]

The recommendation of the Committee, swayed by the strong testimony on behalf of censorship by theatre managers, was that the Lord Chamberlain's Office should continue to licence but that it should be optional whether a manager applied for a licence for any given play or risk being sued for obscenity. In the event, no legislation of any sort followed the report although the Chamberlain did appoint a panel of readers to work with the Chief Examiner. The ferment that inevitably continued was further excited by the astonishingly ill-judged appointment as Examiner in 1911 (Redford having left to become the first Film Censor) of Charles Brookfield, a prolific author of bedroom farces and French adaptations, whose recent attack on contemporary drama in the name of theatre as light entertainment (*National Review*, November 1911) had directed attention to him.

Brookfield's current play, *Dear Old Charlie*, which centred on the escapades of a man who merrily seduced the wives of his friends, was exactly the kind of racy trivia whose easy passage so infuriated the opponents of censorship. A closed-house production of Laurence Housman's *Pains and Penalties*, banned for its representation of Queen Caroline's self-defence against George IV's charges of adultery, fortuitously provided the opportunity for a much reported interval meeting that delivered a spontaneous condemnation of the appointment and, shortly afterwards, the MP Robert Harcourt called in Parliament for the cancellation of Brookfield's appointment, 'in view of the character of the evidence given before the joint committee as to Mr Brookfield's own plays'.[17] The free matinées Granville Barker subsequently staged of Eden Phillpotts' banned play, *The Secret Woman* (February 1912), led to further press reports of the hordes of distinguished people who had attended in an expression, in Barker's words, 'of contempt for the Censorship such as makes it inconceivable that the author of the immoral play now permitted at the Prince of Wales's can dare to tamper any longer with the sincere work of healthy-minded playwrights'.[18]

Although Brookfield continued in office until his death in 1913, identifiable loosening of censorship restrictions did follow with an evident shift to accommodate perceived changes in what the public would accept and the next Chief Examiner, G. S. Street, a man genuinely interested in new dramatic writing, set about licensing previously contentious works, two of the first, in 1914, being *Ghosts* and *Monna Vanna*. New restrictions, unsurprisingly, came into force during the war in the name of national security, but in the immediate post-war years more famously withheld licences were granted, including for *Waste* (1920) and, following the general accolade for *Saint Joan, Mrs Warren's Profession* (1925). *Salomé* followed two years later. While restrictions were relaxed in some areas, however, there were still embargoes in others. A licence was finally granted for performance of *The Power of Darkness* some thirty-five years after the initial application, but performance of a new foreign work, Eugene O'Neill's *Desire Under the Elms*, that echoed the incest and child murder of Tolstoi's play, was forbidden (1925), which suggests that if the now classic status of the older works had reduced their capacity to threaten 'the public peace', new works could still seem dangerous.

Decisions still turned on individual judgements which now sometimes included those of the Chamberlain himself. If Shaw's frank speaking and Wilde's eroticism were tolerated, John van Druten's *Young Woodley* (written 1925), which concerns the infatuation of a public schoolboy with his housemaster's wife, was not – until the Chamberlain, Lord Cromer, saw and was impressed by the subscription performance at the Arts Theatre Club. Similarly, Noel Coward, whose lightness of touch had enabled him to introduce drug addiction and nymphomania into *The Vortex* (1924) and

unpunished female adultery into *Easy Virtue* (1926), was allowed to retain
the whole of the threatened Act II of *Private Lives* (1930), after reading the
act direct to Lord Cromer. But taboos remained. Homosexuality was
outside the limits of the new toleration as Coward discovered with his
Semi-monde which, written in 1926, was not produced until 1977. J. R.
Ackerley's *The Prisoners of War* (1925), set among English officers, whose
internment brings out innate homosexual feelings and, in one case,
obsession leading to mental collapse, was refused a licence after its closed-
house production at the Royal Court. Coward's *Design for Living* (written
1933), however, although delayed for six years, was eventually allowed
following its successful production in America, since the presence in it of
bi-sexuality, nowhere explicit in the dialogue, is merely open to recognition by those of the audience who choose to see it.

As with sex, so with politics. The pre-war *Waste* with its impugning
of the behaviour of Cabinet Ministers might no longer seem a threat to
the system, but sympathetic portrayal of revolutionary politics or Soviet
society, did. Hubert Griffith's *Red Sunday* (1929), a recreation of events
leading to the Russian Revolution, was a notable case in point. Just as
Salomé in its day had ostensibly been banned for its representation of
biblical characters, so Griffith's play was ostensibly forbidden because it
represented historical figures, including Tsar Nicholas, on stage. But Steven
Nicholson, in his investigation of a series of political bans in the inter-war
years, concluded that not only was Russian *émigré* influence brought to
bear in this instance, but that Lord Cromer 'appears to have been ready
to ban a play which caused concern to anyone he thought important'.
Certainly, the rule about historical personages was waived for Housman's
Victoria Regina which, after an initial delay and with the agreement of
Edward VIII, was performed in 1937 in celebration of the centenary
of Queen Victoria's accession.[19]

For all it had relaxed in some areas, then, stage censorship continued
to represent conservative ideas of public decorum against the will to expose
and analyse of the avant-garde. Only with the repeal of the Theatres Act
in 1968 was it abolished, some sixty-six years after the French authorities
had risked taking the same step.

Demands for a National Theatre

If France was something of a model for opponents of British stage censorship, there were also enviable foreign examples for those set on presenting

serious work in a theatre primarily governed by commercial interests and intent on long runs. Paris had two state-supported theatres, the Théâtre Français and the Odéon. The Comédie Française company and its school, the Conservatoire, had been subsidised since the days of Napoleon and, although no actual subsidy was granted to the Théâtre Libre, the Ministry of Beaux Arts did take out four subscriptions. As well as the state-supported Deutsches Theater, numerous German cities regarded support of their local theatre and opera companies as a civic responsibility. Reinhardt's subsidy was maintained throughout the First World War when he did some of his most powerful work and one of the first acts of the Irish Free State was the establishment of the Abbey Company as the Irish National Theatre with an annual subsidy.

Already in 1879 Matthew Arnold, inspired by the quality of the work he had seen during a Comédie Française tour to London, had argued the importance of cultural institutions to a nation's sense of itself, writing that the state 'does well to concern itself about an influence as important to national life and manners as the theatre' and suggesting Drury Lane as the base for a national company with 'a grant from your Science and Art department'. William Archer took up the campaign a decade later, publishing his 'Plea for an Endowed Theatre' which would produce the great dramatic classics and offer a stage to innovatory dramatists. Shaw declared theatre a responsibility of civilised government comparable with public libraries, museums and art galleries and, in 1902, pointing to the subsidised theatres of France and Germany, Archer argued that 'wherever the drama is regarded as a matter of public concern – national or local – it flourishes: wherever it is given over to private enterprise, it more or less obviously falls short of even the most modest ideal'.[20]

With Barker, Archer drew up detailed estimates for a National Theatre. Privately circulated in 1904, these were published in revised form as *A National Theatre: Schemes and Estimates* in 1907. They outlined a programme of thirty-four plays including classics and new work which would not have to sustain long runs but could be kept in repertory for a year, described the kind of building and size of company that would be needed, and estimated costs down to the prices of individual tickets. In 1900 William Poel petitioned the London County Council for support for a reconstructed Globe Theatre and a strong movement to establish a Shakespeare memorial developed, drawing a number of private donors. The various interested parties, including Beerbohm Tree and Pinero as well as Poel, Shaw and Barker and such scholars as A. C. Bradley and Gilbert Murray as well as Archer, came together as the 'Shakespeare Memorial National Theatre Committee'. Although the vote in Parliament in 1913 on a Private Member's Bill to grant state aid to the Memorial Theatre at Stratford was favourable, it was ruled out because there had not been a sufficient number of MPs present and voting, and, with the outbreak of the First World War, discussions were shelved.

The problems of funding serious and innovatory theatre were real. The Independent and New Century Theatres founded in the 1890s were short-lived. The Stage Society, founded in 1899 to mount productions of new plays shunned by the commercial theatre, staged single performances of plays on and off for forty years but, with scant financial resources and no theatre of its own, it could not consistently command strong or even completely competent acting and its productions were often skimpily set. The casting of Poel's ground-breaking Elizabethan Stage Society productions, although including on occasion the likes of Barker, Edith Evans, Robert Speaight, Lewis Casson, similarly depended on who was currently available and prepared to undertake, without prospect of financial return, the demanding rehearsal schedule as well as the eventual performance. Elizabeth Robins, one of the many who for a time committed herself to such activity, subsequently recalled the exacting conditions that eventually led to her own withdrawal:

> Each new play, given outside the established London
> management, meant a new attack and a fresh campaign. It
> meant canvassing the field for a new theatre (the same one
> was seldom available); it meant the delicate, vital business
> of choosing a new cast; it meant 'working in' one's views of
> stage management often with a new stage manager and (as
> part of the general responsibility) trying to arrive at business
> competence under circumstances where artistic
> competence and freedom to increase *that* should have been
> the sole concern.[21]

Independent companies, feeding on the energy and commitment of their members, thrived briefly before exhaustion or disillusion took its toll.

The Barker-Vedrenne seasons at the Court Theatre between 1903 and 1907 were distinct among avant-garde ventures in being fully professional and reasonably financially sound but, even here, this was effected by Shaw's renunciation of royalties. Much more common was a losing battle to make ends meet even where, against the odds, remarkable theatre was being achieved. Barker's own attempt to carry his venture to the West End, with a season at the Savoy backed by the American impresario Charles Frohman in 1909, was financially disastrous and had to be curtailed, the more adventurous works being cut in favour of extra revivals of *Trelawny of the 'Wells'*, which eventually made up one-third of the season. Some of the most renowned achievements of the time were the result of frantic persuasion, individual generosity and calculated risk-taking. Barker had only been able to demonstrate the power of Shaw's work in 1904 by negotiating support from J. H. Leigh for six matinée performances of *Candida* in return for an agreement to direct *Two Gentlemen of Verona*. His ground-breaking production of *A Midsummer Night's Dream* in 1914 was funded partly by a benefactor, Lord Lucas, who sold a pig farm to raise £5,000, and partly by money Barker raised through a successful production of an Arnold Bennett adaptation, *The Great Adventure*, at the Kingsway.

Between 1911 and 1914 Barker and Lillah McCarthy, along with such people as Lena Ashwell and Gertrude Kingston, engaged in a succession of short-term seasons at the Little Theatre, the Kingsway, the Savoy, St James's, working recurrently with the same actors and designers in a programme which, in its alternation of Shakespeare and Ancient Greek drama with modern works, amounted to an unfunded National Theatre experiment. Dennis Kennedy, whose detailed account leaves no doubt as to the wearing effect of the struggle on Barker, quotes him as explaining that he had decided, 'sometime before 1910 that it was futile to plough the sand i.e., in this connection, to make a production and then disperse it, the play to semi-oblivion, the actors to demoralisation'.[22]

In the inter-war period, the Old Vic was the Company which most nearly followed the aspirations of Archer and Barker in presenting the classic repertoire. On inheriting the lease and management in 1912, Lilian Bayliss had determined to turn this South Bank temperance hall into a people's theatre with high standards of plays and performances. By 1918 the Company was playing to packed houses and by 1926, under the direction of Robert Atkins, had staged all Shakespeare's plays at least once, as well as a classic repertoire that in the late 1920s and 1930s, under Harcourt Williams, included Shaw's pre-war writing and plays by Wycherley, Sheridan and Goldsmith. Bayliss brought in a succession of directors to run her seasons and after her death in 1937 Tyrone Guthrie took over as Administrator. The repertoire, acting and production standards, but also the deliberate low pricing and matinées for London schoolchildren, fulfilled something of the National Theatre function although new writing was not part of its schedule, and the inadequate payments that resulted from absence of a subsidy severely limited its ability to retain its actors. While all London's leading actors, including Lawrence Olivier, could boast of having spent at least one season at the Old Vic, few could afford to stay for long.

Barker's Frohman season at the Savoy had demonstrated the difficulties of attempting a commercially based repertory theatre. It was increasingly apparent that the sponsorship of wealthy patrons who believed passionately in theatre was no real solution either. The initial success of the Abbey Theatre depended on the financial underwriting of its activities by Annie Horniman who subsequently took on the funding of the Manchester Repertory Company. She eventually withdrew, much poorer and soured by the failure of the local community that claimed to value the theatre to provide reliable financial support. By 1934, Barry Jackson, having spent some £100,000 of his own money on the Birmingham Repertory Theatre, indicated that the period of private theatre patronage was ending. Already, in 1924, after miserable attendances at productions of Kaiser's *Gas*, he had demanded 4,000 season ticket guarantees before he would agree to continue his operation in Birmingham and in 1935, at his insistence, a Theatre Trust, with him at its head but with representation from the Corporation and the University, the Playgoers' Society and the Rotary Club, assumed responsibility for the theatre. As Shaw perceived, to make a theatre secure in the twentieth-century world, patrons, 'must finally do what Sir Barry has done in Birmingham: that is, hand over his theatre to a volunteer committee of citizens convinced of its public importance'.[23] When Maynard Keynes established the Arts Theatre in Cambridge it was with a comparable group of responsible trustees.

Barker continued the struggle from the study through his books *The Exemplary Theatre* (1922) and *A National Theatre* (1930), an updating of *Schemes and Estimates*, arguing now for two main houses and a third small, experimental theatre. A site for a National Theatre was acquired on the Cromwell Road in 1939 but further development was foiled by the outbreak of war. Activity began again after the Second World War: the Arts Council was established in 1945 and the push towards theatre subsidised by the rates came officially with the 1948 Local Government Act which allowed councils to level up to a 6d rate to be spent on entertainment. The same year, the National Theatre Act provided for up to a million pounds for equipment and a building on the South Bank site which had been provided by the London County Council in 1951, the foundation stone was laid but progress was again halted by the change in government. In 1961, the Royal Shakespeare Company was given state endowment for its work in London and Stratford-on-Avon and in 1964, a company performing under the National Theatre name was established at the Old Vic with Lawrence Olivier as its first Director. In 1969 work began on the South Bank site and the National Theatre building was finally completed in 1976.

The articles and agitation, the pamphlets and public debates no doubt did prepare the way, albeit mighty slowly. For all the excitement of the campaigns, the continually embattled situation was wearing for those closely involved. Although Shaw seems to have delighted in the fight, the frustrations of fighting for serious commitment to the arts and against censorship as well as the repeated shelving of his National Theatre scheme, clearly played their part in Granville Barker's exhausted withdrawal from practical theatre after 1914. The losses to British theatre, as the hopes and courage of enterprising theatre people were ground down in their struggle for the resources to develop new work and new theatrical styles, are not calculable.

Notes

1. *The Hawk* (17.6.1890).
2. *The Weekly Comedy* (30.11.1889). See, too, J. T. Grein, 'Again the Théâtre Libre', *Life* (31.5.1890) and, for a detailed discussion of the Théâtre Libre and its European impact, J. Chothia, *André Antoine* (Cambridge, 1991).
3. Introduction to J. T. Grein, *The World of Theatre* (1921), n.p.
4. *The Daily Telegraph* (14.3.91); cf. *The Daily Chronicle* and other newspapers for 14.3.1891.
5. S. Hynes, *The Edwardian Turn of Mind* (1968), pp. 307–8. For discussion of attacks on artistic innovation and foreign influences see, too, J. Stokes, *In the Nineties* (Hemel Hempstead, 1989), for example, p. 26.
6. See, for example, Mona Caird, 'Ideal Marriage', *Westminster Review*, 130 (1888); Blanche Crackanthorpe, 'The Revolt of the Daughters', *The Nineteenth Century* (January 1894); Sarah Grand, 'The New Aspect of the Woman Question', *North American Review* (May 1894); Alice Gordon, 'The After Careers of University Educated Women', *The Nineteenth Century*, 37 (1895).
7. See, for example, V. Gardner, ed., *Sketches from the Actresses' Franchise League* (Nottingham, 1985); J. Holledge, *Innocent Flowers* (1981); Sheila Stowell, *A Theatre of Their Own: Feminist Playwrights of the Suffrage Era* (Manchester, 1992).
8. Quoted, S. Nicholson, 'Censoring Revolution: the Lord Chamberlain and the Soviet Union', *New Theatre Quarterly*, 32, VIII (November 1992), pp. 305–12, p. 306.
9. Quoted, M. Holroyd, *Bernard Shaw, I: The Search for Love* (1988), p. 334. R. Gagnier quotes a letter from Pigott describing *Salomé* as 'written in French – half Biblical, half pornographic', *Idylls of the Marketplace* (Stanford, CA, 1986), p. 171.
10. Evidence quoted, A. Symons, *Plays, Acting and Music* (1909), pp. 145, 146. Figures from J. Woodfield *English Theatre in Transition, 1881–1914* (Beckenham, 1984), p. 112, which includes a full and enlightening discussion of stage censorship in the period.
11. Wilde's observation is noted by K. Worth, *Oscar Wilde* (1983), p. 52.
12. Quoted, Justin McCarthy 'Ibsen's *Ghosts*', Black and White (23.3.1891), p. 222.
13. W. Archer, 'Mr Wilde's New Play', *Black and White* (11.3.1893), p. 290.
14. 'The Independent Theatre', *The Saturday Review* (12.3.1892), p. 299.
15. Quoted, M. Holroyd, *Bernard Shaw, II: The Pursuit of Power* (1991), p. 229.
16. Letter to Galsworthy (August 1909), read to the Committee (12.8.1909).
17. Hansard (30.11.1911) quoted, Hynes, *Edwardian Turn of Mind*, p. 241 whose full account of the appointment and the report of the Parliamentary Committee is one of my principal sources of information about the censorship battles of Edwardian England.
18. *Daily Chronicle* (23.12.1912), quoted, D. Kennedy, *Granville Barker and the Dream of Theatre* (Cambridge, 1985), p. 97, an important source of information about Barker's battles against stage censorship.
19. Nicholson, 'Censoring Revolution', p. 311.
20. M. Arnold, 'The French Play in London', *The Nineteenth Century* (August 1879), p. 242–3; W. Archer, 'A Plea for an Endowed Theatre', *The Fortnightly Review* (May 1889), pp. 615–19; G. B. Shaw, *The Saturday Review* (21.3.1896), *Our Theatres in the Nineties: II* (1932), p. 81; W. Archer, 'The Case for National Theatres', *The Monthly Review* (July 1902), pp. 140–55, especially p. 144.
21. Elizabeth Robins, *Theatre and Friendship* (1932), pp. 188–9.

22. D. Kennedy, *Granville Barker*, p. 199; my account here relies heavily on Kennedy, an indispensable source of information about Barker and his funding struggles.
23. 25th Anniversary message to Birmingham Repertory Company (February 1938), quoted J. C. Trewin, *Birmingham Repertory Theatre, 1913–63* (1963), p. 118.

Part One

An Overview: Plays in Context

Chapter 2
English Theatre in the 1890s

In 1890 a clutch of actor-managers dominated the West End stage. Besides Henry Irving at the Lyceum, the doyen who was celebrated with honorary degrees and, in 1895, the first theatrical knighthood, they included John Hare at the Garrick, Charles Wyndham at the Criterion, George Alexander at the St James's and Beerbohm Tree, whose spectacular Shakespeare productions at the Haymarket continued with ever larger casts and more detailed visual illusionism into the next decade. Theatre and Music Hall were the dominant forms of public entertainment in the country and, as such, offered profits for shrewd businessmen. There were thirty-four theatres operating in central London and ten more in such inner suburbs as Ealing and Hammersmith, and some forty-four principal music halls which often included dramatic excerpts in their programmes. Five new central London houses were opened in the course of the decade, including D'Oyly Carte's Royal English Opera House (1890) on the newly laid out Shaftesbury Avenue, Her Majesty's (1897) and Wyndham's (1898), and twenty-three in such outlying areas as Camberwell, Brixton and Richmond, including, in 1894, the Theatre Royal, Stratford East.[1]

Where, earlier in the century, it had been common for star actors and their leading ladies to appear at provincial theatres supported by the local stock company, now, with the development of the railway network, touring of full cast productions became increasingly common. In 1879 there had been twelve touring companies. By 1901 there were 143, taking London shows for one-week stands to major cities throughout the provinces. Some 205 provincial towns and cities had theatres: Eccles had its Lyceum; Barrow its Royalty; Lowestoft its Marina. There were Theatres Royal famously in Bath and Bristol, but also in Bolton, York and Newcastle, a city which boasted seven other theatres. Manchester had eight theatres and Liverpool twelve.

Audiences included women as well as men; middle as well as working classes. While the rise of the music halls had led to some defection of the working class, the more genteel element had been drawn into the theatre by Charles Kean at the Princesses in the 1850s, whose respectability was reinforced when Queen Victoria watched productions of sentimental melodrama and archeologically accurate Shakespeare from the royal box, and by the Bancrofts in the 1860s and 1870s, with their meticulous productions of Tom Robertson comedies in realistic drawing-room settings at the Prince of Wales's. The growth of the middle-class audience, with more leisure and later dining habits, had been reflected in the introduction, in 1869, of matinée performances and the shift to 8.00pm from the usual 6.30pm starting time. The comfort and complacency of middle-class English theatre-going had led Henry James to label it in 1877 as a 'social luxury not an artistic necessity', its audience, 'well dressed, tranquil, motionless; it suggests domestic virtue and comfortable homes; it looks as if it has come to the play in its own carriage, after a dinner of beef and pudding'.[2] And in the 1890s fashionable society patronised the smartest theatres where, increasingly, they found their manners and style reflected.

Prices as well as programmes determined and were determined by the clientele. The two big popular theatres, the Surrey and the Britannia, the one holding 2,400 and the other 3,600, had a majority of low-priced seats, the stalls in each costing only a shilling. Although the gallery of the 3,540–seater Theatre Royal, Drury Lane, which aimed at a more mixed audience, also cost only pence, its stalls were ten shillings and sixpence each. Henry Irving's Lyceum, where gallery seats cost a shilling, boxes as much as five guineas and evening dress was *de rigeur* in the stalls, drew a comparably more genteel audience and could earn as much as Drury Lane with half its seating capacity.

Theatre was primarily escapist. Adaptation of popular novels and of French plays by Labiche, Sardou, Scribe and Augier was common. Melodrama, farce and musical extravaganza predominated, churned out by such writers as Robert Buchanen, Charles Brookfield, G. R. Sims and Arthur Shirley in endless succession, with an average run of four to six weeks although some closed within days and others managed a run of several months before disappearing, rather in the way of cinema films now. Plays tended to be racier and more sensational in the cheaper theatres, more intricately staged in the dearer ones which also offered spectacular Shakespeare revivals and, increasingly, social-problem melodrama. Although virginity was regularly threatened in melodrama and adultery hinted at in social comedy, serious representation of sexual exploitation or of desire was forbidden in a theatre that cherished respectability and espoused conventional morality, and the active censorship protected audiences from exposure to such dangerous areas as religion and politics.

In 1891, to document one representative year, the Surrey and the Britannia were mainly occupied with revivals of popular mid-century plays featuring sentiment (*Uncle Tom's Cabin* and *The Two Orphans*), comedy (Tom Taylor's *The Ticket of Leave Man*) and Shamrock Isle melodrama (Boucicault's *The Colleen Bawn*). The Novelty was staging an adaptation of that modern blockbuster of female sin and penitence, *East Lynne*, and another piece of Irishry: Boucicault's *The Shaughraun*. The Gaiety offered theatrical burlesques – caricatures – such as *Carmen Up to Data* and *Cinder Ellen*, while successive versions of its own particular brand of farce and melodrama ran at the Adelphi. At the revered Lyceum, Irving alternated Shakespeare (*Much Ado; As You Like It*) with revivals of well-known adaptations from the French, featuring highway robbery (*The Lyons Mail*) and aristocratic feuding (*The Corsican Brothers*) and much ingenious stage machinery. The Criterion's programme of revivals included popular classics (*Wild Oats, School for Scandal* and Tom Robertson's *David Garrick*), while Charles Wyndham, more attentive than Irving to contemporary writing, premièred Henry Arthur Jones' society play, *The Dancing Girl*, at the Haymarket.[3]

Pitted fiercely against all this, at the beginning of the year, was J. T. Grein's matinée production of *Ghosts* for his new Independent Theatre Company, modelled on Antoine's Théâtre Libre and financed, ironically enough, in part by the proceeds of his translation into Dutch of the popular melodrama, *Little Lord Fauntleroy*, and in part by £50 from the Royal Theatre of Amsterdam in appreciation of Grein's part in facilitating production there of the plays of Jones and Pinero. As a private theatre club, the Independent Theatre escaped the ban on public production of Ibsen's play, which was defiantly offered by Grein as 'a play that has literary and artistic rather than commercial value'.[4] The production created a furore of hostile and partisan excitement, generating some 500 newspaper articles: a response out of all proportion to its two rather amateurish matinée performances, but signalled in the 3,000 applications for the 657 seats.

Interest in Ibsen had been stimulated by translations which had begun to appear in the late 1870s, articles by Edmund Gosse and William Archer,[5] and the delivery and subsequent publication of George Bernard Shaw's Fabian lecture, *The Quintessence of Ibsenism* (1890; 1891). The name of Ibsen had gained notoriety through scandalised English press accounts of the Théâtre Libre production of *Ghosts* in Paris, and through the outrage and excitement stimulated by the Charles Charrington and Janet Achurch matinée production of *A Doll's House* in 1889 at the Novelty Theatre whose small but influential audience had included such individuals as Grein, Shaw, Wilde and Elizabeth Robins, all of whom would help shape the theatre of the 1890s.

That the Independent Theatre's production of *Ghosts* attracted commentary in editorials as well as in theatre columns demonstrated the extent of its reverberation and further fixed the battle lines of the Ibsenites and their denouncers. While *The Pall Mall Gazette* was favourable, the wide-circulation *Daily Telegraph*, in the outraged tone that would recur throughout the 1890s, led the attack with the claim that:

realism is one thing; but the nostrils of the audience must
not be visibly held before a play can be stamped as true to
nature. It is difficult to expose in decorous words the gross
and almost putrid indecorum of this play. (14.3.1891)

The play, moreover, was read by far more than had the opportunity to see
the production: Archer's 1892 edition of *Pillars of Society, Ghosts* and *Enemy
of the People*, for example, sold 14,000 copies over the next six years.[6] The
production of *Ghosts* was followed in April 1891 by Elizabeth Robins' production of *Hedda Gabler* and by revivals of *A Doll's House*. By the end of
the year, preparations were in hand for the Independent Theatre's production of Bernard Shaw's first play, *Widowers' Houses*. In the events of
this one year, at the opening of the decade, the struggles, varying values
and development of the theatre of the next fifty years is already suggested.

As the occurrence of *Carmen Up To Data* among the productions of
1891 indicates, theatrical events were often reflected in that popular Victorian form, the burlesque, which parodied other literary and theatrical works
in doggerel, far-fetched plotting, comic make-up and excruciating puns.
In this instance, it was the new opera, Bizet's *Carmen*, that was travestied,
but W. S. Gilbert's travesty of *Hamlet*, titled *Rosencrantz and Guildenstern*,
was also playing in 1891 and J. M. Barrie's first success, *Ibsen's Ghost, or
Toole Up To Date*, which opened at Toole's Theatre on the day *Hedda
Gabler* closed, in a set remarkably similar to the one Robins had used, ran
for thirty-seven performances. Barrie's convoluted plot, beginning with
the marriage, after Hedda's death, of Tesman and Thea, introduced themes
of emancipation and heredity with echoes of *Ghosts, The Wild Duck* and
A Doll's House as well as *Hedds Gabler* and figured, after a cry of 'Ghosts,
ghosts', the appearance of the actor-manager Toole, transformed with
Ibsen wig and glasses into a simulacrum of the writer.[7]

Despite the scores of new plays performed every year, Grein's Independent Theatre was essential because commercial managers were not adventurous in what they were prepared to stage. Actor-managers looked for
plays that offered them appropriate central roles because stars were what
the public came to see. While they and speculative backers would invest
in elaborate staging of productions that might repay them hugely, they
were reluctant to risk work without a pedigree. The ever-growing London
suburban class and the continually improving public transport systems to
bring it into the metropolis, enabled the long run to become a feature of
the early 1890s and managers looked to the profits that resulted. Toga
dramas of Christian persecution and miraculous conversion set in the
Roman Empire, such as *The Sign of the Cross* (1895) served just such a
purpose for Wilson Barrett; *The Only Way* (1899), an adaptation of *A Tale
of Two Cities*, for Martin Harvey, while Beerbohm Tree achieved huge
success as the mesmerist Svengali in George du Maurier's *Trilby* (1895).

Barrie's second play, *Walker, London* (1892) continued for a thousand performances with a second company at Toole's, while the original cast toured it to the provinces. One of the few farces of the period that is still regularly performed, Brandon Thomas's *Charley's Aunt* (1892), with its rigmarole of flirtation, misunderstanding and practical jokes among university students and its spectacular piece of comic cross-dressing in which a student transforms himself into a maiden aunt, produced at the Royalty in December 1892, was forced to transfer in January because of the pressure for seats. It ran for four years. Mrs Patrick Campbell, having found stardom in Pinero's *The Second Mrs Tanqueray* (1893) was then cast as the heroine of Henry Arthur Jones' *The Masqueraders* which became one of the long-running successes of 1894. Some theatres employed what were virtually house writers: the Adelphi had long runs with G. R. Sims' succession of formula melodramas; a new play by Jones could all but guarantee Charles Wyndham a full house and a writer such as Sidney Grundy, who had nine plays with runs of over a hundred performances, was demonstrably a safe bet.

By no means was every play successful. If profits promised, the cost of production meant losses threatened too. As Shaw pointed out, while a dramatist would be delighted to sell 20,000 copies of a play in two years, a manager would need to see 'some probability of from 50,000 to 75,000 people paying him an average five shillings a piece within three months' before he could risk production. Archer estimated that a run of fifty nights was needed to break even and that, between 1893 and 1897, there were 235 new plays of which sixty-five were successes, fifty-four doubtful and 116 failures. But the prospect of huge rewards for success encouraged writers to offer, and managers to accept, work with a very limited range. As Granville Barker would put it later, 'if you are looking for these plays, you get this sort of play written'.[8]

Although melodrama, farce and extravaganza which had dominated English theatre in the middle years of the century continued to be produced and plays by dramatists who had flourished earlier, such as Sims, Tom Taylor, F. C. Burnand and, indeed, W. S. Gilbert, were regularly revived, 1890s theatre developed its own emphases as the dominant figures of the previous twenty years faded. The prolific melodramatist, Dion Boucicault, had died in 1890 and, despite the success at the beginning of the decade of Gilbert and Sullivan's *The Gondoliers*, which ran from 1889 until well into 1891 and was Commanded for the first Windsor performance since the death of the Prince Consort, the heart had gone out of the collaboration whose comic operas had been a feature of the London theatre since the production of *Trial by Jury* in 1875. Neither *Utopia Limited* (1893) nor *The Grand Duke* (1896) caught the temper of the time. While what Archer labelled the 'jingle, frivolity and mild topical allusion'[9] of such extravaganzas as Adrian Ross's *GoBang* (1894) came to dominate the musical stage, Henry Arthur Jones and Arthur Wing Pinero emerged as the leading dramatists of the decade. Moving drawing-room plays up the social scale, they offered Society Drama with panache, much seriousness of purpose and extremely glamorous dresses. Sidney Grundy and other 1880s writers of light comedy were quick to adapt their material to the new interests.

In a period in which journalism flourished, theatre criticism played a vital role in shaping taste and raising expectations. Clement Scott, critic of the *Daily Telegraph* from 1871 to 1898 and, from 1879, also editor of the illustrated magazine *The Theatre*, was tremendously influential. As Shaw put it:

> Other men may have hurried from the theatre to the newspaper office to prepare, red hot, a notice of the night's performance for the morning's paper; but nobody did it before him with the knowledge that the notice was awaited by a vast body of readers conscious of his personality and anxious to hear his opinion, and that the editor must respect it, and the sub editor reserve space for it, as the most important feature of the paper.[10]

An admirer of Irving and deeply hostile to Ibsen and other advanced European imports, Scott cast himself as spokeman for the middle-class audience and champion of theatre as simple entertainment exemplified in such Adelphi melodramas as his own *Swordsman's Daughter* (1895) and such adaptations of Sardou as his *Diplomacy* (1894, from *Odette*). Critics who, by contrast, encouraged more avant-garde drama included Grein and A. B. Walkley as well as William Archer who, besides translating the plays, turned out hundreds of articles on dramatic topics, consistently arguing the importance of Ibsen. In a class of his own was George Bernard Shaw, initially a music critic, who succeeded Archer as theatre critic of the *Saturday Review* in 1895 but had already developed his credo of the drama in *The Quintessence of Ibsenism*. Shaw's lively, often penetrating and sometimes unjust, reviews have had a major role in shaping subsequent accounts of 1890s theatre, including this one. The sharpness of his insights and his intolerance of sentimentality and humbug changed the way a generation saw theatre. As he cheerfully acknowledged, his reviews were nothing less than a 'siege laid to the theatre of the XIXth Century' through which he accused his 'opponents of failure because they were not doing what [he] wanted, whereas they were often succeeding very brilliantly in doing what they themselves wanted'.[11]

Whereas Shaw waged war on the moral and structural conventionality of Society Drama, Archer and many of his contemporaries regarded Pinero as an important initiator of change in the theatre. In his *English Dramatists of Today* (1882), the first critical, as opposed to biographical or anecdotal, study of contemporary drama, Archer welcomed writing which seemed to bring a new attention to realistic representation and a more serious engagement with contemporary problems. This has created some confusion in terminology. Several commentators have registered the prevalence of the adjective 'new' in *fin de siècle* journalism. 'New Journalism' was found in *The New Review* and *The New Age* as well as in *The Pall Mall Gazette*. It labelled political and social reform movements, 'New Unionism', 'New Women', and was quick to name plays concerned with sexual aberration and threatened contravention of codes and rules the 'New Drama'. As Shaw put it in the preface to *Plays Unpleasant*, 'we called everything adanced "the New" at that time'.[12] But, whereas the plays of Antoine's avant-garde theatre set themselves fiercely, in form as well as content, against the *pièce bien faite*, the well-made play, the first wave of English 'new drama' shamelessly utilised the formula, with its pattern of exposition, complication, climax and revelatory denouement and its shaping tricks of mistaken identities, overhearings, mislaid letters, fortuitous entrances and coincidental meetings. Although some plays of this wave of 'New Drama' seemed to echo Ibsen in their posing of moral questions, they invariably included a *raisonneur* figure, a commentator who presented a comforting perspective on the action and prepared the way for the revelation of the truth in a climactic *scène à faire*, activity which led to the denouement. The morally reassuring conclusion of such works would be fiercely resisted by Shaw and the young turks of the next decade, whose new 'New Drama' supplanted the novelty Pinero and Jones had offered in their high-society problem plays.

Society Drama

The setting which gave Society Drama its name, was most frequently an upper-class drawing room, often varied with splendid ballroom or party scenes, thus providing the glamour expected of an evening at the theatre as did the costumes, hairstyles, jewellery and social *caché* of the, usually titled, characters. Wyndham had raised the stakes when, in 1889, he used Worth gowns and settings by Liberty for a revival of Tom Taylor's *Still Waters Run Deep*, and leading English fashion houses quickly saw the advantage of using close association with a particular theatre as a show case for their gowns.[13] The tension-raising musical chords of melodrama are replaced by the strains of dance music to accompany splendid ballroom scenes or by an on-stage piano, played by a heroine trained in the finer social arts. Besides the glamour, the frisson of excitement came from the introduction into this world of socially risqué characters and situations and of ingenious twists in the formula. Such plays purported to show society as it was, not to reform it. As Noel Coward would later put it:

> The characters in them were, as a general rule, wealthy, well-
> bred, articulate and motivated by the exigencies of the
> world to which they belonged. This world was snobbish,
> conventional, polite, and limited by its own codes and rules
> of behaviour, and it was contravention of these codes and
> rules – to our eyes so foolish and old fashioned – that
> supplied the dramatic content.[14]

The dramatists whose work has survived the fashion, Wilde and Shaw, like Coward after them, utilised their familiarity with such conventions for their own comic and subversive ends.

The codes, character types and class barriers contravened in Jones's *The Dancing Girl* (1891) are a simpler version of much that follows. Drusilla the Quaker girl, loved by the sturdy seaman, John Christison, is seduced by a cynical dandy, the Duke of Guisebury. Her ruin is made clear and public in a climactic scene in which she performs a fantastic dance for the entertainment of Guisebury at the very door of the meeting-house from which John, emerging, observes her. While John finds happiness with her pure sister, Faith, Drusilla drops from the play after abandoning the ruined Duke in Act III. As the Duke, saved from suicide by the intervention of his wise friend Sybil, reformed and turned to good deeds, marries Sybil, news comes of Drusilla's miserable death in poverty. Guisebury, like many of Jones's male characters, may have been weak and fallible but, whereas the erring woman is finally ostracised or dead, usually by suicide as here, redemptive possibilities exist for the man in the love of a good woman, although he loses much of his flippant wit in the course of redemption.

The obsessive topic of 1890s' theatre, feeding a seemingly insatiable demand, is the 'Woman Question' in its various forms: female transgression of society's moral code; the anomalies of the 'double standard'; women's attempts at self-definition and the threat their claims to education and emancipation posed to family, society and traditional perceptions of fixed gender roles. Recurrent plots concern the attempt of a 'fallen' woman, outcast by a shameful past, to 'get back' into her former social sphere or show a woman persuaded back from the abyss of contravening the code of female sexual purity. The very titles, Jones's *The Dancing Girl, Michael and his Lost Angel* (1896) and *Mrs Dane's Defence* (1900), Pinero's *The Second Mrs Tanqueray* (1893) and *The Notorious Mrs Ebbsmith* (1895), as well as Wilde's *Lady Windermere's Fan* (1892) and *A Woman of No Importance*

(1893), emphasise the fascination with figures who are in some way compromised.

Two European plays, Ibsen's *A Doll's House*, produced in London in 1889 and Dumas *fils' Lady of the Camellias*, toured by Eleanora Duse in her triumphant London debut in 1893, stimulated, fed and helped polarise this interest, their themes being variously resisted by and absorbed into the writing of English Society dramatists. While Ibsen was championed by the small body of socialists, feminists and others committed to a theatre of art rather than commerce, the Dumas *fils*, only now licensed for performance in London but well known through many adaptations and as the source of the opera, *La Traviata*, offered the glamour and sentiment that packed West End theatres. In addition, the excitement of the famous Italian actress displaying her genius in a role widely identified with the even more famous French actress, Sarah Bernhardt drew the crowds.

A Doll's House, shifting attention from matters of courtship and adultery to the problematic nature of the marriage relationship in a world in which women without independent means are essentially kept by men for the services they provide, directly challenged current gender and power relations and in doing so made a claim for the theatre as a place where important questions of self and society might be addressed. *The Lady of the Camellias* offered a splendid male fantasy, flattering those who wept for the admittedly fallen but remorseful and generous spirited woman who was prepared to sacrifice even the good opinion of the man she loved for the benefit of the man himself. Walkley's description recreates the virtuosity of Duse's performance:

> How infinitely touching her death scene. She creeps into her lover's arms, like a tired child and nestles there. With her back turned towards you, she lies quite still. You could hear a pin drop. Then slowly, slowly, one arm relaxes and falls. . . . There are not many dry eyes at the Lyric when Marguerite Gautier dies.[15]

It fell in exactly with and provided further impetus for Society Drama.

Arthur Wing Pinero

Pinero's move away from farces such as *The Magistrate* and *Dandy Dick*, with which he began his writing career, was confirmed by the huge excitement that met his 1893 social problem play, *The Second Mrs Tanqueray*. Opening three days after Duse's London debut in *The Lady of the Camellias*, the play gained international celebrity when Duse shortly afterwards took it and the role of Paula Tanqueray into her repertoire.

The Second Mrs Tanqueray was thought particularly advanced because the husband in it knew of his wife's past when he married her. Aubrey Tanqueray's bold decision to face the censure of the world is called into question by the reaction of his virginal daughter, Ellean, and his own perceived need to protect her from his wife's sophistication. Paula Tanqueray comes to realise that when sexual attraction has faded there will be nothing – precisely the argument which vanquished Marguerite Gautier. In the culminating *scène à faire* in which she recognises Ellean's fiancé as her own former lover, she realises she can never attain the place she craves in respectable society. Having cried remorsefully, 'Oh God, a few years ago!' in response to Aubrey's evocation of the pure innocent she herself once was, she says simply, 'I'm sorry, Aubrey' and goes to an off-stage suicide, leaving Ellean to penitent acknowledgement of her own failure of generosity.

A reviewer recorded that 'the shock caused by the realism of the subject might be described as electrical'. 'At last', wrote another, 'an English play has been produced which can be seriously saluted as a work of art', and, endorsing this view, Archer claimed that it satisfied 'the intelligence more completely than any other modern English play'. Forty years later he still looked back on it as 'a milestone on the path of progress'.[16] Henry James took Paula's suicide as a brave rejection of the conventional happy ending, describing it as 'momentous' and most commentators agreed with him. Walkley, like others who criticised the ending, nevertheless admired the general thrust of the play. His suggestion that rather than death, 'a life of dismal monotonous suffering for her own past would have been a more truly tragic expiation', assumes that the play is a tragedy and 'expiation' is necessary. Shaw, coiner of the term 'Pineroticism' as a riposte to *Punch*'s 'Ibsenity', more alert to the pattern, was one of the few to identify the extent to which the seemingly sad ending served to gratify the current moral code and to note how thoroughly conventional suicide was for a character who had erred and how fully Paula was made to participate in Society's view of her situation.[17]

Arthur Symons' account of the 'profound tragedy' Duse's acting brought to the role puts a finger on the specifically linguistic limitations of the play, since:

> frankly, the play cannot stand it. When this woman bows
> down under her fate in so terrible a spiritual loneliness,
> realising that we cannot fight against Fate, and that Fate is
> only the inevitable choice of our own natures, we wait for

the splendid words which shall render so great a situation;
and no splendid words come. The situation to the dramatist
has been only a dramatic situation.[18]

But it is important to register that, as the widespread claims to realism and
artistic achievement make clear, Pinero's play *seemed* new and significant
to most of its original audience; nothing less than an adaptation to the
English stage of Ibsen's exploration of female destiny.

The titillation and capitulation of Pinero's next play, *The Notorious Mrs
Ebbsmith* (1895), are even more striking and the structure of feeling of the
play more difficult to determine. Again, the play nods towards advanced
ideas. The position of the heroine, Agnes, a free-thinker living openly with
a married politician, Lucas Cleeve, in Venice, is allowed full expression in
the first act but her emancipated status is subverted by information that
her days as 'mad Agnes', the platform woman, are behind her and
that Lucas' dependence on her is grounded in her significantly womanly
selfless nursing of him.

The action turns on Agnes's eventual renunciation of her life with her
self-centred lover and of her own beliefs. At the climax of the second act,
having realised that Lucas's feeling for her is primarily physical, she seeks
to hold him by age-old feminine wiles, appearing not in her habitual plain
brown dress but in an erotically cut evening gown. At the climax of Act
III, having – momentarily Hedda-like – thrust a bible into the fire, she
immediately repents and – most unlike Hedda Gabler – burns herself in
saving it. Finally, although tempted by desire to retain Lucas by becoming
his covert mistress while his wife stands publicly by him, she renounces
both that humiliating role and her former free-thinking beliefs and retires
to live in rural seclusion with a modest friend and her parson brother.
Her capitulation 'broke the heart' of Stella (Mrs Patrick) Campbell, who
created this role too, and, as recent research has suggested, played against
the grain of the piece, undermining it with the implication that Agnes
was disgusted by the glamorous dress and those who admired her in it.[19]

Pinero's emancipated woman has more in common than might at first
appear with the stereotype mocked throughout the 1890s in conservative
journals, such as *Punch*. Reproduced on the comic stage, she was immediately recognisable, as in the cartoons, by her frumpish dress and unkempt
hair as well as her tendency to smoke and adopt other male mannerisms.
Sidney Grundy's play, *The New Woman*, produced the year before *The
Notorious Mrs Ebbsmith* is an altogether lighter piece which derides the
very idea of female emancipation, representing its exponents as squabbling
over whether women should be allowed to be as sinful as men or men be
made as virtuous as women. The elderly men-folk in the play seem to
be endorsed as they comment lasciviously on the young women's figures

and faces and, with heavy-footed humour, mock the aspirations to equality of the feminist circle and the books they possess:

COLONEL (reads):
   'Man the Betrayer' by Edith Bethune.
SYLVESTER:
   Oh I know her. She comes to our house.
COLONEL:
   And has a man betrayed her?
SYLVESTER:
   Never. Not likely to.
COLONEL:
   That's what's the matter perhaps – 'Naked and Unashamed – a Few Plain Facts and Figures'. Mary Bevan M.D. Who on earth's she?
SYLVESTER:
   One of the plain figures.

(Act I)

Discontented, disrupting the *status quo*, emancipated women are represented as neurotic or perverse. They are either frigid or possessed by voracious sexual appetite, sometimes, bizarrely, both. Like Hardy's Sue Bridehead, described in the Preface to *Jude the Obscure* (also 1895), as 'one of the intellectualised bundles of nerves', Agnes Ebbsmith is neurotic, her dubious sexuality evident in her horror of sexual passion and her proposal to Lucas that they live platonically. More crudely, Grundy's new woman, Mrs Sylvester, cold towards her husband, pretends to a relationship of the mind with the hero, Gerald, but in reality is set on sexual seduction. A minor character, Elaine, in Jones's *The Case of Rebellious Susan* (1894), '*a raw, assertive, modern young lady, with brusque and decided manner*', is challenged by the play's *raisonneur* who, representing the commonsense viewpoint, rehearses a famous question:

What is it that you ladies want? You are evidently dissatisfied with being a woman. You cannot wish to be anything so brutal and disgusting as a man and unfortunately there is no neuter sex in the human species. What do you want?'

(Act III)

Similarly, although Lucas is indicted for moral weakness, Pinero's play endorses him when to Agnes's cry, 'I believe to be a woman is to be mad', he replies, 'No, to be a woman trying not to be a woman, that is to be mad' (Act III).

These plays show indeterminate or sexually voracious freaks defeated by womanly women. Margery, in Grundy's play, having declared herself simply what God made her – a woman – tells her feminist rival, 'you have your books, your sciences, your brains. What have we? – nothing but our broken hearts' (Act III), and eventually wins the day through her self-abnegating devotion. More sympathetically conceived emancipated women, such as Agnes, discover their true – feminine – selves in the course of the action. Lucas cries joyfully, 'you really love me, you mean – as simple tender women are content to love' (Act V).

As with the women so with the men, challenges to the *status quo* are diffused by insinuation of sexual divergence. Although Jones's character declared 'there is no neuter sex', men who sympathised with the women's ideas were invariably portrayed as effeminate and, like the caricature aesthetes, Postlethwaite Maudle and Cimabue Browne in *Punch*, were given silly names to emphasise the point. Elaine's admirer, Fergusson Pybus, is effete, aesthetically dressed and with mincing speech. A hanger on in *The New Woman* is called Percy Pettigrew while the feminisation of Gerald is signalled visually in the opening stage direction. His room is '*somewhat effeminately decorated. The furniture of the boudoir type, several antimacassars and a profusion of photographs and flowers*' and his uncle says explicitly, 'these people are a sex of their own. They have invented a new gender. and to think my nephew's one of them' (Act I). Agnes Ebbsmith's lover is feminised in that he is described as 'a highly strung emotional creature'; Agnes 'can hear his nerves vibrating'.

Daring, within fixed limits, is the hallmark of Society Drama. The seeming sympathy with Agnes's emancipated stance in the opening scenes of the play made Pinero appear more advanced than his colleagues but, by the end of the play he is found to share their perspective. As Shaw pointed out, his plays reassured his audience 'whilst persuading them that such appreciation was only possible from persons of great culture and intellectual awareness' (16.1.1895).

Henry Arthur Jones

For all their similarity of subject matter, plays by Jones and by Pinero are tonally different. Pinero, who was a member of the Independent Theatre seems, at least on the surface, to allow more generous space to advanced ideas. Jones's plays, as Russell Jackson has observed, have 'an edge of scepticism';[20] his characters are more sketchily drawn, and as the need to conclude a play presses, problems and the fraught emotions associated with them evaporate. Jones's writing increasingly veers towards cynical comedy. Although his 1890s plays end with rocky marriages stabilised, they rarely suggest that marriage offers a simple happy ending, rather that for most it is a matter of compromise and self-interest. His male characters, several of whom are morally very dubious, form a freemasonry that tolerates male 'flirtation' and condemns female 'affairs'. Women often find themselves in disappointing marriages but, however bad their lot, by the end of the play, they have learnt to accommodate themselves to their situation, often using devious means to restore the *status quo*.

The *Masqueraders* (1894) which features the mercenary, loveless marriages of a particularly frivolous, effete aristocracy is a curiously muddled play although one which, according to Archer, worked its audiences up 'to a very high pitch of excitement'.[21] Dulcie is married to a complete bounder who drinks and, it is implied, beats her. Also an inveterate gambler, he pits his wife and child against the fortune of David, his wife's admirer, and loses. The planned elopement of the lovers is prevented by a familiar trope, the melodramatic appeal in the name of motherhood made by Dulcie's sister to the lover to 'keep her pure for her child':

> Save her to be a good mother to that little helpless
> creature she had brought into the world, so that when
> her girl grows up and she has to guide her, she'll not
> have to say to her child: 'You can give yourself to this
> man, and if you don't like him you can give yourself to
> another, and to another, and so on. It doesn't matter. It
> was what I did.'

> (Act IV)

But as he leaves, having renounced Dulcie, David gives her his mother's wedding ring saying, 'with this ring I thee wed. As she that bore me was pure, so I leave you pure, dear. Kiss me once – I've held you sacred': an odd renunciation that claims both marriage and purity on the equivocal grounds that they have not in fact slept together.

The implication of *The Case of Rebellious Susan* (1894) is that the sin resides less in the doing than in the being found out. The material for a fierce parody of Society Drama is here but, as developed by Jones, is dissipated. The heroine, furious at the discovery of her husband's philandering, although warned by the play's *raisonneur* that, 'what is sauce for the goose, will never be sauce for the gander', and advised by one woman friend to nag for a fortnight and then forget it and by another to be 'mutely reproachful' and wear her prettiest frocks, nevertheless does assert herself and, at the end of Act I defiantly joins a woman friend on a trip to Egypt. Returned in Act II, it is evident from dropped hints that she has enjoyed a passionate affair, made more titillating for the audience by the suggestion that it was consummated while her female companion was at church. After she is persuaded to return to her husband in Act III, the interest of the play shifts from the woman's experience and dilemma to the frenetic farce of the defence of her reputation by friends who recognise that if scandal attaches to her, her husband cannot take her back. The play ends in reconciliation and the husband's promise to buy Susan the biggest jewel he can find. The audience, who customarily applauded statements of principle they approved, evidently approved this enthusiastically.

This play's history, incidentally, gives insight into the power structures of the theatre and the constant constraints on a writer who wanted to see his work performed. Charles Wyndham accepted the work on condition that cuts blurred the suggestion that Susan had repaid the adultery in kind and expressed astonishment that Jones should imagine he could 'induce married men to bring their wives to the theatre to learn the lesson that they can descend to such nastiness as giving themselves up for an evening of adulterous pleasure and then return safely to their husband's arms, provided they are clever enough, low enough, and dishonest enough to avoid being found out'. Jones acquiesced, claiming, 'I would at some violence to my own convictions, remove any scene that would hurt the natural reverence of any spectator'.[22]

There were no such objections to *The Liars* (1897), despite its curious tone. Sexual relationships are more than ever presented as a game. The women are trivial; most of the marriages façades only, the partners cynical about marital and sexual relationships. The married heroine, Lady Jessica, plays at love, but her would-be lover, Falkner, is serious and, although his emotion threatens to cast him as a blackguard in Society's eyes, he emerges as the most decent of the group. Act III again turns on the frantic efforts of Lady Jessica's friends to prevent her churlish husband understanding the extent of the flirtation. Tension and absurdity mount as untruths proliferate and the tissue of lies grows increasingly liable to shredding until the climax in Falkner's entrance when, asked by Lady Jessica, he tells the truth of his devotion to her. But the play ends with Lady Jessica and her husband reasserting the respectability of their lives and Falkner heroically departing for his great work in Africa. The advice to the husband about women, 'humour them, play with them, buy them the toys they cry for', is heeded: in this case the conciliatory promise is of dinner at the Savoy. For all Coward's dismissal of Society Drama, it is a short step from such a play to his 1920s comedies.

Many plays included shades of melodramatic villainy with aristocratic male wastrels such as Jones's Guisebury or Wilde's Illingworth, and Jones had a line in cruel or, more commonly, boorish husbands, but the moral consciousness of Society Drama nevertheless was usually male. Israel Zangwill pointed out at the time that all the men in *The Second Mrs Tanqueray* showed to great advantage:

> One covers the rags of a female reputation with the cloak of chivalry; another leads a forlorn hope, and frankly confesses his weakness to his fiancée; a third – Cayley Drummle, an admirably drawn and admirably acted character – is everybody's good genius; the worst of the batch – a baronet – marries a vulgar actress, but still marries her.[23]

Cayley Drummle, like Sir Richard in *Rebellious Susan*; Sir Christopher in *The Liars*; Sir Daniel in *Mrs Dane's Defence*, is the play's *raisonneur*, its guiding moraliser: a man-about-town of charming good-humour and wisdom learned from a past that, it is implied, was probably rather colourful but, as Sir Christopher puts it, never involved wrong to 'any *friend's* sister or daughter or wife'. Wilde gave the character wit. Even his apprentice plays from the early 1880s, *Vera* and *The Duchess of Padua*, featured a Wildean figure, commenting on the action with cynical or flippant observations that quickly became known as 'Oscarisms' and were widely, though rarely as pithily, imitated by other dramatists. In the figure of Lords Goring and Darlington, he is evidently a dandy although still fundamentally staunch and vulnerable to tender passion. The role was invariably taken by the actor-manager and one of the moral certainties voiced by such *raisonneurs* and endorsed by the endings of play after play was that, while it might be regrettable, the double standard was an unshakeable fact of public life and social survival depended on recognition of this.

Oscar Wilde

European initiatives and *fin de siècle* decadence almost touched English theatre with *Salomé* (1891), the play Wilde wrote in French for Sarah Bernhardt. In constructing his drama of desire defeated – Herod's lust for Salomé but also Salomé's for Jokanaan (the Baptist) – Wilde drew on the symbolism and use of dance of Maeterlinck's *La Princesse Maleine* and on the sensuousness of Paul Fort's short-lived Théâtre d'Art, which he had attended in Paris. The recurrent references to the moon, to colours, jewels and precious metals, and the curiously stilted syntax, both of Wilde's original French and the Wilde and Alfred Douglas English translation, gives a uniformity to the dialogue and a remoteness to the characterisation which is emphasised by the studied pictorialism of the visual effects.

In performance, bodies were to have been posed, colour used express-ively and mood suggested by staging. The white moon that shone on Salomé's declaration of obsessive passion for Jokanaan and on the young Syrian's suicide for love of her, was to have turned blood red for her dance before Herod and her subsequent demand for the beheading of Jokanaan. Finally, it would have been covered by a black cloud as she was crushed to death under the shields of Herod's soldiers. The play was banned while in rehearsal, ostensibly for its portrayal of biblical figures. Although it was performed in Paris in 1896 by the Théâtre d'Oeuvre, awareness of the play in England was fleeting, stimulated more by the association with Bernhardt and by Beardsley's scandalous illustrations for the 1894 English translation, than regret for its disappearance from the stage. Once the ban was lifted, however, in 1927, productions at the Gate (1929) and Festival (1931) Theatres stimulated new interest in this venture into eroticism and death, and the severed head theme, symbolism and use of dance in Wilde's piece informed a spate of plays by W. B. Yeats: *The King of the Great Clock Tower* (1934), *A Full Moon in March* (1935) and *The Death of Cuchulain* (1939).

Wilde's Society plays, written in a period of intensive creativity between 1892 and 1894, were, by contrast, immediately successful despite, perhaps because of, the strong element of parody in them. *Lady Windermere's Fan* (1892); *A Woman of No Importance* (1893) and *An Ideal Husband* (1895) are oddly patchy works. The familiar patterns of social-problem melodrama are both relished and exposed; audience expectations flattered and mocked. Certainly, the costumes warranted admiration and pictures of them were widely reproduced in the illustrated papers. In some ways Wilde's Society plays are more old-fashioned than those of Jones and Pinero in that he relies heavily on soliloquy and staccato asides as well as on *raisonneurs* to explain motives and press the plots forward. His plots, too, as C. E. Montague and many subsequent critics have observed, are 'propelled by theatrical commonplaces'.[24] Derivative situations recur. In one, *Lady Windermere's Fan*, a fallen woman tries to get back; she infiltrates the company of the daughter who has idealised her memory; a letter is intercepted; a mislaid fan threatens to destroy a reputation; a woman is saved by the heroic sacrifice of a woman she has spurned. In the next, *A Woman of No Importance*, a chance encounter reveals paternity; a betrayed woman, insulted by her former lover, strikes him with her glove; an overheard conversation effects a change of heart; a cry from a woman in distress alerts one man to another's villainy; a man learns that the man he has just challenged is his father. And in the third, *An Ideal Husband*, ancient shady financial dealings return to haunt a man on the brink of a brilliant political career; a letter is misunderstood; a blackmailer is foiled. The lessons of the French well-made play have been gleefully absorbed.

The tone of *A Woman of No Importance*, the weakest of the three plays, is erratic. Wilde shows just how thoroughly he has absorbed the tricks of the trade but seems uncertain of whether his audience is to laugh at them or take them seriously, as, for example, with the arrantly melodramatic climax when Gerald is prevented from avenging Lord Illingworth's insult to Hester by Mrs Arbuthnot's cry: 'Stop, Gerald, stop. He is your own father' after which she '*sinks slowly to the ground in shame*' (Act III) and the curtain falls. In much the same way, Wilde has Mrs Arbuthnot outdo all rivals in claiming her position as the classic fallen woman:

> her life was ruined, and her soul ruined, and all that was sweet and good and pure in her ruined also. She suffered terribly. She suffers now. She will always suffer. For her there is no joy, no peace, no attonement. She is a woman who drags a chain like a guilty thing. She is a woman who wears a mask like a thing that is a leper. The fire cannot purify her. The waters cannot quench her anguish. Nothing can heal her. No anodyne can give her sleep, no poppies forgetfulness! She is lost! She is a lost soul!
>
> (*A Woman of No Importance*, Act II)

The imagery and self-blame; the staccato phrases and the iterations of the lamentation are true to type. The problem is that Wilde seems to invite the audience to revel in the excessive expression at one moment and to take the characters seriously and be moved by their plight the next. The witty characters, in this play, tend to exist in separate compartments from those who carry the plot, and the epigrams, perhaps because less germane to the action, are, with a few exceptions, less well charged than elsewhere.

Both the current of feeling and the jokes work to undercut the sanctity of the social law in the more fully achieved *Lady Windermere's Fan*. The audience is drawn to laugh *with* the sinful mother, Mrs Erlynne, who mocks the very genre in which she finds herself, forcing recognition of its fictionality when she refuses to '. . . weep on her neck and tell her who I am, all that kind of thing', or to 'retire to a convent or become a hospital nurse or something of that kind as people do in silly modern novels' (Act IV). Wilde's closest model, as critics from his own day on have perceived, was Pierre Leclerq's *Illusion*, which ended with the penitent mother returning dressed in widow's weeds which she declares:

> my costume til I die . . . Yes. I have disposed of all I possess to found a home for others who have been as

I have been, who would be as I will be. I am penniless.
Thank God. – My past is black. My future shall whiten
it.[25]

Mrs Erlynne, by contrast, observes that, 'if a woman really repents, she
has to go to a bad dressmaker, otherwise no-one believes her. And nothing
in the world would induce me to do that'.

Lady Windermere's closing declaration that Mrs Erlynne is 'a very good
woman' underlined the doubling possibilities of the subtitle, 'A Play About
a Good Woman' and reverberated mischievously on the scandal that had
erupted the previous year – 1891 – around Hardy's subtitling of his novel,
Tess of the D'Urbervilles: 'A Pure Woman'. But Wilde does offer reassurance
even while teasing his audience. Mrs Erlynne can be seen to be following
conventional wisdom in ensuring that her errant daughter returns to her
marriage before reputation is damaged and, if she has not succumbed to
the Leclerqian ending, the husband she has ensnared is an evidently silly
man and she will have to leave the country to enjoy his wealth.

At the end of each play, though, handwringing is replaced by resistance.
Not only do the upright puritans, Lady Windermere, Hester and Lady
Chiltern, learn generosity towards human failings as, indeed, in her smaller
way Ellean does in The Second Mrs Tanqueray but, in each, the melodramatic
climax is prepared and then thwarted. Mrs Erlynne refuses the touching
reconciliation scene with her daughter and ensures that heroics are avoided
through her insistence that husband and wife keep their own counsel.
Even in the weakest of the three, Mrs Arbuthnot refuses marriage with
the father of her child while, in An Ideal Husband, Sir Robert Chiltern,
instead of squaring up to the anticipated confession and noble acceptance
of its consequences, finds a way of forgiving himself that is not far removed
from the complaisant accommodations of the shocking plays of Théâtre
Libre naturalism. Both James and Shaw found the tone of Wilde's plays
unfeeling,[26] but I suspect that the two-dimensionality of the characters,
the fast movement of the dialogue and the parodic version of the genre is
what enables even the weakest of his plays to seem as unmawkish as they
do in revival.

But it is with the play which appears to break away from the Society
formula altogether, The Importance of Being Earnest (1895), that Wilde
achieves a classic comedy. In this last work to be produced before trial and
imprisonment ended his brief career as a dramatist, the guilty secret, past
indiscretion and the double standard all figure but so refashioned that the
play separates itself from any other work of the time, mocking received
ideas and engaging with the assumptions and hypocrisies surrounding
contemporary attitudes to sexual relationships, the education of young
women and the marriage market. There is no evident raisonneur. John Jack
Worthing, the likeliest candidate, is an inveterate liar and each character

is notably egocentric. The funniest interchanges insist that both characters and audience are conscious of the social games that are being played. As a contemporary reviewer, recognising a 'genuinely comic farcical situation', perceived:

> Never perhaps in the records of the drama has a joke at once so colossal and so frivolous as Wilde's new play, *The Importance of Being Earnest*, been perpetrated on the stage. Its title is a pun, its story a conundrum, its actors are lunatics, its dialogue is galimatias, and its termination is a 'sell'. It kept, nonetheless, the St James's audience simmering with delight, and it will probably count among the chief attractions of the approaching season.[27]

Wilde's abortive libel action against the Marquess of Queensbury that erupted into one of the scandals of the decade with his subsequent arrest and trial for 'gross indecency' in the summer of 1895 and the harsh sentence of two years' penal servitude brought his short career as a dramatist to an end. Although the run of *The Importance* had continued during the trial, the dramatist's name was removed from the posters and programmes and, with the guilty verdict, the play was taken off and there were no further productions of Wilde's work in England during the rest of the century. George Alexander wrote of the work now widely acknowledged as one of the greatest English comedies, 'personally, of course, I wish I had never seen it. The scandal came and a heavy loss with it'.[28] The heavier loss was Wilde's: broken by the experience and by hard labour in Reading Gaol, he wrote no more plays before his death in France in 1900.

Guy Domville (1895)

Wilde's interest in theatre is one of the many signs of change in the 1890s. It was because he was perceived to be, as Peter Raby has pointed out, 'the first major English literary figure to write a comedy for years'[29] that Henry James, another aspirant, wrote to Elizabeth Robins before the production of *Lady Windermere's Fan*:

> One thing I do wish you would do – tell me three words about Oscar W's piece – when it is produced, and if in particular the *subject* seems to discount my poor three year

old (or almost) that Hare will neither produce nor part with.[30]

James's attempt also occurred at George Alexander's theatre in 1895. For James, who had devoted the five years from 1890 to writing plays, it was a baptism by fire. His adaptation of his novel, *The American*, into a melodramatic comedy with Robins as Madame de Cintré had had a reasonably successful short run, but *Guy Domville* was conceived and written as a play. It succeeded Jones's *The Masqueraders* at the St James's and, after the near riot of the first night, sustained a reasonably respectable short run before being replaced by *The Importance of Being Earnest*, but it has gone into theatrical history, partly as a result of James's own retelling of the event, as a fiasco of the first order.

The choice the hero faced between participation in life or withdrawal from it into the priesthood, was only part of the problem. James was not wholly in control of dialogue or characterisation and, in an evident sop to what he thought the public taste, included a long, clumsy scene of drunkenness as the second act of the play. Guy, on accession to his title, suddenly and implausibly having become a man of the world is about to marry Mary whose lover, Thomas Round, has, just as implausibly, moored his boat at the bottom of Guy's garden and, according to H. G. Wells, came and went 'with great freedom and pertinacity through the conservatory'. Wells, in the audience as a fledgling reviewer, recapitulated the events of this 'hopeless' act for his readers:

> Then followed a remarkable scene: Round pretends to be
> drunk and tries to make Guy Domville really so; Domville
> perceiving his intention, pours away the wine into a bowl
> of flowers, and also pretends to be drunk. His pretence
> successfully deceives Round but not Mary. However, after
> numerous exits and entrances it ends happily in Domville
> understanding how matters lie, and Round retires to his boat
> for the last time through Domville's appartments, with
> Mary, presumably to fly to Twickenham and marry'.[31]

Besides Wells, Walkley and Arnold Bennett were among those who, despite clear perception of its weaknesses, wrote largely positive reviews. Shaw, in his *Saturday Review* article, praised the 'rare charm of speech' and the 'delicate inflexions of feeling conveyed by the cadences of the line'. Berating those who booed, he suggested that the real argument was between the highbrow and the philistine; those who believed that, as in the Renaissance, there was still a place for 'serious' plays and those who insisted on theatre's role as a cultural safety valve, a place of light entertainment and escapism (6.1.1895).

For James, the reversal was such that it was twelve years before another play of his was produced, in the wake of the changes brought about by the Stage Society and the theatrical activity of Shaw and Granville Barker. Although his plays did not themselves contribute to those changes, the *occasion* of *Guy Domville* and its championing by the reformers did. It functioned as a rallying point for those who believed that established writers had a part to play in the imminent dramatic revival. The defiant literary element in the audience of *Guy Domville* applauding ostentatiously at the jeering gallery and defending the play in their subsequent reviews were the champions not so much of James's play as of the *idea* that theatre could be reclaimed and that serious writers must contribute to this reclamation.

Ibsen and new initiatives

It was in direct response to *Mrs Tanqueray* and the Dumas *fils* revivals and fired with the enthusiasm expressed in his *Quintessence of Ibsenism* (1890–91) that Shaw wrote his second play, *Mrs Warren's Profession*, late in 1893. This play pushes the debate about the double standard and male-female relationships on to new ground, introducing questions about the interactive structure of power and economic dependency that compels women at any level of society to survive by being, in Mrs Warren's words, 'good to some man that can afford to be good to her'. The audience is asked to recognise that the desperate conditions of a society's poor are what underpin prostitution and other exploitations of the capitalist system. Shaw's perspective makes a claim for sharper insight and more challenging analysis than anything offered by the supposedly modern themes of contemporary plays which, having appeared to threaten, reassuringly endorsed the received code.

Again, a woman with a past encounters her grown-up child: the one, Mrs Warren, is a vulgar business woman, with brothels in every European city, the other, Vivie, a free-thinking new woman but one initially as innocent as Lady Windermere or Ellean Tanqueray of her mother's past and profession. Shaw uses Mrs Warren's rejection of honourable poverty to interrogate assumptions in the language. There is certainly no sighing 'a few years ago – ':

> How could you keep your self-respect in such starvation
> and slavery? And whats a woman worth? whats a life

worth? without self-respect. Why am I independent and able to give my daughter a first-rate education, when other women that had just as good opportunities are in the gutter? Because I always knew how to respect myself and control myself. Why is Liz looked up to in a cathedral town? The same reason. Where would we be now if we'd minded the clergyman's foolishness? Scrubbing floors for one and sixpence a day and nothing to look forward to but the workhouse infirmary.

(Act II)

In the course of the play, the audience is educated with Vivie in economic realities, is asked to see the complicity of everyone in the wrongs of the economic and social system. Vivie's personal crisis is of a different kind from that of Ellean Tanqueray or those men who discover their wives' past indiscretions. Brought to recognition of the terrifying absurdity of her situation she neither learns retrospective generosity nor yields to male authority, unlike the caricature new woman parodied in her straight-talking and her hefty handshake, cigarette-smoking and mathematical prowess. Although the play dangles both options, Vivie rejects the demands of mother and of sexual relationship. As this play has been a consciously distorted echo of the Society Drama, so the final stage direction offers an equally conscious tribute to Ibsen's *A Doll's House* as, '*Mrs Warren goes out, slamming the door behind her. The strain on Vivie's face relaxes; her grave expression breaks up into one of joyous content*', and she immerses herself in her work.

After the fun, the unexpected twists of the plot and the strong characters with their lively tirades, the audience is left with disturbing questions about the relationship between such rejections and the capacity to live. The paradoxical recognition remains that Vivie is only who and how she is because her mother made money. She can renounce the money but not her educated mind and social values, nor would she want to. It was crucial to Shaw's challenge to the audience that there is no catharsis; the bad are not punished in any material way and the good are inevitably compromised. Mrs Warren, a representative of a society in which the self-serving flourish, continues to be prosperously immoral to the end of the play. It is a fiercely polemical work. How could the censor have failed to ban it?

Among the attacks that Ibsen's plays habitually stimulated, a particular strain which Shaw gladly responded to here, reiterated the threat to English domestic life of the perceived message of emancipation. In response to the 1889 production of *A Doll's House*, *Queen* magazine had warned that, 'the result of preaching the doctrine that every woman ought to emancipate herself' would be 'a dangerous general rebellion of women' and Clement Scott denounced the play's promotion of a 'new creed of selfishness' in which the ideal of woman was no longer to be 'a fountain of love, and forgiveness and charity . . . but a mass of aggregate conceit and self sufficiency' who, and this is the real horror which the heroine of Jones's *Masqueraders* would reject, 'leaves her home and deserts her friendless children because she has *herself* to look after'. The 1892 testimony of the Examiner of Plays to the Select Committee on Censorship included the opinion that:

> All the heroines are dissatisfied spinsters who look on
> marriage as a monopoly, or dissatisfied married women in
> a chronic state of rebellion against not only the conditions
> which nature has imposed upon their sex, but against all
> the duties and obligations of mothers and wives.[32]

While these attitudes were reflected in the caricature new women of Society Drama, those promoting Ibsen did so in terms directly opposed to those of Scott and the Examiner of Plays, emphasising the clash between different perceptions of the function of theatre. 'The stock vocabulary of the old judicial school of criticism' had, according to Walkley:

> absolutely no meaning for those of us who think that literary
> criticism is not some dominie-business of assigning good
> and bad marks, but the art of enjoying masterpieces. *Hedda
> Gabler* is a masterpiece of piquant subtlety, delicate
> observation and tragic intensity, and I take leave to enjoy it.
> Its heroine may be, as our judicial critic asserts, 'a monstrous
> specimen of unfettered womanhood', but I can only ask,
> 'What then – so long as she is interesting?'.[33]

Frustration with the limited range of female roles in West End theatre and the dependent status of the actresses who played them motivated Elizabeth Robins and Marion Lea in their 1891 co-production of *Hedda Gabler* (playing Hedda and Thea respectively). As Robins wrote of the excitement of creating the role, 'she wasn't on the scene sixty seconds before it was clear she knew there was joy in life she hadn't been able to grasp, and that marriage only emphasised what she was missing'.[34]

Rosmersholm and *The Lady from the Sea* joined the other 1891 productions. *A Doll's House* was revived in 1892. *The Master Builder* was produced as soon as Ibsen had finished writing it, in 1893, and Beerbohm Tree brought the phenomenon into mainstream theatre with his special matinée performance of *An Enemy of the People*, the same year. Since none of the other managers followed his initiative, this did not quite 'mark the acceptance of the great Norwegian within the official circle of the London managers', as one critic claimed (*Black and White*, 24.6.1893) but, with its impressive crowd scenes and with Tree dressed and made up to look like Ibsen as Stockmann, it did attract a somewhat different audience although it also, perhaps, endorsed that audience's interest in personality rather than play.

'An English Théâtre Libre'

Although the Independent Theatre (1891–97) never had more than 175 members, among them were such luminaries as Hardy, Meredith, Pinero, Gilbert Murray, William Archer, Henry James as well as its founder, J. T. Grein and his close advisers, George Moore and Bernard Shaw. After *Ghosts* in 1891, it performed some twenty-one plays, many of them one-act pieces, usually for two matinées. While these included several translations of Théâtre Libre plays, which suggested man is shaped by his environment and life is a struggle for survival, and that classic of contemporary alternative theatre, *The Wild Duck* (4.5.1894), new English work was disappointingly sparse despite Grein's manifesto intention of stimulating 'a native unconventional school, and to give a hearing to those who strive to foster the undeniable renaissance of the drama'.[35]

If nothing else, the Company was responsible in December 1892 for Shaw's debut as a dramatist, *Widowers' Houses*; the play's subtitle, 'an Original Didactic Realistic Play in Three Acts', already signalling the mercurial Shavian manner that, in representing slum landlordism, would demand laughter as well as indignation from its audience. It was followed in 1893 by four new full-length plays, George Moore, *The Strike at Arlingford* (21.2.1893); Elizabeth Robins and Gertrude Bell, *Alan's Wife* (28.4.1893); 'Michael Field', *A Question of Memory* (27.10.1893) and John Todhunter, *The Black Cat* (8.12.1893), but none of these led far and Grein shied away from *Mrs Warren's Profession* even before the Lord Chamberlain's Office refused it a licence.

Moore's play might seem to have broken new ground in that its central plot, which concerned the desperate love of a socialist for a colliery owner, Lady Anne, brought issues of Capital and Labour on to the stage but it made surprisingly little of this. The plot is melodramatic and the situation between the lovers includes Anne's clichéed cry, 'Gone, gone, I shall never see him again', the moment before he returns to admit his love. *Alan's Wife*, more genuinely innovative, stood out in the 1890s as a rare play that, for all it included an infanticide, explored the feelings of a mother for her child and created belief in the maternal bond. It was also exceptional in a period in which Ibsen was despised for offering 'suburban' settings in being set among working-class people. Its three-scene episodic structure deliberately rejected the smooth dovetailing and preparatory clues of the well-made play. At the end of Act I in which a group of women have chatted and a wife prepared her husband's meal, the body of the husband is brought home, killed and hideously damaged in an industrial accident. It emerges in Act II that, perhaps as a result of the shock, the child she was carrying has been born cruelly deformed and, at the end of the act, she smothers the child. In the final act, set in prison, Jean refuses to repent her action before going out to be hanged.

Motherhood might have been adduced in Society plays but in no way did they engage with its realities: only token children appeared, to tug the characters', and the audience's, heartstrings and, in the face of seduction, to remind mothers of their primary duty. Dependency and the relationship of parent to child assumed a new and embarrassing force in a play located, as *Alan's Wife* was, among working people. If things went wrong in this other, harsher environment, there would be no retreat into another room, or wing; no handing the intrusive child over to a nurse, or sending it away to school, and even the Independent Theatre audience were not ready for that kind of realism. In a statement that, despite itself, gave testimony to the play's power, Walkley endorsing the general claim that such a thing should not have been shown on stage, wrote that:

> Life presents us occasionally with cases of unspeakable
> calamity for which there can be no compensation; wrongs
> that can never be righted; hopeless, heartless, odious things
> which put the glib commonplaces of the pulpit and the
> copybook to rout and leave poor mocked mankind shaking
> their fist with impotent rage.[36]

The Independent Theatre's achievement was limited probably because, unlike Antoine in Paris, Brahm at the Freie Bühne in Berlin or Stanislavski at the Moscow Art Theatre, Grein and his colleagues seem to have had little real stage sense: the initiative was more literary than theatrical. The productions seem to have showed scant ability to use movement and spatial relationship on the stage, or to develop sets which would create mood and atmosphere and an acting style appropriate to the lower-key writing. Indeed, although some of its actors were better than competent – Elizabeth Robins gave a particularly powerful performance as the main character of *Alan's Wife* – others were willing but not very competent amateurs. As one contemporary critic observed of the pioneering revival of *The Duchess of Malfi*: 'It was quite worth reviving. . . . But if worth reviving, it was worth reviving with better actors' and 'the young men of the cast were for the most part ludicrously bad' (*Black and White*, 29.10.1892). It is in no way unfair to argue, as John Stokes has done, that 'Antoine's specific achievement – the materialization of the naturalist aesthetic in the actual staging of the play' was 'only slightly apprehended or absorbed' by his English imitators.[37]

The figure of the director, alert to the possibilities of staging and responsible for all aspects of performance – casting, acting standards, overseeing the designs and the lighting and shaping the play through rehearsal – was emerging in avant-garde theatres throughout Europe. Antoine and Stanislavski were among the first so identified. It is ironic that, for the moment, such values were not apparent in English independent theatres: it was W. S. Gilbert at the Savoy and Irving at the Lyceum, who were the important English forerunners in their attention to production detail. Although Antoine had been amused by Irving's histrionics and, for example, by the shaft of moonlight that illuminated the stage beautifully but had no realistically possible source, he found the Lyceum's stage pictures and the creation of mood through lighting effects revelatory, and it was to these that he turned for inspiration when he produced his own *King Lear* in 1905. Pinero, who had briefly worked with Irving at the Lyceum, as indeed had Edward Gordon Craig, followed his lead in overseeing the production of his plays as, later, Shaw would do.

The Independent Theatre did, however, focus attention on Ibsen and place a marker for the future. As Shaw put it, 'the modern manager need not produce *The Wild Duck*; but he must be very careful not to produce a play which will seem insipid and old fashioned to playgoers who have seen *The Wild Duck*, even if they have hissed it'.[38] It also imported the notion of alternative theatre into Britain and gave some writers, notably Shaw and Elizabeth Robins, an opportunity to experiment before an audience.

Its initiative also stimulated other avant-garde productions. Its one Jacobean effort, *The Duchess of Malfi* (1892) was directed by William Poel who, with his Elizabethan Stage Society, would foster the return to full texts and Elizabethan scenic simplicity in his authentic Shakespeare productions. William Archer's Minority Theatre, grew from a production of *Little Eyolf* at the Avenue in 1896. The optimism apparent in its renaming as the 'New Century Theatre', preparatory to the formation of a National Theatre early in the next century, was short-lived. The New Century's manifesto, announcing that it was not 'in search of the esoteric, the eccentric, or the mystic' but would welcome 'all *acting plays*, of a certain standard of intrinsic merit, which are likely to interest the intelligent public',[39] strove to meet criticism of the Independent Theatre while making it clear that it, too, wanted new writing and addressed a similar audience. The centrality of Ibsen is evident in the group's production of *John Gabriel Borkman* (1897) and its announcement of a *Peer Gynt*, although this never materialised. Other productions included, in 1899, Stevenson and Henley's, *Admiral Guinea* and Edward Martyn's *The Heather Field*, which would become one of the standbys of the Abbey repertoire. Having generated even fewer satisfactory plays than the Independent Theatre, however, the Company became dormant towards the end of 1899.

Florence Farr's management of the Avenue Theatre in 1894, heralded three separate strands of things to come with her presentation of a double bill of W. B. Yeats's mystical Irish play, *The Land of Heart's Desire*, and Shaw's satirical comedy, *Arms and the Man*, financed by Annie Horniman, the future supporter of W. B. Yeats and the Abbey Theatre and founder of the Manchester Repertory Company. Shaw's play, with its contrast between Bluntschli, the realist professional soldier, who hides from pursuit in a lady's bedroom and wolfs down chocolate creams, and Sergius, the heroic cavalry officer, who makes love to the maid in the garden, was his first theatrical success, its run of fifty nights suggesting that he probably did have a future as a dramatist.

The close of the century

In mainstream theatre, the decade went out with lavish show. On the one hand, Beerbohm Tree, in his spectacular *Julius Caesar* at the Haymarket (1898) outdid anything Irving had managed and, on the other, what William Archer described as a 'vulgar, religious piece', Wilson Barrett's toga melodrama, *The Sign of the Cross*, in which a Roman patrician is won by the truth of a simple Christian woman, having transferred to the Lyric from St Louis, ran for a year in 1896–97 with the equally melodramatic, *Prisoner of Zenda* rivalling it at the St James's and four versions of *The Three Musketeers* playing in London and the immediate suburbs. Shaw, still indefatigable in denunciation, reiterated his theme of the beginning of the decade:

> If every manager considers it due to himself to produce
> nothing cheaper than *The Prisoner of Zenda*, not to mention
> the splendours of the Lyceum, then goodbye to high dramatic
> art. The managers will, perhaps, retort that, if high
> dramatic art means Ibsen, then they ask for nothing better
> than to get rid of it. I am too polite to reply, bluntly, that
> high dramatic art *does* mean Ibsen; that Ibsen's plays are at
> this moment the head of the dramatic body; and that though

an actor manager can and, often does, do without a head,
dramatic art cannot. (30.1.1897)

And in 1899, William Archer, so optimistic about the prospects for theatre
at the beginning of the decade, lamented that now he could see 'no
movement whatever in that "spangled firmament" but only a monotonous
glittering stagnation'.[40] But for all that, there was movement and on two
separate fronts: from the Irish Literary Society and the English Stage
Society.

Yeats had founded the Irish Literary Society at the beginning of the
decade to revive interest in Irish legend and folk-tale and encourage
the writing of literature of an Irish character. Despite the production of
his *Land of Heart's Desire*, he found the emphasis on Ibsen and realism
among the English theatrical avant-garde irksome and, having been
impressed by Villiers de l'Isle Adam's symbolist *Axel* in Paris in 1894, and
by Maeterlinck's 'interior drama', *Pelléas et Mélisande* in 1895, he instigated
a different kind of venture and one that was specifically Irish. In 1897 a
letter signed by Yeats, Lady Gregory and Edward Martyn, inviting support
from various businessmen, announced:

> We propose to have performed in Dublin in the spring of
> every year certain Celtic and Irish plays, which whatever be
> their degree of excellence will be written with a high
> ambition, and so to build up a Celtic and Irish School of
> dramatic literature. We hope to find in Ireland an
> uncorrupted and imaginative audience trained to listen by
> its passion for oratory, and believe that our desire to bring
> upon the stage the deeper thoughts and emotions of Ireland
> will ensure for us a tolerant welcome, and that freedom to
> experiment that is not found in theatres of England.[41]

The importance of language is already identified in that 'passion for
oratory' and of allegiance to the growing Irish Nationalist Movement in
the reference to Celtic plays and the reiteration of the word 'Ireland' in the
manifesto. In 1899, the group produced Martyn's *The Heather Field* and
Yeats's *The Countess Cathleen*, with Florence Farr in the title role, at the
Antient Concert Rooms in Dublin. George Moore joined them in
the same year and *Beltaine*, the theatre's journal, edited and largely written
by Yeats, began publication.

The mainly Fabian English Stage Society was founded to give a stage
to 'uncommercial theatre' and to plays 'of power and merit' ignored by
West End managements or banned public but permitted private performance.[42] The ideals were comparable with, but the circumstances distinct
from, those of the Independent Theatre and its short-lived successors, on

whose work it built. Quickly reaching its proposed maximum membership of 300 two-guinea-a-year subscribers, it produced eight plays including Shaw's, *You Never Can Tell* and *Candida* as well as plays by Ibsen, Maeterlinck and Hauptmann, in 1899–1900, its first season. Granville Barker, who had made his mark as Richard in William Poel's Elizabethan Stage Society production of *Richard II* in 1899, turned in a memorable performance as Marchbanks in *Candida* and gained his first experience as a director with three short plays, Maeterlinck's *Death of Tintagiles* and *Interior* and, from the Celtic fringe, *The House of Usna*, by Fiona Macleod. Already an able actor, alert to the importance of Ibsen, ready to invest his energies in the production of new writing and possessed of a genuine theatrical sense, Barker, backed by the Stage Society, was the needful catalyst through whose means the tentative experimentation of the 1890s could become the dramatic achievements of the next decade.

Notes

1. Information is drawn mainly from lists in Allardyce Nicholl, *A History of late Nineteenth Century Drama* (Cambridge, 1949), pp. 214–22.
2. *The Galaxy* (May 1877).
3. Information here is largely drawn from the British Theatre Association William Archer collection of cuttings and theatre programmes.
4. J. T. Grein, 'The Independent Theatre', *Black and White* (14.3.1891), p. 167. Grein's dealings with the Dutch theatre are discussed in J. Woodfield, *English Theatre in Transition, 1881–1914* (Beckenham, 1984), p. 43.
5. See E. Gosse, 'Ibsen the Norwegian Satirist', *The Fortnightly Review* (January 1873); W. Archer, 'Ibsen and English Criticism', *The Fortnightly Review* (July 1889), pp. 30–5.
6. Information is from an unpublished Cambridge PhD thesis, Sara Jan, 'Ibsen in England, 1889–1914' (1993), p. 3.
7. See *The Era* (6.6.1891) and Penny Griffin, 'The First Performance of *Ibsen's Ghost*', *Theatre Notebook*, 33, pp. 30–7.
8. Shaw, Preface to Archer, *The Theatrical World of 1894* (1895), p. xix; Archer, *Theatrical World, 1897* (1898), p. 376; G. Barker, 1908, quoted Woodfield, *English Theatre*, p. 5.
9. Archer, *Theatrical World, 1894*, p. 84.
10. *Saturday Review* (30.5.1896); repr. G. B. Shaw, *Dramatic Opinions and Essays*, p. 442. Shaw's reviews are collected in *Dramatic Opinions and Essays* (New York, 1906) and *Our Theatres in the Nineties* (1932); there is also a selection in The World's Classics, Bernard Shaw, *Plays and Players* (1952). Subsequent quotations from Shaw in this chapter are from *The Saturday Review* unless otherwise stated. Date of publication will be noted in the text after the quotation.
11. 'Author's Apology', *Dramatic Opinions*, p. xxi.
12. *The Plays of Bernard Shaw*, Vol. 1 (1926), p. x. See, too, Holbrook Jackson, *The 1890s* (1913); John Stokes, *In the Nineties* (1989).

13. The recently published, J. Kaplan and S. Stowell, *Theatre and Fashion* (Cambridge, 1994), investigates the link brilliantly.

14. Noel Coward, *Play Parade* II (1939), p. ix.

15. A. B. Walkley, 'The Drama', *Black and White* (3.6.1893), p. 681.

16. Reviewers cited, *The Era* (3.6.1893), *Pall Mall Gazette* (29.5.93); Archer, *Theatrical World, 1893*, p. 131, and *The Old Drama and the New* (1923), p. 316.

17. James to Pinero (2.5.1893), quoted, L. Edel, ed., *The Complete Plays of Henry James* (1949), p. 455; Walkley, 'The Drama', *Black and White* (3.6.1893), p. 681; Shaw (February 1895), *Dramatic Opinions*, p. 39.

18. A. Symons, *Plays, Acting, Music* (1909), p. 61.

19. Mrs Patrick Campbell, *My Life and Some Letters* (1922), p. 98; and see J. Kaplan, 'Pineroticism and the problem play: Mrs Tanqueray, Mrs Ebbsmith and "Mrs Pat" ', pp. 49–58, in R. Foulkes, ed., *British Theatre in the 1890s* (Cambridge, 1992) and see Kaplan and Stowell, Chapter 2.

20. Introduction, Russell Jackson, *Plays by H. A. Jones* (Cambridge, 1982), p. 24.

21. Archer, *Theatrical World, 1894*, p. 312.

22. Wyndham quoted, Penny Griffin, *Arthur Wing Pinero and Henry Arthur Jones* (1991), p. 37; H. A. Jones, *The Renascence of the English Drama* (1895), p. 50; full account in Doris Jones, *The Life and Letters of Henry Arthur Jones* (1930), p. 166ff.

23. Israel Zangwill, 'Without Prejudice', *Pall Mall Magazine*, 1 (1893), p. 598.

24. C. E. Montague, *Dramatic Values* (1911), p. 180.

25. Identified by A. B. Walkley and by Hesketh Pearson, *A Life of Oscar Wilde* (1946), among others; quoted, Kerry Powell, *Oscar Wilde and the Theatre of the 1890s* (Cambridge, 1990), p. 25, detailed discussion, pp. 22–6. For other sources see R. Ellmann, *Oscar Wilde* (1988), p. 348.

26. James to Florence Bell (8.2.1892), quoted, L. Edel, ed., *Selected Letters* (Cambridge, MA, 1987), p. 152, also p. 253; Shaw, for example, reviewing *The Importance of Being Earnest*, *Saturday Review* (23.2.1895).

27. Unsigned review, 'The Play', *Black and White* (23.2.1895), p. 240.

28. Quoted, George Rowell in Foulkes, ed., *British Theatre in the 1890s*, p. 36.

29. Peter Raby, *Oscar Wilde* (Cambridge, 1984), p. 90.

30. Henry James to Elizabeth Robins (7.8.1893), quoted Elizabeth Robins, *Theatre and Friendship* (1932), p. 112.

31. H. G. Wells, 'A Pretty Question', *Pall Mall Gazette* (7.1.1895); Arnold Bennett described the act as 'invertebrate, long winded and impossible', *Woman* (16.1.1895).

32. *Queen* (15.6.1889), Scott (July 1889), reprinted in M. Egan, ed., *Ibsen: The Critical Heritage* (1972), pp. 106, 114; E. F. S. Pigott, quoted, Samuel Hynes, *The Edwardian Turn of Mind* (1968) pp. 308–9.

33. A. B. Walkley, *Playhouse Impressions* (1892), p. 58.

34. Robins, *Theatre and Friendship*, p. 29, *Ibsen and the Actress* (1928), p. 20.

35. J. T. Grein, 'The Independent Theatre', *Black and White* (14.3.1891).

36. *The Speaker* (6.5.1893), quoted, Archer, preface to *Independent Theatre Series, 2: Alan's Wife* (1893), p. xliv. *Alan's Wife* and *The Strike at Arlingford* are discussed further in Chapter 8.

37. J. Stokes, *Resistible Theatres* (1972), p. 125.

38. Shaw, *Our Theatres, I*, p. 165.

39. Quoted Robins, *Theatre and Friendship*, p. 192.

40. W. Archer, 'Plays of the Season', *Fortnightly Review* (July 1899), pp. 132–9, p. 132.

41. Quoted, Lady Gregory, *Our Irish Theatre* (1914), pp. 8–9.

42. Incorporated Stage Society, *Ten Years, 1899–1909* (1909), p. 7.

Chapter 3
1900–1920 The New Drama

A dinner, held on 7 July 1907, to celebrate the persistence and theatrical energy of the collaboration of Harley Granville Barker and the entrepreneur J. E. Vedrenne at the Court Theatre between 1904 and 1907, was one of those remarkable Edwardian occasions on which almost everyone of significance in contemporary English drama was present. Among the guests were not only dramatic critics such as Archer and Grein, theatre people as diverse as William Poel and Bram Stoker, Beerbohm Tree and Annie Horniman, but many of the new actors and writers whose work would possess the stage in the years up to the First World War. Predominant among them was George Bernard Shaw whose plays had finally found such an audience at the Court Theatre that productions of them underpinned the Court programme and helped subsidise the work of other younger dramatists.

Some dozen years after avant-garde theatres were established in France and Germany, the concurrence of confident new writing that engaged in a challenging way with social issues, an audience receptive to it, and a producing agency that, by believing in the new work, helped stimulate both writers and audiences, had made the long-mooted revival of the English drama a reality. In the Vedrenne-Barker venture the English-speaking theatre finally had an independent theatre operating, albeit precariously, on a professional basis. As Shaw put it:

> The Court Theatre has had to cut its coat according to its cloth; and it has never really had cloth enough. But it has paid its way and made a living wage for its workers; and it has produced an effect on dramatic art and public taste in this country which is out of all proportion to the mere physical and financial bulk of its achievements.[1]

The tentative progress of the 1890s towards the New Drama; the availability of published versions of plays which could not find a stage, and the adventurous productions of Ibsen, now came to fruition. Despite his appeal for new native drama, many of the plays produced by Grein's

Independent Theatre had been translations from the French and others had been slight, one-act pieces, but he had indicated the possibility of serious theatre and set Shaw, at least, writing. The Stage Society, the immediate progenitor, had encouraged innovation and, as it grew in confidence, defied the prohibitions of the Lord Chamberlain with its closed-house Sunday evening or Monday matinée performances of avant-garde foreign plays and such 'uncommercial' native drama as Barker's own *The Marrying of Ann Leete* (1902), Maugham's *A Man of Honour* (1903) and, among numerous works by Shaw, the English première of the banned *Mrs Warren's Profession* (1902). Whatever their differences, Stage Society plays were notable as a group for their rejection of the contrived plotting of the well-made play genre and their emphasis on realism of language, social setting and event. Both Shaw and Barker had developed their directing skills in Stage Society productions and, through its activities, had gathered around them a group of actors committed to reform of the theatre as well as a willing and well-informed audience. Each complimented the other. Having acted Marchbanks in the 1900 Stage Society *Candida*, Barker, in 1904, made it a condition of his agreement to direct *Two Gentlemen of Verona* that the production be accompanied by matinées of Shaw's play. On the success of these matinées the Barker-Vedrenne collaboration at the Royal Court Theatre was founded. The success of Shaw's *John Bull's Other Island* (1904) established the Court in public consciousness, in its first season. Not only did Beatrice Webb, pursuing the Fabian policy of 'permeation', take the Conservative Prime Minister, Balfour, to see it, but he, in his turn, took the Liberal leaders, Asquith and Campbell-Bannerman and, in 1905, a special performance was arranged for Edward VII.

The Court's policy specifically encouraged new writing. Barker stressed the centrality of the author's text, insisting that actors knew the whole play not just their own part in it. A play would be introduced initially for six or seven matinée performances. If these proved successful, it was transferred for a short two-to-three-week evening run. An effect of the repertory system with its quick succession of plays was that playwrights learned from each other's work – cross-fertilisation of subject, tone and method is everywhere apparent – but also, encouraged to attend rehearsals, they learned through performance of their work and were able to rewrite before the evening transfer. Rehearsal experience was, as Shaw advised H. G. Wells, 'a part of the dramatist's experience that is worth a good deal of solid gold'.[2]

Barker, unlike Grein, not only brought a strong theatrical sense to his staging of the plays, but attended to acting style and, particularly, clarity of diction, insisting that attention be paid as much to small as to central roles. His pressure on actors to project their sense of their characters beyond the confines of the play gave an impression of psychological depth in performance. 'The average of acting all round at the Court', according to Rupert Brooke, was 'exactly four times as high as at any other theatre in London. Each character is perfect.'[3] Plays were blocked and lines learned early in rehearsal, the emphasis thereafter being on ensemble and developing an impression of the reality of the stage world. Although the dominant acting style was low-key in keeping with the socially committed realistic style of most of the Court plays, the repertory system provided each actor with a multiplicity of roles. Experience with Shaw's rhetoric, with Gilbert Murray's translations of Euripidean verse, and with Alfred Sutro's version of Maeterlinck's symbolist poeticisms, helped develop the versatility for which Court acting became famous.

Although Barker did not yet succeed in the campaign for a National Theatre, the achievements of the Court seasons did prove generally enabling. Not only were there further Barker seasons, at the Savoy (1907–08) and the Duke of York's (1910–11), but Vedrenne leased the Haymarket to present work by Shaw, Housman and Masefield; Lena Ashwell at the Kingsway, and Gertrude Kingston at the Little Theatre ran seasons of New Drama; Edy Craig founded the largely feminist Pioneer Players, and repertory companies were founded in the provinces. Lewis Casson, Harcourt Williams, Louis Calvert and other actors who had worked with Barker, took his acting styles and directing methods into the West End as well as into the repertory theatres and, after its foundation in 1906, into the Royal Academy of Dramatic Art and subsequently the Guildhall and Central Schools, which between them provided the basis for the remarkable quality of English acting that developed in the years after the First World War.

The Court and Stage Society plays generated a new excitement about theatre. They widened the potential audience with their appeal to younger, more socially conscious and politically alert groups. The aristocratic figures of Society Drama were satirised in the writing of the new dramatists or were replaced by characters who reflected the new audiences and their aspirations, who talked about books, music, education, politics and included liberals and socialists, feminists and university-educated women. New stereotypes appeared: conservative, narrow-minded and complacent characters were immediately identified by their trivial conversation, their card-playing and their over-indulgence in food and drink. A warm response was guaranteed for such a self-referential exchange as Barker's:

JESSICA:
    Got over your anger at the play last night?
THOMAS:
    Oh, sort of play you must expect if you go to the theatre
    on a Sunday.

                             (*The Madras House* (1910), Act II)

On the West End stage, emancipated women were still derided as the reference point for all things alien, but their male associates, no longer Wildean aesthetes, were now identified as Shavian vegetarian-socialists, as a speech in Pinero's *Mid Channel* (1909) demonstrates:

PETER:

> I'm referring of course to real men and women. I don't include persons in petticoats with flat chests and no hips; nor individuals wearin' beards and trousers who dine on a basin of farinaceous food and a drink o' water out o' the filter. They belong to a distinct species.

(Act I)

'Frocks and frills' drama[4] still dominated the commercial theatre, musical comedy flourished at the Gaiety, and Pinero remained the leading West End dramatist, still turning out such fallen-woman pieces as *Mid Channel* throughout the first decade of the century. Theatre remained for many an ephemeral, after-dinner entertainment of light comedy and familiar Society themes, with evening dress *de rigueur* in the stalls and circle as well as on the stage. The social acceptability of the actor-managers was reinforced as, one after another, Charles Wyndham, John Hare, George Alexander, Beerbohm Tree and Johnston Forbes Robertson chalked up knighthoods; as, indeed, did the playwrights W. S. Gilbert, Pinero and Barrie, and (final accolade) when Irving died in 1905 he was buried in Westminster Abbey. But, even here, ripples of Stage Society and Court performances were felt if not acknowledged. Jerome K. Jerome's hugely successful *The Passing of the Third Floor Back* (1907), in which the selfish, bad-tempered residents of a boarding house are transformed by the advent of a stranger who sees only the better self of each of them, is a softened, anglicised version of Gorki's *The Lower Depths*, produced by the Stage Society three years earlier. But in the second decade of the century, Shaw, scarcely performed before the advent of the Stage Society, became the most performed dramatist on the English stage, outstripping even Pinero.

From the outset, Shaw had proved the most successful and prolific of the Court dramatists. Indeed, eleven of the thirty-two plays produced, 701 of 988 performances, were of his work. New Shaw plays included *John Bull's Other Island* (1904), *Man and Superman* and *Major Barbara* (1905) and *The Doctor's Dilemma* (1906). But there were also plays by Yeats, St John Hankin, Masefield, Robins and Galsworthy, among others; translations of Ibsen, Hauptmann, Maeterlinck, Schnitzler and, each year, a new translation of Euripides, while there was, as yet, very little consciousness of Strindberg or Chekhov, Ibsen was now widely acknowledged as the major contemporary European dramatist.[5]

Harley Granville Barker

The issues addressed in Court and Stage Society plays shifted the parameters of what could be represented on stage. Barker in particular, a committed socialist from 1904, brought topics of current debate on to the stage in the four plays he wrote in this period, as well as in his direction of the work of other writers. For all his first performed play, *The Marrying of Ann Leete* (1901), is set in the eighteenth century, it has a strong interest in eugenics and in the ousting of old ideas by new. Its notably modern heroine not only rebels against her tyrannical father's plans to commit her to a useful political marriage but, while the rain falls on the previously parched garden in a play dense with images of degeneration and fertility, she abandons aristocratic life to marry where she sees strength, with the gardener, the rather embarrassingly named, John Abud.

In the subtler *Voysey Inheritance* (1905), Edward Voysey, a youthful idealist like Ann Leete, also rejects the corrupt morality of his family, but the rejection is more complex and the play's symbolism less obvious. Edward's father dies, having confessed to his son not only his long-standing financial fraud but also, like Shaw's Mrs Warren, his continued fraudulence when direct financial need no longer demanded. Edward is left with the choice between the simple course, which immediately occurs to him, of keeping his own hands clean by rejecting his inheritance, exposing the fraud and declaring the firm bankrupt, and the more morally problematic one, which he eventually adopts, of preserving the firm's name for honesty and continuing to manipulate the finances until all the creditors are repaid.

Terms like 'honesty', 'duty' and 'trust' are problematised in the shady world of stock-market profits and financial dealing that Barker portrays, and there are no scapegoats whose removal will resolve the problem as there were in Society Drama. Old Voysey, whose portrait, like General Gabler's, dominates the family living room in the last act, is revealed as merely one of the most effective of those who have embraced the capitalist ethic. Not only have previous generations of the respected Voysey firm exploited the resources of the unproductive people who live off inherited money, but other layers of dishonesty and connivance are exposed in the dealings of the Peaceys, trusted head clerks, father and son, in the blind eye turned on the sources of her husband's affluence by Mrs Voysey, and in the private arrangement for which the chief creditor bargains.

Although Acts II and IV are set in the work place, the Voysey office in Lincoln's Inn, the action of three of the five acts takes place, as in many of the realist plays of Antoine's Théâtre Libre, in the heart of the family home, around and sometimes across the large dining table that fills the central acting area. The hearth and the table, indeed, become recurrent features of the set of subsequent realist drama. Public and private worlds participate in the corruption and are equally usurped by it and, alongside the financial issues, the normal miseries of family life – a bitter feud between father and eldest son, a spinster sister whose life is withering away, a breaking marriage, a bullying husband – continue.

The domestic scene, and the representative nature of it, is, however, an area of difficulty as well as of interest in Barker's writing. Although his plays repeatedly feature family, inheritance and the idea of 'the House of . . .', the relationships seem curiously unfamilial. The echo of Ibsen in the use of the Voysey portrait serves to emphasise the difference. We accept that Ann Leete is daughter of her father's house because we are told that this is so, but little in her world-view, or the speech in which it is expressed, endorses this. Philip Madras in *The Madras House* has little in common with either his whining mother or his dashing, self-centred father, and Edward Voysey's three brothers are rather representative types of the law, the army and the arts (failed) than convincing siblings and have little in common with Edward, the only one with much complexity. The variations might help to suggest that these families in some way figure England – the stage settings insist on the typical nature of the rooms shown – but the absence of a growing sense of relationship prevents belief in a shared past that might interact, as it does in Ibsen's drama, in strange but convincing ways with the present. For all the intelligence of observation in Barker's plays, this lack of familial texture leaves an impression of thinness.

Waste (1907), Barker's next play, was banned while still in rehearsal on account of its 'extremely outspoken reference to sexual relations'.[6] In it, Trebell, a politician, has an affair which would have been the whole matter in a conventional social-problem play. Here, the married woman involved becomes pregnant and, realising there is no love in the case, has an abortion which kills her. The emotional and personal life of the characters affects and is affected by the public and intellectual one. Trebell is a liberal thinker and, with his fall, his plans for the Disestablishment Bill and reforms in teacher training and educational policy fall too. This is what catches Barker's imagination as the play veers away from its initial suggestion of interest in the relationship and the issues involved in the unwanted pregnancy to the man's destroyed career and the implications of that for society. The play in no way argues for sympathy with the idea of abortion. Amy is called 'a pretty little fool' by Trebell and nothing in the representation of the character contradicts this. Indeed, despite the franker treatment of sexuality, it is hard to avoid a Pinero-like moral that the man should not have yielded to his sexual attraction for a woman less than perfect in her moral behaviour. Of the various possibilities suggested by the 'waste' of the title, the loss of Amy's life seems to be the least considerable. What is condemned, besides her action, is the triviality that results from lack of education and the valuation of women based primarily on their decorative quality and sex appeal.

The frustrated lives of women without independent means is a recurring feature of Barker's plays. Edward Voysey's spinster sister, Honor, functions essentially as the family servant. Without status, she is at the beck and call of mother and brothers. Even Frances, wise sister of Trebell in *Waste*, acknowledges her own limited scope when she comments ruefully, 'until I was forty I never realised the fact that most women must express themselves through men'. There is a fuller representation of this in *The Madras House* (1910), which has much the widest range of female characters, socially, economically and in their various idiosyncrasies and attitudes, of all Barker's work and which, in successive scenes, demonstrates the constraints on and pretensions of women in the current organisation of society.

Structurally the most adventurous of Barker's plays, *The Madras House* consists of four juxtaposed episodes. The life of every character is shaped by his or her particular relationship to the couture firm, the Madras House, whether or not they are actually employer or employed or merely supported by profits from the business, and all come under the cool scrutiny of the central character, Philip Madras, an anti-*raisonneur* who shares ground with such sceptics as Ibsen's Dr Relling in *The Wild Duck*. The play has no ostensible plot although it is acutely alert to the range of roles and restrictions society's construction of gender imposes on women.

In Act I, set in the home of Philip's uncle and business partner, Henry Huxtable, we learn that Philip's libertine father, Constantine, is to return for the proposed sale of the business and that one of the firm's sales assistants, Miss Yates, has become pregnant. Act II moves to Huxtable's business premises, the retail drapery side of the firm, where, besides a fierce indictment of the 'living-in' system for shop workers, a subject of literary denunciation since the publication of H. G. Wells' novel *Kipps*, in 1905, there is a set-to between Miss Yates, the man wrongly suspected of being her lover, that man's outraged wife and the housekeeper whose task it is to oversee the morals of the employees. Worker and overseer are equally cowed in the presence of Philip's smart, bored wife, Jessica, who appears at the end of the act. In Act III, set in the inner sanctum of the high-fashion Bond Street premises of the Madras House, the new season's stock is displayed through a mannequin parade before the prospective purchaser of the firm and the sale is agreed. In the last act, in Philip's own drawing room, Constantine meets his aggrieved wife and Philip reiterates his determination to stand for the County Council and warns Jessica that their income will be considerably reduced, as a result of which she seems to see her own role of cossetted wife with new clarity. Possible plot lines are repeatedly glimpsed in all this but are not developed: the relationship between Philip's wife and friend remains at the level of the laziest flirtation; there is no hitch in the proposed sale of the firm, we simply catch stages towards completion; Constantine and his wife have no means of communicating with each other but though there is resentment there is no explosion. There is no resolution for any of the characters in marriage, divorce or suicide, and even the pregnancy of Marion Yates and her refusal to name the father of her child results in no denouement. The identification of Constantine Madras as her seducer is made between the lines and serves less to excite emotion than to undercut any sense of glamour that might have attached to his theories about women and his accounts of his Eastern harem.

Acts I and III, which include the most trenchant social comment, are also the wittiest. The limitations on the lives of the six unmarried Huxtable daughters, whose ages range from 26 to 39, are demonstrated in their adolescent excitement at the most trivial events and in the repetitive mundanity of the polite formalities that make up much of their conversation. Barker's ironies are rife in the conversation of the male characters in Act III while, subject to their collective gaze, the mannequins parade in gowns made fashionable by French courtesans and now intended for the wives of wealthy and respectable English businessmen. The prospective buyer rhapsodises about 'what Goethe refers to as the woman spirit . . . drawing us ever upward and on' but also outlines a scheme he has for replacing mannequins with automata. Meanwhile the models circulate: clothes-horses for the absurd gowns on view.

Elizabeth Robins and the suffrage dramatists

While the frustrations of middle-class women facing spinsterhood had been a recurrent theme throughout Barker's writing, the self-sufficiency of Marion Yates who, with no private income determines to bring up her child herself, is new in his work, as is the tentative move towards recognition of her gender role by Jessica. It suggests the impact on him of contemporary plays by women dramatists, as well as reaction against the vogue for rags to riches shop-girl musicals such as Leedham Bantock's *The Girl Behind the Counter* (1906) or the Gaiety's *Our Miss Gibbs, or The Girl at the Stores* (1909) which included a chorus of happy mannequins.

Elizabeth Robins' *Votes for Women* (Court, 1907), had offered a feminist version of matters raised in *Waste* and a positive image of women more markedly different from the 1890s subjection to male values and social control than anything yet written by her male colleagues. The experience of an abortion, suffered before the action of the play begins by its heroine

Vida Levering after she had been abandoned by the leading male character, now the up-and-coming Tory MP, Geoffrey Stonor, is given full weight in terms both of the loss to the woman and her capacity to absorb and learn from the loss. The play begins conventionally enough with a country house party and a prospective engagement. Vida is not only, as Mrs Pankhurst and many of her colleagues famously were, glamorous enough to draw compliments from a dreadful old chauvinist, but is also self-sufficient and politically active, as is demonstrated in her winning Stonor's support in the final act for the suffrage cause. It is demonstrated even more effectively in her passionate address to a suffrage meeting which, taking up the whole of Act II, caused a sensation at its first performance with its startling re-presentation of a real suffrage meeting in Trafalgar Square. With red banners flying, the speakers addressed the teeming, motley crowd and, over their heads, the audience as if they were an extension of the crowd. Act II's dramatic power derives from the intercutting of the public occasion with the private drama. The male perspective is mocked as Stonor, silenced at the edge of the stage, looks upstage towards the woman who speaks from a position of strength, her clear ringing tones combining a moving version of their intimate story with general arguments about gender injustices and witty responses to hecklers in the crowd, while his fiancée is simultaneously fired by the political message and brought to realisation of the realities of Stonor's past.

Robins subtitled the play, 'A Dramatic Tract in Three Acts' but, while the play clearly proselytises on behalf of women's suffrage, it is not merely propaganda. The conventions of Society Drama are wittily subverted in Acts I and III, telling use is made of the stage space, and details of relationships between the characters are sharply observed. While Githa Sowerby does not mention the suffrage cause in her gritty *Rutherford and Son* (1912), the hard-headed bargaining by the heroine as she makes conditions with her bullying father-in-law demonstrates a parallel mode and plot device.

Indubitably, Robins' play and its Trafalgar Square scene was a force behind the establishment the following year of the Actresses' Franchise League, of which the playwright was a founder member. With over 900 members, some 400 of whom wrote plays, the AFL assumed an important role in the suffrage movement and was responsible for the production of countless plays between 1909 and the outbreak of war in 1914 in an astonishing outpouring of energy and activity. Some plays were full length, like Cicely Hamilton's *Pageant of Great Women* (1910), a parade of famous women from history in celebration of women's achievements, which included the actress Ellen Terry appearing as herself; many, much more amateur, were only a few minutes long, written to be performed between speeches on suffrage platforms. Unashamed propaganda, most take the form of conversion or reconciliation narratives in which characters initially passive, like Geoffrey Stonor's young fiancée or hostile, like Stonor himself, are won to the cause. *Mrs Appleyard's Awakening* by Evelyn Glover, for example, ends with the heroine, appalled by the bigotry shown by an anti-suffrage visitor, asking her maid to retrieve previously discarded suffrage leaflets; in Gertrude Jennings' *A Woman's Influence*, first played at the Women's Social and Political Union exhibition in 1909, a husband is convinced by argument and evidence, and in Joan Dugdale's comedy, *10, Clowning Street*, the daughters of the Prime Minister outwit their father – essentially blackmailing him into a promise to bring in a female franchise bill.[7] It is unsurprising that Shaw wanted to play, too, opening his *Press Cuttings*, written in 1909 as a challenge to the Censor, with the cry 'Votes for Women!'.

In many of these plays, as in others not strictly concerned with the suffrage cause but written for one or another of the new producing agencies, single women figure as heroines. They celebrate Vivie Warren's or Vida Levering's choice of education, a career and a single life. Their self-sufficiency is applauded. Beatrice Webb had a point in her criticism that Barker and Shaw, 'both harp on the mere physical attractions of men to women, and women to men, coupled with the insignificance of the female for anything but sex attraction with tiresome iteration'.[8] The perceptions, even of these advanced writers, are shaped by the assumptions of their time and sex. The women dramatists, Robins, Elizabeth Baker and Cicely Hamilton develop the perceptions introduced by Shaw and Ibsen about the bad faith implicit in the married relationship where women are not able to be self-supporting. As Hamilton's Georgiana says in *Just To Get Married* (1911), 'Surely you're not romantic enough to imagine that all the married women of your acquaintance have selected their more or less unsuitable husbands out of pure affection' (Act I). But there are also single working women among their characters who face a choice of marriage or independence.

Working life is by no means glamorised in Elizabeth Baker's *Chains* (1909): income from letting off a room is necessary, the tedium of daily commuting stretches unrelievedly into the future with already low wages liable to be docked when the firm's profits sink but, while one sister holds her husband by announcing her pregnancy, shop work, however irksome, allows the other freedom to resist the marriage trap. The central figure of Cicely Hamilton's sharp comedy, *Diana of Dobson's* (1908) defies the moral-ising and restrictions imposed on a group of live-in shop assistants in a scene that surely informed that of Miss Yates' defiance in Act II of Barker's *Madras House*, which was produced in the following season. After this forceful opening scene, set in the shop workers' bleak living-in dormitory, Diana, backed by a small legacy, is rediscovered masquerading as a rich widow in a Swiss resort where she is courted by and rejects both the owner of the firm for which she previously slaved and a careless young fortune hunter. Hamilton's characters acknowledge love away from the drawing room, in unlikely situations, where they see each other clear, without the trappings of costume, jewellery and hairdressing: on a bench on the Embankment among the down and outs, in *Diana of Dobson's*; in a station waiting room, having been drenched by the rain, in *Just To Get Married*. Her heroines do accept marriage but on terms of mutual respect and honesty: the position, indeed, to which Philip and Jessica seem to be moving at the end of Barker's play.

The Court dramatists: Galsworthy, Masefield and Hankin

In nineteenth-century melodrama there were bandits, sailors, landowners, milkmaids, but they were only involved in their *métier* in a general kind of way. The earning of money was no more discussed in Society Drama than it would have been at a polite dinner. In the New Drama, there are jobs and money; work occurs frequently and is often crucial to the dramatic conflict. Those with jobs are pitted against those with an easy life from inherited wealth. But, equally, work is essential to the creation of environment: people must earn a living to survive and where and how they do so affects who they are and how other characters see them. Marion Yates' pregnancy is the more shocking because she is 'not a chit of a girl, but first hand in our Costume room' and marked for promotion to Buyer, while Brigstock, the putative father of her child, is 'third man in Hosiery'. Where, previously, the lower classes had appeared most commonly as blandly loyal or humorously insouciant personal servants, careful distinctions are now made between the functions and status of different servants, and the particular rankings and responsibilities of policeman, shop assistants or office clerks.

As in the nineteenth-century realist novel, even the well-off have derived their money in some specific way: by inheritance, by land, through trade, through investment. Even more than those of Granville Barker, the plays of John Galsworthy fix attention on the power wealth can wield, on the dishonesties and exploitation involved in making money, and on how people who do not have it manage. We are made conscious of the price of things and the commercial valuation of lives; made aware that actions have unforeseen implications in the lives of other people. His plays consistently indict complacency and self-interest, particularly of the middle classes, whose morality and respectability is demonstrably bolstered by money and influence. They also attest to the existence of the working classes and to the damaged condition of lives on the poverty line.

In Galsworthy's first play, *The Silver Box* (1906), a man and woman are taken away by the police accused of burglary by Barthwick, a Liberal MP. At the end of Act II the Barthwicks are seen listening guiltily to the off-stage crying of the small child who waits in vain for its mother's return. Denying responsibility with an 'Ah, but it's out of our hands', Barthwick blocks his ears. The denial is emphasised by the gesture and also by its positioning at the end of an act. Act I had ended with Barthwick's shrug of doubt at Mrs Jones's denial of theft, and the last and, for the audience the most devastating shrug, ends the play when, faced with Mrs Jones's appeal after Jones has been sentenced, Barthwick *'makes a shamefaced gesture of refusal, and hurries out of court'*. The audience is both punished and liberated by what it must recognise as self-deception and the inequity of life chances as the on-stage middle-class characters shamefacedly acknowledge or guiltily refute their own part in the misery of less fortunate people.

Recognition of the gulf between the haves and have-nots is pointedly spoken in the dialogue as well as being built into the structure of the play. 'Why a poor man who'd behaved as you've done', says Barthwick to his son, 'd'you think he'd have any mercy shown him?' (I. iii.) Just as drunken spite motivated middle-class Jack Barthwick to steal a purse, so it motivated working-class Jones to steal the silver box as well as the purse but, whereas Jones is condemned to hard labour, Jack is protected from the exposure of a court case by his father's ability to pay off the owner of the purse and use his influence to mobilise the assistance of a cunning lawyer. Similarly, in *The Eldest Son* (1912), a landowner, who had insisted on pain of dismissal that one of his underkeepers marry the village girl he has made pregnant, insists equally strongly, on pain of disinheritance, that his son abandon the maid servant whose pregnancy threatens the family honour. The 'proper pride' of the working man's rejection of 'a charity marriage' for his daughter shows where real honour lies. Such patterning, pressurising the audience, is most obviously present in *The Silver Box*, although it is characteristic of all Galsworthy's plays.

The sharp contrast offered between the straitened circumstances of the Joneses and the comfortable lifestyle of the Barthwicks is more thoroughly worked into the structure of *Strife* (1909), Galsworthy's play about the last day of a damaging strike and the stand-off between the charismatic strike leader, David Roberts, and John Anthony, the iron-willed Chairman of the Trenartha Tin Plate Works. The conflict between the two sides is expressed directly in the dialogue:

ROBERTS:
    All those demands are fair. We have not asked anything

that we are not entitled to ask. What I said up in
London, I say again now: there is not anything on that
piece of paper that a just man should not ask, and a just
man give.

ANTHONY:

There is not one single demand on this paper that we
will grant.

(Act I)

The organisation of the scenes and their parallel settings and action
demonstrate the contrast in life chances of the two sides. At the beginning
of Act I, the Board of Directors, all men, discuss the badness of the hotel
dinner and the good lunch in prospect, and call for screens to protect
them from the heat of the fire. There is just bread and cheese on the table
at the opening of Act II, which takes the audience into a worker's cottage,
and talk between the characters, who are all women, soon turns to practical
ways of lessening the hunger pangs. The stage direction asking for a
'meagre' fire is reinforced when a character comments, 'there ain't much
'eat to this fire. Come and warm yerself, Mrs Rous, you're lookin' as
white as the snow, you are'. But the parallelism goes further than this. In
each scene a group discussion which demonstrates communal strength
gives way to a more intimate duologue in which the vulnerabilities of
each side are exposed. The voice of opposition within each side is most
strongly expressed by a woman, each of whom enters the enemy's camp
and is rebuffed. It becomes clear that both the Board and the workers
want compromise but are prevented from it by the opposed ideological
stance of the two leaders. The immediate causes of the final compromise
are both medical: Roberts' wife has a weak heart and needs the nutritious
food denied her by the strike, while Anthony has been warned about
strain by his doctor: evident plot indicators to an audience attuned to the
devices of the well-made play, of which Galsworthy always made more
free than Barker. That he has recourse to each of these medical problems
at successive climactic moments makes the parallel plotting too obvious
and mars an otherwise powerful play.

The public and private, social and emotional levels of *Strife* coincide in
the second scene of Act II, the strike meeting, which is the most compelling sequence of the play. Out of the quarrelling and alternation of voices,
Roberts speaks, gradually gaining control through the power of his oratory
which is addressed directly to the audience as well as to the crowd who,
as in the Trafalgar Square scene of *Votes for Women*, face up-stage to listen.
The Defence Counsel's address in *The Silver Box* had already demonstrated
Galsworthy's relish for rhetoric and his skill with it is freshly evident here.
With interruptions, Roberts' speech takes up three pages of the printed
text. Alternating question and statement, long and short sentences, repeat-

ing key phrases in an anaphoric display, he denounces Capital, emphasises the importance of unity in the present fight, derides the would-be appeasers and, looking to the future and those that come after, reaches a messianic climax in which the actor's delivery is skilfully shaped by Galsworthy:

> They're welcome to the worst that can happen to me, to the worst that can happen to us all – aren't they? If we can shake (*passionately*) that white-faced monster with the bloody lips, that has sucked the life out of ourselves, our wives and children, since the world began. (*Dropping the note of passion but with the utmost weight and intensity.*) If we have not the hearts of men to stand against it, breast to breast, and eye to eye, and force it backward till it cry for mercy, it will go on sucking life; and we shall stay forever what we are (*in almost a whisper*) less than the very dogs.
>
> (II. ii)

The single figure addressing a crowd and gaining their attention, absorption and then total acquiescence, a scenic image that derives in the English theatre from Mark Antony's address to the Roman mob in *Julius Caesar*, is used to powerful effect here, but as the shout for Roberts goes up news comes that his wife is dead. Directly contrary to the Shakespearean model, this abrupt turn of fortune, subverts the effect of Roberts' oratory and, in the sudden anticlimax, control passes to the appeasers.

The anti-heroic final scene in which agreement is reached, over the heads of the displaced Roberts and Antony, to the terms drawn up before the beginning of the strike, seems to endorse the argument for compromise and Galsworthy clearly took pains to be even-handed to Capital and Labour in the structure and dialogue of the play. But this is to reckon without the emotional impact of contrasting conditions of food and warmth in the opening scenes; the novelty of the scene in which the working-class women discuss the exigencies of the strike; the fiery loyalty to her husband of the suffering Annie Roberts, and the sheer theatrical energy attaching to the scene of the strike meeting. It is, surely, these scenes that remain in the mind and that led Conrad to comment that, 'the murmurs against *Joy* shall be drowned in such a shout around *Strife* as this country has not heard for a hundred years or more', and Emma Goldman to write that, 'not since Hauptmann's *Weavers* was placed before the thoughtful public, has there appeared anything more stirring than *Strife*'.[9] Indeed, the fact that a revolutionary such as Goldman spent time writing *The Social Significance of Modern Drama* (1914) is itself a demonstration of the impact drama was making in these years.

That John Anthony dismisses his daughter's plea for the workers with a 'read your books, play your music', guarantees reaction from an audience concerned with suffragism and the woman question. Similarly, the talk from both sides of who is up, who down, resonates in the context of contemporary discussion of Social Darwinism, survival of the fittest and the growth of trade unionism. As contemporary politicians argued, Labour, could it but be fully organised and united, threatened to disrupt the comfortable existence Capital had made for itself. The whole of *Strife* is dense with such contextual references and the play prepared the way for an extraordinary number of strike plays in the next two decades (see, Chapter 8). The paradox of committed writing in which social rather than experiential issues are addressed is that precisely those elements which make the piece so immediate will also leave it seeming thin and dated once the context has changed. The most powerful realist writing is perhaps of necessity locked into its own period.

In play after play, sometimes as the central issue, sometimes merely glimpsed as a background to other matters, Galsworthy presents the harshness of life on the breadline, of conditions which brutalise men and leave women with little alternative but the streets. There is, moreover, a generalising tendency in his plays. By beginning the trial scene of *The Silver Box* with another case in which poverty and drunkenness have ruined a family, he implies that Jones's case is representative of the successive miseries of any court and of countless families. Similarly, in the second of the two prison scenes of *Justice* (1910), as the governor makes his rounds, the audience recognises the desperation not just of Falder, whose story they have followed, but of three other men variously tormented by incarceration.

Galsworthy researched the prison scenes of *Justice* with Zolaesque rigour. He visited prisons and interviewed prisoners. Beatrice Webb who had thought other plays of her Fabian colleagues insufficiently geared to the advocacy of social causes, welcomed the plea for specific reform of the penal system that she found in this play and Winston Churchill, then Home Secretary, famously saw the play four times and acknowledged the impact of the solitary confinement scene on his subsequent programme of prison reform. But the power of the piece lies less in the documentation than in the way what he had seen fired Galsworthy to remarkable dramatic invention.

Already, when the solitary confinement scene begins, the turns and tensions of the plot have enlisted audience sympathy for Falder. Direct appeal to emotion is made first in a touching scene between Falder and Ruth, the married woman he loves, in which she describes having run away from her brutal husband in terror the previous night. Then Falder, in what becomes an increasingly tense detection scene, is exposed as having forged a cheque to enable him to take Ruth and her children away, and, finally, in the course of the Act II trial scene, Galsworthy further loads the dice with an eloquent plea for mercy from Falder's young defence counsel and, lest audience sympathies might be alienated, clear testimony that Ruth and Falder have not yet slept together. But the plea is rebuffed by the judge who censures what he describes as theft to further an immoral relationship and condemns Falder to three years' penal servitude.

The first shock of the scene (III. iii) is that the stage space is reduced to thirteen feet by seven, to suggest the dimensions of Falder's cell, the next is that no words are spoken. Falder's mime, foregrounded in the immediately preceding scene in the hysterical anxiety of his responses to the governor's questioning, and now charted in Galsworthy's stage directions, reveals the increasing desperation of the imprisoned man as he goes round and round his tiny cell, body tense and hands pressed against the walls. The off-stage sound of distant pounding on a cell door mounts and seems to get nearer until, at its loudest Falder, too, 'panting violently, flings himself at his door, and beats on it'.

Eugene O'Neill, just beginning his own career as a playwright, was one of those deeply impressed by the play. He wrote to a friend that:

> My advice is keep to the main idea – the injustice of Justice. It's big. It's fundamental. Too much can't be said about the farcicality of man-made laws. Can the sentiment. Write impartially and make your facts, your characters, drive home the point. Galsworthy's *Justice* is a model of what I mean.[10]

Galsworthy's point is driven home because the audience, unlike the other on-stage characters, are made party to the details of the doomed Falder's circumstances. Their inwardness with his anxieties and his sense of responsibility is what makes them acutely conscious of the blindness of the justice meted out. This establishment of emotional commitment is a crucial part of Galsworthy's dramatic method.

Another cause recurrently fought by Galsworthy is signalled in the condemnation by the judge in *Justice* of what he labels immorality. The question of loveless marriage and the assertion of marital rights is central in the plays Galsworthy sets among the respectable middle classes. *Joy* (1907) presents the hurt and jealousy felt by the eponymous heroine as she is forced to acknowledge her mother's love for a man other than her estranged husband. But, having created the situation, Galsworthy shies away from real examination of it, resolving Joy's problems through her own awakening to love for the young man who has assiduously courted her through the earlier scenes. The first act of *The Fugitive* (1913), however, a much darker play, unequivocally demonstrates the revulsion of its heroine, Clare, from her obtuse upper middle-class husband and culminates in her insistence on a separation. The act ends with a lengthy stage direction, after Clare's exit to her room, in which the estranged husband moves restlessly around the stage, seems about to leave and then resolutely opens the door to his wife's room. In the shaft of light, the audience glimpses her '*unhooking a necklet*' before '*he goes in, shutting the door behind him with a thud*' and the curtain falls. An audience familiar with the miseries of Irene and Soames Forsyte in Galsworthy's hugely successful novel, *The Man of Property* (1906), would have had little difficulty in recognising this as a prelude to marital rape, particularly since Act II begins with Clare seeking refuge with her bohemian writer friend. The abandoned husband's continued destructive hold on Clare's fate, evinced in the recurrent presence of detectives set to watch her, and the effects of the vengeful divorce settlement, underlies the subsequent action of the play.

Less theatrically compelling than either of these plays, although worthy in its attempt to show the failure of a marriage from the bereft husband's point of view, is *A Bit o' Love*, produced at the Kingsway two years later. There seems to have been a good deal of wish-fulfilment in this play. At immense emotional cost to himself, the hero, a West Country curate, not only accepts his wife's wish to leave him but also, despite the destructive mockery of his parishioners, refuses to revenge himself on her and her lover by suing for divorce. The curate's saintliness is cloying, as is the obviousness of the symbolism that attaches to his flute-playing and his St Francis-like feeling for dumb animals. His wife gone, he whispers to himself, 'never cage any wild thing', his earlier reprimand to one of the village children, while a youth who has seen him seeking comfort in his flute reports that he saw Orpheus charming the animals down 'Mr Burlacomb's long medder'.

The Fugitive helps to focus some of Galsworthy's limitations. It is not just that the plot too evidently shapes the action, rather that, for all he berates the middle classes, his is an evidently class-bound perspective. His working-class figures are almost uniformly pathetic, the women hard-working, anxious for their children, subject to male violence; the men spineless, finding oblivion in drink, albeit usually under the pressure of unemployment. The class stereotyping limits the depth of representation. It is significant that the fiery Roberts in *Strife* is differentiated from the other men from the outset: he is trained, an engineer. The implication of *The Fugitive* is that Clare is fundamentally different from the shop girls with whom she has had to work; that the humdrum routine and the 'working *under* people' (III. i) is worse for her than for them. Moreover, it is the fact that she is so evidently 'a lady' that touches the heart of the youth who picks her up when, at the point of despair in the final scene of the play, she tries to sell herself; and it is those finer feelings that lead her to swallow poison rather than accept an unwanted sexual liaison as working-class Ruth in *Justice* evidently had done. *The Fugitive*'s closing tableau of the dead Clare, the young man with head in hands, a waiter crossing himself, a languid lord twisting a gardenia in his fingers and his partner stooping to kiss Clare's forehead, has a facility worthy of Henry Arthur Jones, as does the final exchange:

LANGUID LORD:
  Friend of yours?
YOUNG MAN:
  My God! She was a lady. That's all I know about her.
LANGUID LORD:
  A Lady!

(Act IV)

These plays are fiercely moralistic. Although they often have upper-class settings, the challenging nature of the problems and the conclusions drawn distinguish his plays from Society Drama. He commented that 'every grouping of life and character has its inherent moral; and the business of the dramatist is so to pose the group as to bring that moral poignantly to the light of day',[11] which is even more appropriate to John Masefield's plays than to his own.

Like Galsworthy, Masefield puts working-class characters on the stage, although his are the rural poor. In both *The Campden Wonder* (1907) and *The Tragedy of Nan* (Pioneers, 1908, directed by Barker) the issue is capital punishment. The thrust of the argument against it is that innocent people might be hanged. Not only is the innocence demonstrated by Masefield's plays but sympathy is wrung for their bereft families. Nan's father, hanged for stealing a sheep, is subsequently shown to have been the victim of a false accusation. In *The Campden Wonder*, a desperate man, revenging himself on his brother, confesses, to the incredulity of the local people, that he, his brother and mother have murdered Harrison, a missing man. In the last scene, which takes place in prison, all three, the two protesting innocents and the hypocritically penitent, perjured man, are taken out in turn to be hanged. In the ironic coda to the play, Mrs Harrison runs in to say, too late, that all can be freed since the supposedly murdered man has returned home.

The failing minister of God, the subject of fierce dramatic irony, deriving probably from Ibsen's Pastor Manders but chiming with contemporary intellectual scepticism, is a recurrent figure in turn-of-the-century drama. 'It's little the likes of him knows of the ways of the sea', says Maurya in accurate dismissal of the priest's reassurances in Synge's *Riders to the Sea* (1904). The Reverent Colpus in *The Voysey Inheritance* looks to his profits as assiduously as the next man and, albeit credulous rather than grasping, the parson in *The Campden Wonder* is wholly deceived by the wicked brother's supposed penitence:

PARSON:
> There is joy, John, over one sinner that repenteth. God's
> mercy is infinite. Put your trust in him.

JOHN:
> Ah, sir. I do feel it in my heart. It be a glow like.
>
> (sc. iii)

Masefield's plays are certainly poignant but the moral is brought to the light of day through plots that are complicated rather than complex. The moral scales are heavily weighted. Even more evidently than in Galsworthy's, the working-class characters are presented as victims. They don't fight the system, but are crushed by it and, like Mrs Harrison at the end of *The Campden Wonder* or the heroine of *The Tragedy of Nan*, they kill themselves because they can't bear to live in the wicked world in which they discover themselves to be.

St John Hankin, by contrast, brought satirical humour to an upper middle-class milieu, particularly as embodied in that recurrent New Drama character, the repressive father. His most interesting characters are idiosyncratic resisters of Society's demands. As a contributor to *Punch*, Hankin had written a series of 'Dramatic Sequels' to various famous plays, including *Caste* and *A Doll's House* and this experience tells in his full-length plays whose setting and plot development have much in common with Society Dramas but whose bitter edge, sharp analysis of social aspiration and disconcerting endings offer a direct contrast of tone and perception. All feature conflict between parents and the adult children who challenge their belief systems.

The wastrel anti-hero of *The Return of the Prodigal* (1905), playing on the political ambition of his authoritarian father and the social aspirations of his philistine brother, induces them to pay him to stay out of their lives in a mocking reversal of the biblical story of the Prodigal Son. As his family lives off their work-people so he proposes to live off them. The daughter of the family, Violet, who has appeared content, is revealed as trapped, like Honor Voysey or the Huxtable daughters, by the social proprieties attaching to marriage and social intercourse. In the last act, she registers her situation with a bitterness Barker's women never quite express:

> It's all very well for Henry. He is a partner in the
> firm. He will be a very rich man. He can marry Stella
> Faringford. Oh, we are to be great people! But you
> don't find Sir John Faringford's son proposing to *me*.
> No! He wants a girl of his own class or else an heiress,
> not a manufacturer's daughter with a few thousand
> pounds. So the great people won't marry me and I
> mustn't marry the little people.
>
> (Act IV)

The comedy of the early scenes of the play evaporates before the pain of her seemingly unalterable situation. Unlike her wastrel brother, she has no means of relaxing her father's iron authority. But such unalterability is precisely what is challenged by the spirited heroines of Robins, Hamilton and Sowerby in the next five or six years. The daughter of the house, early in Sowerby's *Rutherford and Son* echoes Violet's cry precisely, saying 'I don't know anybody – you know that. No-one in Grantley's good enough for us, and we're not good enough for the other kind', but, in the last act, turned out by her father, she is more defiant than crestfallen. The resilience and capacity for self-assertion of Sowerby's female characters no doubt contributed to the 'realistic grasp' Emma Goldman attributed to this play in her book on drama and its social significance.[12]

Hankins' *The Cassilis Engagement* (1907) is a more problematic play whose detailed social observation sets up expectations not met by the development of the plot. The discomfiting of a fortune hunter, Mrs Borridge, and her daughter, Ethel, by Mrs Cassilis, who thwarts her son's plans to marry Ethel but retains his affection for herself by extending to the enemy a most generous-seeming hospitality in which their social incompetence is demonstrated and the impropriety of the match revealed, is a classic comic situation and is presented as such by Hankin. The difficulty is that Hankin's satire is unbalanced by the grossness of the caricature of the lower middle-class Mrs Borridge and the lightness, if it is satire at all, of his presentation of the possessive Mrs Cassilis whose cool head and cold heart – 'I want them to feel thoroughly at home. Vulgar people are so much more vulgar when they feel at home, aren't they?' (Act II) – seem to be endorsed. Moreover, the potentially sympathetic characteristics he gives Ethel are not developed although they must have raised expectations in the Stage Society audience. The comedy admits no regret at the loss to the Cassilis house of Ethel's loyalty, implicit in her protectiveness of the much mocked Mrs Borridge, or her sense of purpose, for it is she who eventually acts to break off the engagement. There is no challenge to her Act II statement, 'I've been to school and been taught things. But what's education? It can't alter how we're made, can it?', and her spirited singing of a vulgar song to relieve the boredom of the country house party, for all it lifts the scene, is offered as a demonstration of her unsuitability rather than as criticism of the genteel clique. Any criticism of the endless round of riding and card parties of which life in the country seems to consist, and the presumption of maternal right of interference in a son's most intimate relationships, remains latent. Hankin, who is no Shaw, makes little of it. The Stage Society audience, sensitised to issues of class snobbery, unsurprisingly found the play embarrassing or trivial in its development and, although it did become one of the most frequently revived productions of the Birmingham Repertory Company, it was not performed again in London.

There is no such opacity of tone in Hankin's next and final play before his premature death. *The Last of the De Mullins* (1908), is a very direct representation of the preoccupations of the new drama: a tyrannical father is again challenged, middle-class pretentions and limitations on personal freedom are clearly derided, and the impact of the growing feminist movement is felt in the spiritedness of this heroine. Disowned by her ancient county family eight years previously when she became pregnant, Janet, now a successful hat-shop proprietor, is summoned to the bedside of her dying father, Hugo. Won by her energy and liveliness, the once dictatorial Hugo proposes to forgive her and recognise her son as his grandson and the last of the De Mullins, a title he had previously assumed to be his own. Janet, debilitated by the repressive atmosphere of the family home, rejects the offer and the name, as well as the snobbish prejudice against trade, reasserts her New Womanhood and returns to the city life she has established for herself. She returns, too, to contented single motherhood, having, like Vida Levering, rejected the half-hearted offer of marriage from her one-time lover on the grounds that he is not interesting enough. Hankin is most effective when, as here, he subverts from within.

George Bernard Shaw

Shaw's praise of Hankin as 'a most gifted writer of high comedy of the kind that is a stirring and important criticism of life', echoed the younger writer's claim on Shaw's behalf that 'a play may be a serious work of art and yet remain amusing . . . people laugh abundantly at the plays of Mr Shaw although he is almost our only "serious dramatist" '. Shaw's claim to seriousness was challenged by those who, like Beatrice Webb, found him fundamentally flippant, 'gambling with ideas and emotions in a way that distresses slow-minded prigs like Sidney and me and hurts those with any fastidiousness'.[13]

Although he shared intellectual ground with them and challenged the contemporary organisation of society and gender relationships at least as fiercely, Shaw's dramatic method subverted the earnest social realism of the younger Court dramatists. His villains prove philanthropic, his brothel-owner endows scholarships, his arms-dealer provides model living conditions for his workers, his reformers find themselves wrong-footed and, among his liveliest characterisations, are those he labels 'the undeserving poor'. Where Galsworthy's Jones is by turns pitiable and brutish, Doolittle in *Pygmalion* (1914) has real wit and self-sufficiency; where Hankin's Mrs Borridge is merely grotesquely vulgar, Shaw's Mrs Warren has dramatic energy and the capacity to startle her audience into admiration, however short-lived. Just as *Mrs Warren's Profession* was his response to the success of *The Second Mrs Tanqueray* and 1890s woman-with-a-past drama, so *Fanny's First Play* (1911) parodies the new plays of middle-class emancipation and *Misalliance*, premièred in the same season as *The Madras House*, is an absurdist reworking of the class and generation conflicts of St John Hankin and Barker. Shaw's audience, constantly stimulated by the uncertainties and mockeries he introduces, can never relax into the complacency and self-admiration to which a coterie audience is often prey.

The paradoxical tone of Shaw's plays had confounded criticism from the outset but, by 1905, the provision of a performing base by the Stage Society and the Court Theatre had demonstrated that they were eminently performable: audiences returned to be challenged by the dialectic and amused by the wit even when directed against themselves. *Candida* (Court revival, 1903), *John Bull's Other Island* (1904), *Man and Superman* (1905) having all had huge success, J. T. Grein could write in *The Sunday Times* that Shaw was 'acknowledged at home and abroad as the most original English dramatist of the day' (3.12.1905), a claim that would be reiterated more often than it was disputed throughout the next half-century. Premières of successive new plays and revivals or first London performances of the 1890s works meant that for a decade from 1904 there was virtually always some Shaw in performance in London, including the 623 performance run of *Fanny's First Play* (1911), wryly described by Shaw as 'the *Charley's Aunt* of the new drama'.[14] This culminated in the doubtful apotheosis of the West End staging of *Pygmalion* (1914) with Beerbohm Tree and Mrs Patrick Campbell, in the leading roles, persistently distorting Shaw's anti-romantic ending into the promise of marriage between Eliza and Henry Higgins.

The repertory movement and the Manchester School

Many of Barker's actors moved into the repertory companies that, influenced by the values of the Stage Society and Vedrenne-Barker seasons, were established in various cities outside London. The impetus came, once more, from private money: from Annie Horniman who had earlier been an anonymous benefactor of new theatre when she funded the 1894 Avenue production of *Arms and the Man* and *The Land of Heart's Desire*.

Although she continued her support for Yeats' drama with subsidies of the Irish Players, her relationship with the Dublin Company, which foundered completely in 1911, was always difficult. Arguing that there must be an audience for repertory in a big provincial centre like Manchester, with its flourishing Hallé orchestra, fine public libraries and famously liberal newspaper, *The Manchester Guardian*, she demonstrated her case by founding the Playgoers' Theatre Company (1907) which soon became known as the Manchester Repertory Company. The audience according to Basil Dean, for a time one of her actors, consisted of:

> intellectuals from the university, vegetarians, nature lovers,
> weekend hikers in the Derbyshire hills and general marchers
> in the advance guard of public opinion.[15]

Dean left the company in 1910 to found the Liverpool Repertory Company and groups with similar programmes were founded in Glasgow, Sheffield, Bristol and, in 1913, Birmingham which, funded by Barry Jackson, was the only other company with comparably secure financial backing. *Widowers' Houses, You Never Can Tell, The Voysey Inheritance, The Tragedy of Nan, Strife, The Silver Box*, became repertory company staples.

These theatre companies made it possible for new London work to be seen by audiences in the provinces but also for writing to emerge from the provinces. Horniman appealed to playwrights to send in scripts, promising to read everything she received. Plays with characters involved in trade and mill-work, speaking bluntly with more than a touch of regional accent or dialect and demonstrating hard-headed Lancashire qualities, were seized on. Schools of local colour realism began to develop around the Reps., notably in Glasgow and Manchester, and work was passed between the companies and taken up beyond them. Not only was Masefield's *The Witch*, directed by Barker for Glasgow in 1910, before transfer to London, and *Justice* premièred simultaneously in Glasgow and London but at least two playwrights of the 'Manchester School', Harold Brighouse and Stanley Houghton, both *Manchester Guardian* journalists, found fame and an audience in London and with other provincial companies. The Lancashire idiom of Brighouse's *The Price of Coal* (1909), for example, was translated 'freely into Lanarkshire' for its première in Glasgow. After a series of one-act plays for Birmingham Repertory Company, John Drinkwater's full-length chronical play, *Abraham Lincoln* (1918), ran for a year after its London transfer.

Drinkwater's play which, in a series of episodes introduced by verse choruses, presents Lincoln as a man fighting to preserve the democratic system from the cunning and malice of self-servers, now seems very much a period piece but the sense of fun and dry humour of Brighouse's and, even more, Houghton's writing remain remarkably fresh. Houghton's plays are written in a Lancashire idiom. His sharp ear for register and the shifting texture of regional and class markers in northern industrial speech gives his dialogue an unusually life-like ring. Language is closely observed as a note in the first edition of *Hindle Wakes* (1912) informs readers:

> In the smaller Lancashire towns it is quite usual for well-to-do persons, and for persons who have received good educations at grammar schools and technical schools to drop more or less into dialect when familiar or when excited, or to point a joke. It is even usual for them to mix their speech with perfect naturalness.

Houghton handles matters of staging and debate that preoccupy his contemporaries with good humour and an element of parody. In *The Younger Generation* (1910), for example, he does what Antoine, for all his development of realistic staging never did: he sets a fender and fire irons and a red glow in the centre front of the stage so that the audience watches as if from behind the fireplace in the fourth wall. In this play, too, the generational conflict and that recurrent theme of New Drama from *The Marrying of Ann Leete* and *The Voysey Inheritance* through *The Return of the Prodigal* and *The Eldest Son*, the discovery that the pompous *pater familias* has feet of clay, is the central matter of the comedy as submissive wife and adult children, guilty of a range of offences against his code, combine to defy and tame the domestic tyrant. Houghton's female characters speak out the *Doll's House* message: the importance of self-knowledge and truth to oneself, with an enviable strength of mind. The suffragette heroine of his first play, *Independent Means* (1909), takes responsibility for herself and her family when her husband's business fails, declaring, 'I will not be bound by you or your ideas. I must think for myself', while in *The Perfect Cure* (1912) Martha, an energetic Lancashire woman, opens the window to let the fresh air in on her London suburban cousins, telling her niece that, 'it's your duty and everybody's duty, to be free, first of all'. But it is with *Hindle Wakes* that Houghton claims more permanent notice.

A great upset is caused in a Lancashire mill town because Fanny Hawthorn has spent a weekend away at the seaside with Alan Jeffcote, the son of the local mill-owner. The central scenes of the play are preoccupied with successive confrontations between the adult children and their parents; between the two sets of parents, and between Alan and the fiancée he has betrayed by his fling, who, self-sacrificing like a true Pinero heroine, declares she must renounce him to the woman he has wronged. The liberal audience might well be expected to side with the mill-owner's arguments that his son has a responsibility to the girl he has compromised, a responsibility phrased here, as so often in the New Drama, in terms of class as well as gender, since Fanny is a worker in Jeffcote's mill. When

Fanny finally gets the chance to speak for herself, however, the problems and heart-searching dissolve before the mirth of the real new woman as she derisively refuses the offer of marriage the parents have extorted from the young man:

ALAN:
But you didn't ever really love me?
FANNY:
Love you? Good heavens, of course not. Why on earth should I love you? You were just someone to have a bit of fun with. You were an amusement – a lark.
ALAN (*shocked*):
Fanny! Is that all you cared for me?
FANNY:
How much more did you care for me?
ALAN:
But it's not the same. I'm a man.
FANNY:
You're a man and I was your little fancy. Well, I'm a woman, and you were my little fancy. You wouldn't prevent a woman enjoying herself as well as a man, if she takes it into her head?

(Act III)

The audience, taken off guard by the emphasis on marriage and personal responsibility, by the skill with which the various subterfuges are unmasked, and by the realism of the nicely differentiated responses and interactions of the other characters, discovers that it too has fallen into the trap of the double standard. We realise that everyone but Fanny has been given the opportunity to voice an opinion. As Emma Goldman pointed out, the startling 'social lesson' of the play was that a woman 'has the right to satisfy, if she so chooses, her emotional and sex demands like any other need of her mind and body'.[16]

For all the intensity of the play's arguments and decisions, the tone of the ending has been prepared in the dialogue whose comic texture derives from the individual attitudes and turns of phrase of the characters, and from the bizarre flippancy of some features of the plot. Fanny's subterfuge is revealed in Act I because Mary, the friend supplying the alibi, was unfortunately drowned in Blackpool while Fanny, unaware, was in Llandudno. Having served its purpose, this sad event is only referred to again in a brief exchange in Act III where the interest is scarcely in Mary. Houghton ensures that in their response to Mary's catastrophe the various characters reveal themselves succinctly:

FANNY:

> If Mary hadn't been drowned you'd never have found out about it. I'd never have opened my mouth, and Alan knows that.

MRS HAWTHORN:

> Well, Mary's got her reward, poor lass!

MR HAWTHORN:

> There's more in this than chance it seems to me.

MRS HAWTHORN:

> The ways of the Lord are mysterious and wonderful. We can't pretend to understand them. He used Mary for an instrument for His purpose.

JEFFCOTE:

> Happen. But if He did it seems cruel hard on Mary, like.

As they do so the seriousness of the event is subverted.

The fiercest, funniest and most touching clash between domineering parent and strong-minded offspring comes in Harold Brighouse's dramatisation of his novel of obstinacy and forgiveness, *Hobson's Choice* (1916). The blunt-speaking, strong-minded Maggie Hobson could be Fanny ten years on. After years of running her father's house and business with little reward or acknowledgement, she rebels, proposes marriage to her father's best workman, Willie Mossop, shocking both Willie and her sisters with the impropriety of such a match. Turned out by her furious father she proceeds to make a man of Willie and a success of the boot and shoe business they build up in competition with her father. Fighting the class as well as the gender war, she gains respectful treatment for Willie from her sisters in exchange for so manipulating events that their father not only allows them to marry their suitors but is compelled to provide marriage portions as well. This comic reworking of the plot and family relationships of *King Lear* culminates, after an abortive love test, in the curmudgeonly old man's acceptance of the 'kind nursery' of the daughter he originally scorned but, as the title has foreshadowed, only on her terms.

The Irish drama

The success of the Irish Literary Theatre, founded in Dublin by Yeats, Lady Gregory and Edward Martyn in 1898, was the other spur for the provincial repertory theatres. It was reconstituted as the Irish National Theatre Society with Yeats as President in association with the Fay brothers, although the 'Irish' was later dropped from the title and the Fays from the very disputatious Board. From 1904, the Company operated rent free from the Abbey Theatre, provided by Annie Horniman who also subsidised salaries until resentments having become too strong, she withdrew. The Abbey Company's repertory plan was to stage a different play each week of a ten-month season, a more predictable pattern than at the Court, and one subsequently adopted by most of the English provincial repertory companies. The remit, to produce new plays by Irish writers, was remarkably fulfilled: not just in the Irish peasant plays of Augusta Gregory, Padraic Colum, William Boyle and T. C. Murray, the bread-and-butter work of the theatre, but in Yeats's own poetic plays of Irish legend and, although they were markedly different from anything Yeats had imagined in founding the theatre, in the prose comedies of J. M. Synge.

The emphasis in all the writing, varied as it was, was on what was notably Irish in tradition, language and history. In contrast with the New Drama developing simultaneously in England, it was not a social realist theatre. Particularly after George Moore and Edward Martyn withdrew in 1903, there was little interest in issues of social reform, class conflict, feminism or the operation of Capital; action was located in villages or the countryside rather than cities, and expressive language, accentuated by Frank Fay's insistence on clear melodious speaking, was relished. As Arthur Symons commented:

> The Court Theatre has given us one or two good realistic
> plays, the best being Mr Granville Barker's, besides giving
> Mr Shaw his chance in England, after he had had and taken
> it in America. But is there anywhere but in Ireland, an attempt
> to write imaginative literature in the form of drama? The
> Irish Literary Theatre has already, in Mr Yeats and Mr
> Synge, two notable writers, each wholly individual, one a
> poet in verse, the other a poet in prose.[17]

Or, in Synge's own words in the Preface to *The Tinker's Wedding* (1907), 'drama is made serious' not by being taken up with serious problems but 'by the degree in which it gives the nourishment, not very easy to define, on which our imaginations live'.

Although many of the Abbey plays demanded a realistic setting, it was a bare peasant realism of scrubbed – or, in Synge's shebeen, squalid – surfaces; household activities attentively reproduced, and poor but carefully observed costumes. But Yeats shared the reaction against realism of European stagecraft that was quite distinct from the English New Drama. Lugné Poe's symbolism was more suggestive to Yeats than Antoine's realism and

Gordon Craig's ideas about stage design, neglected by the London avant-garde, were given a hearing. Having made his mark with his designs for the Purcell Society *Acis and Galatea* in 1900 and *Dido and Aeneas* two years later, Craig was invited to design the costumes for the 1904 Dublin production of Yeats's mythic Cuchulain play, *On Baile's Strand* and sent a set of screens to the Abbey in 1906. Although Craig was to realise very few of his ideas in production, his screens, supplying an alternative to the illusionism of painted scenery were welcomed by Yeats as enabling the 'rhythm, balance, pattern, images that remind us of vast passions, the vagueness of past times, all the chimeras that haunt the edge of trance'.[18] Screens were used, as was incantatory speech for the 1911 production of Yeats's *The Hour Glass*, and became part of the regular equipment of the Abbey up to the outbreak of war. Charles Ricketts's symbolist designs for the Literary Theatre's closed-house production of Wilde's *Salomé* in 1906 were similarly suggestive and, in the 1916 production of *At the Hawk's Well*, Yeats's first play after Ezra Pound had introduced him to Japanese Noh drama, screens were replaced by the symbolic folding of various coloured cloths. On-stage musicians functioned as a chorus; the characters accompanied the chanted verse with stylised gestures, and the Guardian of the Well, in flowing robes and huge hawk wings designed by Ricketts, distracted Cuchulain and an Old Man, seekers of the waters of immortality, with a ritualistic, free-form dance. This play was conceived less for the public stage than for the chamber and, indeed, sign of the way Yeats's drama was developing, had its first performance in a private drawing room in London.

The cultural and communal role the Abbey Company assumed in Dublin was such as most alternative and avant-garde theatres only dream of. It was not wholly absurd for Yeats to ask about his *Cathleen ni Houlihan* (1902), whose closing call to heroic action for Irish freedom was uttered in performance by the revolutionary, Maud Gonne:

> Did that play of mine send out
> Certain men the English shot?
> > ('The Man and the Echo', in *Last Poems* (1939))

At the very least, the play had excited the Dublin audience as had Augusta Gregory's *The Rising of the Moon* (1907) in which a policeman acknowledges the claims of his own Irishness over those of his English masters and so allows the escape of a Nationalist prisoner. The specifically Irish claims of the theatre at a moment when demands for independence from English rule were becoming insistent, led to an alliance with the Nationalist movement which, while it guaranteed an attentive audience, was not always in the theatre's interest. Whereas Lady Gregory's short farces, which derived from a specific incident and proliferating local responses to it, and her longer plays, *Dervorgilla* (1907) and *Kincora* (1909), which set crucial events in Irish history among simple but fundamentally heroic people, pleased, the imaginative energy and teasing tone of Synge's comedies brought opprobrium from the outset.

Arthur Griffiths, writing in the *United Irishman* in 1903, attacked Synge's first performed play, *In the Shadow of the Glen*, on the grounds that the old peasant's feigning death to test his wife's fidelity and her subsequent abandonment of her joyless husband for a passing silver-tongued tramp, demeaned Irish womanhood and fed anti-Irish prejudice. Although Synge's tragedy of attrition, *Riders to the Sea* (1904) in which, with ballad-like simplicity, Bartley, an Aran Islander, crosses the sea despite a brooding storm and his mother's premonition, and is drowned, was well received, his three-act comedy, *The Well of the Saints* (1905) was barely tolerated. Response to *The Tinker's Wedding* (written, 1905) whose anarchic characters not only thieve, fight and swear but, to avoid paying for the marriage licence, torment the grasping priest who retaliates with a loud Latin malediction, was not tested since the first Abbey performance was delayed until 1971, but the first night of his last completed play, the wonderful full-length comedy, *The Playboy of the Western World*, in 1907, ended in notorious riots which were repeated at each performance for a week and again in New York, in 1911, when the Company took the play on tour.

Although the use on stage of the word 'shift', in Christy Mahon's refusal to give up Pegeen even for, 'a drift of chosen females, standing in their shifts itself, maybe, from this place to the eastern world', was the sparking point for the riot, the ironic tone of the humour; the tedium, violence and squalor of the life based on the Mayo shebeen, implied in the references and metaphoric texture of the characters' speech, and the irreverent presentation of heroising and religion in the play, no doubt supplied the fuel. As a commentator, P. D. Kenny suggested in a remarkable contemporary analysis in the *Irish Times:*

> The merciless accuracy of his revelation is more than we can
> bear. Our eyes tremble at it. The words chosen are, like
> the things they express, direct and dreadful, by themselves
> intolerable to conventional taste, yet full of vital beauty in
> their truth to the conditions of life, to the character they
> depict, and to the sympathies they suggest. It is as if we
> looked into a mirror for the first time, and found ourselves
> hideous. We fear to face the thing. We shrink at the word
> for it. We scream. (30.1.1907).

The closely observed realism of the costumes, domestic interiors, daily activities of Synge's Aran Island or County Wicklow peasants give a rootedness to his stage worlds, in which various outcasts: beggars, tramps or fugitives, interact with, disrupt and are eventually ejected by rural communities. This rootedness underpins the truth to conditions, character and sympathies that Kenny perceived and, coexisting with the anarchic action, makes its cruelties and perceptions the more uncomfortable. While eschewing, except in his unrevised tragedy, *Deirdre of the Sorrows* (performed posthumously, 1910), Irish legend and the verse Yeats hoped to restore to the theatre, Synge's plays, as their subsequent performance history makes clear, fulfil more thoroughly than any of the other writing for the theatre Yeats's promise in the Irish National Theatre's journal, *Samhain*, of an Irish drama that should be 'joyful, fantastic, extravagant, whimsical, beautiful, resonant'.

Peter Pan (1904)

Left out of this account so far is J. M. Barrie who stands between the Society Dramatists and the writers of minority drama whose themes he often absorbed into lighter, less testing plotting and characterisation, in, for example, his series of comedies including *What Every Woman Knows* (1908) and *The Twelve Pound Look* (1910), in which women have the initiative. His fundamental acceptance of contemporary class and sexual relationships, though, pins Barrie's writing to its period. In *Peter Pan* (1904), he found a form and a subject that allowed his narrative and inventive skills full range and contained the complacent gentility and coy humour that mars so much of his other work. *The Admirable Crichton* (1902) challenged its first audiences with its master-servant role reversals, and became a staple of the radical amateur repertoire of the 1920s and 1930s. But the uncritical assumption that society will have strict class differences, necessarily associated with authority or obsequiousness both of manner and language, leaves later audiences squirming. The running commentaries to the reader with which Barrie accompanies the dialogue in the printed form of the plays have a joviality and self-satisfaction which makes them scarcely readable. 'His plays', as Graham Greene has written, 'are cloyingly sweet'.[19] Why, then, did *Peter Pan*, which shares all these features, survive? What led to the absorption of its characters and events into the imaginative lives of countless British children and to its Christmas revival annually for some sixty years?

Victorian melodrama having largely given way to farce and drawing-room comedy in the commercial theatre, the place for theatrical spectacle was either the music hall, with its Paris-derived dancing choruses, or the

Shakespearean theatre of Beerbohm Tree. *Peter Pan* brought the magic and fantasy of nursery tales – pirates, indians, orphans, wolves, fairies, mermaids, a crocodile – on to the stage but did it with a remarkable mixture of humour and psychological suggestiveness. The treatment of the fantastic and the topsy turvy as if they were quite natural contributes to the charm of the piece. A shadow is, of course, trapped when a window closes on it. Nana, the children's nurse, is a dog. The fantasy figures are all inventively extended: the fairy, TinkerBell, represented by a darting point of light, is bad-tempered, rude and full of spiteful tricks; a loud ticking heralds every appearance of the crocodile because it once swallowed a clock, and, most famously, Captain Hook, the pirate chief, who speaks an astonishing mixture of public schoolboy slang and Shakespearean pastiche, has a flowing, black, Stuart wig and an iron claw instead of a hand. Fearsome himself, Hook pursues Peter Pan and his tribe of lost boys but is terrified of the crocodile and is tormented and eventually defeated by the Puck-like antics of Peter.

At a time when the serious drama assiduously refused to admit the presence of the audience, Barrie uses the direct address and audience involvement of pantomime as a crucial element of his plot: most memorably, TinkerBell survives only if the audience acknowledges sufficiently enthusiastically its belief in fairies. Three very ordinary children are central figures of the action that revolves round fantasy games and role-playing and, through their anxious, then elated, discovery that they, too, can fly, the flying spectacle of pantomime is brought within everyone's reach.[20] The audience, moreover, does not have to read the saccharine commentary included with the printed version, nor need it, in all the excitement, probe too deeply the disturbing representation of human relationships that shadows the play in which the mother, Mrs Darling, is grossly sentimentalised and the female role in the person first of Mrs Darling and then of Wendy, is seen entirely in terms of mating and maternity while contriving to be quite sexless; the father, as Hook, is killed by Peter and, as Mr Darling, is mocked for his pomposity, humiliated and made to live in the dog kennel, while the central figure, Peter, who ran away the day he was born in order not to have to grow up, never touching nor touched throughout the play, finally, Huck Finn-like, although with none of the resilience or mental complexity Mark Twain gives Huck, rejects the offer of a home and civilisation, to stay playing forever in his Never Never Land.

As the discussion of the work of the Abbey Players suggests, there were other seekers of colour in the theatre and, by 1910, when Anna Pavlova and a small company from the Russian Imperial Ballet danced in London, the English theatre began to be alerted to new approaches to theatre being developed in Europe. Diaghilev's Russian Ballet returned in 1912 to overwhelm its audience with *L'Apres Midi d'un Faune, The Firebird* and *Petrouchka* with music by Debussy and Stravinski and choreography by Njinsky and Fokine. In 1913, another Russian, Chaliapin, sang the role of Boris Gudonov at Covent Garden. The 1910 and 1912 Post-Impressionist Exhibitions excited interest in abstraction and decoration in painting, complementing Gordon Craig's theories of stage decoration which had begun to be known through his magazine, *The Mask*, and his work with Yeats. While William Poel's ideas on Elizabethan staging of Shakespeare were becoming more widely known and appreciated, Reinhart's production of *The Taming of the Shrew*, with symbolic backcloths, toured to London in 1909 suggesting still other ways of engaging with classic texts. In 1911 Reinhardt's more fully abstract spectacle, the wordless Arabian Nights play, *Sumūrun*, played at the Savoy and *The Miracle* was staged at Olympia. His staging of *Oedipus Rex* (1912), incorporating recent ideas about Ancient Greek staging suggested by German archeologists, put the chorus into a space that projected into the audience, thus altering its habitual relationship with the stage.

The impact of these events was felt first in Shakespearean production, feeding into Barker's revelatory versions of *Twelfth Night* (1912) and *A Midsummer Night's Dream* (1914) at the Savoy and stimulating plans for open air and arena productions. How far plays written for the British theatre might have been affected by the impact of new theatrical experience cannot be known. The inflow of vital work from Europe was stemmed by the outbreak of war in 1914.

The First World War and its devastations stands as a clear barrier between two periods. After an abortive production of Hardy's *Dynasts* (1914) Barker left for an American season, returning at the end of the war married to a new wife and in retreat from the theatre to the study. The London theatre scene continued, albeit in diminished form, as actors left for the Front, and the emphasis was more than ever on light, escapist plays. Miles Malleson's short play *'D' Company*, written in 1914 in an attempt to recreate his army experience was not produced and when *Black 'Ell*, his study of a disillusioned and shell-shocked returning DSO, was published in 1916 it was seized by the police as a deliberate calumny on the British soldier. The Actresses' Franchise League collapsed in the face of the need for war work and the activity of the repertory theatres shrank. As part of the war effort, Horniman's policy in Manchester was to play 'cheery' works – Pinero, Maugham and Shakespearean comedy – but, despite this, and the free seats given to those in uniform, the Manchester Repertory Theatre finally folded in 1917 and despite hopes of renewal after the war, Horniman, with her private funds drastically diminished and no civic support forthcoming, was obliged to sell the Gaiety Theatre in 1920. Birmingham Rep did just manage a holding operation. Although

Barry Jackson himself left for the Navy, performances continued spasmodi-cally with actors not at the Front contributing to the war effort through Sunday voluntary work at an armaments factory.

The development of the newly burgeoning form, the cinema, was also affected by the war. By 1913, Greater London had had 600 cinemas – vaudeville theatres, music halls, old gas works, factories, boat houses – any possible space was converted for travelling cinema shows. Purpose-built cinemas had begun to appear from 1908. The Elstree site developed as studios from 1913 and the Neptune Studios from 1914 so that, immediately pre-war, the British silent film industry was flourishing. But the work of these new studios was drastically cut under the impact of the Entertainment Tax, levied during the war, and the disappearance of personnel to the Front. The demand for cinema shows continued unabated, however. Hollywood, unaffected by the war, not only continued to develop but seized on the British market as an outlet for its own products and also, from its growing position of strength, seized on the talent of British actors, writers and directors, in a pattern that has continued ever since.

All of Ibsen's modern prose dramas as well as *The Pretenders*, *The Vikings at Helgeland*, *Brand* and *Peer Gynt* were performed in London between 1900 and 1914. Ibsen's drama had been deeply influential on the new English drama and the widely available translations of his plays at the turn of the century had been a major factor in creating an audience for the Stage Society and the Barker-Vedrenne venture. But although Ezra Pound claimed in 1916 that 'more than any one man, it is he who has made us "our world", that is to say "our modernity" ',[21] at the time when prose fiction and poetry were about to undergo transformation at the hands of the modernists, and the American drama was just coming into being through the Provincetown Players' productions of Eugene O'Neill and Susan Glaspell, the new spirit and passion for social reform which had brought an excitement and seriousness unknown for years to the English theatre, engaging its audiences and creating partisans as it would not again until the late 1950s, was fading. Only Shaw, with his own very particular kind of modernism, survived to develop into the next two decades and even he held back *Heartbreak House*, written in the early years of the war, until 1919 before allowing it to be produced.

Notes

1. *Programme of a Complimentary Dinner at the Criterion* (7 July 1907), pp. 11, 16, 15.
2. G. B. Shaw to H. G. Wells, quoted, J. Woodfield, *English Theatre in Transition,*

1881–1914 (Beckenham, 1984), p. 79; Woodfield includes a full list of Stage Society productions as an Appendix.

3. T. F. Evans, ed., *Shaw: The Critical Heritage* (1976), p. 163.

4. So-called by Archer and Barker, echoing the title of Grundy's fashion plate play, *Frocks and Frills* (1902), *Appeal for a National Theatre* (1904), p. 7.

5. Figures for performances, 1910–19: Pinero, 1078; Shaw, 1482; Galsworthy, 230; Barker, 129; from Ian Clarke, *Edwardian Drama* (1985), pp. 22–3; figures for Court from Woodfield, *English Theatre in Transition*, p. 78. The growing acceptance of Ibsen's drama is charted in the last chapter of Sara Jan's unpublished Cambridge PhD thesis, 'Ibsen in England, 1889–1914' (1993).

6. Censor's description, C. B. Purdom, *Harley Granville Barker: Man of the Theatre, Dramatist and Scholar* (1955), pp. 73–4.

7. Made newly available by various recent editions: D. Spender and C. Hayman, eds, *How the Vote was Won and Other Suffragette Plays* (1985); V. Gardner, ed., *Plays of the Actresses' Franchise League* (Nottingham, 1985) and L. Fitzsimmons and V. Gardner, eds, *New Woman Plays* (1991). No date is recorded for first performance of the plays by Glover and Dugdale but they were in performance *c.* 1910.

8. Beatrice Webb's 'Diary', March 1910, quoted, S. Hynes, *The Edwardian Turn of Mind* (1968), p. 129.

9. Conrad to Galsworthy, 1909; E. Goldman, *The Social Significance of Modern Drama* (1914), p. 108.

10. Letter to Felton Ellis, June 1925, quoted, Travis Bogard and Jackson Bryer, eds, *The Selected Letters of Eugene O'Neill* (1988) p. 70.

11. Quoted, Ian Clarke, *Edwardian Drama*, p. 54. Sowerby's play proved itself stage-worthy in the National Theatre revival, 1994.

12. E. Goldman, *Social Significance*, p. 130.

13. Shaw: obituary notice for Hankin, 1909, quoted, Jan MacDonald, *The 'New Drama'* (1986), p. 149; Hankin: quoted, Evans, ed., *Shaw: Critical Heritage*, p. 173; Webb, 'Diary' (29.11.1905), quoted, Evans, ed., *Shaw: Critical Heritage*, p. 147.

14. Quoted, Purdom, *Harley Granville Barker*, p. 129.

15. Quoted, S. Goodie, *Annie Horniman, Pioneer in the Theatre* (1990), p. 115.

16. E. Goldman, *Social Significance*, p. 129.

17. A. Symons, *Plays, Acting and Music* (1909), p. 209.

18. W. B. Yeats, 'The Tragic Theatre' (1910), in *Essays and Introductions* (1961), p. 243. Craig's impact on Yeats is discussed further in Chapter 7.

19. G. Greene, *British Dramatists* (1942), p. 42.

20. Barrie added the Act I sprinkling of 'fairy dust' to his text for revivals of the play, to deter copy-cat flying attempts.

21. 'Mr James Joyce and the Modern Stage' (February 1916), reprinted Forrest Read, ed., *Pound/Joyce* (1967), p. 51.

Chapter 4
1920–1940 Between the Wars

The First World War led to profound disruption in British life, accelerating the social and political changes already begun before its outbreak. The Irish Free State was established in 1921. Full male suffrage and the first step towards women's suffrage having come in 1918, the vote was finally extended to all women over the age of twenty-one in 1928. But in the immediate aftermath of the war, while the country was experiencing financial boom and slump and problems of employment for the men returned from the Front to the labour market, London's West End was one of the few places where the clock seemed not just to have stopped but to have gone backwards. Seeming to have lost all consciousness of its own past achievements, it was dominated by drawing-room comedy and social drama set among the glamorous and ruling class although, in the 1920s, this at least meant upper middle-class rather than aristocratic characters and settings.[1]

Modernist experiment was transforming the more private literary arts of poetry and prose fiction but inconsequential entertainment dominated mainstream English theatre epitomised in *Chu Chin Chow*, the long-running musical set in a Never Never Orient. Having opened in 1916, this work reached its 2,000th performance in 1920. Margaret Kennedy's *The Constant Nymph* (1926), adapted from her best-selling sensational romance, ran for more than a year and Somerset Maugham's plays with their fashionable cynicism and *risqué* language, that introduced words like 'slut' to the stage, provided a frisson of daring without much risk to the intellect or emotions. The theme of Maugham's *Our Betters* (1923), is the attempt of knowing American heiresses to infiltrate aristocratic society. The self-satisfaction of the English characters is apparent and seems to be endorsed by Maugham who has a snobbish American boast (for the derision of the audience) that 'everyone took me for an Englishman'.

With censorship still very much in place and no public subsidy to encourage new or experimental work, London theatre was scarcely touched by the theatrical revolutions which were taking place in Europe under the impact of developing ideas about staging, of the movement away from fourth-wall realism, of Strindberg's chamber plays and of revolutionary politics. Avant-garde French staging, Soviet experimental work, the expressionism of Kaiser and Toller, Marinetti's futurism, only seeped in here and there through the activities of such directors as Terence Gray at the Festival Theatre, Cambridge (1926–32) or Peter Godfrey at the Gate (1925–34). Godfrey staged Kaiser's *From Morn til Midnight* (1925) and some startling new writing from America. O'Neill's *The Emperor Jones* and *All God's Chillun Got Wings* and, later, Clifford Odets's *Waiting for Lefty*, did get a hearing through productions at small theatres away from the West End but, although Copeau's Vieux Colombier Company toured to the Arts Theatre in 1931 and Pitoeff's two years later, the writings of Brecht, of Pirandello and, later, of Lorca and the practice of Piscator, of Tairov, of Meyerhold, even indeed, of Gordon Craig, were scarcely known to London audiences.

Whereas the new literary works with their difficulty and subtle allusion, Eliot's *The Waste Land* or Joyce's *Ulysses* (both 1922), could address themselves to a small avant-garde readership, West End managements, saddled with large theatres and conscious of the need to attract a wide audience and to compete with the new medium of cinema, looked to the erotic charge that live actors could bring to the witty persiflage of drawing-room comedy or to dark, fast-moving thrillers. Sensation was at a premium in commercial theatre. When Patrick Hamilton's *Rope*, the great theatrical success of 1929, which presented the motiveless murder of a contemporary by two Oxford undergraduates, was broadcast, the public was enticed beforehand with the warning:

> If you have weak nerves, if you don't read murder stories in
> bed late at night, if you are genuinely afraid of the dark,
> or if you feel that murder is too serious a subject to be dealt
> with anywhere except at the Old Bailey, then you had
> better give this play a miss.[2]

And, as Sean O'Casey wrote in 1934 of the sexual titillation offered in the commercial theatre by the likes of Frederick Lonsdale and Somerset Maugham:

> The stage is fully furnished now if it bears on its breast a
> bottle of champagne, a box of cigarettes, and a coyly
> covered bed. Not a bed for glorious love as in *Romeo and
> Juliet*, nor a bed for terrifying lust as in *Desire Under the
> Elms*, but a bed for a mean and half-hearted pastime. The
> pomp and circumstance of life have been degraded down
> to the pomp and circumstance of a bed.[3]

Plus ca change . . ., it might seem, but the real change in the British theatre scene in these years is indicated in my need to use the distinguishing term 'commercial theatre'. Popular fiction, after all, flourished alongside *Ulysses* and *The Rainbow.* Unlike novelists, writers of unpopular, 'resistible' theatre, needed not just a sympathetic publisher but a venue, actors and stage technicians before their work could be realised and these were to be found now consistently, if often precariously, beyond the West End. The fragmentation of theatrical activity, begun in the 1890s and furthered in the first decade of the century by Barker, the Stage Society and the suffragettes, became the evident condition of British theatre in these years and has remained so since.

It is not simply that exciting theatre work increasingly happened outside the West End, although it did. It is also the extent and range of dramatic activity that marks the altered circumstance. On the production side, numbers of small committed theatre companies after the Stage Society or Court Theatre models: the Hampstead Everyman; the Arts Theatre Club; the Gate Theatre Studio; 'Q' at Kew Bridge, appeared in London while, in the provinces, where in the past the mainstay had been tours out of London, of pre-London try-outs or of West End successes, the repertory theatre movement, following the trail of the Abbey Theatre and the handful of pre-war repertory companies, was again burgeoning after the hiatus of the war years, creating local theatres with stable companies and often sponsoring work by local dramatists and providing an inlet for foreign plays. Where, in 1914, there had been 170 touring and twelve stock (locally based) companies, in 1934, there were as many provincial repertory as touring companies, thirty-seven of each. Underpinning this activity and, no doubt, also stimulated by it and by the regularity with which new plays were now published, was an upsurge in amateur theatre, over 700 local amateur groups being affiliated to the British Drama League in the 1920s.

In addition to this multifarious dramatic activity, the new visual medium of cinema offered scope to writers and theatre practitioners, as well as audiences, more particularly after the passing of the Cinematograph Films Act in 1927. Its stipulation that a minimum twenty per cent of cinema output and distribution must be of British origin stimulated the reviving British film industry, that had been badly damaged by the virtual cessation of film-making during the war and the consequent advance of the Ameri-can cinema with its unmatchably costly spectaculars like *Ben Hur* (1926) and such comedies as Chaplin's *Gold Rush* (1925). The stipulation led to the cynical production of 'quota quickies' but, for all their shabbiness, these gave openings to actors, writers and technicians. In 1927, *The Jazz Singer* starring Al Jolson, heralded the arrival of the 'talkies' with their voracious appetite for plots and dialogue. The advertising slogans for Hitchcock's *Blackmail* (1929), 'the first full length all talkie film made in Great Britain': 'See and Hear it. Our Mother Tongue As It Should Be –

Spoken,'[4] was a call answered by playwrights and actors as well as audiences. From the mid-1920s, moreover, the development of sound broadcasting brought the idea of drama into every home and to countless people who had never been inside a theatre, increasing the demand for scripts and creating a new outlet for experimental writing.

Despite the establishment by the newly independent Irish Free State of the Abbey Company as Ireland's National Theatre (1925) with an annual subsidy from 1926 of £1,000 a year, no equivalent government subsidy was forthcoming to sustain a British National Theatre, but the ground laid earlier in the century by the Stage Society and the Court Theatre was developing towards that end, albeit mighty slowly because it was under-resourced. Inspired by the achievements of the pre-war 'new drama', of the early Abbey Theatre, and of the practice and writing of Barker and Poel, the numerous small companies that appeared were committed, in the words which regularly appeared on the programmes of the Birmingham Repertory Company, to 'serve an art instead of making that art serve a commercial purpose'.[5]

Repertory theatres, independent theatres and theatre festivals

Innovation and experiment, as I have suggested, came from the repertory and independent theatres. Among the most notable, Nugent Monck's Norwich Company moved in 1921 into the tiny Maddermarket Theatre which, with gallery, thrust stage and largely Elizabethan repertoire, enabled thorough testing of Poel's ideas about Shakespearean staging. J. B. Fagan at the Oxford Playhouse opened (1923) with a revival of Shaw's *Heartbreak House* and developed an ambitious programme of international classics that included Strindberg and Sophocles as well as Ibsen, Shaw and Synge. A triumphant *Cherry Orchard* (1925) with the young John Gielgud as Trofimov, marked the advent of Chekhov into British consciousness. Transferring to the Lyric Hammersmith, it convinced its audiences of the power of the play that had failed dismally in its 1911 Stage Society production, and spurred the Russian *émigré* director, Theodore Komisarjevski, to further productions of Chekhov. At the Festival Theatre, Cambridge, Terence Gray, influenced by the writings of Gordon Craig and Adolphe Appia, broke the dominant realistic stage convention. He used screens and rostra for non-naturalistic settings and, when there was scenery, a stage revolve so that scene changes happened speedily and in front of the audience. He also installed a cyclorama, a rounded back wall off which expressive lighting effects could be played, and utilised the choreographic talents of his cousin Ninette de Valois in a succession of remarkable productions, not just of Aeschylus and Aristophanes but of avant-garde European drama – Kaiser, Toller and Pirandello; American expressionism in the form of Elmer Rice's *The Adding Machine* and O'Neill's *The Emperor Jones* and *The Hairy Ape*, and two scarcely performed dance dramas from the National repertory, Wilde's *Salomé* and Yeats's *On Baile's Strand.*

The Birmingham Repertory Company also staged brave productions of foreign work, including Capek's *Insect Play,* Giradoux's *Amphytrion 38* and Pirandello's *Right You Are, If You Think So* but, unlike the Festival Theatre which rarely handled new British plays, was also responsible for numerous premières (in Birmingham, London or Malvern), including Shaw's *The Apple Cart* (1929) and *Too True To Be Good* (1932). Some were evidently aimed at the box office, including Eden Phillpotts' undisturbing 'honey and cream' family plays and Rudolph Besier's romantic melodrama about the Brownings' elopement, *The Barretts of Wimpole Street*, which, with stereotype Victorian father and dashing hero, ran for 529 perform-ances in London. But they also supported more daring ventures, including plays by such feminists as Elizabeth Baker and Cicely Hamilton and the full version of Shaw's mammoth *Back to Methuselah* (1923), licensed on condition that Adam and Eve be dressed decently, the paraphrase of the Athanasian creed be omitted and two of the characters not to be made up to look like Lloyd George and Asquith. The Company, moreover, satirised the vogue for historical chronicle plays with its brilliant *1066 and All That* created from the Sellar and Yeatman cod-history in which the forerunner of the Common Man in Robert Bolt's *A Man for all Seasons* (1960) and the Bargee in John Arden's *Sargeant Musgrave's Dance* (1959) appeared, the plain Englishman of ten centuries, who linked the episodes of Good and Bad Kings as England struggled to be 'Top Nation'.

The beginnings of collaboration of civic and private patronage enabled the development of the Festival idea, also initiated by Jackson in 1929 with his annual festival at Malvern where six new Shaw plays as well as revivals and other Birmingham Rep works were performed and, in the 1931, 1932 and 1933 seasons, British plays from the Middle Ages to the present were staged. The great coup of the Canterbury Festival, also founded in 1929, which had revived Tennyson's *Becket* (1932), was persuading T. S. Eliot to write a play on the martyrdom of Thomas à Becket for the 1935 Festival. Eliot had already experimented with dramatic form in the fragmentary, *Sweeney Agonistes* (Group Theatre, 1934), and in the choric sequences of *The Rock*, E. Martin Browne's religious event produced at Saddler's Wells earlier the same year. Now, in *Murder in the Cathedral*, he adapted the forms of the liturgy: sermon, antiphony and choric response, into a work with the narrative, colourful history and episodic structure of a pageant and the intellectual excitement and mounting suspense of a stage play which made an impact beyond Anglican circles when it transferred from Canterbury Cathedral to Ashley Dukes' Mercury Theatre in London. It impressed W. H. Auden and Christopher Isherwood, then engaged in their own attempt at socially committed poetic drama, and had Yeats standing to applaud with cries of 'Magnificent! Magnificent!'. Eliot's primary attention, indeed, from the late 1930s shifted from poetry to drama, although never again with the liveliness of the *Sweeney* fragment or the coherence and confidence of the Canterbury piece.

If London generated few outstanding plays in the inter-war period, it did boast an extraordinary crop of actors who in many ways were the product of the earlier campaigning by Barker, Poel and Shaw for drama schools, for a more highly disciplined but more informal acting method and for the revaluation of assumptions about the performance of Elizabethan drama. They included Sybil Thorndike and Lewis Casson, from Barker's pre-war companies; William Poel's discovery, Edith Evans, and the generation, trained at the newly instituted schools, RADA or the Central, including Ralph Richardson, Lawrence Olivier and Peggy Ashcroft as well as John Gielgud who had come through the repertory movement. The West End provided the bread and butter, but the opportunity to develop their talents and acting skills came through work with Lilian Bayliss's Old Vic, Nigel Playfair's Lyric, Hammersmith, the Arts Theatre Club (founded, 1927), the Gate and the repertory companies (Ashcroft made her debut at Birmingham and Olivier, Gwen Ffrangcon Davies, Edith Evans and Cedric Hardwicke all performed there early in their careers). 'It was', as Gielgud put it, 'no fun earning a big salary in a bad part', and Dukes wrote of Mercury that it was 'better to struggle with the help of a cultivated audience in a side street than to flourish on a main street with the aid of movie millions'.[6]

If the main street sparkled it was because its actors had the opportunity to hone their skills in the side streets. In the six years before bankruptcy ended the Arts Theatre venture, there were productions of plays by Claudel, Sudermann and Strindberg and a first Quarto *Hamlet*, and it functioned as the corridor through which new writing emerged. Plays which now seem to epitomise the inter-war theatre, Van Druten's *Young Woodley* (1928), Reginald Berkeley's Florence Nightingale play, *The Lady With the Lamp* (1929), and Gordon Daviot's history play, *Richard of Bordeaux* (1932), directed by Gielgud and staged with simple settings but rich fabrics and colours by the Motleys design group, were launched at the Arts before sustaining significant West End runs. Like the Stage Society before it, the Arts Theatre Club could evade censorshp by offering closed-house productions. Hubert Griffith's Russian Revolution play, *Red Sunday*, with Gielgud as Trotsky and Athene Seylor as the Czarina, was forbidden a transfer by the Censor despite howls of protest from Shaw, among others.

Gielgud's account of Komisarjevki's direction of this play suggests something of the appeal of working at the Arts. He was, he wrote:

> more than ever impressed by [Komisarjevski's] handling of the actors, and with his acute musical sensitiveness, which always enabled him to 'orchestrate' a scene to perfection allowing the actors to feel instinctively that the pauses and business sprang naturally out of the dialogue and process of the action. The result was closely patterned rhythm flowing backwards and forwards between the characters, covering any weakness in individual performance, and shifting the focus of attention continually without breaking the illusion of continuous life and movement on the stage.[7]

O'Casey and the Abbey Theatre

The Abbey, flagging after the death of Synge, had gained fresh life following its establishment as the Irish National Theatre. By contrast with London's struggling independent theatres, it was clearly the leading Dublin theatre, a position further strengthened by the discovery of Sean O'Casey whose two-act *Shadow of a Gunman*, in which a pedlar and a poet share a Dublin tenement room and through their fears and fantasies bring about the death of a romantic innocent, was produced in 1923. The comic action of the first act in which the poet Donal Davoren, colludes in his neighbours' mistaken supposition that he is an IRA gunman on the run, turns unexpectedly grim in Act II when the girl whose admiration he has won is killed in an attempt to protect him.

The closely observed urban working-class setting and the marked social commitment demonstrated in O'Casey's representation of Independence struggle, Easter Rising and civil war in his three Dublin plays was very different from the kind of work dreamed of by Yeats and Lady Gregory, but there is something of the spirit of Synge in the tonal shifts of O'Casey's plays and his presentation of the coexistence of fantasy and reality.

Increasingly recognising that his own plays about the kings and peasants of Irish legend could expect only a coterie audience, Yeats turned his attention to chamber drama, staging his plays for sympathetic audiences in such places as Coole Park. But, although his *Plays for Dancers* using movement, masks and music as complements to the words were not addressed to the Abbey audience, he was able to recognise the vitality of

O'Casey's reflections of and on recent Irish history and tenement life in *Juno and the Paycock* (1924). With its verbal liveliness intermixed with popular song and oratory, this was a play of a different quality from anything currently playing and, astonishing and absorbing its audiences, it became the greatest success the Abbey had so far known.

Fierce protest against contemporary living conditions is implicit in the action of *Juno and the Paycock*. Continual interruptions by neighbours and street hawkers, intermittent sounds of off-stage voices and knockings on the shared front door, and the observed activities of daily existence, create a remarkable image of the reality of tenement living and the struggle for survival. Financial penury and the lack of any welfare support of the family and their neighbours are apparent in Juno's scrimping and in the loans, pawnings and repossessions witnessed in the course of the play; apparent, too, in the details of slum life indicated by the set and the contrast of the Act II stage when, the family briefly thinking itself rich, the same room is crowded with new possessions and small luxuries and the anxieties of daily living give way to a celebratory party with neighbours. Violent resistance to the terms of settlement of the new Irish Free State, and the sectarian slaughters between 'Statesers' and 'Die-hards', only recently stilled when the play was written, are also indicted in the play.

The action shifts between the straight drama of love and loss of Juno and her children and the anarchic comedy of her husband, the peacock, and his side-kick, Joxer. The juxtaposing of the two kinds of action creates disturbing echoes between them which gives ironic force to the final repetition of Boyle's catchphrase, 'the whole world's in a terrible state of chassis'. O'Casey extends Shaw's tendency to use popular type-figures, introducing the music hall double act into his plays, but Joxer and Boyle are by no means simply lovable clowns whose irresponsibility is fun. They include much darker shades than ever attach to Shaw's undeserving poor. Their action is often funny, their energy enlivening. We can even be drawn briefly into their schemes to avoid work and deceive Juno; enjoy Joxer's hasty departure through the window; the leg pains that smite Boyle so conveniently at any mention of a job, and the airs he assumes in response to his supposed wealth, but Boyle also plays a significant part in the developing action of the play and Joxer contributes not a little to the impression of the tenement community. Boyle's comic vanity, characterised by his habits of speech and the '*slow consequential strut*', the initial stage directions instruct the actor to adopt, have their logical extension in his vicious denunciation of his daughter's pregnancy, his role-playing in his self-centred assumption of the part of offended patriarch, and his sloth in the eventual exhaustion of affection and collapse of the family. Joxer can only be played as a feckless charmer if the '*habit of constantly shrugging his shoulders with a peculiar twitching movement, meant to be ingratiating*' that O'Casey directs for him is ignored and the shifts from self-demeaning flattery of Boyle to sudden quick acts of malice, self-serving or petty theft are blurred by the actor.

It is the interaction of the comic stereotypes with these more sinister elements that give Joxer and Boyle their peculiar piquancy. Recreated in the roles of Fluther and Flynn in *The Plough and the Stars* and of Simon and Sylvester in *The Silver Tassie*, they are less disturbingly interactive with the structure of feeling of the play. Reworked by other dramatists, they recur as Jock Smith and Tam Pettigrew in Joe Corrie's *In Time o' Strife*, in the multiple pairings of O'Neill's *The Iceman Cometh*, and as Didi and Gogo in *Waiting for Godot*.

The sharp social and political commentary of *Juno and the Paycock* had an immediacy and specificity unlike anything else that had played in the theatre: the off-stage Republican funeral, the mother's lament for her dead son, is as much a symbolic cry for Ireland torn by civil strife as Yeats's *Kathleen ni Hoolihan* in the early days of the Company had been a call to arms, but the mother here is the clearly individualised Mrs Tancred, whose son is dead because betrayed by a neighbour; the man taken for summary execution by former comrades is Johnny Boyle whose fearful attempt to withdraw from action after being maimed in earlier strife has been witnessed by the audience. And along with this specificity is a passion never realised in Yeats's drama.

O'Casey's next play, *The Plough and the Stars* (1926), set during the 1916 Easter Rising, moved even further from the images of heroic Ireland that the Nationalists expected from the Abbey. Its action included neighbours bickering and squaring up for drunken brawls; a prostitute attempting to solicit on stage; a public house setting with the Irish flag carried in and a baby abandoned on the floor while its mother flouts a rival, and Irishmen taking advantage of the chaos to engage in looting. The oratory of the Republican leader, Padraic Pearce, heard off-stage as if addressing a meeting, must compete with the rowdy drinkers in the public house and is seen only hazily through the frosted glass of the pub window. Far from glorifying the heroes of the Rising, the play attends to the victims and presages the civil war that followed Independence.

The furore which broke out at the opening performance rivalled the *Playboy* riots and drew Yeats's famous angry upbraiding of the audience, 'you have disgraced yourselves again. Is this going to be a recurring celebration of Irish genius?'.[8] But the incident seems to have made Yeats more wary and, notoriously, just as he had refused Synge's *The Tinker's Wedding*, so he refused O'Casey's next play, *The Silver Tassie* (1928), which charts the experience of Harry, the triumphant winner of the football cup, the silver tassie, in Act I, through action at the Front (Act II) and recognition that he is crippled in the Act III hospital scene, to his final sense of futility and rejection as, returned home, he is the bitter spectre at another celebration. The refusal, on the grounds that O'Casey wrote out of opinion not experience of the First World War,[9] marked the break between O'Casey and the Abbey and the end of the Abbey as an important source of new drama.

In 1929, the board refused Denis Johnston's play about the patriot Robert Emmet, initially called *Shadowlands*. Johnston, one of the advocates of O'Casey's play, had, like O'Casey, been impressed by the London Gate Theatre's 1925 production of *From Morn to Midnight* and his play is expressionist in structure, though with more vivid individual life and sharper humour than was characteristic of Toller's play. After an opening playlet, which is a pastiche of the romantic verbiage of such Irish poets as Todhunter, Mangan and Thomas Moore, the play presents a collage of twentieth-century Dublin as if through the unconscious mind of Emmet. Retitled derisively, *The Old Lady Says 'No'*, Johnston's play was performed by the newly opened Dublin Gate Theatre, founded by Michael MacLiammoir to enable production of new European drama.

Johnston's next play, *The Moon in the Yellow River*, set in a '*shockingly untidy*' dwelling in an old fort, turns on an attempt to blow up a power station erected with German expertise at the mouth of the Liffey. Like O'Casey's Dublin plays, it includes a variety of visitors and passers-by and interrogates the Free State's myths of freedom fighting and Sinn Fein heroism. Although a chastened Abbey staged it in 1931 and, despite outraged protests from churchmen and patriots, staged *The Silver Tassie* in 1935, the theatre thereafter settled back to a safe repertoire of plays with quaint and comfortable peasant settings. It had anyway, following the success of Yeats's version of Sophocles' Oedipus plays (1926 and 1927), increasingly become, like the Old Vic, an agency for revivals rather than for the discovery of exciting new writing. O'Casey, who had moved to England, did not write for the Abbey again.

It is a critical commonplace that the *fracas* damaged O'Casey's writing since, while *The Silver Tassie* was staged successfully in London in 1929 with designs by Augustus John and Charles Laughton in the role of Harry Heegan, O'Casey, without the needful performance base, grew away from the realities of theatre.[10] It is true that, although he became a member of London Unity Theatre, his subsequent plays were all, like *The Silver Tassie*, published before they were performed without the opportunity for honing and development that the rehearsal process gives. But it is at least arguable that the breach was a necessary one which enabled O'Casey to break away from the trammelling expectations of Company and audience and explore the different possibilities of dramatic structure and language that are signalled in the satire and symbolism of the second act of *The Silver Tassie* to which Yeats took such exception.

Although, with distance, the action might seem hectic and the political argument crude, *Within the Gates* (1934) and *The Star Turns Red* (1940) proved revelatory to some at least of their contemporaries, including three of the leading theatre critics of the time. Ivor Brown wrote of O'Casey's revolt from realism in *Within the Gates* that he had 'gone a long way further than he did in *The Silver Tassie* towards a theatre of poetic power as well as prosaic fun' (*Observer*, 11.2.1934) and Brooks Atkinson commented after the New York production of this play:

> Out of the dead print of the text a glorious drama rose last evening with songs and dances, with colours and lights, with magnificent lines that cried out for noble speaking. For Mr O'Casey is right. He knows that the popular theatre is withered, and he also has the gift to redeem it with a drama that sweeps along through the loves and terrors of mankind. (*New York Times*, 23.10.1934)

James Agate commented that he found the later piece with its 'verbal splendour' to be 'a *magnum opus* of compassion *and* a revolutionary work', adding, 'I see in it a flame of propaganda tempered to the condition of dramatic art, as an Elizabethan understood that art' (*Sunday Times*, 17.3.1940). These are hardly small claims and serve as a reminder that these plays are among only a handful in English which show a lively sense of the theatrical ideas currently being explored in Europe. There are grounds for gratitude that, as John Arden, who claims O'Casey as a strong influence on his own writing, has commented, 'O'Casey's exile caused him to write like a European rather than an Irishman'.[11]

Mainstream theatre

What I dismissed earlier as the 'inconsequential entertainment' of mainstream theatre warrants a closer look since the movement of actors and the West End transfers of independent and repertory theatre productions created a degree of cross-fertilisation. Indeed, the first successes of all the long running dramatists of the period had begun outside the West End. Acclaimed plays of the period include Shaw's *Saint Joan* (1924) and his extravaganza, *The Apple Cart* (1929), as well as R. C. Sherriff's *Journey's End* and the work of Noel Coward.

With *Saint Joan*, as so often previously, Shaw was taking up and transforming a current dramatic mode. *Abraham Lincoln*, which had carried Drinkwater from Birmingham Rep to the London stage with huge success, was a historical chronicle play. Although masquerading under those colours, *Saint Joan* was a play about dissent and personal responsibility. Just as in the 1899 *Caesar and Cleopatra*, Desmond MacCarthy noted, Shaw here 'scrubs at the patina of time, 'til contemporary life begins to gleam through its surface unfamiliarly'.[12] Careful of historical fact and innovatory in his return to original documents as the basis of the trial scene, Shaw, nevertheless, fills his play with spiritual anachronisms creating a very contemporary debate between internal authority and the authority of institutions such as church and state. His Joan says, 'God speaks to us through our imaginations' and is twice described as a 'Protestant'. The effect of the play, however, perhaps because of the impact of Sybil Thorndike's performance as Joan and the staging with its tapestries, stained glass and intensely coloured costumes, designed by Ricketts after Flemish primitive paintings, was a further crop of history plays with defiant heroes – Gordon Daviot's *Queen of Spades* (1934) as well as Eliot's *Murder in the Cathedral*.

Although Granville Barker had retreated into the study and the two plays he did write, *His Majesty* and *The Secret Life*, pale shadows of his former work, remained unperformed, his influence was omnipresent in the production values of the alternative companies. Plays of 'modern ideas' did still appear. Galsworthy reworked his themes of the strong and the rich imposing on the less fortunate in *The Skin Game* (1920) and *Loyalties* (1922) but, even more evidently than in the pre-war years, his writing presumes a shared viewpoint with his bourgeois audience: the tribulations of a prisoner on the run, traced in *Escape* (1926), are relieved by recognition by the comfortably off people who help him that he is, fundamentally, 'one of us'. Issue plays from the younger generation, however, were more sexually and sometimes more socially challenging.

Although Shaw's Joan was recognised at once as displaying the Pankhurst spirit – her claims to the practicality of trousers for a working woman being one of the multitude of glancing contributions to contemporary social debate which made the play seem so fresh to its contemporary audience – feminist drama as such had vanished with the outbreak of the war and had not resurfaced after it. But a number of women dramatists now not only wrote for the Arts, the Lyric or the New but achieved West End transfers and overnight acclaim. In her best known play, *Bill of Divorcement* (1921), Clemence Dane engaged with the contemporary debate about the divorce law, focusing on the clause in the 1920 Bill that gave vicars the right to refuse their churches for the remarriage of divorcees. The somewhat contorted plot, set twelve years in the future, includes the return after fifteen years in an insane asylum of a man whose ex-wife's divorce had been delayed and whose remarriage has now been postponed by clerical recalcitrance. In a touching central scene, he pleads and she, overcome, opts for self-denial while their free-thinking, sturdy-spirited daughter, who refuses to go to church and declare herself a 'miserable sinner', faces the fact of hereditary madness. The ostensible message is spoken in well-made play style, if not sentiment, with mouthfilling rhetoric by the *raisonneur*, a doctor:

> That young, young generation found out, out of their own
> unhappiness, the war taught them, what peace couldn't
> teach us – that when conditions are evil it is not your duty
> to submit – that when conditions are evil, your duty, in
> spite of protests, in spite of sentiment, your duty, though you
> trample on the bodies of your nearest and dearest to do it,
> though you bleed your own heart white, your duty is to see
> that these conditions are changed. If your laws forbid you,
> you must change your laws. If your church forbids you,
> you must change your church; and, if your God forbids
> you, why then, you must change your God.
>
> (Act II)

But the conclusion in which daughter persuades mother not to sacrifice happiness, then shoulders the care of her father herself, rejecting marriage on eugenic grounds, begs the very questions the play would resolve.

Clemence Dane's penchant for the powerful situation and strong female character is evident, too, in *Granite* (1926). The play's language and imagery, its isolated setting on Lundy Island, the characters' biblical names and the demonstration of thwarted emotion in this play all echo O'Neill's *Desire Under the Elms*, although without the incest and child murder which had led to the banning of O'Neill's play and without the extreme economy of O'Neill's vernacular style. As in the American play, where Ephraim says, 'God's hard and lonesome. God's in the stones', landscape reflects spiritual condition. The heroine, Judith, says:

> Stone walls. . . . Even the walls are on his side. Oh God I've
> sat here ten years between stone walls, beside a stone
> man . . . it's killing me, the sea and the gulls screaming and
> Jordan's silences and Jordan's face, set, set, set, on his work
> like granite . . . you can't wreck this house, its roots are in
> the granite.
>
> (Act I)

It is forceful writing but the supernatural dealings of Judith, at whose summons the devil appears and brings about the death of each of her husbands, pushes the play into sensation and melodrama at the expense of characterisation.

If the modernist poets caught one kind of post-war mood – of personal futility within 'a botched civilization' – it is in the best plays of Coward and certain works by Maugham that what Pound labelled the 'accelerated grimace' of the age found its clearest image.[13] Coward's touch was lighter than Maugham's with always a lurking note of self-parody, and his own performances brought a remarkable panache to a string of successful productions in the 1920s beginning with *The Vortex* (1924). This drama of gossip, maternal deprivation and the insecurity of approaching old age which, according to John Gielgud created an 'extraordinarily tense' atmosphere in the auditorium of the Hampstead Everyman,[14] was still running in 1925 in the West End to which it had quickly been transferred, when first *Fallen Angels* and then *Hay Fever* and the revue, *On with the Dance*, opened.

Noel Coward

A writer of immense facility, Coward borrowed from and wrote variations on other plays, much as Oscar Wilde had done before him. His first play, *The Young Idea*, was heavily derivative of Shaw's *You Never Can Tell* in its treatment of relations between the generations; subsequent borrowings and parodies were much more adroitly handled. In Act II of *The Vortex*, as in Act II of *Much Ado About Nothing*, the action is carried in snippets of dialogue during a dance in which, '*everyone must appear to be talking at once, but the actual lines spoken whilst dancing must be timed to reach the audience as the speakers pass near the footlights*'. *Easy Virtue* (1926; New York, 1925) reworks the classic fallen woman plot but, whereas Mrs Tanqueray longed to be loved by her pious step-daughter and accepted by respectable society, Coward's Larita speedily recognises the mistake of marrying into the philistine English middle class and the play lights up when she turns their hypocritical words mockingly back on to them, a position endorsed, moreover, when the *raisonneur* Sarah, a healthy but unusually perceptive product of the husband's world, observes, 'I used to be awfully fond of him, but he's shrunk over this beyond all recognition – gone tiny' (Act III). *Bitter Sweet* (1929) is a Franz Lehar operetta and *Cavalcade* has as its fourth scene an unusually long quasi-extract from a romantic musical.

Coward filled theatres, particularly when, as often, he directed and performed the lead part himself, but the common epithets of contemporary criticism were, 'trivial', 'light', 'inconsequential' and many of his pieces confirm such judgements. *Bitter Sweet*, which had a budget of £20,000 and ran for two years is saccharine. Coward invites his audience to wallow in nostalgia in the central sequences which flash back to a *fin de siècle* setting and shamelessly uses the romantic convention of a heroine in straitened circumstances and her lover's touching death in a duel. The interpolated tribute to Oscar Wilde in the quartette sung by a painter, a poet, a dilettante and a playwright:

> Faded boys, jaded boys, womankind's,
>   Gift to a bulldog nation,
> In order to distinguish us from less enlightened minds,
>   We all wear a green carnation
>
> (I. iii)

and the good tempered fun with which the 'ladies of the town' sing of their profession are worlds away from Wilde's own social insights and from the disconcerting harshness characteristic of the presentation of the prostitute's lot in the Brecht/Weill *Threepenny Opera*, produced in Berlin the previous year. Similarly, despite the claim in the closing stage directions of *Easy Virtue* that Larita feels 'hopeless sadness', the stated intensity of her love for the feeble John has not been credible and the strongest feeling as she quits the mean-spirited bourgeois household is relief.

Where Coward makes his continuing claim to attention is in his wonderfully symmetrical comedies of egoism, desire and bad manners: *Hay Fever* (1925), *Private Lives* (1931) and *Blithe Spirit* (1941) and the somewhat shakier, *Design for Living* (1939; New York, 1933) and *Present Laughter* (1942). Played with panache by a team of actors (Gertrude Lawrence, Jessie Matthews, Jack Buchanen, the Lunts, as well as Coward himself) skilled in delivery of the well-bred insults and discourteous frankness that characterise the staccato dialogue, they are works that perceive the absurdities of sexual relationship and social organisation.

War plays and patriotism

Coward's assault on contemporary mores is much fiercer in *Post Mortem* (written, 1930), a rawly didactic play, as yet unproduced professionally, which he wrote after a brief spell acting in a touring production of R. C. Sherriff's First World War play, *Journey's End*. Initially rejected by one theatre after another, Sherriff's play, after a single Stage Society performance in 1928, became the runaway success of 1929 when, under pressure from Shaw, it was produced at the Savoy and subsequently made into a film. While the honour and glory of dying for one's country were recorded on public memorials in towns and villages throughout the country as well as at the centre of government in Whitehall, writers recorded the waste, futility and individual cost of what, as already registered in the war poems of Siegfried Sassoon (1919) and Wilfred Owen (1920), was increasingly coming to be seen as a great *débâcle*. The myth of the Great War was examined in a near simultaneous crop of literary works at the end of the 1920s which, besides Sherriff's play, included such autobiographical fiction as Ford Maddox Ford's four Tietjens novels (1924–28). The next year, 1929, came Richard Aldington's *Death of a Hero*, Robert Graves' *Goodbye To All That* and, telling a remarkably similar story from the other side, the English translation of Erich Maria Remarque's *All's Quiet on the Western Front*, and then Hemingway's *A Farewell to Arms*. In 1930 Sassoon's, *Memoirs of an Infantry Officer*, whose autobiographical hero renounces war, appeared. On the stage, the sounds of low-flying aircraft and explosions that concluded Shaw's wartime play, *Heartbreak House*, presaged the coming destruction, the dislocation and breakdown within the house, the lack of direction of the British state. Miles Malleson's two war plays, *'D' Company* and *Black 'Ell*, had been seized on publication in 1916 for defamation of the British soldier, and its treatment of homosexuality had led to the banning of Ackerley's *The Prisoners of War* in 1925, but Reginald Berkeley's *The White Chateau*, which gave an account of successive waves of wartime destruction and ended with a vision of hope in the newly established League of Nations, was broadcast on radio to an already expanding national audience, on Armistice Day the same year.

The Silver Tassie and *Journey's End*, both written in 1928, recreate in their very different ways the tedium and devastation of life at the Front: the one through expressionistic images, chanting and action, the other with a realistic account of the tensions and gestures of mutual humanity of a group of men, vulnerable and awaiting the inevitable slaughter in a dugout. While O'Casey pursues his soldiers back into the scrap heap that is their civilian life, Sherriff's ends cataclysmically with the ordering from above of a raid the characters know will be futile, the collapse of the dugout under a shell blast, and the off-stage rattle of machine-gun fire. The action, in each case, works as an indictment of those running the war and of their carelessness of the lives of serving soldiers.

All these plays demand recognition of the stupidity or ruthlessness of the commanders running the war and of the sheer exhaustion that besets the Front-line troops. Most include indignation at the ignorance of people at home, but, of all of them, only *The Silver Tassie* and *'D' Company* are set among common soldiers rather than officers. O'Casey introduces a political awareness, voicing the ironic hostility of the men to the officer-, inspector- and official visitor-class:

1ST STRETCHER BEARER:
    The red-tabbed squit.

2ND:
> The lousy map-scanner.

3RD:
> We must keep up, we must keep up the morale of the
> army.

2ND:
> Does 'e eat well?

THE REST:
> (*in chorus*): Yes, 'e eats well.

2ND:
> Does 'e sleep well?

THE REST:
> (*in chorus*): Yes, 'e sleeps well.

2ND:
> Does 'e whore well?

THE REST:
> Yes 'e whores well.

2ND:
> Does 'e fight well?

THE REST:
> Napoo; 'e 'as to do the thinkin' for the Tommies.

> (Act II)

The rage behind this scene excoriates.

Coward's play, less controlled than any of the others, opens and closes
with the mortal wounding and death of its officer hero at the Front in
1917. The intervening scenes project him into the future that is 1930
where the self-seeking and triviality or the jaundiced clarity of those who
survived him provide a bitter answer to his question about the purpose of
life and of his own death in war. The sour note is shared by Somerset
Maugham's *For Services Rendered* (1932) which, set in the present, figures
a First World War hero, blinded like Ted in *The Silver Tassie*. He spends
his life in knitting, tatting and sardonic recognition of the wasted lives
around him. A friend, awarded the Distinguished Service Order for wartime bravery, commits suicide to avoid the shame of peacetime bankruptcy.
Maugham's play, unlike Coward's, was produced but the jaundiced tone
made it the least successful of his plays.

In contrast with *Post Mortem*, Coward's *Cavalcade* (1931), was an assured
and reassuring piece that won instant acclaim, praise from George V and
a command performance for the Hollywood film version. Taking his
history from the *Illustrated London News*, Coward sketched in shared
moments of national joy and shock, with a series of *coups de théâtre* (the
announcement of the relief of Mafeking interrupting a musical comedy;
a honeymoon couple suddenly revealed to be on the doomed Titanic)

and of brilliantly orchestrated crowd scenes set in such notably English places as Kensington Gardens, an Edwardian ball, a seaside resort and Trafalgar Square on Armistice Day. The illusion is of a wide-ranging reflection of the life of the nation but the perspective is one-sided and, for all its sequences of private grief and its First World War scene of soldiers marching continually uphill, it is unduly complacent. The working classes appeared in stereotypical guises and recognisable theatrical situations (the kitchen below stairs, a street scene with shoppers in shawls, pearly costers dancing and a Salvation Army band); references to the socially divisive General Strike and the current Depression were avoided, and the upwardly mobile working-class girl's singing of the 'Weary Twentieth Century Blues' number towards the end was juxtaposed with the upper middle-class woman's brave toast to the future and 'the hope that one day this country of ours, which we love so much, will find dignity and greatness and peace again' (III. i), a sentiment reinforced by the concluding stage direction, in which '*the Union Jack glow[ed] through the blackness*', lights came up on the tiered ranks of the company and all sang 'God Save the King' together. It is an astoundingly blithe conclusion at the moment when British unemployment had reached twenty-one per cent, there had been a run on the pound and the Government had just fallen.

Elizabeth Robins could write with some justification in 1932 of 'these times, theatrically so calm, if not becalmed'.[15] The nature of the issues dealt with in mainstream theatre and the tendency to facile resolutions demonstrate the mismatch between it and the state of the nation. Churchill's return to the Gold Standard in 1925, bitterly attacked by John Maynard Keynes, led to a period of high interest rates and low growth. The attempt to cut miners' wages resulted in the General Strike of 1926.[16] The turmoil was international: overvaluation of the dollar and the resultant Wall Street Crash, the collapse of confidence and economic dislocation created the Depression that affected all the Western world, most terrifyingly, in the triumph of Nazism in Germany, signalled by the election of Hitler in 1933.

Rodney Ackland and J. B. Priestley

Almost contemporaneously, two dramatists appeared who did respond in some degree to the impact of such events. J. B. Priestley followed the dramatised version of his novel *The Good Companions* (1931) with *Dangerous Corner* (1932) and was to write some forty-nine plays. Though Rodney

Ackland's output was smaller and is now much less well-known, the impact of *Strange Orchestra* (1932), the first piece of new writing to be directed by John Gielgud, was immediate, and *The Old Ladies* (1935), also directed by Gielgud, which gave Edith Evans a wonderful part as a covetous old gypsy woman, was a *succès d'estime*.

While the large claims that have recently been made for Ackland's plays[17] may be overstated, the rejection of glamorous and escapist settings and the interweaving of the experiences of convincingly individualised characters suggest that they have a greater potential for revival than most of the long-running contemporary successes. *Strange Orchestra* presents what might be thought of as the darker side of the Noel Coward world. Set among aimless, indigent young people who quarrel, make love, play the gramophone and behave sometimes appallingly, sometimes heroically, it was immediately labelled Chekhovian and has something of that complexity, although it lacks Chekhov's speed of movement from laughter to tears and back.

Priestley was prepared to experiment with form and to address pressing issues of the contemporary world. *Dangerous Corner* includes the repetition of part of the first act in the second which offers a different version of the same events, a technique subsequently developed by Alan Ayckbourn. In *Cornelius* (1935), the title role (played by Ralph Richardson in the first production) faces the prospect of the collapse of his small business and the consequent unemployment of his loyal workforce. He voices the dismay of a generation at the realities of unemployment when he says,

> I can't believe it. If you're willing to work hard, willing to take risks, ready to be scorched or frozen, drowned or sent half-mad with thirst, there must be openings somewhere for you in the world. They can't have closed everything up so that we're bees in a glass case. It's unthinkable.
>
> (Act I)

But Priestley retreats from reality in his ending in which a newly determined Cornelius, far from meeting the situation, sets out to look for the lost city of the Incas.

Virtually all his plays include a strong moral statement as one or more of the characters, usually speaking the language of Priestley's own socialism with the insight and idealism of the younger generation, make a claim for social responsibility. In *I Have Been Here Before* (1937), Yorkshire villagers' hostility to a foreigner provokes the hero to cry:

> All over this rotten world now they're slamming the doors in the faces of good men. But we've still a door or two

open here. We can't bang them in the face of this man,
who's done none of us any harm.

(Act II)

Clifford Odets, Priestley's American contemporary, in such plays as *Awake
and Sing* (1935) and Arthur Miller, in his first stage success, *All My Sons*
(1947) share the same rhetoric and the idealism.

Another hallmark of Priestley's writing is that, like the dramatists of
the pre-war Manchester School, he replaces the stereotypical comic voices
and clumsy behaviour of the West End representation of northerners with
something more credible. Unlike them, he also uses the dramatic frame
playfully. Certain devices recur: temporal disjunction compels the audience
and sometimes the characters themselves to see the central figures in a
new light or, in its mildest form, to become conscious of the artifice of
stage time. In *Dangerous Corner* and again in *An Inspector Calls* (1946), each
act begins with the words with which the previous one ended, the interval
the audience has just experienced being eclipsed by the repetition. A leap
forward twenty years in Act II of *Time and the Conways* (1937) means that
we watch Act III, which begins at the point where Act I ended, with sad
recognition of the disappointed hopes and attrition of years that faces the
characters. In *An Inspector Calls* the moral guilt of every character and
the failures of humanity which have resulted in the suicide of a young
woman are exposed in the inspector's interrogation. As the play seems to
come to its conclusion, following the departure of the inspector, with the
characters blindly grasping at the reassurance that there has not been a
death and ready, therefore, to deny responsibility, the telephone rings. The
curtain line, 'that was the police. A girl has just died – on her way to the
Infirmary – after swallowing some disinfectant. And a police inspector is
on his way here – to ask some – questions', reveals the action to have
been not the cruel hoax they supposed but a strange premonition.

Such undermining of audience perceptions is a feature even of Priestley's
lightest works. In the detective extravaganza, *Laburnum Grove* (1933), a
man of sterling worth but boring suburban lifestyle is suspected of being
a master criminal. He allows the suspicions to linger as a comfortable
means of freeing the family from self-interested, not to say parasitic,
relations and an unpleasant prospective son-in-law. The absurdity of the
fears and suspicions having been made clear and the relations, son-in-law
and last policeman having departed, Priestley has the man spring into
action to make good his escape with his ill-gotten gains. This formal
insouciance is what enabled Graham Daldry's recent (1993) hugely successful adaptation of *An Inspector Calls* for the National Theatre to seem fresh
while retaining a truth to the play. The post-modernism that places the
family in a frame within the proscenium arch and allows the inspector to

move between the two worlds is an updated version of precisely the temporal tricks and framing devices that surprised Priestley's first audiences.

Problems arise when his fascination with contemporary theories of time, is insufficiently absorbed into the texture of the play. In *I Have Been Here Before*, for example, the credibility of the action turns on acceptance of an untenable theory, deriving in this case, as Priestley's prefatory note indicates, from 'P. D. Ouspensky's astonishing book, *A New Model of the Universe*'. It is presumably this work which is confusingly offered as reassurance in Act II of *Time and the Conways*. Alan tells his sister:

> It's hard to explain – suddenly like this – there's a book I'll lend you – read it in the train. But the point is, now, at this moment, or any moment, we're only a cross-section of our real selves. What we really are is the whole stretch of ourselves, all our time, and when we come to the end of this life, all those selves, all our time, will be us – the real you, the real me. And then perhaps we'll find ourselves in another time, which is only another kind of dream.
>
> (Act II)

The effect is as dulling as when a figure or event in fiction must be accepted as unquestionably supernatural and not in any way an emanation of the character's unconscious fears or desires.

James Bridie was somewhat in the same mould as Priestley, although his base was Scotland rather than Yorkshire. With such plays as *The Anatomist* (1931), *The Black Eye* (1935) and *Mr Bolfry* (1943), another of those flirtations with the supernatural so current in this period, Bridie was the chief among a group of dramatists, including Robert Maclellan and Gordon Bottomley, through whose writing the Scottish National Players hoped to establish a Scottish theatre comparable with the Abbey in Dublin. There was a short period of animation, including productions of Bottomley's two curious Shakespearean prequels, *King Lear's Wife* and *Gruach*, a girlhood-of-Lady-Macbeth play, but no Synge or O'Casey emerged although the Players did help prepare the ground for Glasgow Unity Theatre and place a marker for such later Glasgow-based companies as the Citizens and 7:84.

Following in the wake of *The Good Companions* and *Strange Orchestra* came a much more direct encounter with the world of unemployment and Depression. Ronald Gow's adaptation of Walter Greenwood's novel, *Love on the Dole*, produced by Manchester Repertory Company in 1934 and then toured, played continuously somewhere until the summer of 1937, with stagings in London, New York and, wonderfully retitled *Rêves sans Provisions*, in Paris. Although it contains moments of optimism and a notably escapist sequence on a mountain in the Peak District, the play is finally deeply pessimistic about the prospects for working people. The sensitive socialist leader, Larry Meath, who believes that saving oneself is not enough, is killed by police while attempting to control a demonstration, leaving his bereft fiancée, Sally Hardcastle, to accept the favours of a self-serving smart alec, as the only way out of the Salford slum.

Political theatre: the Group

Gow and Greenwood's play represents a surfacing into mainstream theatre of another area of 1930s dramatic writing: that of political commitment. In the aftermath of the Russian Revolution, plays that presented the new Soviet regime in any way favourably were banned from public performance,[18] but one effect of the Depression and the rise of fascism in Europe was a surge of interest in and enthusiasm for socialism and specifically the Soviet regime which, with the reported success of the Five-Year Plan, appeared to be succeeding where Western capitalism was evidently failing the mass of its people. Socialism flourished among the new generation of writers and in the colleges and universities, as well as among the politicised working classes. Although there were internecine struggles, the various left-wing groups increasingly followed continental models in cooperating to form the Popular Front with, in 1934, a massive anti-fascist demonstration in Hyde Park and, in 1936, the Cable Street 'They Shall Not Pass' demonstration against Mosley's anti-Semitic brownshirts. By this time there was a Popular Front government in Spain and impassioned support for it when Franco's fascist forces attempted its overthrow. Although the participation of numbers of young writers in the International Brigade which fought in the Spanish Civil War between 1936 and 1939 has implied it was a poets' war, some eighty per cent of the 2,000 British members of the International Brigade were working class. That some 500 of the British contingent were killed and 1,200 injured suggests the scale and horror of the slaughter.[19]

Anthologies, essays, the journal *New Left Review*, (1934–38) and the poetry of W. H. Auden and the New Country writers bear witness to the politicisation of literature. Everyone's attention had moved in the direction of reality, as Wallace Stevens wrote in 1936 of a parallel movement in America. The New Country group, impressed by the dramatic writing of Yeats and Eliot, and looking to address a wider and more immediate audience than they could through their poetry, joined forces with Rupert Doone, whose Group Theatre had been founded in 1932, to restore music and dance to the English drama. The membership included Eliot and Masefield, Havelock Ellis and Vanessa Bell, Henry Moore and Adrian Stokes, as well as such theatre people as Tyrone Guthrie and the dancers, Anton Dolin and Doone himself, but the presence of the New Country writers from 1934 onwards shifted the Group towards the production of socially engaged verse drama. The motivation was summarised by John Lehmann in 1940:

> the poets felt that the established theatre had become too much a slave to rigid and empty formulas to welcome the experiments in language and shape they were interested in, and too deeply involved in flattering the principles of the middle classes to want to have anything to do with their explosive social criticism: new channels, therefore, were urgently needed.[20]

Auden's political allegory, *The Dance of Death* (1934), directed by Tyrone Guthrie, was a startling example of experiment in language and shape. Evidently following Cocteau's emphasis on the sensuous power of the human body, Yeats's ideas about dance and Eliot's use of the rhythms of jazz and popular music in *Sweeney Agonistes*, it intermixed Brechtian polemic and choric techniques picked up from contemporary agitation-propaganda theatre. A lively rag-bag, the piece addresses, with some ferocity, the crisis of Western capitalism and the predicted end of the bourgeoisie and, more uncertainly, heralds a new socialist future. The Dancer having collapsed, the action, which has been characterised by cries from figures placed in the audience, vaudeville routines and other disruptive methods, ends with the momentary appearance of Karl Marx who declares, notably unpoetically, 'the instruments of production have been too much for him. He is liquidated'.

Buried guilt is exposed in both *The Dog Beneath the Skin* (1936) and *The Ascent of F6* (1937), but the argument of both is confused. Individuals seem to symbolise the deep inner corruption of society, but there is little of the convincing political analysis the plays seem to promise. *The Ascent of F6*, indeed, which initially seems to be an indictment of the ways in which the state misuses the talents and aspirations of its people, proves in the end to have offered an embarrassingly obvious autobiographical presentation of obsession with the maternal principle, as its mountaineer hero, having climbed Brand-like up the mountain, dies collapsed before the spectre of his all dominant mother. In *On the Frontier* (1938), written with Christopher Isherwood, people are revealed as conditioned by their culture, less free than they had assumed:

We cannot choose our world,
Our time, our class. None are innocent, none.
Causes of violence run so deep in all our lives
It touches every act.

(On the Frontier, III. iii)

But although this dramatisation of hostilities between two fictional warring nations is evidently offered as an allegory of the forthcoming European calamities, it remains imprecise. As in the rest of Auden's drama, the method demands an energetic use of theatre, but the development of thought and action in the piece remains confusing. What is clear, throughout, is anger against the moral bankruptcy of contemporary society which clings to its myths of Empire and respectability and an Establishment that is complacent although many people live in economic misery and a new war looms.

Political theatre: the Workers' contribution

A more evidently working-class political theatre had been developing simultaneously. The Manchester Theatre Union, London Unity Theatre, Merseyside Left Theatre Club, Glasgow Workers' Theatre Group, were only the most famous of some 300 'Left' theatre groups active throughout the country by the late 1930s. Twenty-two groups sent representatives to the Workers' Theatre Movement National Conference. At first sight the proliferation, splintering and reformation of radical theatre groups in the late 1920s and 1930s is bewildering, but it represents a remarkable area of theatrical activity. While much of its output was crude, ideologically simplistic, hastily assembled, clumsily performed, some good new writing was generated and the emphasis of some of the companies on ensemble, the physical skills of the actors and the importance of creating dialogue close to common speech, gave their work vitality. Although shockingly neglected in most theatre histories,[21] what for ease of reference I will call 'Workers' Theatre' was a vital element in the British theatre scene and an important forerunner of the post-Second World War revival of English drama.

O'Casey's influence was ubiquitous although the political allegiance of his plays was not sufficiently clear cut for many in the movement. Joe Corrie, a Fife miner who was greatly impressed by the Dublin plays, wrote his first play, the one-act *Hogmanay* in 1926. Clearly drawing its inspiration from the Act II celebration scene in *Juno and the Paycock*, it portrays drinking, talking and singing, including the recurrent pitting of 'The Red Flag' against songs by Burns, to evoke a mining family's New Year during the six-month lockout that followed the General Strike of May 1926. He followed it with *In Time o' Strife* (1927), a dramatisation of the impact of the strike on the local community and the pressure to return to work on men whose families are starving. The local amateur group, the Bowhill Players, turned themselves into the professional Fife Miner Players in 1929 to tour this remarkable work to music halls throughout Scotland.

Corrie's realistic recreation of the texture of working-class life is typical of only one strand of left-wing theatre. Although Corrie was bewildered by an expressionist version of *In Time o' Strife* that he saw in Leipzig which included crowds shouting slogans and pictures flashed up on a screen, new ideas from Continental Europe and from America were embraced willingly by other Workers' Theatre practitioners, some twenty of whom had attended the International Olympiad of Workers' Theatre in Russia in 1933, where they encountered the work of Meyerhold and Piscator. Indeed, the Soviet and, after 1933, the exiled radical German theatres, exerted a strong influence on their British counterparts. The various groups gathered under the Workers' Theatre Movement banner between 1926 and 1936, were anti-naturalistic, developing an agit-prop style as a way of attacking the capitalist system. Sketches were performed, as in Russia, by touring groups at factory gates, strike meetings and to dole queues. After 1933, the drive became fiercer and, after the outbreak of the Spanish Civil War, was strongly directed towards raising consciousness about, and indeed funds for, Spain.

The roots of Joan Littlewood's Theatre Workshop, which was founded in 1945, were in the Manchester region in the 1930s where one Jimmy Miller co-founded the Red Megaphones (1931) whose street theatre involved 'mass declamation' – essentially slogan shouting in protest against unemployment, poverty and capitalist exploitation. In 1934, Ewan Mac-Coll, as he had then become known, formed the narrative, didactic and expressionist 'Theatre of Action' with Joan Littlewood, newly out of drama school and working as Stage Manager with Rusholme Rep, with whom he had worked on a BBC documentary. Initially amateurs, the group developed in 1936, into the more fully professional Theatre Union, follow-ing a taste of repertory theatre the previous year when Ernst Toller had invited them to add some rough authenticity to his stokehold play, *Draw the Fires*, which he was directing for Rusholme Rep. The thrust was political, 'facing up to the problems of our time', according to their manifesto, and addressing plays of social significance to the 'widest possible public, particularly that section which has been starved theatrically' but, importantly, the venture was also committed to the attempt 'to solve our own theatrical problems both technical and ideological'.[22] In the course of the next three years, Littlewood and MacColl worked with their companies on movement and voice, used Stanislavskian exercises and investigated masks, lighting effects and back projections. Their productions included Spanish Civil War sketches and the first British performance of Lope de Vega's, *Fuente Ovejuna*, the Spanish classic in which a village community rebels against a cruel tyrant. Among other British premières they presented *The Good Soldier Schweik* (in the version dramatised for Piscator) and developed their own version of that specifically 1930s dramatic form, the Living Newspaper.

The Living Newspaper, developed by the American Federal Theatre Project in such works as *Triple A Ploughed Under* (1936) and *One Third of a Nation* (1938), utilised lighting and other theatrical effects to argue a case, alternating the bald statement of potent facts with dramatised scenes and song. Home-grown versions included London Unity's *Busmen* (1938) and MacColl and Littlewood's, *Last Edition* (1940). MacColl's account of this dramatisation of events from the Depression to the Munich Agreement, summarises the range of theatrical activity involved, as well as providing a strong indicator of Theatre Workshop's post-war style:

> Everything we had learned of theatre and politics in the years
> of work was now to be put to use – the mass-declamatory
> form, the satirical comedy style of agit-prop, the dance drama
> of *Newsboy*, the simulated public meetings of *Still Talking*
> and *Waiting for Lefty*, the constructivism of *John Bullion*, the
> expressionism of *Miracle at Verdun*, the burlesque comedy
> of *Lysistrata*, the juxtaposition of song and actuality from the
> Spanish Civil War pageants and the fast moving episodic
> style of *The Good Soldier Schweik*.[23]

One of Littlewood and MacColl's most successful productions, Clifford Odets's episodic dramatisation of the taxi drivers' strike, *Waiting for Lefty*, borrowed from the New York Group Theatre, with its final resonant call to strike action, was also produced by London Unity Theatre where it generated *Where's that Bomb?* (1936), a comparably structured piece written by two London taxi drivers, Roger Gullan and Buckley Roberts. Unity, whose driving interests were the Spanish Civil War and advocacy of the Popular Front, was a force to be reckoned with. Like Theatre Union, it used a diversity of dramatic forms, revues, sketches, mass chants, pageants but, although it commanded the services of some excellent actors and directors, it concentrated, unlike Theatre Union, on the political message at the expense of theatre skills. It was, though, considerably better endowed with a 323–seater London theatre of its own (in St Pancras) from 1937, and with a General Council whose members included Stafford Cripps, Harold Laski and Victor Gollancz, as well as O'Casey, Michel St Denis,

Miles Malleson, that energetic and ubiquitous 1930s figure Tyrone Guthrie and, as its president from 1937, André van Gyseghem.

Gyseghem's career is indicative of the interactive nature of radical theatre of the time. Beginning from a Co-operative Movement drama class, he moved to RADA and then into the professional theatre, where his work included directing Paul Robeson in O'Neill's *All God's Chillun Got Wings* at the Embassy Theatre, Swiss Cottage. He worked on voice and move-ment with the Rebel Players who performed agit-prop pieces at factory gates. After attending the Moscow Olympiad as a delegate, he spent a year with Piscator's International Union of Revolutionary Theatre in Moscow, then, having visited New York to see the work of the Group Theatre and Federal Theatre Project, he founded Left Theatre in 1936 where he directed various Federal Theatre pieces, Gorki's *Mother* and Montagu Slater's play about the Welsh miners' strike, *Stay Down Miner* (1936). In 1937, he became president of London Unity. Robeson, turning down West End offers, joined the Company in 1938.

Unity's programme was eclectic. It gave the first ever British perform-ance of a full-length Brecht play in 1938 – his rather undistinguished piece about the Spanish Civil War, *Senora Carrar's Rifles* – and at Christmas of that year one of its greatest successes, the satirical *Babes in the Wood*, which adapted traditional pantomime to its own political ends: the babes were Austria and Czechoslovakia, the wicked uncle, Neville Chamberlain, and the robbers Hitler and Mussolini. With six performances a week, the piece ran from Christmas 1938 until May the following year. Seen within the context of Unity, contemporary claims to the dramatic power of the current work of O'Casey, a writer experienced in the possibilities of theatre and responsive to the political moment, have a new force. The immediate performance experience deriving from the combination of social satire and vivid effects in Unity's 1940 production of *The Star Turns Red* is inevitably lost in a bare reading of the script. John Lehmann recalled that, 'for sheer dramatic excitement', he knew 'of nothing to beat the scene in Act III when the two factions cross swords over the bier of the first victim on the workers' side'.[24]

If the mass declamation of the Red Megaphones derived in part from Soviet propaganda theatre, the political pageants performed at the end of the decade also drew on the elaborate dance routines of Hollywood musicals and the newly celebrated folk song and dance of British popular culture. The Women's Co-operative Pageant at Wembley in 1938, used declamatory speech, processions, dancing, rousing music and thousands of people on a huge circular stage in the middle of the stadium to chart the rise of everyman through folk festivals of the Middle Ages, via communal machine wrecking, to the emergence of the industrial working classes, trade unionism and the foundation of the Co-operative Movement. Gyseghem, the director, recalled the visual and emotional impact:

Theatre is a weapon, and we were using it in numerous forms. A film was made of the performance, mostly taken from the air so that you could look down and see the patterns made. I was pleased because the patterns made by the living people on this film reproduced exactly the coloured chalk marks I had made for the groups on the pre-rehearsal plans. And there you saw it live, worked out by thousands of living people.[25]

In 1939, the 100th anniversary of the Chartist Movement was celebrated in another pageant by the same team and, in May, the South Wales Miners' Federation staged its Pageant of South Wales with 2,000 people performing in each of three different localities – Abertillery, Pontypool and Ystradgyn-lais – simultaneously.

These mass spectacles, curiously revived in recent years in the national-istic opening and closing ceremonies of successive Olympic Games, were valued by their initiators as 'co-operation of all for the sake of all',[26] but there is an abnegation of thought in the combination of simplistic political message and synchronised physical movement. The claim is to an alterna-tive to the allegiances of commercial or high culture, but the style and method comes uncomfortably close to those of the mass rallies of contem-porary totalitarian states.

Much of the output of the radical theatre groups of the late 1920s and 1930s was hasty, ideologically simplistic or clumsily performed, but there was life and imaginative energy in much of it which, in the seriousness of its representation of issues, registered and contributed to a shift in national and cultural consciousness and made a claim to social and political aware-ness that was missing from mainstream theatre.

The advent of radio

In 1920, the Marconi Company began broadcasting from Chelmsford with two thirty-minute sessions daily of news, live music and gramophone records, public attention being attracted to radio in June of that year when Northcliffe papers engaged Dame Nellie Melba for a broadcast *Daily Mail* concert. The first transmission from Marconi's London studio, 2LO, came in May 1922 and public interest was further stimulated in the autumn when the Prince of Wales's speech to boy-scouts at a rally at Alexandra Palace was broadcast. The British Broadcasting Company was formed in

October with J. C. W. Reith as its General Manager – it became a Corporation in 1927 and Reith its Director General – and, after the licence permitting 'news, information, concerts, lectures, educational matter, speeches, weather reports, theatrical entertainments, and any other matter permitted', was finally granted early in 1923, it began regular transmissions.

The first dramatic pieces broadcast were excerpts from well-known plays – the quarrel scene from *Julius Caesar*, the trial scene from *The Merchant of Venice*, scenes from *Henry VIII* and *Much Ado About Nothing* and highlights from current London plays but, after protests from London theatres anxious about the new form of competition, a drama department was formed under the direction of R. E. Jeffrey. The first broadcast play, specifically written for radio, Richard Hughes' short piece, *Danger*, was broadcast early in 1924 with the first full-length play, Reginald Berkeley's plea for the renunciation of war, *The White Chateau*, following on Armistice Day 1925. By 1930, radio was producing some fifty plays a year and *The Times* was beginning to print reviews of radio plays. Val Gielgud, who had succeeded Jeffrey as Head of Drama in 1929, received over 12,000 letters in response to his 1934 request to listeners to:

> Write to us and say, as candidly, as clearly and as categorically as you can what you feel about the whole question. Are there too many plays broadcast? Are there too few? Do you hear the sort of plays you want to hear?[27]

Only 323 of the replies seem to have been hostile. The number of plays broadcast rose to 200 a year by 1938 and close to 400 by the end of the war which created what Gielgud later described as the 'insoluble problem' of finding 'a sufficient quantity of material of quality'.[28]

Many of the hundreds of plays written for radio in the inter-war years were slight, offering the passing entertainment regularly found in the theatre. Thrillers were particularly preferred, as if there was a special thrill in encountering frightening things in the security of the home. Adaptations of novels or stage plays took up a deal of air time and Shakespearean drama worked well, probably because, being written for a largely bare stage, its verbal language is expressive: its scenes are set and characters repeatedly named *in* the dialogue which facilitates aural location and identification. But there were also numbers of original plays written in response to the challenge posed by the new medium – a medium which not only denied actors the responsive presence of a live audience, but denied its audience communal engagement as well as the visual presence of set and characters and the spatial relationships between them. By the same token, though, it was a medium not subject to the financial and visual restraints of staging.

British radio was free, too, from the demands of sponsors that afflicted

American productions or of government that, in the 1930s, increasingly pushed the previously inventive German radio services towards propaganda. Programming, in the inter-war period, was scheduled around play length rather than, as often with American radio stations, play length fitted into preordained time slots.

Not all freedoms, however, were as real as might at first appear. While radio drama was not subject to the Lord Chamberlain's veto, it was subject to internally imposed checks. The BBC's own managers, watchful of its licence and of offending its broad-based public, seem to have allowed hardly more rein than existed in the theatre. As Gielgud put it, 'the amber warning lights at the crossroads of Sex, Religion, and Politics' flashed red 'with disquieting rapidity'.[29] A further, less obvious, constriction was associated with voice. The enunciation of announcers and of most actors was a very specific clipped form of Received Pronunciation. Heard now on records in the BBC's Sound Archive, dialogue from the period sounds remarkably slow and stilted, often lacking the elisions, redundancies and repetitions that have suggested speech in fluent stage dialogue from the earliest times.

Despite the restrictions, writers did respond to the challenge to discover what could be made of this new form, that was dependent on the single sense of hearing as that other new, mechanised form, the silent film had been on sight. Like the silent film it was a necessarily short-lived medium, bound to be eclipsed when developing technology introduced sound to the one and vision to the other, but, like that medium, radio for a short period had the advantage of novelty and a distinct kind of availability that gained it both a huge popular audience and some inspired practitioners. With its emphasis so firmly on language, it offered writers dramatic possibilities different from the theatre. It also offered the remarkable prospect not just of a huge audience but of a unitary one.

Until the Second World War when the need arose to provide both home and forces broadcasting – subsequently the Home and Light services – any given broadcast play would be heard by anybody listening in on that evening. The subsequent addition of the Third Programme to which the serious music, talks and the more troubling experimental drama could be assigned, brought the division into high- and low-brow, alternative and mainstream, familiar in the theatre, to the airwaves – to the relief, it should be said, of many listeners who were bewildered or irritated by experimental work, as well as some drama producers, beleaguered by the results of audience research, which began in the late 1930s and often indicated hostility to avant-garde work. But there would not be again, after the Second World War, that sense of addressing a nation which must have accompanied the performance of *The White Chateau*, on Armistice Day 1925, or the various plays on religious themes specially commissioned for broadcast on holidays during the period: *Unto Us* devised by R. Ellis

Roberts, (broadcast, Christmas 1935; repeated, Christmas, 1936) or Dorothy L. Sayers', *He That Should Come* (Christmas, 1938). The culmination of such work came in 1941 with Clemence Dane's series of seven plays on English heroic themes that included *Alfred the Great*, *England's Darling* (Elizabeth and Essex) and a First World War play, *The Unknown Warrior*, and with Sayers' sequence of plays on the life of Christ, *The Man Born to be King* – neither overtly propagandist but each, in its sense of national unity and shared values, offering a significant contribution to the war effort on the Home Front.

Perhaps because so many on the production side of radio also tried their hand at writing – Lance Sieveking's *Kaleidoscope* was broadcast in 1928; Gielgud's discussion play, *Red Tabs*, in 1930; Cecil Lewis's *Pursuit* in 1932 – technical advances were immediately reflected in radio plays. Certainly writers and producers had to work closely together. With the introduction and perfection in 1927–28 of the Dramatic Control Panel, the operator had control of several different elements. He could intercut dialogue produced in different studios and blend in sound effects and music, the last a particularly important consideration since, before the advent of tape recording, musical contributions to theme and mood were provided by gramophone or by a live orchestra. The move to Broadcasting House, in 1932, gave the department two floors with two Dramatic Control Panels, five speech studios, an effects studio, two echo rooms and a music studio, all with intercommunication and access by microphone for the producer. Useful in even the most run-of-the-mill work, such equipment stimulated the dramatic activity and experimentation of those at the centre.

Kaleidoscope is a case in point. Advertised not as a play but as 'A *Rhythm* representing the Life of Man from the Cradle to the Grave', it exploited the opportunities the medium offered blending words, effects and music. It was not published, as Sieveking later wrote, apart from a brief extract, 'because it was the epitome of a radio play – there is nothing to print'.[30] Only about twenty per cent of what was heard in the one and a half hours of broadcasting time was ever written on paper but that and what has since been retold of it suggests the daring of the drama department as well as its enclosed nature. Val Gielgud produced, his brother, John, being drafted in as the Voice of God. Sieveking acted as announcer and then moved over to operate the control panel. The risk of such a work is that it functions primarily as a show piece for the technology and, for all its immediate impact, is more than usually ephemeral. Val Gielgud's retrospective analysis was that, 'the theme if grand was also, perhaps, both grandiose and trite. The more obvious classics of music and literature had been drawn upon.' Although he also insisted that the work was not 'mere pastiche' and achieved a 'remarkable sense of flow and rhythm',[31] the temptation to go for effect at the expense of exploration of idea and emotion is evident.

Most prolific of radio writers was L. du Garde Peach who wrote dozens of short sketches as well as a series of ballad operas and several full-length radio plays. Among the most notable of these were *Ingredient X* (1929), *The Marie Celeste* (1931), to huge acclaim, and *The Path of Glory* (1931) which was chosen for reprise in a festival of twelve notable radio plays broadcast in 1932 which, as well as *Danger; The White Chateau; The First Kaleidoscope; Pursuit* and *Red Tabs*, included Tyrone Guthrie's *The Flowers Are Not For You To Pick* (1930). Guthrie wrote other experimental pieces for radio including, *The Squirrel's Cage* (1929). Other celebrated radio plays include occasional borrowings from foreign broadcasting companies. A translation from German of Ernst Johannson's *Brigade Exchange* (1930), was described by Raymond Postgate as 'by far the most important thing I have ever heard upon the radio'. It seemed so perhaps because, like *All Quiet on the Western Front*, it revealed the likeness to ourselves of the enemy. In 1937, Archibald Macleish's verse parable about dictatorship, *The Fall of the City*, originally written for CBS with Orson Welles as the narrator, was broadcast on British radio.[32]

Necessarily a broad church during its first twenty years, radio was one of the great technological extenders of culture beyond a limited class and the metropolitan centres. Through its means, people who had not before had access to theatre, became familiar with the play form. It helped supply the need of the still not achieved National Theatre with its offerings not just of Shakespeare but other Elizabethans, Aeschylus and Euripides, as well as more recent European and British dramatists. In 1934, for example, there were radio productions of five Shakespeare plays, two Chekhov and two Ibsen as well as five adapted novels. During a single week, in 1933, Hardy's vast, unwieldy *Dynasts* was performed with a success that had eluded Granville Barker's stage production in 1914. New stage drama, too, reached a wider audience via radio. Not only Shaw but T. S. Eliot's *Murder in the Cathedral*, for instance, and Yeats's *The Words Upon the Window Pane* were broadcast (1936 and 1937). The disembodying of the words seems to have given a validity to verse drama that was not at ease in the twentieth-century theatre.

A wide range of forms, then, came under the head of 'radio drama' and shortly before the war, the notion of the 'microphone serial', a novel dramatised in several parts, was introduced with, in 1938, a twelve-part adaptation of Dumas' *The Three Musketeers*, forerunner of serialisations of Galsworthy, Dickens, Trollope, Scott, as well as a tremendously popular Francis Durbridge detective serial, *Send for Paul Temple*. Serials quickly came to seem one of the most natural modes of radio drama as did 'features' which were programmes primarily concerned with fact although offered in a dramatised form. Initially part of the Drama Department, a separate Features Department was established in 1934, under Lawrence Gilliam, although there remained a sizable area of overlap and both departments drew on the same group of actors and shared some technical facilities. From the later 1930s, indeed, the more interesting radio increasingly came from Features. An anonymous commentator in *The Listener*, probably Val Gielgud himself, already in 1933 looking nostalgically to the early experimental period, wrote that:

> the possible danger of increasing popularity of radio drama
> is that once a public has been won over to listening
> regularly, it may then demand simply more of what it has
> already liked, and so discourage that continuous experiment
> which has been so necessary to bring radio drama as a
> medium separate from stage drama into existence at all.[33]

Certainly, Gielgud's policy became increasingly conservative. Tyrone Guthrie's third radio play, *Matrimonial News*, was not broadcast until 1938, seven years after it had been written, and *Traveller's Joy* was rejected in 1939 on the grounds that it was too abstruse. An attempt to hold the line was made in October 1937 when an 'Experimental Hour' was specially designated for the CBS *Fall of the City*. The Columbia Broadcasting Station, indeed, in the late 1930s and early war years took over from the BBC as major begetter of lively English language radio drama, with Irwin Shaw's *Bury the Dead* (1938), in which the dead of the Great War rise up in protest against the squalor of the world for which they died, and Orson Welles' notoriously convincing broadcast of H. G. Wells' *The Martians are Coming*.

If the impetus had gone from the Drama Department, Features in the late 1930s and early 1940s was a centre of creative activity. At just the time when documentary forms were being exploited in the theatre, dramatised documentaries, such as *Tunnel* (1934), dealing with the building of the Mersey Tunnel, D. G. Bridson's *The March of the '45* (1936), 'a radio panorama in verse and song' of the Jacobite rebellion, and *Coal* (1938), about the Durham miners, were a particularly successful British radio form. Usually demonstrating a strong social conscience in their narrative of actual events, they juxtaposed factual information with song and dramatised scenes, very much in the manner of the Living Newspapers of radical theatre, although usually without the evident polemic. They, in their turn, fed back into the practice of London Unity and, subsequently, of Theatre Workshop. Importantly, they introduced new voices on to the network.

Coal begins with miners from Willingham Colliery singing the industrial ballad, 'Follow the horses, Johnnie me laddie', formal questions of miners about details of their work – pitheads, cages, conditions, pit ponies – by the interviewer, Joan Littlewood. This gives way to miners speaking freely about their world: one tells a ribald story about his 'marra' (mate), another, having talked of the dangers concludes that, 'the only way to be really safe is to let the flamin' coal stay there'. It was Archie Harding, a Manchester based producer committed to replacing theatrical stereotypes with authentic working-class and regional voices, who brought Ewan MacColl and Joan Littlewood together to work on *Tunnel*. Other producers developed the idea of using real voices within dramatic presentations. Western Region's *The Life of Walter Barnes* (1938) uses dramatised scenes, intercut with snippets of recordings made on the waterfront and, narrated by Barnes himself, recreates his sixty-three years as a Brixham fisherman.[34] Ewan MacColl's own account of *The Chartists' March* (1938), a history of Chartism, gives the flavour of these drama documentaries:

> That was exciting because we had actors in every studio in the country, we followed the line of the march and brought studio after studio in, and finally brought them all in together to London. I wrote the words for the songs, and Benjamin Britten wrote the music.[35]

In the period immediately after the war, with the creation of the Home, Light and, in 1946, the Third programmes, there was much more specific targetting. Experimental drama, hived off to the Third programme, regained some of its earlier freedom even while it lost the wider audience. Although operation of the control unit passed from the hands of the producer to programme engineers and the 10–14 day pre-war rehearsal period for drama gave way to a week on the Third and 2–4 days on the Home Service, there were productions to come that stemmed from and marked the culmination of the experimentation of the pre-war years. Initially, the most notable dramatic works of the post-war period, including Louis Macniece's *The Dark Tower* (1946), Henry Reed's dramatisation of *Moby Dick* (1947) and Dylan Thomas' *Under Milkwood* (1954), appeared under the auspices of Features. But, in the late 1950s and early 1960s, the Third Programme, which broadcast Beckett's radio play *All That Fall* in 1957, was to function as an important alternative theatre offering space to new writers who would have had difficulty convincing mainstream theatre managers of the viability of their work, among them Harold Pinter (*A Slight Ache*, 1959; *The Dwarfs*, 1960) and Tom Stoppard (*The Dissolution of Dominic Boot*, 1964; *If You're Glad, I'll be Frank*, 1966).

Cinema

In only one area did British cinema in the inter-war years share the inventiveness of radio and this, too, was documentary. The common language had resulted in domination by the better funded American industry despite the protectionist attempt of the British Cinematograph Film Act. British feature films of the time were as limited as the commercial drama and, indeed, many of the better known films were versions of stage plays. A film of *The Constant Nymph* (1928), with full orchestral accompaniment, became the most popular British silent film. *Young Woodley* and *Journey's End* were among the first talkies (1930–31). There followed film versions of *The Farmer's Wife*, *The Skin Game*, *Juno and the Paycock* (directed by Alfred Hitchcock), *Easy Virtue* and *Private Lives* (all 1931). These adaptations revealed differences between live theatre and the cinematic medium. Shaw had allowed Cecil Lewis to make a film of *How He Lied to Her Husband* in 1931 on condition that there were no cuts. The fixed camera for this and *Arms and the Man* (1932) resulted in a stilted artificiality of speech and plot development that was acknowledged in Shaw's agreement to allow Anthony Asquith a freer adaptation of *Pygmalion*. The result is a far more achieved film (1938).

Alexander Korda's *The Private Life of Henry VIII* (1933) with Charles Laughton as the king, and the six suspense films made by Hitchcock between 1934 and 1939, which included *The Thirty Nine Steps* (1935), *The Lady Vanishes* (1938) and *Jamaica Inn* (1939), stand out among the films that were produced in Britain, although recent trawls through the remnants of thousands of 'quota quickies' – 'B' films made in a week to twelve days to satisfy the requirement that a certain proportion of British films be included in cinema programming – suggests there are a few gems among them, including films by Michael Powell and Bernard Vorhaus, such as *The Love Test* (1935). But the output of the British industry, though extensive was largely dismal and successful work usually resulted, as in Hitchcock's and Korda's cases, in offers from and eventual removal to the much better endowed Hollywood. Michael Balcon, who founded Gainsborough Pictures, worked with Gaumont and MGM and gave Hitchcock his first directing opportunities, subsequently regretted the triviality and escapism of British cinema in the 1930s, noting that 'hardly a single film of the period reflects the agony of those times'.[36]

This is not true of documentary cinema and, interestingly enough, a Balcon production, Robert Flaherty's spare account of the struggle for survival on the outer edge of the British Isles, *Man of Aran* (1934), has rightly become one of the classics of the movement. Flaherty, a rare reverse immigrant, had moved from Hollywood to what he saw as the greater freedom of England. John Grierson at the G.P.O. Film Unit which he helped establish in 1932 was at the centre of the documentary film movement. Much influenced by Soviet cinema, Grierson demanded of documentary, 'no more than that the affairs of our time shall be brought to the screen in any fashion which strikes the imagination and makes observation a little richer than it was'.[37]

Some 300 British documentary films were made between 1929 and 1939. The justly celebrated *Night Mail* (1936), directed by Basil Wright and Harry Watt, with a rhythmic verse commentary by W. H. Auden, follows the nightly journey of the mail train from London to Scotland, charting the places through which it passes and the impingement of the mail services on the lives lived there, as well as the actual activity of sorting and delivery. *Housing Problems* (1935), directed at Grierson's instigation by Edgar Anstey and Arthur Elton for the British Commercial Gas Company, movingly presents the faces and voices of slum dwellers speaking in the miserable conditions of their homes. The film, in what must have been one of the first examples of *cinema vérité*, endorsed Grierson's definition of documentary form as 'the creative interpretation of actuality'.[38] Paul Rotha's *The Face of Britain* (1935) exposed social inequalities with irresistible images.

All these works, which consciously make statements about the state of the nation, demonstrate a patriotism as sure as anything in *Cavalcade*, for all the difference of perspective. The claim is to community, the valuation of all lives and the insistence that a society with extremes of affluence and hardship lacks self-respect. As will be apparent, there was overlap in method, often in social commitment and sometimes in personnel, with the work done by the Features Department of the BBC and in the experimental drama of Theatre Union, the Group and Unity Theatre.

The suffragette theatre movement turned its resources to the war effort after 1914. After the outbreak of the Second World War, the contribution of film to the war effort was based in the work of the documentary movement, leading to Humphrey Jennings' wartime films, *Listen to Britain* (1941) and *A Diary for Timothy* (1945) and a new brand of British film with dramatic stories set within realistic, documentary-style settings. These are notably films which appreciate the lives of working men and women and convey a strong expectation of social change in the post-war era.

Notes

1. See Harold Hobson, *Theatre in Britain* (Oxford, 1984), p. 18.
2. Quoted, Val Gielgud, *British Radio Drama* (1957), p. 166.

3. Reprinted in Nesta Jones, ed., *File on O'Casey* (1986), p. 86.
4. Poster reproduced in Patricia Warren, *Elstree, The British Hollywood* (1983), p. 42.
5. Quoted, J. C. Trewin, *Birmingham Repertory Theatre* (1963), p. 3, to which my discussion of Birmingham Repertory Company is indebted.
6. J. Gielgud, *Early Stages* (1939; repr., 1990), p. 89.
7. Gielgud, *Early Stages*, p. 88.
8. Reprinted in Robert G. Lowery, *A Whirlwind in Dublin* (Greenwood, CT, 1984), p. 31; see too, D. E. S. Maxwell, *Modern Irish Drama* (Cambridge, 1984) and H. Hunt, *The Abbey, Ireland's National Theatre* (Dublin, 1979) for accounts of the riot.
9. Yeats's letter to O'Casey 20.4.1928, reprinted N. Jones, ed., *File on O'Casey*, p. 36.
10. Argued in, for example, J. B. Priestley, *In Our Time*, V (1945–46), p. 238; J. L. Styan, *Modern Drama in Theory and Practice* (1981), p. 104; Maxwell, *Modern Irish Drama*, p. 107.
11. J. Arden, *To Present the Pretence* (1977), p. 23.
12. D. MacCarthy, *Drama* (1940), p. 277.
13. See Ezra Pound, *Hugh Selwyn Mauberley* (1919) section V; II.
14. Gielgud, *Early Stages*, p. 59.
15. Elizabeth Robins, *Theatre and Friendship* (1932), p. 75.
16. See Barry Eichengreen, *Golden Fetters. The Gold Standard and the Great Depression, 1919–1939* (Oxford, 1992) for a recent analysis.
17. Notably in the obituaries for 6.12.1991, for example, Hilary Spurling, *The Guardian*; Sam Walters, *The Independent*.
18. Steve Nicholson, 'Censoring the Revolution', *New Theatre Quarterly*, 32 (November 1992), pp. 305–12.
19. James Klugmann, 'Crisis in the Thirties: a View from the Left', in Jon Clark, Margot Heinemann, David Margolies and Carole Snee, eds, *Culture and Crisis in Britain in the Thirties* (1979), p. 20.
20. John Lehmann, *New Writing in Europe* (1940), p. 65. *The Dance of Death* is discussed at greater length in Chapter 7.
21. But for excellent recent work, see Clarke et al., *Culture and Crisis*; Howard Goorney, *Theatre Workshop Story* (1981); Howard Goorney and Ewan MacColl, eds, *Agit Prop to Theatre Workshop* (Manchester, 1986); Linda Mackenney, ed., *Joe Corrie: Plays, Poems and Theatre Writings* (Edinburgh, 1985), from which most of the information in this section is gleaned and see, too, Chapter 8.
22. Quoted, Goorney and MacColl, *Agit Prop to Theatre Workshop*, p. xxxix.
23. Goorney and MacColl, *Agit Prop to Theatre Workshop*, p. xliv.
24. Lehmann, *New Writing*, p. 138.
25. Gysegham, in Clark et al., *Culture and Crisis*, p. 217.
26. Gysegham, in Clark et al., *Culture and Crisis*, p. 218.
27. Val Gielgud, quoted Asa Briggs, *The History of Broadcasting in the United Kingdom*, Vol. II (1965), p. 263.
28. Val Gielgud, *British Radio Drama*, pp. 73, 74.
29. Gielgud, *British Radio Drama*, p. 36.
30. L. Sieveking, *The Stuff of Radio* (1934), p. 29. An extract from *Kaleidoscope* printed as an appendix in Sieveking's book is its only published form.
31. V. Gielgud, *British Radio Drama*, p. 29.
32. R. Postgate, in *The Listener* (2.4.1930), p. 613. The BBC production by Peter Cresswell of *The Fall of the City* and extracts from *The Squirrel's Cage* are among the few recordings from this period that survive. They are in the BBC Sound Archive.
33. 'Twelve Radio Plays', *The Listener* (22.11.33), p. 776.
34. *Coal* (LP 3138); *The Life of Walter Barnes* (T28016), both in BBC Sound Archive.

35. Ewan MacColl, 'Grass Roots of Theatre Workshop', *Theatre Quarterly*, III, 9, pp. 58–68, p. 67.
36. Quoted, D. Robinson, *A History of the Cinema* (New York, 1973), p. 209, which includes an excellent chapter on the documentary movement.
37. Quoted, Robinson, *History of the Cinema*, p. 211.
38. Quoted, Edgar Anstey, 'John Grierson, Founder of the Film Documentary', in Ann Lloyd, ed., *Movies of the Thirties* (1983), p. 103.

Part Two

Closer Readings of Some Significant Works and Topics

Chapter 5

Four Comedies

In a certain sense Mr Wilde is our only thorough playwright. He plays with everything: with wit, with philosophy, with drama, with actors and audience, with the whole theatre. Such a feat scandalises the Englishman, who can no more play with wit and philosophy than he can with a football or a cricket bat. He works at both. (G. B. Shaw)[1]

Dramatic comedy is what principally survives from this period. Intriguingly, the most effective practitioners, Wilde and Shaw, Synge and Coward, came from outside established English culture. Like Congreve, Farquhar, Sheridan and Goldsmith before them, Wilde and Shaw were Irishmen writing for the London theatre. Noel Coward, like Oscar Wilde, was homosexual at a time when this was thought a shocking perversion. However fully absorbed into society these writers might have seemed, they all retained the satiric distance of the observer. They also shared a tendency to use and subvert traditional theatrical structures.

Wilde and Coward, contributing to and apparently working within the conventions of mainstream theatre, transcend them. Identifying Wilde's capacity to transform clichés, proverbial sayings and platitudinous ways of thinking into sharp and often stinging epigrams, Shaw cut to the heart of his originality with his observation that Wilde played with everything, not just with wit and philosophy but dramatic mode, actors and audience. For all his use of nineteenth-century theatrical devices, Shaw himself presents not only a more bizarre and idiosyncratically comic perception than any of his models, but also an innovative capacity for social commentary. Different again, J. M. Synge, an Anglo-Irishman well-versed in European Symbolism and urban culture, writing in Ireland for the new Irish theatre demonstrates a comparable transforming force when he offers his version of the Catholic peasant world that is sentimentalised or rendered quaint in the work of his Abbey contemporaries. Synge's *Playboy of the Western World* is a work of dramatic power which stands with *The Importance of Being Earnest* as one of the greatest comedies ever written in English. Noel Coward's *Hay Fever* and *Private Lives* run them close.

Although these works shine out from among their contemporaries, a remarkable vein of comedy runs through the period as it did in the Restoration and late eighteenth century. Henry Arthur Jones is more convincing as the author of cynical comedies of aristocratic high life than of such would-be tragedies as *Mrs Dane's Defence* or *Michael and His Lost Angel*. Despite its sentimentality, *Trelawny of 'The Wells'*, Pinero's period tribute to Tom Robertson and cup-and-saucer comedy, has proved more revivable than his social-problem plays. The vitality of young people in rebellion against the strictures of their elders in the domestic comedies of Stanley Houghton and Harold Brighouse, restored a source of comic action exploited in drama from Shakespeare to Goldsmith, while St John Hankin turned a satiric eye on social climbing, snobbery and class consciousness. With a zany energy matched only in Brandon Thomas's *Charley's Aunt*, Ben Travers reinvented farce offering virtually one a year throughout the 1920s including *A Cuckoo in the Nest* (1925), *Rookery Nook* (1926) and *Thark* (1927). His refusal to moralise in his blackly comic *Plunder* (1928), for example, in which the two murderer heroes escape unscathed, makes him a notable forerunner of Joe Orton. The work of Sean O'Casey, like that of his great mentor, Shaw, is alive with comic perception and expression.

The Importance of Being Earnest (1895)

Wilde's last play has marked symmetry of plot and character. Not only do its settings alternate town and country, indoors and outdoors, but two heroes with different but parallel secret lives are matched with two heroines who fantasise and idealise along remarkably similar lines. At its core is a dual absurdity: far from roses smelling as sweet by any other name, neither woman will marry a man whose name is not Ernest and both men unquestioningly accede to the preposterous demand. There are two proposals of marriage; one refusal of consent is matched by another. Each man plans independently to resort to christening to acquire the appropriate name; the women, first enemies then allies, act together to resist the blandishments of any but the fictional Ernest.

Traditional comic elements recur, writ larger than ever before. A host of monster-dowagers, including the Marchioness in Robertson's *Caste*, are subsumed in Lady Bracknell. The most banal of food jokes gain a new absurdity: having eaten his way through the cucumber sandwiches in Act I, Algernon eats his way through the muffins in Act II. As well as comic pairings, there are mistaken identities and startling revelations which come thick and fast, notably at the climax of the play when what was lost is found and everything falls satisfactorily into place: Lady Bracknell recognises in Miss Prism her family's long lost children's nurse; the orphan Jack Worthing is not only discovered to be the child she mislaid long ago and therefore Algy's actual brother but is found – although only after speedy checking of the army lists, which happen to be to hand – to have indeed been christened Ernest, and Miss Prism's equally long lost three-volume novel is restored to its author. What is distinctive is the panache with which these elements are combined and the remarkable control Wilde exerts over the proliferating complications and absurdities.

The dialogue moves fast largely because the scenes fall essentially into consecutive duologues between ever-changing partners punctuated by occasional large group scenes dominated by the monstrous Lady Bracknell, in which much of the plot information is given and the discoveries made. The exchanges of Act I run: Algy and his butler; Algy and Jack; a group scene; Jack and Gwendolen Fairfax; Jack and Gwendolen's mother, Lady Bracknell; then Algy and Jack again; and the next two acts follow much the same pattern culminating in the full group revelation scene that ends the play.

Plot markers, echoes and repetitions with notable variation and certain running jokes, bind the scenes into a developing and proliferating action. For example, since the supposed Ernest has already revealed his subterfuge and his real name, Jack, to Algy in the second duologue, the charge is strong when Gwendolen proclaims in the third, 'my ideal has always been to love someone of the name of Ernest', and reverberates into Act II and Cecily's sudden remark to Algy, 'besides, of course, there is the question of your name'. The audience, on familiar ground, is ready for her elaborating, 'there is something in that name that seems to inspire absolute confidence. I pity any poor married woman whose husband is not called Ernest.' In the first proposal scene, Gwendolen, having already announced her determination to accept, insists on playing out her scene:

JACK:
　　Gwendolen!

GWEN:
　　Yes, Mr Worthing. What have you got to say to me?

JACK:
　　You know what I have got to say to you.

GWEN:
　　Yes, but you don't say it.

JACK:
　　Gwendolen, will you marry me? (*Goes on his knees.*)

GWEN:

> Of course I will, darling. How long you have been
> about it. I am afraid you have had very little experience
> in how to propose.
>
> (Act I)

In the second proposal scene the wind is taken out of Algy's sails when his attempt to do the thing properly is, by contrast, cut short by Cecily's matter-of-fact announcement that they have been engaged for four months already. And the joke is extended with her revelation that she has already provided herself with the ring, keepsakes and a set of sentimental letters: girlish fantasy has been developed literally.

The individual duologues are elaborately set up and staged virtually as 'turns'. Lady Bracknell sits, Jack stands in their Act I encounter as she prepares, through catechizing him, to discover whether or not to permit his suit for her daughter. She produces notebook and pencil to record his answers. The absurdity of her opening question after this palaver 'do you smoke?', is capped by her bizarre response to his affirmative, 'I'm glad to hear it. A man should always have an occupation of some kind'. When she eventually turns all but satisfied from such trivialities to the 'minor matter' of his parentage, the revelations she unleashes, astonishing to the audience as well as herself, build to the climactic statement that Worthing was not only a foundling but one whose very name was derived from a railway station. But what most resoundingly appals Lady Bracknell, always responsive to the least significant matter, is the fact that he was abandoned in *a handbag*. The sequence culminates in Jack's wonderfully earnest response to her insistence that he find at least one parent: 'Well, I don't see how I can possibly manage to do that. I can produce the handbag at any moment. It is in my dressing room at home. I really think that should satisfy you, Lady Bracknell'.

Delayed by mistakes, and after numerous other surprises and recognitions, the play ends with a proliferation of marriages in which not only the young lovers but, with Gilbertian symmetry, the elderly Miss Prism and Reverend Chasuble fall into each other's arms. The revelation scene draws on the familiar nineteenth-century pathetic sequence in which the abandoned child discovers its distressed missing parent and the equally conventional discovery, reminiscent of Oliver Twist's that the supposed orphan is, by remarkable coincidence, already in the bosom of his own family. But comedy subverts pathos. Miss Prism retreats angrily before Jack's sentimental cry of 'Mother!' and is further insulted by his offer to forgive her unmarried state:

> Unmarried! I cannot deny that is a serious blow. But after
> all who has the right to cast a stone against one who has
> suffered? Cannot repentence wipe out an act of folly? Why

should there be one law for men and another for women?
Mother I forgive you!

(Act III)

There is no mistaking the parody of melodramatic language and attitudes here.

Such dialogue invites the audience of *The Importance of Being Earnest* to participate in the developing jokes. Wilde's sense of timing had been used to good effect in his earlier plays, both in creating anticipation and in thwarting expectation: Lady Windermere was not discovered in her hiding place behind the curtain because Mrs Erlynne stepped in at the vital moment and took the guilt on herself. While this generated tension, it was neither funny nor subversive of the convention it exploited. But when, in *The Importance*, following Jack's confession of the fictionality of 'Ernest' and Algy's overhearing and ostentatious noting on his cuff of Jack's country address at the end of Act I, Algy not only appears in that country garden in Act II but passes himself off as Ernest, the audience is thrown into a state of anticipation which Wilde rewards with the appearance of Jack dressed in full mourning. The implications of the costume convulse the audience even before the words which confirm that he has indeed killed off the fictional brother are spoken. The audience, ahead of each, anticipates the meeting of the two masqueraders. Wilde then plays the sequence over again, as it were, in the meeting and misunderstanding of Jack's ward, Cecily, with his fiancée, Gwendolen, in which each, believing herself engaged to the mythical Ernest, attempts to outface the other.

Anticipation makes this entrance effective, too. Cecily's supposition, when Miss Fairfax is announced, that she must be 'one of the many good elderly women who are associated with Uncle Jack in some of his philanthropic work in London', prepares the moment of silent mutual appraisal when fashionable city sophisticate and pert country miss first become conscious of each other's existence. The joke is extended when the short-sighted Gwendolen asks permission to view Cecily through her lorgnette and, having done so, comments merely, 'you are here on a *short* visit I suppose'.

In a play so concerned with appearance, Wilde compels the audience to attend to what it sees. The cuff, the mourning dress, the lorgnette, properly interpreted, put the audience ahead of the action. The formality of the tea table, laid out by silent servants, is an appropriate context for the barbed politeness of the duel of words between Cecily and Gwendolen. Alone in possession of the truth, the audience can enjoy the visible representation of antagonism behind the smiles and polite conversation as Cecily ostentatiously over-sugars Gwendolen's tea and helps her to a large piece of cake, instead of the bread and butter for which she has specifically asked. What is seen interacts creatively with what is said.

The play is notably epigrammatic and paradoxical. There are brilliant puttings-down such as Gwendolen's riposte to Cecily's claim to call a spade a spade: 'I am glad to say I have never seen a spade. It is obvious that our social spheres have been widely different.' But the epigrams and paradoxes, besides contributing to the mood of the play, are much more fully tied in to situation and character than they were in Wilde's earlier plays. Although it is sometimes claimed that Algy and Jack are indistinguishable, all the outrageous remarks come from Algy who lies instinctively, however large or small the issue – about dining, about Bunbury, about the lack of cucumber sandwiches – while Jack, apart from his one great Ernest-in-the-town, Jack-in-the-country subterfuge, is honourable in word and deed. Jack contradicts Algy's more flippant remarks, calling them nonsensical. He dismisses cynicism as too easy while Algy speaks up for it. Algy carries an affectionate echo of Restoration Comedy into such comments as, 'the amount of women in London who flirt with their own husbands is perfectly scandalous'. The two characters are both witty, as are the women, but each is distinct from the other. As C. E. Montague put it in an early analysis:

> In the French slang of the theatre, the *mots d'ésprit* have become *mots de situation* also, and, to some extent, *mots de caractère* too; the verbal good things, besides their first glitter, take value from where they are placed in the play, and often give value by making someone's mood or character divertingly apparent.[2]

The action, indeed, is of a part with the linguistic texture of the play. Attention is frequently drawn to the treacherous doubling capacity of words, as with Miss Prism's self-correction, 'the manuscript unfortunately was abandoned. I use the word in the sense of mislaid'; the absurd explanation the Reverend Chasuble offers to excuse his Freudian slip in, 'Were I fortunate enough to be Miss Prism's pupil, I would hang upon her lips. I spoke metaphorically. – My metaphor was drawn from bees'; and Lady Bracknell's disconcerting tendency to take the use of such words as 'explode' literally and fear imminent revolution.

The characters themselves often recognise and enjoy the wit. Both young women are fascinated by their own diaries: Cecily consciously preparing hers for publication, Gwendolen holding on to hers as 'something sensational to read in the train'. It is rare that an aphorism passes without comment or elaboration, although few are as direct as the discussion that follows one of Algy's more mordant remarks. It contains enough perverse logic and enough truth to have entered the language but it is also absorbed into the ongoing dialogue of the play:

ALGY:

> All women become like their mothers. That is their tragedy. No man does. That is his.

JACK:

> Is that clever?

ALGY:

> It is perfectly phrased! and quite as true as any observation in civilised life should be.

JACK:

> I'm sick to death of cleverness. Everybody is clever nowadays. You can't go anywhere without meeting clever people. The thing has become an absolute public nuisance.

(Act I)

It is at once a meta-theatrical comment on the Wildean epigram and a fully integrated signal of Jack's irritability. The exchange is elaborated in Act II by Gwendolen's comment agreeing that the beauty of an answer is not diminished by its probable untruth, since 'in matters of grave importance, style, not sincerity is the vital thing'. But, in point of fact, the audience in all these instances responds not just to the elegant balance but also to the fleeting sense of having caught a truth, an arrant and provocative untruth, or an implication worthy of further argument.

Wilde's verbal agility is the more evident in the light of contemporary imitations. Henry Arthur Jones, especially in the later 1890s, seemed to aim for Wildean wit in such exchanges as the following from *The Liars* (1897):

LADY JESSICA:

> Oh, I've got a splendid idea.

LADY ROSAMUND:

> What is it?

LADY J:

> A new career for poor gentlewomen. You found a school and carefully train them in all the best traditions of the gentle art of husband baiting. Then you invite one of them to your house, pay her, of course, a handsome salary, and she assists you in 'the daily round, the common task' of making your husband's life a perfect misery to him. After a month or so she is played out and retires to another sphere, and you call in a new – lady help.

LADY R:
> Oh, I don't think I should care to have my husband
> systematically hen-pecked by another woman.

LADY J:
> No, especially as you do it so well yourself.

> (Act I)

Not only is Jones's lead-in to the epigram laboured, but the characters are
mouthpieces, as Wilde's never are, for opinions they could not themselves
convincingly hold. His aphorisms, too, miss Wilde's remarkable balance.
A character in *Rebellious Susan* comments that it takes twelve months for
newly-weds to settle down, 'in all well-regulated households, for the
woman to learn that she has got a master. In all ill-regulated households
for the man to learn that he has got a master': a pronouncement which
lacks the surprise and compression, the need for the listener to be interactive with the idea, of even so slight an exchange as Wilde's:

LADY STUTFIELD:
> The world was made for men not women.

MRS ALLONBY:
> Oh, don't say that, Lady Stutfield. We have a much
> better time than they have. There are far more things
> forbidden to us than are forbidden to them.

> (*A Woman of No Importance*, Act I)

The Liars, indeed, with its suggestions of decadence, cynical humour and the
sexual aggression of some of the young women, bears a more convincing
relationship with Coward's drama than with any of Wilde's plays.

Absurdities abound. The Reverend Chasuble's last cathedral sermon
was 'on behalf of the Society for the Prevention of Discontent among the
Upper Orders'; Aunt Augusta rings the bell in a 'Wagnerian manner', and
not only is the stern schoolmistress the authoress of a three-volume romantic novel that she has mistaken for a baby in her care and left in a pram,
but her teaching, shaped by her quirky turn of mind, includes, for example,
the instruction that Cecily omit the chapter on the Fall of the Rupee
from her Political Economy text book, it being 'somewhat too sensational'.
For all the fun, though, there is a wry social or political edge to most of
the sallies.

There is a sound, underlying moral consciousness evident in Wilde's
writing. The wit may be sharp but, unlike Jones's, it is never sour. Among
the sparks, truths are spoken, often very straightforwardly and lines are
held. Lord Darlington's rebuke to the intolerance of Lady Windermere's
moral code, 'I think life too complicated a thing to be settled by these
hard and fast rules' (Act I) is exemplified in the whole action of their play.

At a time when loveless mercenary marriages recur on the stage, the couples in *The Importance* are unswerving in their attachments. Jack repudiates cynicism. Society's representative, Lady Bracknell, on the other hand, is characterised by an incapacity to distinguish between the trivial and the significant in the things she approves and disapproves. Snobbery and intolerance are continually mocked; the sharpest satire is directed against Lady Bracknell's reliance on matters of status and wealth in judging people and assessing the appropriateness of a match, and the audience is left in no doubt as to the miserable life led by the ailing, 'entirely unknown', and always off-stage Lord Bracknell.

The self-possession of Gwendolen and Cecily marks them as modern young women of notably decided opinion whose very presence satirises the sweet English roses of melodrama and farce. Unlike the caricatured new women in contemporary plays, they are allowed to understand the implications of what they say and, doing so, to make serious points. To Miss Prism's, 'I suppose that you know where socialism leads?' after a suspect remark of Cecily's, her charge replies, 'Oh yes! That leads to Rational dress, Miss Prism. And I suppose that when a woman is dressed rationally, she is treated rationally. She certainly deserves to be.' Which is not to say there are not concomitant jokes for the enjoyment of an audience that persisted in finding women's education a matter of hilarity: Cecily prefers the excitement of her own diary to the tedium of the political economy she studies, and the excuse for Gwendolen's absence in the country is attendance at an unusually long lecture at the University Extension Scheme.

Charges of plagiarism dogged Wilde in his own day, from Sidney Grundy's specific complaint that he could not stage a revival of *The Glass of Fashion* 'because Mr Oscar Wilde did so, under the title of *Lady Windermere's Fan*'[3] to Clement Scott's more sweeping claim that Wilde was wholly dependent on his predecessors. Recent research, which has unearthed an astonishing number of sources in Restoration as well as contemporary drama, not merely for Wilde's plots but for his characters and patterns of action, demonstrates that Wilde had a magpie mind and sprang his own plays off other works. Most obviously, *Lady Windermere's Fan* and *A Woman of No Importance* rework the woman-with-a-past tropes, and *An Ideal Husband*, those of financial chicanery. *The Importance of Being Earnest* is spun from foundling plays and situations common in farce from Gilbert to Lestocq and Robson, whose 1894 farce, *The Foundling*, was pretty thoroughly absorbed and reworked by Wilde. This play offered itself, complete with male adult orphan, objections by the mother of the girl he wished to marry to his lack of a name and a compensatory christening scheme. Platitudes and popular literature energised Wilde's imagination. In Kerry Powell's words, 'to turn the ordinary idea or expression inside out was the habit of Wilde's paradoxical mind'.[4]

The uncertainty of tone sometimes apparent in the earlier plays, has gone from *The Importance*. Whereas formerly, melodramatic commonplaces uttered by Wilde's characters at moments of emotional intensity were not always ironised, in *The Importance* such language, sententious thinking and the kind of works in which they appeared, are consciously subverted. Jack Worthing's greeting of Miss Prism as his supposed long-lost mother is an obvious case in point. None of the many works from which Wilde drew fire shares his sparkle; none has the capacity of *The Importance* to surprise its audience and stimulate thought with the sting in the tail of the passing aphorism. Wilde's audience is compelled to interact with the text. The truth is that while Wilde was remarkably eclectic, taking over, absorbing, reworking suggestions from other works, it was and is his transforming inventiveness that delights. As the critic of the *Pall Mall Gazette* commented with feeling, 'more humorous dealing with theatrical convention it would be difficult to imagine. To the dramatic critic especially, who leads a dismal life, it came with a flavour of rare holiday' (12.2.1895).

The final line of the play, Jack's 'I've now realised for the first time in my life the vital Importance of Being Earnest', not only offers the culminating Ernest/earnest pun with a repetition of the title as silly as the last line of John Ford's *'Tis Pity She's a Whore*, although much more knowingly so, but also functions as a parodic version of the tendency of contemporary farce to wise conclusions in which the hero, returned to sobriety, moralises.

Secrecy had been a recurrent subject in Wilde's drama. In his earlier plays he reworked conventions of deceit common in French and English Society Drama: Mrs Arbuthnot disguised her past with a life of good works, Sir Robert Chiltern covered an early financial fraud with a life of ostentatious propriety. But secrecy and invention, fantasy and fiction are the very stuff of his last play. Jack can kill Ernest off at will and Ernest can be revived; Cecily registers her engagement before ever meeting Algy and he simply fits into her plot. References to Wilde's own double private life and homosexual philandering, identified in the place-names used and the notion of Bunburying, have been the subject of recent discussion. If the name 'Ernest' was, as some have pointed out, a covert term for homosexuality among Wilde's close circle, there would have been a *frisson* of recognition for them in the final line of the play,[5] but such encoding can only have been apparent, as is usually the case with autobiographical references, to a tiny fraction of the contemporary audience. The present-day *reader*, aware of Wilde's own story and the imminent trial that ruined him, might find a shadow of consciousness cast over such speeches as Gwendolen's:

> Men of the noblest possible moral character are extremely susceptible to the influence of the physical charms of others.

Modern no less than ancient history, supplies us with many
most painful examples of what I refer to.

(Act II)

But, in the speed and pressure of performance, I suspect that only a
directoral decision would nudge an *audience* in this direction.

For the majority of Wilde's original audience, delight in the reworking
of recognisable theatrical tropes and specific contemporary clichés would
doubtless have extended to the rejoinder Gwendolen delivers to the heavy-
footed humour of such as Grundy and Jones against emancipation, and the
supposed feminisation of its male supporters when, beautiful and evidently
intelligent, she observes:

The home seems to me to be the proper sphere for the man.
And certainly once a man begins to neglect his domestic
duties he becomes painfully effeminate does he not? And I
don't like that. It makes men so very attractive.

(Act III)

Whereas Jones caricatures aestheticism in the person of Fergusson Pybus,
the dress, hairstyle and beautifully furnished rooms of Algy signal that he
is certainly an aesthete but, neither mincing nor effete, he is also presented
as a man of sharp wit and vigorous life.

It is a mark of the achieved work of art that its audience is not distracted
by private references. *The Importance of Being Earnest* is such a work. In
whatever complex way private experience has acted as a spur to the
creative imagination, the secret self of the writer has been absorbed into
the work.

The Playboy of the Western World (1907)

Wilde was among the writers John Millington Synge read in his period
of self-education in Paris in the later 1890s. *The Importance of Being Earnest*
is set among the English upper classes, Synge's *The Playboy of the Western
World* among Irish peasants, but each is a notably enclosed and self-
sufficient world. Both plays are concerned with fiction and fantasy and
the role of language in the creation of experience. *The Playboy of the
Western World* is more direct in its exploration of the human need for and
delight in fiction and powerful words. The telling not the doing of the

deed; the fantasy and the tale that is elaborated round it, are what charm the peasant community into which the stranger, Christy Mahon comes. But since Christy's father, unlike Ernest Worthing, actually exists and the blow Christy tells of, albeit not fatal, really was struck, Christy never has Jack Worthing's freedom; he is more evidently at the mercy of events, the fiction he develops more vulnerable to the intrusion of reality.

All Synge's comedies share the *Lower Depths* theme: the intrusion into a small community of outsiders – tramps, tinkers or, in the case of Christy, a fleeing murderer – who, even if threatening, bring life and stimulate excitement, usually through their linguistic flights and capacity to fire the imagination. As Molly Byrne, '*half-mesmerised*' by Martin Doul's attempt to woo her in *The Well of the Saints* says, 'it's queer talk you have if it's a little old shabby stump of a man you are'. In each case, too, the community eventually turns on and ejects the stranger, leaving a sense of loss as well as relief in the return to normality. Whereas the community reverts, essentially, to its starting point, the incomers, having in some way found themselves, move on.

In *Playboy*, Synge uses a succession of traditional farcical situations: of two timorous young men, one refuses to spend the night alone with his fiancée for fear of the priest, the other, clings to her for protection at the sound of a sudden knock at the door; two women claim a man literally, each having seized an arm, pulling him in opposing directions; village girls line up in a row to peer at their young hero through a chink; a supposedly dead man appears, not once but twice; and father and son engage in knockabout and mutual verbal abuse. There is even a comic chase, when son, brandishing a loy, pursues father, and a moment of transvestism when the village women attempt to dress their hero in petticoats to facilitate his escape. The activity is of a kind. In Act I Shawn, the timid fiancé, with a sudden movement, '*pulls himself out of his coat and disappears out of the door, leaving his coat in Michael's hands*', only to run back in moments later terrified of the 'queer dying fellow' on the road. The anticlimax, after Shawn's terror, of the entrance of the thing he feared, Christy, slight, dirty, obviously frightened, is humorously extended when the fearsome newcomer sits by the fire moaning to himself and, oblivious of the others in the shebeen, proceeds to gnaw on a turnip.

The hyperbole and inventive glee, of each of these sequences is crucial to the central action of the play. That it is the community which creates or at least brings out Christy's verbal gifts is demonstrated in the first act as the people in the shebeen, sensing an excitement to brighten their dull lives, probe the reason for Christy's flight and, each contributing, speculate increasingly fantastically on the nature of his crime – perhaps he followed after a woman? maybe it was the bailiffs, agents or landlords? perhaps he forged golden guineas, or married three wives, or fought bloody wars for

Kruger and the freedom of the Boers? – until speculation is interrupted by Pegeen's taunting scepticism which finally compels an announcement:

PEGEEN:
> You did nothing at all.

CHRISTY:
> That's an unkindly thing to be saying to a poor orphaned traveller, has a prison behind him and a hanging before, and hell's gap gaping below.

PEGEEN (*with a sign to the men to be quiet*):
> You're only saying it. You did nothing at all. A soft lad the like of you wouldn't slit the wind pipe of a screeching sow.

CHRISTY:
> You're not speaking the truth.

PEGEEN (*In mock rage*):
> Not speaking the truth, is it? Would you have me knock the head of you with the butt of the broom?

CHRISTY:
> Don't strike me. I killed my poor father, Tuesday was a week, for doing the like of that.

(Act I)

What the printed text loses is the grinning, listening crowd, to whom Pegeen is playing, gathered round, willing her to draw out the answer and triumphant when she does. The confidence Christy gains from the heroising that follows releases his capacity for highly figured speech.

The activity of the community is used in varying forms by Synge, throughout the play. It is echoed in the second act, where four village girls arrive to present, in turn, their tributes to Christy – a brace of duck eggs, a pat of butter, a piece of cake and a cooked pullet – and listen to him tell of his mighty exploits, which telling, like the homely gifts, Synge casts into splendidly mock-heroic form. In Act III, there is a startling shift of mood. The folk again act as one, cheering on Christy's genuine success in the country sports which happen off-stage, but, following the touching scene in which Pegeen and Christy, briefly alone on stage, declare their love, they become suddenly altogether more sinister. When Christy's romantic tale seems to have become reality and threatens to incriminate them all, they turn into a vengeful lynch mob.

It is an enclosed world, riddled with superstition and limited in opportunity. Its demons and legendary figures are 'Red Linahan, has a squint in his eye and Patcheen is lame in his heel, or the mad Mulrannies were driven from California and they lost in their wits'. In Wilde's play there are serio-comic topical references (to the dramatic fall of the Indian Rupee and the, oddly prophetic, fear of the aristocrat that educating the working classes might lead to 'rioting in Grosvenor Square'). Here, more darkly in the face of grimmer realities, memorable expression is given to Irish peasant fears of the English soldiery ('the loosed khaki cut-throats', the 'thousand militia . . . walking idle through the land'), and to the pressure to migrate in pursuit of work ('the harvest hundred do be passing these days for the Sligo boat'). Similarly, the title words, 'playboy' and 'western world' have their purely local meanings, the one an expression of admiration of a 'tricky rascal'[6] the other indicative of the west coast region but, as each is reiterated in the course of the play and used in Pegeen's closing cry of loss, they take on a wider, more general suggestiveness.

There is an undercurrent of earthiness and brutality to the play that comes to the surface in the final sequence, and a suggestion of bizarre behaviour, offset at times by the fleeting impression of strange logic, as, for instance, in Pegeen's accusation against the Widow Quinn: 'you reared a black ram at your own breast, so that the Lord Bishop of Connaught felt the elements of a Christian, and he eating it after in a kidney stew.' Entertainment in this bleak region is often disturbingly violent. Vanished heroes include Daneen Sullivan, 'knocked the eye from a peeler', and Marcus Quinn who got six months 'for maiming ewes'; another vlllager having hanged his dog 'had it screeching and wriggling three hours at the but of a string and himself swearing it was a dead dog and the peelers swearing it had life', and one of the girls drove ten miles to see 'the man bit the yellow lady's nostril on the northern shore'. What is offered in such moments is not just vivid words but what C. E. Montague described as 'the harsh crab-apple tang of peasant cruelty'.[7] Violence and drunkenness is habitual: Pegeen fears the tinkers camped in the East Glen as well as the casual harvest labourers with 'their tongues red for drink', and Old Mahon is warned that 'them lads caught a maniac one time and pelted the poor creature till he ran out raving and foaming and was drowned in the sea', while Michael James, incapacitated by drink at Kate Cassidy's wake, left other men 'stretched out retching speechless on the holy steps'. Yeats noted with approval the realism of Synge's incorporation of the vehemencies and violences of life, 'all that is salt, all that is rough to the hand',[8] but he also seems to have feared the shock effect. He was reluctant to play the piece as written: violent oaths and disturbing phrases, including the references to Widow Quinn breast feeding the black ram, were cut from the Abbey production, by his and Lady Gregory's order, although Synge restored them to the published text.[9]

There is much talk about talk in Synge's plays. Eloquence is admired. As Pegeen tells Christy, 'any girl would walk her heart out before she'd meet a young man was your like for eloquence or talk at all', and he is delighted by her 'voice talking sweetly'. Speakers, in a constant state of discovery about themselves, know or learn the value of their own linguistic capacity. In *The Well of the Saints* Martin Doul tells Molly, 'let you not put shame on me and I after saying fine words to you and dreaming dreams' (Act II). In *Playboy*, Old Mahon, who has already gained free bed and board on the strength of his story during his pursuit of Christy across Ireland, recognises at the end of the play that their experience can be reworked. Together they will have 'great times from this out telling stories of the villainy of Mayo and the fools is here', and Christy, having found himself 'a likely gaffer in the end of all', is ready to 'go romancing through a romping lifetime' leaving Pegeen and her community to their own devices.

Synge incorporates a degree of self-mockery even into that last state-ment of Christy: the excess of the 'romancing/romping' alliteration is a reminder that dubiety as well as admiration attaches to fine talk. Earlier, Christy's romantic vision of 'the lovelight of the star of knowledge shining' from Pegeen's brow, has been sardonically undercut by Widow Quin's comment, 'there's poetry talk for a girl you'd see itching and scratching, and she with a stale stink of poteen on her from selling in the shop'. As Martin and Mary Doul, in *Well of the Saints*, make their way south looking forward to the great times they'll have yet and the 'great talking before we die', the audience is reminded of the risk of deep rivers and floods they will have to cross to get there. But while there is disparity between image and reality, neither is privileged as more true. The emotion of Christy and Pegeen is genuine and their mutual wonder at it touches the audience, even if it is not shared by the Widow.

The creative imagination is both celebrated and found lacking. Stories fail at crucial points. They have the power to sustain the teller but not the listener. Molly Byrne mocks Martin Doul before her lover, for thinking 'he's only to open his mouth to have a fine woman, the like of me, running along by his heels', and Pegeen Mike loses faith in Christy at the moment when it matters. Shocking Christy by her betrayal and the audience by the sudden passage from comedy to something much blacker, it is Pegeen who leads the assault on Christy, declaring that there is 'a great gap between a gallous story and a dirty deed'. It is she who drops the noose over his head and she who, vengeful at the collapse of the fantasy that attached to him, wields the brand with which his leg is burnt. Whereas Nora in *In the Shadow of the Glen* joins her lot with the storyteller, saying, 'you've a fine bit of talk, stranger, and it's with yourself I'll go', Pegeen is left with her lamentation, 'I've lost him surely. I've lost the only Playboy of the Western World'.

While the intruding strangers in each play are the notably fine speakers, the dialogue of any character is likely to include telling images and such sharp sensory perception as Shawn's, 'I could hear the cows breathing and sighing in the stillness of the air, and not a step moving any place from the gate to the bridge'; or Old Mahon's humorously observed account of his son as, 'a lier on walls, a talker of folly, a man you'd see stretched the half of the day in the brown ferns with his belly to the sun'. Synge relishes language and the way particular configurations and juxtapositions challenge loose speech and create new significance. 'Is it killed your father?' Christy is asked, getting the reply, 'With the help of God, I did surely', a particularly taut version of the joke against the casual use of religious language that recurs throughout Synge's writing. Pegeen's father accepts Christy as husband to Pegeen with the words:

> A daring fellow is the jewel of the world, and a man did
> split his father's middle with a single clout should have the
> bravery of ten, so may God and Mary and St Patrick bless
> you, and increase you from this mortal day.
>
> (Act III)

The effect is that the audience is drawn into listening for meaning and into hearing the metaphor usually left dormant in the language.

The original manifesto of the Irish Literary Theatre cited as one of Ireland's advantages a potential audience 'trained to listen by its passion for oratory', and Synge repeatedly emphasised his good fortune in setting his plays among people whose language, because 'rich and living' as he put it in the Preface to *Playboy*, allows a writer to be 'rich and copious in his words' that will nevertheless seem realistic to the audience. But as Nicholas Grene has pointed out:

> It is not merely that Synge luckily came upon a language
> that was still poetic. It is a matter of credibility. An audience
> is prepared to accept that the Irish people do – or did –
> naturally use a vivid and unselfconscious dialect and
> therefore the flow of language in Synge's characters does not
> seem false or inappropriate.[10]

For all Synge's protestations that he had heard virtually every phrase he used spoken by country people, the speech that is so vivid in Synge's plays, sounds merely quaint or mundane when written by such contemporaries as Lady Gregory or Padraic Colum.

Synge selected, reworked, shaped, the idiom and structures he encountered and, by translating certain Gaelic constructions directly into English, he created a language that *sounds* authentic and is consistent but is as much his own as Wilde's was his. A simple example illustrates this. A phrase in a letter he received about a death: 'isn't it a sad story to tell? But at the same time we have to be satisfied because a person cannot live always',[11] is transformed by its new cadence and its position in the play when it recurs in Maurya's final speech in *Riders to the Sea* as, 'what more can we want than that? No man at all can be living for ever, and we must be satisfied'. The dying fall on the last word while making it sound final drains it of any note of contentment. As this suggests, it is less the occasional highly coloured speeches than the overall rhythm and use of imagery that empowers Synge's language. As Yeats observed, 'he made his own selection of word and phrase, choosing what would express his own personality. Above all he made word and phrase dance to a very strange rhythm'.[12] The brutality and strangeness as well as the exuberant response to the natural world helps establish the credibility of this world and this dialogue as remote from but coexistent with the audience's own.

The claims Synge made for his plays were not small. Ben Jonson and Molière are held up as his models in the Preface to *The Tinker's Wedding*, where he also wrote that:

> The drama is made serious – in the French sense of the word
> – not by the degree in which it is taken up with problems
> that are serious in themselves, but by the degree in which it
> gives the nourishment, not easy to define, on which our
> imaginations live.

And in the Preface to *The Playboy* he dismisses the two main streams of contemporary advanced writing, Ibsen and Zola, for their 'joyless and pallid words'; and Huysmans, Maeterlinck and, by implication, Yeats too, for their 'elaborate books that are far away from the profound and common interests of life'.

Synge brings the tramp and the outcast into the drama in English. Such figures, already present in Maeterlinck's *Les Aveugles* and Jarry's *Ubu Roi*, symbolist works staged by the avant-garde theatres Synge knew in the 1890s, and hovering at the edge of Yeats's *On Baile's Strand* as the Old Man and the Fool, populate the post-Second World War 'absurd' drama. As Katherine Worth has pointed out, the missing link between 1890s France and post-Second World War Britain is the Irish drama of the beginning of the century.[13] The two blind beggars who sit by the roadside and talk in *The Well of the Saints* are evident forerunners of Beckett's Vladimir and Estragon. In a period when kings have lost power and aristocracy with its superficial relationship to society may evoke gossip or envy of possessions but can hardly carry symbolic force, other universalising figures are sought. If the imagination can't go up, it can go down to tramps, beggars, blindmen. The prototype is the scene in *King Lear* on Dover cliffs between mad man, blind man and bogus madman which, at once grotesque and deeply moving, has become a paradigm for twentieth-century drama. It is with Synge and Yeats that it comes into twentieth-century English language drama.

Hay Fever (1925) and *Private Lives* (1930)

Noel Coward's comedies have none of the depth or apparent freedom of range of Synge's. Like Wilde, he presented himself as an entertainer and wrote for performance in mainstream theatre. Like Wilde, he was a remaker: his audiences recognise familiar tropes and relish the ingenious thwarting of expectation. Unlike Wilde, Coward did not produce notably epigrammatic dialogue, although his comedy is self-consciously artificial. Where Synge engaged with ideas of art and the artist, Coward introduced personality, famously creating an on- and off-stage persona for himself, marked not just by the dressing gown and cigar but by a careless sophisti-cation. Wilde indicted the society he depicted, mocking its pretensions and absurdity. Coward's position, like that of his American contemporary, Scott Fitzgerald, was more equivocal.

The pleasure principle is dominant for Coward's characters: they use their charm as a way of surviving; they have no responsibilities (the few children who appear being already grown up) and no commitments to anyone except themselves. Unusually, and this is one of the most interesting aspects of Coward's plays, the women are as self-assertive, independent and as likely to seethe with sudden desire as the men, so that courtship and the battle of the sexes is waged on strictly equal terms. The plays, essentially, consist of encounters of these selfish egos in a series of permutations. *Hay Fever* and *Private Lives* are the most successful because the egos are most sharply portrayed and the permutations most speedily enacted.

Role-playing disguised the double lives of Jack and Algernon in *The Importance of Being Earnest*, and Christy Mahon became the chief character in his own fiction in *The Playboy of the Western World*. Since the main characters of *Hay Fever* are an actress and a novelist, theatricality and fictive invention are even more apparent. If he is, in his own way, a feminist, Coward also figures as a kind of modernist in his insistence that his audiences are conscious of the artifice of theatre. His plays are alert to the glamour of the stage and to the eroticism of beautiful and beautifully dressed actors displaying themselves to an audience. The lure of such glamour, of fame generally and of the admiration they stimulate, is robustly treated in the absurd house party of *Hay Fever* in which the four guests independently invited by the four members of the Bliss family are neglec-ted, tormented, swept off their feet and humiliated by their hosts and finally creep surreptitiously away while the family is locked deep in argument with each other. If the pretensions and vanities of the family are satirically treated, so is the sycophancy of the supposedly more normal guests, who initially seemed to be the audience's representatives.

The play abounds in theatrical jokes. It is not only that Judith's world is so limited by the theatre that she exclaims at the mention of Sandy's boxing match that she must attend his first night, or that the characters continually respond to events and emotions either through direct quotation of Judith's roles or through improvised parodies of them; but Coward also slips in allusions beyond his characters' frame of reference when, for instance, he gives Judith's star vehicle, *Love's Whirlwind*, the title of Arkadina's in *The Seagull*, or echoes the closing line of Act III of Wilde's *A Woman of No Importance* to close the supposed extract from *Love's Whirlwind* and the second act of his own play, 'Don't strike. He is your father'.

The action meanwhile sweeps breathlessly on. Coward's plays are characterised by continual motion. *Hay Fever* is set entirely in the hall of the Bliss's country place, and for much of the play, the suitcases of characters arriving or about to depart are on view. In other plays, characters are caught while dressing to go out; are obliged to borrow pyjamas when they find themselves sleeping in unexpected places, or, ill-equipped, they make hasty exits. Arguments erupt; dialogue gives way to physical action; couples fall into embraces but, equally readily, into the tangle of arms and legs of a physical fight. The impression is of life lived on the hoof; of impulsive reactions; of imminent collapse or unmasking. While much of this is common to traditional farce, there is a new directness of statement and openness about the pressures of desire and about promiscuous or adulterous activity.

Courtship behaviour and sexual attraction and commitment are subjected to sharp scrutiny in *Hay Fever*, primarily through the tendency of the Bliss family to say what they think without recourse to common politenesses or subterfuge, to act on signals, and to read flirtation literally. When Myra flatters him, David disconcerts with a 'shall we elope?'; when Richard kisses Judith, she announces that her life is transformed. Caught in flirtation with one of their guests, any member of the Bliss family will switch into melodramatic confession or renunciation mode. The tropes and clichéd language of popular fiction and drama are reworked to the amusement of the audience, who recognise what is happening, and the horror of the guests, who do not. Sorel confesses her love for her mother's admirer with a 'Mother, say you understand and forgive', and Judith, having discovered her husband embracing Myra, announces:

JUDITH:
> The time has come for the dividing of the ways.

MYRA:
> What on earth do you mean?

JUDITH:
> I mean that I am not the sort of woman to hold a man against his will.

MYRA:
  You're both making a mountain out of a molehill. David
  doesn't love me madly, and I don't love him. It's –
JUDITH:
  Ssshh! – you do love him. I can see it in your eyes – in
  your every gesture. David, I give you to her – freely and
  without rancour. We must all be good friends always.
DAVID:
  Judith, do you mean this?
JUDITH (*with a melting look*):
  You know I do.
DAVID:
  How can we ever repay you?
JUDITH:
  Just by being happy.

                   (Act II)

While the guests are disconcerted by such exchanges, the bonds of family
understanding and of audience participation in the family's performances
are reinforced.

Such participation stimulates audience receptivity. As the play progresses
the rapid shifts from affection to irritation, hostility to understanding, are
found to be habitual, a more frenetic version of family relationships in the
real world. The Bliss family dynamics are a parodic version of those of
any close-knit, mutually dependent group. It might be difficult to imagine
a play more different in tone from *Hay Fever* than *Long Day's Journey Into
Night*, the most achieved play of Coward's near contemporary, Eugene
O'Neill. Like *Hay Fever*, however, the American play uses actor-characters
with a tendency to role-play and quotation and gives dramatic form to
the mutual needs and hostilities, the rhythms of daily intercourse of a
nuclear family, albeit it does so in a deeper and darker way.

It is impossible to say whether O'Neill picked up such metatheatrical
usage direct from Coward, although it is clear that Coward enjoyed a joke
in the opposite direction. Francis Gray's perception that the situation of
the heroine of *Design For Living* (written 1933), whose relationships shift
between three differently disposed potential lovers, is a comic reworking
of that in O'Neill's mammoth *Strange Interlude*, is irresistible.[14] The role of
O'Neill's heroine, Nina Leeds, had been created by Lynne Fontanne, five
years before Coward wrote the role of Gilda for her. Such reworking is
characteristic of Coward's use of personality and his propensity, as Shaw
wrote of Wilde, 'to play with the whole of theatre'.

The danger in Coward's writing is that the charm can very easily break,
the playfulness seems trivial: mishandled by actors or by the writer, what
should be most compelling is what irritates most. While there is mockery

in the representation of glittering empty people, there is also admiration and, between the early *Hay Fever* and the later *Design for Living*, the balance has shifted from the one to the other, to the detriment of the comedy. Whereas the intrusion of Wilde's personality decreased as his plays became more confident, the single epigrammatic *raisonneur* of the earlier plays giving way, most notably in *The Importance*, to a stage full of observant and observed figures, all equally linguistically adept, the Coward persona is given increasing prominence in his plays and treated with increasing indulgence. This culminates in the playwright characters, Leo in *Design for Living* and Garry Essendine in *Present Laughter*, written as star vehicles for Coward himself, as the other roles in these plays were written for his friends. The glamour of such self-referentiality has to carry too much. The credibility of the action of *Design for Living* suffers because, much as the characters admire themselves, the charm and unconventionality of the lead roles has to be taken largely on trust. Too much is invested in the audience's appetite for gossip and the sex appeal of the individual performers.

The wit of the characters in *Design for Living*, moreover, is limp. Otto's identification of Scotland as a country, 'with the banshees wailing and the four leaved shamrock', and Gilda's response, 'That's Ireland dear' (II. ii), has an obviousness that would shame Henry Arthur Jones, let alone Wilde. For all the claim that the characters are artists, the attention is always on what success can buy, never on the experiencing or making. There is little in the dialogue or action to convince that there is more to them than is expressed in Leo's credo:

> Let's be photographed and interviewed and pointed at in
> restaurants. Let's play the game for what it's worth, secretaries,
> fur coats, and de luxe suites in transatlantic liners at minimum
> rates. Don't let's allow one shabby perquisite to slip through
> our fingers.
>
> (II. iii)

The self-knowledge suggested by such words as 'game' and 'shabby' is belied by the gusto of such a speech. Although there are several suggestions that their work, though successful, is not first rate, these characters are not placed as the Blisses were: the very titles of David Bliss's novels *Broken Reeds* and *The Sinful Woman*, the melodramatic clichés of the quotations from them and from Judith's roles, subvert any pretentions to art. Coward ends the earlier play with the wonderfully ironic exchange when the appalling Bliss family interrupt their argument to register the departure of their guests:

SOREL:
> They've all gone!

JUDITH:
  How very rude!
DAVID:
  People really do behave in the most extraordinary
  manner these days.

(Act III)

There is no such ironising of behaviour in *Design for Living*. Sean O'Casey
wryly noted the absence of criticism of the commonplace intolerance of
Otto's self-defensive speech which begins, 'we're not doing any harm to
anyone. We're not peppering the world with illegitimate children', and
observed, 'surely Mr Coward and the characters in his play, so much above
the ordinary opinions and practices of ordinary life, should know that
there are neither legitimate nor illegitimate children – there are only
children'.[15] And there is nothing in the surrounding dialogue to suggest
that words like 'rich' and 'thrilling' in Otto's conclusion ('the only thing
left is to enjoy it thoroughly, every rich moment of it, every thrilling
second') are intended to be spoken sardonically.

In *Private Lives*, however, the balance is held remarkably. It is a comedy
of anticipation and coincidence but it increasingly becomes clear that the
coincidences derive from the shared attitudes and nostalgia of the glamorous divorced couple who meet again on the terrace of adjoining rooms
of the honeymoon hotel where they are separately arrived with their
newer, safer partners.

Much of the fun as well as the poignancy of the play resides in the
absurdly symmetrical action. Anticipation is established by parallel action:
Amanda goes in from her terrace, saying she will bring the cocktails out;
a moment later, Elyot comes out on to his carrying cocktails. Amanda
declares to her husband that they must leave for Paris, immediately and in
his turn Elyot draws the same conclusion. The echoic patterning of the
dialogue contributes to the effect. The mutuality of Amanda and Elyot is
registered in their conversations with their new spouses, before the audience sees them together. It is not just that each defends the other and
makes it clear how strong the sexual attraction once was, but they clearly
talk the same language; both enjoy the sun and are eager to swim; Elyot's
new love is 'cosy and unflurried by scenes and jealousy', Amanda loves
Victor 'more calmly'; each new spouse is wrong-footed in consecutive
opening exchanges, exposed as attempting to impose their strait-laced
conventionality on their partners. Amanda's response to Victor's excla-
mation that she is 'so sweet', 'thank you, Victor, that's most encouraging',
is as sardonic as Elyot's description of Sibyl as 'a completely feminine little
creature' and his offer to try to master pipe-smoking. Amanda's later wry
characterisation of Victor's threat to knock Elyot down as 'rugged grandeur', compliments Elyot's, 'If he comes near me I'll scream the place

down'. The pressure is, therefore, on the audience to recognise Elyot and Amanda as the natural partners.

The long duologues make performance a *tour de force*, as Coward acknowledged when he wrote of the forty minutes of duologue between Elyot and Amanda in Act II that, 'taken all in all it was more tricky and full of pitfalls than anything I had ever attempted as an actor'.[16] The talk is compelling for the audience because of the remarkable way it dramatises pragmatics: the recognition that we often speak words which substitute for what we are actually thinking; that the primary function of conversation is frequently not the exchange of substantive information; that what is understood in an exchange differs from the paraphrasable meaning. Hence the pitfalls but, providing the actors are fully attentive, the audience needs no sophisticated theory of language usage to recognise in the series of banal questions-and-answers in which Elyot and Amanda engage in their Act I exchange on the terrace, the search of each for his or her feeling about the other and the progress of their mutual emotion. Elyot has travelled since the breakdown of the marriage:

AMANDA:
   How was it?
ELYOT:
   The world?
AMANDA:
   Yes.
ELYOT:
   Oh, highly enjoyable.
AMANDA:
   China must be very interesting.
ELYOT:
   Very big, China.
AMANDA:
   And Japan –
ELYOT:
   Very small.
AMANDA:
   . . . How was the Taj Mahal?
ELYOT (*looking at her*):
   Unbelievable, a sort of dream.
AMANDA:
   That was the moonlight I expect, you must have seen it in the moonlight.
ELYOT (*never taking his eyes off her face*):
   Yes, moonlight is cruelly deceptive.

(Act I)

It is the mercurial speed and shifts of understanding rather than Wildean wit that keeps the audience alert in this play.

A marriage rather than a courtship play, *Private Lives* is concerned with passion and with long-term commitment. Amanda and Elyot both try to substitute a commonsense marriage for the intensities and endless quarrels of their earlier failed relationship. The play just predates and, in its film version (1931) must surely have been influential on, what Stanley Cavell has identified as a Hollywood genre, the crop of comedies of remarriage including *Philadelphia Story* and *Adam's Rib* that appeared between 1934 and 1941, but it differs from them in its refusal to work through to mutual forgiveness and new harmony.[17] The intercourse of Amanda and Elyot shifts from tenderness to harsh abuse and a vicious fight on the floor, and nothing suggests the future offers anything more mature. Indeed, the longer they are together the more the fights and disagreements flare, and any audience tendency to sentimentality is dispelled. Although the tone of the play is light, the underlying suspicion is grim. Could this couple, so well matched that they cannot live together but are miserable apart, represent an accurate image of love? Lest the safer might seem the better option, the ending re-uses the conclusion of *Hay Fever*, except that here it is the 'normal' couple who engage in bitter argument while Amanda and Elyot slip away hand-in-hand.

Traditionally, comic plots have resolved themselves in marriage or in multiple marriages, in a reassertion, however ironically shadowed, of belief in the institution with its bonds and promises rather than impulse and anarchy. This is as true of *The Importance of Being Earnest* as it is of *The Way of the World* or *Much Ado About Nothing*. This does not happen in Synge's play which, proving not to have been centrally concerned with courtship, ends with Christy's exit to independence and Pegeen's howl as she recognises the extent of her loss. Coward does not offer even this shaping. The topsy-turvy events and relationships, the continual changing of partners in the dance, look set to continue at the end of his plays. This may be the inevitable result of positing thorough-going social, personal and economic equality of sexual partners, or an effect of the covert treatment of homosexual attachment, or of a detached reading of hetero-sexuality, or it may simply be the effect of the invasion of comic form by a realism that resists the shaping comfort of art. I suspect something of each of these contributes; certainly marriage is presented as part of the chaos. The young people in *Hay Fever* retreat from possible liaisons; the formal bond of *Design For Living* has no power against the desires and jealousies of the troilism that defies Societys' code; new ties in *Private Lives* are dissolved in favour of the earlier and evidently unsustainable one. It is, at times, achingly funny.

Notes

1. G. B. Shaw, *Saturday Review* (21.1.1895).
2. C. E. Montague, *Dramatic Values* (1911), p. 187.
3. Sidney Grundy, quoted K. Powell, *Oscar Wilde and the Theatre of the 1890s* (Cambridge, 1990), p. 14.
4. Powell, *Oscar Wilde*, p. 118. For discussion of *The Foundling*, see Powell, *Oscar Wilde*, pp. 2, 108. There is extensive discussion of Wilde's borrowing in, among others, Walkley's reviews; the biographies of Wilde by Hesketh Pearson (1946) and Richard Ellmann (1987); Katherine Worth, *Oscar Wilde* (1983) and, most thoroughly, Powell, *Oscar Wilde*.
5. See R. Ellmann, *Oscar Wilde* (1987), p. 399; Jonathan Dollimore, 'Different Desires: Subjectivity and Transgression in Wilde and Gide', *Textual Practice*, 1, 1 (1987), pp. 48–67; J. Bristow, ed., *The Importance of Being Earnest* (1992), p. 208. This text reprints the first published edition, 1899, from which quotations here are taken.
6. See Nicholas Grene, *Synge: A Critical Study of the Plays* (1975), p. 5.
7. Montague, *Dramatic Values*, p. 6.
8. W. B. Yeats, *Essays and Introductions* (1961), p. 326.
9. Account given in A. Gregory, *Our Irish Theatre* (1914), pp. 133–4.
10. Grene, *Synge: A Critical Study*, p. 159.
11. Quoted, D. E. S. Maxwell, *Modern Irish Drama* (Cambridge, 1984), p. 47. The best discussions of Synge's language are, Alan J. Bliss, 'The Language of Synge', in Maurice Harman, ed., *J. M. Synge Centenary Papers* (Dublin, 1971); Grene, *Synge: A Critical Study*, Chapter 4, and a fine early analysis in Montague, *Dramatic Values*.
12. Yeats, 1905, reprinted in *Essays and Introductions*, p. 299.
13. K. Worth, ed., *Beckett the Shape Changer* (1975), p. 4.
14. F. Gray, *Noel Coward* (1987), p. 160.
15. S. O'Casey, *The Green Crow* (1957), p. 98.
16. Quoted, Sheridan Morley, introduction, Coward, *Plays*, Vol. 2 (1986), p. x.
17. See S. Cavell, *Pursuits of Happiness: The Hollywood Comedy of Remarriage* (Cambridge, MA, 1981).

Chapter 6

George Bernard Shaw

VAUGHAN:

> I've repeatedly proved that Shaw is physiologically incapable of the note of passion.

BANNAL:

> Yes, I know. Intellect without emotion. That's right. I always say that myself. A giant brain, if you ask me; but no heart.

> (Epilogue, *Fanny's First Play*, 1911)

The inescapable figure who straddles this period, from the publication of *The Quintessence of Ibsenism* in 1891, through the assault on contemporary theatre in the columns of *The Saturday Review* in the mid-1890s and the achievement of the Stage Society and Court Theatre productions after the turn of the century, to the huge success of *Saint Joan* in 1924 and the Malvern Festival productions of the next decade, is George Bernard Shaw. Stimulating, disruptive and worryingly unsatisfactory in a multitude of ways – his plays are among the few from the period which retain their capacity to excite, engage and annoy; which have entered the international repertoire, and which invariably draw audiences when revived.

Shaw's targets were theatrical as well as social. His characteristically questioning engagement with ideas is as evident in his deliberate reworking of subjects and attitudes that recurred in contemporary drama as in his frank representation of aspects of sexual, political and religious experience that had habitually been banned from the English stage. The early works, *Plays Pleasant and Unpleasant* (1898) and *Three Plays for Puritans* (1901), launched a polemic against contemporary social organisation but also against the cynical practices and unreal action of contemporary theatre whose 'whole difficulty' he claimed, 'had arisen through the drama of the day being written for the theatres instead of from its own inner necessity'.[1]

Shaw's claim to address reality, to show things as they are, in the 1890s plays, is made through the introduction and subversion of familiar devices and plot-lines and the conventional morality they presupposed: the emphasis was not on sentimental poverty but slum landlordism; not penitent fallen women but prostitution; not glamorous costumes and settings but the damage and corruption of the capitalist system which supplied them to the few through exploitation of the bodies and minds of the many. Gender stereotypes were challenged when dashing heroism was mocked in *Arms and the Man* (1894), or the guise of angel in the house revealed as camouflage for the new woman in *Candida* (1895).

Like Ibsen, but markedly unlike most contemporary English play-wrights, Shaw also provided excellent female roles in his first dozen or so plays and very little that might appeal to actor-managers. On the few occasions when he did attempt to write for specific theatres and performers – *You Never Can Tell* (written, 1896) bright, witty, good-humoured, seems to have been conceived for the Haymarket, and *The Man of Destiny* (written, 1897) in the serious hope that Irving would play it – his own inner necessity invariably won out. The usurpation of family values, in the one, when the rude old man is revealed to the family as their defaulting father, proved too bizarre, and Shaw can hardly have believed Irving would relish the teasing feminine baiting of Napoleon in the other.

Shaw coolly acknowledged that the 'stage tricks and suspenses and thrills and jests' on which he drew were in vogue when he was a boy, but as W. B. Yeats observed, if he took his 'situations from melodrama', as he frequently did, he 'called up logic to make them ridiculous'.[2] Mistaken identities, delayed disclosure, startling recognitions do recur but their placing within a network of unconventional perceptions draws attention to the artifice of theatrical plotting and creates a consciousness in the audience quite different from that assumed by the plays from which they derived. Specific sources have, indeed, been identified for many of the plots and details of the action. Thomas Holcroft's *The Road to Ruin*, revived in 1891, fed into *Mrs Warren's Profession* (written, 1893) as did Janet Achurch's *Mrs Daintree's Daughter*, but Shaw himself pointed to the difference. His claim that the play 'skilfully blended the plot of *The Second Mrs Tanqueray* with that of *The Cenci*',[3] not only characteristically aligns his own with a substantial literary work but with one recently driven to a closed-house production in defiance of the Censor's ban.

The Devil's Disciple (1899) shamelessly lifted the gallows substitution from *A Tale of Two Cities*, whose most recent adaptation, Freeman Wills's *The Only Way*, had appeared earlier the same year, but instead of the tear-jerking 'far, far better thing', Shaw's play has its hero deconstruct the execution scene and indict the solemnity of an occasion got up to impress the people with 'Handel's music and a clergyman to make murder look like piety'. In *Major Barbara* (1905), Cusins' ingenious repudiation of the legitimacy of his parents' marriage clears his way to an inheritance:

CUSINS:
    Here they are outcasts. Their marriage is legal in Aus-

tralia but not in England. My mother is my father's deceased wife's sister and in this island I am consequently a foundling. Is the subterfuge good enough Mac-chiavelli?

(Act III)

The blithe speciousness of the argument acknowledges realistic motive even while enjoying a thrust at both the absurd contrivances of foundling plots and an absurd English marriage law. *Androcles and the Lion* (1914) draws both on Christmas pantomime, with its anthropomorphised animals and spectacular transformation scenes, and on the conventional plot line of 1890s toga plays, in which the steadfastness of Christian faith wins out over Roman duty. But in Shaw's play a leading Christian runs amok and slaughters the gladiators and the hero, Androcles, is 'desperately frightened' as he goes to face the lion. W. S. Gilbert is the most obvious forerunner but Shaw's iconoclasm is fiercer: with *his* topsy-turvy humour goes a propensity, as he put it in *The Quintessence of Ibsenism*, to convert the audience 'from the ordinary acceptance of current ideals as safe standards of conduct, to the vigilant openmindedness of Ibsen'.[4]

'Intellect the surest tool'

As Shaw's own phrase suggests and as Brecht later argued, Shaw's is intellectual drama in its unhesitating appeal to the reason[5] but, although ideas are fiercely discussed, there is rarely a clearcut message, unless it is the overriding one that the system is deeply corrupt and none of us in it can afford to be complacent. Even more than in Brecht's drama, the expression of contrary positions is crucial to the effect of Shaw's. As early as 1904, A. B. Walkley noted that it 'delights by its dialectic'.[6] Strong-minded characters recognise each other and, although cast as opponents, are glad to see dunderheads and time-servers bested even when ostensibly allied to them, and the audience is led to share the triumph. Moments such as the following from *The Devil's Disciple* in which the judge, Burgoyne, appreciates Richard's defiance of the fanatical Swindon, recur:

SWINDON:
Do you mean to deny that you are a rebel?
RICHARD:
I am an American, sir.

SWINDON:
> What do you expect me to think of that speech, Mr Anderson?

RICHARD:
> I never expect a soldier to think, sir.
> (*Burgoyne is delighted by this retort, which almost reconciles him to the loss of America*).

(Act III)

A quarter of a century later, his Inquisitor in *Saint Joan* will similarly acknowledge the robustness of Joan's common sense rebuttals of the interruptions of the bigotted English Chaplain, de Stogumber.

But the audience, including those whose politics and cultural attitudes might seem to make them Shaw's natural allies, may be disconcerted by being made to laugh as well as to think. Although Shaw's debut was with the Independent Theatre (*Widowers' Houses*, 1892), his next two plays, *The Philanderer* and *Mrs Warren's Profession*, proved too strong even for that avant-garde organisation, and I suspect it was the playful tone as much as the subject matter that disconcerted earnest Jacob Grein, since the audience of each play is made at least partly complicit with a central character whose behaviour is immoral. Elements of the *Punch* stereotype of the new woman are evident in Vivie Warren's hearty hand-shake, dress and failing housewifery, while a Club of teasingly parodied Ibsen enthusiasts is used as a setting in *The Philanderer*.

Similarly, after the turn of the century, commentators accustomed to the clear-cut arguments of committed problem plays, felt that the wit trivialised Shaw's work.[7] They failed to recognise the strong moral consciousness operating throughout: its sharpest barbs always directed against attitudes that, whatever their source, lacked integrity or the 'vigilant openmindedness' he discovered in Ibsen. Whereas Brieux, the leading avant-garde French dramatist of the day, has not survived the problems he so seriously attacked, Shaw's evident survival is largely due to what Brecht recognised as the power of fun, '*späss*', in his drama. And yet it is also true that the element of fun allows writer and audience to avoid confronting horror or despair. Deep levels of grief or joy are not encountered. Shaw himself was clear about his method from the beginning: 'it is by jingling the bell of the jester's cap', he wrote, 'that I, like Heine, have made people listen to me'.[8]

Such jingling is immediately present in the self-referentiality of many of Shaw's plays. William Archer labelled the anti-heroic central character of *Arms and the Man* (1894), 'Captain Bernard Bluntschli-Shaw'[9] and characters that might seem to share his idiosyncratic way of seeing and reasoning crop up repeatedly in the Edwardian plays. In the Court productions, actors playing central figures – John Tanner, Undershaft –

were made up to look like Shaw.[10] While this is, in part, self-mocking – Tanner shows himself terrified of the pursuing female and his propensity to talk is much derided, and Undershaft is a machiavellian arms dealer – the Shavian viewpoint is, on balance, upheld or promoted. In *Caesar and Cleopatra* (1899) Caesar, the first fully developed Shavian rationalist, having been persuaded off the barley water he prefers to wine, agrees to sacrifice his comfort to Cleopatra's wish that he should be for one day, 'like other people: idle, luxurious, kind'. When the vain and scurrilous Louis Dubedat in *The Doctor's Dilemma* (1906) proclaims himself a disciple of Bernard Shaw, the metatheatricality is even more pressing. The Shavian position is mocked and then endorsed in the dialogue that follows the *frisson* induced by the familiar name:

LOUIS:

Of course I havnt the ridiculous vanity to set up to be exactly a Superman; but still, it's an ideal that I strive towards just as any man strives towards his ideal . . .

SIR BERNARD:

Bernard Shaw? I never heard of him. He's a Methodist preacher, I suppose?

LOUIS (*scandalized*):

No, no. He's the most advanced man now living: he isnt anything.

SIR PATRICK:

I assure you, young man, my father learnt the doctrine of deliverance from sin from John Wesley's own lips before you or Mr Shaw were born.

(Act III)

In the Induction to *Fanny's First Play* (1911), the critic, Trotter, repeats the common assertion that Shaw's works are dialogues, exhibitions of character, especially the character of the author, but (even as we watch one) that they are definitely not plays. More defiantly still the most recurrent indictment, quoted at the head of this chapter, that Shaw's work is all head and no heart, is presented for scrutiny in the Epilogue.

In his prefaces and critical writing, Shaw's discussion of the audience is invariably expressed in terms of combat. As early as *The Quintessence*, he noted Ibsen's refusal to supply a trustworthy *raisonneur* and offered an account of Ibsen's method that more accurately described his own:

Ibsen substituted a terrible art of sharp shooting at the audience, trapping them, fencing with them, aiming always at the sorest spot in their consciences. Never mislead an audience was an old rule. But the new school will trick the spectator into forming a meanly false judgement, and then convict him of it in the next act often to his grievous mortification.

(The Quintessence of Ibsenism, 1913, p. 145)

His preface to Plays Unpleasant similarly warns that his attacks are directed against audience, not characters (p. xxvi). And the liberal audience, at least as vulnerable as the conservative, sees its closest representatives wrong-footed: Trench, having learned that he is no better than the rack renter, Sartorius, joins him; Vivie Warren admits her guilt by acceptance; Major Barbara capitulates to her arms-dealing father.

Certain obviously alienatory shifts are introduced: in Man and Superman (1905), Mendoza debates anarchism and social democracy with his bandits as they wait with nails strewn on the road to waylay the next car and, with the arrival of Tanner and Straker, the scene moves from the Sierra Nevada to Hell. Act II of Androcles and the Lion takes places as if in the green room of the Roman amphitheatre, where a Call Boy summons the performers, the net thrower arranges his hair, gladiators preen in front of the mirror, before heading off to their supposed doom. A framing device of puzzled, then derisive, critics begins and ends Fanny's First Play and in his greatest popular success, Saint Joan, Shaw traps his audience into a romantic response which he then subverts. Following the trial and recantation, the emotional power of the rush to the off-stage burning and the hysteria of de Stogumber who repents his part too late, comes the closing exchange of scene vi:

EXECUTIONER:
>Her heart would not burn, my lord; but everything that is left is at the bottom of the river. You have heard the last of her.

WARWICK:
>The last of her? Hm! I wonder!

But the audience, ready to leave the theatre in the glow of an ending satisfactorily tragic but with promise for the future, is compelled to see the curtain rise again on the bedroom and the night-capped figure of Charles VII, and to endure the farcical and deeply disconcerting epilogue in which Joan and the other leading figures in her drama appear again to hash over the martyrdom and its effects. Directors who leave out or somehow gloss over these shifts offer their audiences a smoother, more readily naturalisable experience but, I suspect, one that, if less annoying, is also less stimulating, less memorable.

Shaw frequently evaporates endings. Like Chekhov who, after The Seagull, found low-key alternatives to the final gun-shot of melodrama, he

saw commitment to 'plays that have no endings' as the necessary conse-
quence of resisting the formulaic development of the well-made play. He
avoided strong curtain lines within his plays or, where he did use them,
it was to start hares that were not pursued. Even *Mrs Warren's Profession*
ends anticlimactically with the fizzling out of the interaction between
mother and daughter that had produced such fireworks in the second act,
while the revelation that Frank's father had been one of Mrs Warren's
clients that concludes Act I and that Frank and Vivie may be half-brother
and half-sister that concludes Act III, prove a false trail. With their other
preoccupations, nobody in the final act pays much attention to the possibility of incest. The final act of *The Doctor's Dilemma* finds Dubedat's
widow not only not broken-hearted but happily married to someone else
and, at the end of *The Shewing up of Blanco Posnet* (1909), Feemy simply
says, 'Oh well, here' and the antagonists shake hands. Such endings,
affronting expectations and mocking the attention the audience has given
to the developing plot, are frustrating. They effectively deny the satisfaction
of completed form and thereby put pressure on the audience to relate the
action they have witnessed to the world outside the play. As Shaw wrote
of Brieux' refusal of closure, 'you come away with the very disquieting
sense that you are involved in the affair, and must find the way out of it
for yourself and for everybody else if civilization is to be tolerable to your
sense of honour'.[11]

All of which goes to suggest that the Shaw play works by a process of
leading on and undercutting; inveigling its audience into new – Shavian
– ways of seeing. C. E. Montague having observed such a process at the
Edwardian revival of *Arms and the Man* wrote:

> You will find it pretty clear that a good part of your average
> audience in the first act sympathises warmly with the two
> gas bags then swelling. During the second act it will veer
> round, and in the third the laughter and applause, at the
> right places, may be warm and almost continuous. The
> strange point of view has by that time been attained, the
> idiom of the new commentator on experience been
> mastered.[12]

Just as a much later audience would discover how to engage with a Pinter
or a Beckett play, so Shaw shifted the expectations of his contemporary
audience. The effect was that, although he retained the capacity to surprise,
the interaction became less of an assault on and more of a playing with
and for the newly responsive audience. W. D. Howells observed of the
1916 New York production of *Major Barbara*:

Apparently the spectators missed no point of the author's cutting irony and audacious humour; a constant ripple of enjoyment ran over the house, and the author, if he had been there must have felt that he had come into his own in all the length and breadth of his intention.[13]

Major Barbara (1905)

Following the success at the Court Theatre of *John Bull's Other Island* (November, 1904) and *Man and Superman* (May, 1905), *Major Barbara* (November, 1905) clinched Shaw's arrival as a force on the English stage. Stimulating, compelling, frustrating, the play is representative of the second wave of Shaw's writing; works all but guaranteed a stage and written for performance by a company of actors led by Barker and Lillah McCarthy who were increasingly familiar with the demands of a Shaw play.

The texture of *Major Barbara* derives from a series of dislocations. Some of these operate at a trivial level as large general ideas shift to anticlimactic domestic ones: Lady Britomart interrupts her husband with, 'you can talk my head off; but you can't change wrong to right. And your tie is all on one side. Put it straight' and, with a sting by Shaw out of Wilde, says: 'really Barbara, you go on as if religion were a pleasant subject. Do have some sense of propriety'. But there is a continual modulation of jokes into something much darker. Undershaft, the arms dealer, built up as a stock sinister capitalist before his entrance, proves mild, sensitive, willing to listen to everyone. Once audience and family circle have surrendered to his charm, however, he states his position unequivocally, allowing no mealy-mouthed apologies:

UNDERSHAFT:
> But consider for a moment. Here I am, a manufacturer of mutilation and murder, I find myself in a specially amiable humour just now, because, this morning, down at the foundry, we blew twenty-seven dummy soldiers into fragments with a gun which formerly destroyed only thirteen.

LOMAX (*leniently*):
> Well, the more destructive war becomes, the sooner it will be abolished, eh?

UNDERSHAFT:
>   Not at all. The more destructive war becomes, the more
>   fascinating we find it.

(Act I)

A brief sequence in which Undershaft considers possible careers for his son Stephen, who might, in his settled values, be supposed a *raisonneur*, demonstrates the method. Stephen's evidently slower wit and the stiffness of his rejections of his father's suggestions distance him from the audience, even as they lead Undershaft to observe:

> He knows nothing; he thinks he knows everything. That
> points clearly to a political career. Get him a private
> secretaryship to someone who can get an under secretaryship
> and then leave him alone. He will find his natural and
> proper place in the end on the Treasury bench.

(Act III)

The speedy movement from the epigram, through a joke about political patronage, to the indicting of advancement of mediocre minds in public office, bears enough relation to the truth to hold the audience's attention. Shaw makes Stephen the fall-guy when, far from arguing the point or identifying over-simplifications in his father's commentary, he replies in facilely conventional terms, 'I'm sorry, sir that you force me to forget the respect due to you as my father. I am an Englishman; and I will not hear the Government of my country insulted'. With his fall must go any audience tendency to similarly unthinking patriotic platitudes, and Undershaft concludes the contest with a new thrust: 'Stephen, I've found your profession for you. You're a born journalist. I'll start you with a high toned weekly review.' The way is thus prepared for Stephen's *volte face* at the end of the act when, completely won by his father's efficiently run factory and model town ('Magnificent . . . the administrative capacity, the financial genius, the colossal capital it represents'), his only question is whether such provision for the work force 'may sap their independence and weaken their sense of responsibility', which provides a comic counterpoint to the torment and painful rethinking in which Cusins and, more especially, Barbara must engage. It is not that the play creates revolutionaries of its audience but that its pattern of laughter and disruption of expectations insists that mind plays its part in the audience's response, and plays it in Shaw's way.

The demands made on the audience here are more complex than in the 1890s plays. Undershaft having opted, like Mrs Warren, to be ruthless and rich rather than honest and poor, out-faces the horror of the next generation who learn, like Vivie, that until society finds different means of organising itself everyone is guilty, not just the traders in sex or weaponry but those who help generate the circumstances in which such trade flourishes. By contrast with Mrs Warren, however, whose profession has to be gleaned between the lines, Undershaft wholly believes in the life he leads and continually reminds family and audience of his trade. It is he who spells out to the Salvationist General the brutal slaughter his armaments effect, even as she is taking his cheque; he who celebrates the news in the last act that 300 people have been blown up in Manchuria.

The struggle between Undershaft and Barbara runs, like that between Mrs Warren and her daughter, throughout the play but is resolved differently. Vivie, having ranged from horror to admiration and back, finally distances herself from her mother. Her remark, 'I might have done as you did. But I should not have lived one life and believed in another. You are a conventional woman at heart', gives the audience its let-out. There is no such release in *Major Barbara*. Certain sequences generated cries of blasphemy and excessive violence in an outraged press – among them Barbara's despairing echo of Christ's 'my God, my God, why hast thou forsaken me?' and the ruffian's striking of a woman Salvationist, which Grein for one found 'beyond all bounds of realism in art'. They are crucial elements in the emotional texture of the play. It is convincingly in character, as Max Beerbohm pointed out, that the Christian Barbara, facing spiritual crisis, should 'echo the words of agony most familiar to her', but the familiarity and sacred nature of the words, charges their speaking with an extra-dramatic poignancy.[14] Similarly, the violence, like the stoning of the pram in Edward Bond's *Saved* very much later in the century, assaults complacency and the tendency that might be anticipated in the liberal audience to sentimentalise poverty instead of recognising it as 'the worst of crimes – the one unforgiveable crime that must be wiped off before any virtue can grow', which Shaw claimed was the driving force of this play.[15]

That the indictment is of palliatives, as well as of more evident abuses, is clear from such exchanges as this between Undershaft and the Salvation Army General:

MRS BAINES:
> Let me tell you there would have been rioting this winter in London but for us.

UNDERSHAFT:
> Do you really think so?

MRS B:
> I know it. Remember 1886, when you rich gentlemen hardened your hearts against the cry of the poor. They broke the windows of your club in Pall Mall.

UNDERSHAFT:
> And the Mansion House Fund went up the next day

> from thirty thousand pounds to seventy nine thousand.
> I remember quite well.

MRS B:

> Well, wont you help me get at the people? They wont
> break windows then.

(Act II)

Pressed to engage with the fact of poverty, voiced most passionately not by the Salvationist but by the arms dealer, the audience responds to the commitment of the young Salvationists as well as to the poignancy and humour of the action of the deserving and undeserving poor gathered on stage. But it also remains conscious of the direction and deviousness of Undershaft's questions and the increasingly untenable position of Barbara. The arguments are embedded in the dramatically complex action.

Stage properties contribute to the play's effect: the milk offered to Snobby and Rummy adds realistic detail to the Salvation Army setting and contributes to the scroungers' comedy when they sip it while black-mouthing Army fare, but when, later, a mug of milk saves Peter Shirley from starvation, the reality of destitution is given contrastingly sharp recognition. Sets are made similarly interactive with events. The comfort-able upper-class library of Acts I and III of the play gives way to the shock of the Salvation Army shelter of Act II and the munitions factory of the end of Act III, with its background vision of a model town and its foreground reality of cannons and dummy corpses. The spectacle and stirring sound of the Salvationists' march at the end of Act II are hard to resist, although the effect is complicated because the faithful, banging their tambourines and crying out for joy and glory, are led by the unbelievers, Undershaft on the trombone and Cusins on the drum. The audience, implicated in the ironic context of Barbara's collapse of faith by its response to the activity, is made more acutely responsive when it hears her cry of distress.

Staging and stage directions

Set and staging are integral to *Major Barbara*. Shaw was no stranger to theatrical effects. He played a large part in the direction of his own plays as did Gilbert and Pinero, before him, and his letters reveal close concern not just with acting style but with stage sets and the disposition of actors within them. When it suited his purposes, he could outdo nineteenth-century spectacle with rising and setting moons, huge crowds or a stage lightening to reveal Cleopatra asleep on a bed of red poppies at the feet of the Sphinx (*Caesar and Cleopatra*). He might demand heavy rain and a summer storm (*Pygmalion*) or the appearance on stage of a lion (*Androcles and the Lion*). More disconcertingly, in *Man and Superman*, he allowed the quasi-real Sierra Nevada set to darken to 'utter void. Then somewhere the beginning of pallor, and with it a faint throbbing buzz as of a ghostly violincello palpitating on the same note endlessly' which transported the action to a dream Hell, realised in production by the use of black velvet-covered stools and drapes against a black floor and backcloth. The first black box set? He put a car on to the stage in this play and, revelling in the technological novelty, had it roar off at the end of the act while, in 1910, in *Misalliance*, he introduced the sound and shadow of an overflying aeroplane.

Shaw's use of lengthy, even novelistic, stage directions now so out of favour, demands some explanation. In a period of increasing directoral influence, they put the dramatist's marker on potential future stagings, directing attention to the interaction of verbal with visual image, but, on Shaw's part at least, they were also knowingly aimed at the reader, as the increasingly lengthy, always argumentative and often mischievous prefaces that accompanied each publication demonstrate. When Shaw, pressed by the newly established publisher, Grant Richards, prepared his first group of plays for the press, English plays texts were rarely published except in acting editions bedevilled by technical stage jargon. Although Heinemann had told Shaw that no one bought plays and even Pinero's sold only to amateur companies, *Plays: Pleasant and Unpleasant* (1898) and then *Three Plays for Puritans* (1901) with their readable accounts of location and of behaviour and mood of the various characters, sold well and, along with the new Archer translations of Ibsen, helped to alter perceptions of theatre for readers who had had no opportunity of seeing these works live. Conscious both of the novelty of his chosen method of presentation and its polemical nature, Shaw, in the preface to his first volume, predicted a time when:

> the customary brief and unreadable scene specifications at
> the head of an act will have expanded into a chapter, or
> even a series of chapters. No doubt one result of this will be
> the production, under cover of the above arguments, of
> works of a mixture of kinds, part narrative, part homily, part
> description, part dialogue and (possibly) part drama – works
> that could be read but not acted.
> (*Plays: Pleasant and Unpleasant*, 1898, p. xxiv)

While this has not come about, the habitual publication of reader-friendly playscripts with stage directions bracketted and italicised as devised by Shaw, albeit in much terser form than he envisaged, is a reality.

For all the charm and challenge to the reader of his prefaces, Shaw's plays were very clearly intended for acting. The force of the dialogue and the interactions between the characters drive the plays. He insisted, moreover, that he tried to include in the stage directions only things relevant to the actors' performance and, as actors and designers who worked with him consistently acknowledged, he had a lively sense of the play on the stage, and knew how to 'draw the full value out of a line'.[16] Many of his notes to actors and ideas developed in rehearsal were subsequently incorporated into the stage directions of the printed texts, and his prompt copies for *Caesar and Cleopatra* and *Captain Brassbound's Conversion*, for example, show that he supplied individualised lines to enable the extras to be more convincingly voluble in the crowd scenes. Rehearsal experience led him to recognise that stage directions were suggestions not orders. He told Annie Russell, his first Major Barbara, that a part that was any good could 'be played fifty different ways by fifty different people' and wrote to J. L. Shine, his Larry Doyle in *John Bull's Other Island*:

> Don't worry yourself by trying to carry out my suggestions
> exactly or hampering yourself in any way with them. Very
> likely when you study them over you will be able to improve
> on them. That's all they're for. I think I am probably nearly
> right as to the best changes and stopping places on the
> journey; but as to the way of making them, follow your
> own feeling and make the most of your skill: turn the whole
> thing inside out if you like – in fact you won't be able to
> help yourself when the spirit takes possession of you at full
> pressure – but don't hesitate on my account to make the
> part entirely your own: my idea of having my play acted is
> not to insist on everybody rattling my own particular bag
> of tricks.[17]

But new tricks more often than not proved to have gone against the grain of the play, strengthened as that was by directing experience. While he explained to the Theatre Guild that the sets for *Saint Joan* might be 'reduced to extreme simplicity. A single pillar of the Gordon Craig type will make the cathedral. All the Loire needs is a horizon and a few of Simonson's lanterns', he later objected with some vehemence to the 'feebly stagey' quality of the set the Guild came up with and its failure to respond to such textual demands as that Joan should appear with short hair and in soldier's dress in the second scene.[18]

Shaw recognised the younger Court and Stage Society dramatists as co-conspirators in a Fabian war against the triviality and conservatism of current drama, with its stock characters and its actors' tendency, out of incompetence or vanity, to reduce to type characters that did have potential life. The younger dramatists responded to the polemic, echoing in their plays the strong-mindedness of the female characters, and what they took to be the realistic settings and characters of Shaw's. But the tone and texture of Shaw's writing and his conception of realism as the undermining of romanticised or idealised readings of human action rather than as a portrait of everyday life, are essentially different from theirs. Whereas the Edwardian realists adopted the conventions of European naturalism – a low-key acting style and fourth-wall settings in courtroom, office or drawing room whose appearance and lay-out is detailed in the stage directions – Shaw's actors are involved in role-playing not representation, and his settings are likely to be used parodically or suffused with fantasy.

The absurd possibilities of human existence emerge in increasingly bizarre form, from Sergius' declaration of romantic devotion, in front of a line of washing in *Arms and the Man*, via the rationalist Bishop's detailing of his sceptical view of marriage in *Getting Married* (1908), to the aviatrix who, in *Misalliance*, drops from the sky into an English garden where figures unexpectedly appear out of stone tanks. Hovering often on the verge of consciousness, absurdity breaks out fully fledged in the late 'Extravaganzas' and in the short plays Shaw called 'Tomfooleries'. With a logic worthy of Ionesco or N. F. Simpson, the lover in *Passion, Poison and Petrification* (1905), for instance, having swallowed poison and needing lime as an antidote eats the plaster ceiling then, having drunk water to slake his thirst, solidifies as a statue. The play at an essential level is recognised as playing.

Shaw's dramatic language

The most realistic-seeming play must use artifice to organise its incidents, impressions and ideas meaningfully and is likely to do so more effectively where the dramatist acknowledges this. Recognising from the outset that speakable dramatic dialogue is necessarily different from both written prose and speech, Shaw went neither for poeticism nor verisimilitude in dialogue but for what he called 'audible intelligibility'. Jonson's *Volpone* might be 'detestably unreadable' but it became a 'model of vivid dialogue' when spoken on stage and:

'This my hand will rather the multitudinous seas incarnadine'
is such a polysyllabic monstrosity as was never spoken
anywhere but on the stage; but it is magnificently effective
and perfectly intelligible in the theatre.[19]

Unlike his New Drama contemporaries, therefore, Shaw claimed the right
to use rhetorical devices freely in his stage dialogue. He stressed the
importance of sound and rhythm, demanding, 'a new convention of acting,
rather formal, and tending a little to caricature', and wrote approvingly
that Lillah McCarthy, who had spent five years on the road touring in
Wilson Barrett's *Sign of the Cross*, 'saturated with declamatory poetry and
rhetoric from her cradle, [had] learned her business out of London by
doing work in which one was either heroic or nothing'.[20] Sharing Henry
James's admiration for the Théâtre français actor, Coquelin, he
emphasised the importance of clarity in the actor's speaking of the words and relished the tirade which, building to a climax, allowed individual characters
to possess the stage verbally.

Virtuoso monologues, from John Tanner's harangues to the Inquistor's
three-page disquisition on heresy, are among the most gripping sequences
of his plays but they are part of a complex texture. They give way to
group sequences of short quick speeches or to duets which offer exhilarat-
ing verbal duels, from the revelatory Act II exchange of Mrs Warren and
Vivie, through the jousting of Ann and Tanner in *Man and Superman*
and of Cusins and Undershaft in *Major Barbara*, to the political wrangling
of Cauchon and Warwick in *Saint Joan*. The panache and the verbal
intensity involved in voicing the arguments as well as the very rhythm of
the lines is, I think, what led T. S. Eliot to observe that, however clearly
characters might be distinguished, any speech of Shaw's has 'that unmistak-
able personal rhythm which is the mark of a prose style', and to claim
further that Shaw was, with Congreve, our 'greatest prose stylist in the
drama'. These word-dominated plays act so successfully because Shaw
scored and cast, as he famously claimed, as if for operatic voices and knew
the necessity of varying vocal timbres and types; of patterning the action
into recitative, aria, duet and chorus.[21]

Shaw's engagement with the rhetoric of theatre is evident too in his
representation of dialect and low colloquial forms of speech. Although in
the notes to *Captain Brassbound's Conversion* (1900) he rejected Dickens'
Sam Weller as an appropriate Cockney model for Drinkwater's speech, he
did not look to what was spoken on the streets but to current popular
representations of it: Mr Anstey's dialogues in *Punch* and Mr Chevalier's
coster songs and patter. Stage cockney phrases such as 'Lor bless yer'
and 'Bless yr awt' make it clear that he wants quick recognition not
verisimilitude:

DRINKWATER:

> Clawss feelin! thats wot it is: clawss feelin! Wot are yer,
> arter all, but a bloomin gang o wust cowst cazhls (*casual
> ward paupers*)? Better ev naow fembly, an rawse aht of it,
> lawk me, than ev a specble one and disgrice it, lawk
> you.
>
> (Act II)

Conscious of the staginess of his dialect forms, Shaw was able to use them
to tease his audience. A characteristic disjunction, of the kind later identified as an alienation effect, occurs at the end of the first scene of *John Bull's
Other Island* (1904) when, having let Haffigan spout fairly convincingly in
stage Irish, Shaw exposes him as a fake, self-conscious in his Irishry, and
then puts Tom Broadbent into an Irish context where he figures as a stage
Englishman, deeply complacent and quite without imagination or verbal
dexterity. The joke is rather on the reader when, in the printed text of
Pygmalion (1914), a play centred on the discussion of language and its
social markings, the orthographic representation of Eliza's cockney speech
in the opening scene is suddenly jettisoned, since 'this desperate attempt
to represent her dialect without a phonetic alphabet must be abandoned
as unintelligible outside London'. Previous to this, Shaw had usually
represented dialect orthographically but Synge's example had demonstrated
that actors and readers were quite capable of supplying accent on the basis
of syntactical and lexical markers.

Pygmalion (1914)

Shaw had frequently introduced discussion of language into his dialogue
before *Pygmalion*. 'Never mind him. He likes to talk', says Straker of
Jack Tanner, whose final word in his play is 'talking . . .'; Undershaft,
reprimanded for making speeches, declares he knows no other way of
expressing himself, and Aubrey Bagot in *Too True to be Good* (1931) will
say, 'I must preach no matter how late the hour and how short the day,
no matter whether I have nothing to say'. *Pygmalion*, however, takes the
investigation and deconstruction of language usage as its subject matter.

Higgins' experiment is to demonstrate that language is the 'gulf that
separates class from class and soul from soul'; that flower girl and duchess
are remarkably similar were it not for their language usage. Eliza is to be
absorbed into the bosom of the snobbish Eynsford-Hills while her dustman

father easily transforms himself into an ethics lecturer. Characters notice their own prowess and comment on each other's speech modes even more openly than usual. So Higgins says of Doolittle:

> this chap has a certain natural gift of rhetoric. Observe the rhythm of his native woodnotes wild. 'I'm willing to tell you: I'm wanting to tell you: I'm waiting to tell you.' Sentimental rhetoric.
>
> (Act II)

The audience is invited to admire and enjoy but to keep its critical faculties alert.

Setting the opening of *Pygmalion* in Covent Garden at night in the rain, allows Shaw to bring together an extraordinary social mix. Opera House audience and market traders still at work, wearers of rags and of evening dress, whether gathered for business or pleasure need to shelter. The verbal texture is even more variegated: in the opening exchanges we pick up the cockney liveliness of the flower girl, Eliza, the gauche propriety of Freddy, the urbanity of Pickering, the bad-tempered snobbery of Violet and the brusque forthrightness of Higgins – it is less an operatic than a music hall variety that allows immediacy of identification of voice and type.

Where Galsworthy sentimentalised the poor or represented them as brutalised, Shaw created the idea of the 'undeserving poor', argumentative non-conformists, 'up agen middle class morality all the time' and gleefully adept at turning a dishonest penny. With forerunners in the Salvation Army scroungers, and a successor in Billy Dunn, the incompetent burglar of *Heartbreak House*, Doolittle, is the quintessential version. He appears in Higgins' study ready to claim a price for his daughter. Mocking current dogma about pauperisation, Shaw has him rebut Pickering's suggestion that he will only make bad use of the five pound note Higgins has given him with:

> not me, Governor, so help me I wont. Dont you be afraid that I'll save it and spare it and live idle on it, There wont be a penny left by Monday: I'll have to go to work same as if I'd never had it. It wont pauperise me, you bet. Just one good spree for myself and the missus, giving pleasure to ourselves and employment to others, and satisfaction to you to think its not been throwed away. You couldnt spend it better.
>
> (Act II)

Having regularly and deliberately refused the conventional ending of a love match between the principal man and the principal woman, Shaw altered the ending of this play to prevent the slippage into the morally and theatrically conventional reading given by Beerbohm Tree in its first production. Tree infiltrated the suggestion of Higgins' love for Eliza by expression and gesture, even turning on his final exit to throw flowers to her. To repudiate such sentimentality, and insist on the comic incompatibility of Higgins and Eliza, Shaw added a sequel when he published the play in 1916, explaining that Eliza married the lovelorn Freddy. He also refused Lehar permission to use the work as the basis of an operetta (1921). Having discovered just before the première of the film version (1938) that a screenwriter had been hired to add a 'sugar sweet ending', he had to let it stand but, in 1939, produced his final version:

MRS HIGGINS:

I'm afraid you've spoilt that girl, Henry. I should be very uneasy about you and her if she were less fond of Colonel Pickering.

HIGGINS:

Pickering! Nonsense: she's going to marry Freddy. Ha, ha! Freddy! Freddy! Ha ha ha ha ha!!!! (*He roars with laughter as the play ends.*)[22]

And yet his practice of using and subsequently undermining theatrical conventions gives a hostage to fortune in that it can be subverted by an actor, as determined as Tree, who plays to those elements of the convention Shaw has used and feeds the audience's urge to naturalise the text, or, indeed, by one who unintentionally supplies his own more conventional reading of a role. Shaw found it necessary to complain to Barker when he was preparing the role of Frank in *Mrs Warren's Profession*:

Instead of getting boundless amusement out of everything disastrous, you become the man of sorrows at every exhibition of human frailty, and seem to be bitterly reproaching me all through for the flippancy of my dialogue. Two rehearsals more and you will draw tears even in the third act.[23]

And productions of *Saint Joan* have regularly made the most of the climaxes of the early scenes of the play. The suddenly laying hens, the changing of the wind, Joan rallying the troops with sword raised high, might well be there to trap the audience into the political debate in Scene iv, but they are also gifts to the romatically minded director.

Subverting convention, and some Shavian limitations

In the face of the success of *Arms and the Man*, William Archer had commented on the bloodlessness of Shaw's representation of human relationship, writing:

> it is one thing to argue that the exultations and agonies of
> love are apt to be morbid, factitious, deliberately exaggerated
> and overwrought, and quite another to represent life as if
> these exultations and agonies had no existence whatever.[24]

Where sexual feeling does appear in a Shaw play it is commonly exposed as self-deceivingly romanticised (Sergius, Freddy Eynsford-Hill, Ellie Dunn), self-interestedly vain (Hector Hushabye) or demonstrably driven by a Darwinian urge to reproduction (Ann and Tanner). The love story anticipated in the title *Caesar and Cleopatra* is thwarted by its Cleopatra being represented as in early adolescence and its Caesar as immune to her precocious charms and, in many subsequent plays, one at least of a possible pair resists sexual attraction. The characters in whom Shaw is most interested are either fundamentally impervious because emotionally self-sufficient, like Caesar and Higgins, or, like Eliza finding her true voice and using it to protest, are passionately alert not to another person but to a newly achieved sense of self. John Tanner's declaration that 'moral passion is the only real passion' holds good for Shaw.

For all the sprightliness of Shaw's resistance of convention there is weight in Archer's criticism because, at times, he does gesture towards other sorts of depth and then his thought and expression, so sinewy in argument and polemic, seems 'emotionally inadequate'.[25] The vapidity of Joan's recantation speech is a notorious example: the actress must make what she can of the romatic pathos of 'the larks in the sunshine, the young lambs crying through the healthy frost', and, in revivals, directors have been tempted to supply the need with swelling background music.[26] Having established the ironic texture so effectively in *Major Barbara*, for example, he seems to want the play to end with new hope. His stage direction '*she is transfigured*', asks the actress to give meaning to the obfuscating speech. This leaves the audience puzzled as to the tone of the final moments of the play, an impression compounded by the bathos of Barbara's evocation of her 'dear little Dolly boy' in her final line. In other words, although he found Wilde's plays lacking in feeling and Elizabeth Robins inadequate 'in sympathetic parts where wisdom of heart and sense of identity and common cause with others' was wanted,[27] his own writing is blank in just such areas. He never quite moves on to the deeper plane he seems to suggest is there. Similarly, his very mockery of convention, as in the denial of sexual relationship between Caesar and Cleopatra, can be read as avoidance. Horror is not encountered and emotional suffering is short-lived in Shaw's universe. Feelings of loss that might accompany bereavement are invariably turned aside, as when we meet the newly buoyant widow of Dubedat.

Scenes of close personal encounter which are not ironic or of a teacher-pupil kind prove embarrassing. The final stage direction of *Candida*, '*but they do not know the secret in the poet's heart*', applies to audience as well as characters and, in representing the love between Vivie Warren and Frank, Shaw not only steers away from the dilemma of the incest relationship that lurks harrowingly behind Ibsen's *Ghosts*, but has them engage in little boy/little girl slush without the parodic edge that would place the exchanges as confidently satiric. The deeper pains and joys of relationship are not experienced although such sequences gesture towards them. When his lovers stop sparring with each other, they have nowhere to go; there is little of the silence that accompanies wonder or mutual recognition, no equivalent, for example, of the still moment between Beatrice and Benedick which follows Benedick's suddenly serious question, 'Think you in your heart the Count Claudio hath wronged Hero?' (*Much Ado About Nothing*). There is genuine passion in the expression and exchange of ideas and what Shaw named 'the search for enlightenment',[28] but we don't encounter 'the foul rag and bone shop of the heart' in Shaw's writing, as we do, for example, in the last act of O'Neill's *Long Day's Journey Into Night*.

Heartbreak House (1921)

Shaw's subtitling his wartime play, *Heartbreak House*, 'A Fantasia in the Russian Manner on English Themes' has proved something of a red herring, leading critics to debate the play's likeness or unlikeness to Chekhov.[29] Very different from anything Chekhov wrote, the play is more usefully seen as Shaw's assimilation of his encounter with Chekhov's drama than as a failed attempt at imitation. Shocked when the audience hissed the Stage Society production of *The Cherry Orchard*, which he thought an exquisite play, Shaw incorporated certain elements into his first country-house play, *Misalliance*. The daughter, Hypatia, expostulates in Chekhovian pastiche:

If you all sat in silence, as if you were waiting for something
to happen, then there would be hope even if nothing did
happen. But this eternal cackle, cackle, cackle about things
in general is only fit for old, old, OLD people. I suppose
it means something to them: theyve had their fling. All I
listen for is some sign of it ending in something; but just
when it seems to be coming to a point, Johnny or papa
just starts another hare; and it all begins over again; and I
realise that it's never going to lead anywhere and never going
to stop.

(Act I)

The Polish aviator, Lina Szczepanowska, has a comparable role in the plot
to Hilde Wangel, as repeated references to Ibsen's *Master Builder* make
clear, but her prowess in juggling and acrobatics also link her to the strange
foreign governess in *The Cherry Orchard*. *Heartbreak House* is much more
thoroughly sprung off it. The quasi-allegorical status of the house and
orchard in Chekhov's play, and the emphasis on group rather than individual action, gave Shaw the basis and shape of his condition-of-England
play through which he attempted to encounter the forces and the drift
that had led the nation into the disastrous First World War.

The first two acts share the same set, although the set has various acting
areas, including some potent ones off-stage. Its allegorical potential is
declared both in its strange appearance (a room built to resemble the after
part of an old fashioned high-pooped ship) and in the dialogue which
increasingly associates the House with 'the ship of state' and 'this soul's
prison we call England'. But the play is not entirely an indictment, since
the inventiveness and sheer fun of much of the action lead the audience
to watch the characters and their bizarre interactions with fascination.
One contemporary reviewer caught the tone when he described 'the
inmates' of the House as having 'a butterfly air', but added that 'their
sentimentality grows around a pretty hard core of selfish indulgence' as
they engage in 'a riot of talkative flirtation'.[30] As Ellie Dunn, the incomer,
charmed as well as infuriated by the life and chaos in the house, puts it,
'this silly house, this strangely happy house, this agonizing house, this
house without foundations' (Act III). The brief last act moves through the
glass doors to the garden and, for all the Preface to the play insists on its
importance, consciousness of the war figures only in the closing moments
of the play when first its language becomes suffused with images of
torpedoes, wrecks and destruction, and then a dull distant explosion is
heard and instructions come that lights must be extinguished. Disobeying,
the characters let the lights blaze out as they wait for destruction to engulf
them.

The action turns on Hesione's determination that her young friend,

Ellie, shall not sacrifice herself to the marriage with the Philistine industri-
alist, Mangan, that her weak father, Mazzini Dunn, has engineered. Initially
innocent, Ellie's eyes are opened by a succession of unmaskings: neither
the romantic Hector nor the practical Mangan is what he had appeared.
Captain Shotover, Hesione's father and owner of the house, is evidently
in the line of Shavian characters that includes Caesar, Tanner, Larry Doyle
and Undershaft, lucid thinkers all, who cut through illusion and self-
deception. But in this play he is more markedly eccentric than usual,
admits to being on the edge of his dotage and, quite unlike his famously
teetotal creator, gains his inspiration, his 'seventh degree of concentration'
from copious draughts of rum. Although his self-presentation as a dreaming
drunkard is not the whole story, he is certainly not the rock of wisdom
Ellie imagined him to be. His daughters – Ariadne, returned home after
twenty-three years, and Hesione, permanently ensconced there – seeming
so different at first, prove to be demonstrably from the same stable. Differently styled, each dyes her hair. One may have rejected the other's bohemian lifestyle but they are equally outspoken and self-centred. Shaw gleefully
puts into the mouth of the initially more sympathetic Hesione such
outrageous remarks as her complaint to Shotover, 'living at the rate we
do, you cannot afford life-saving inventions. Cant you think of something
that will murder half Europe at one bang?'

The play addresses serious matters of betrayal, self-deception, misplaced
idealism, false government, and the potential slaughter of millions but does
so through an action as absurd as anything in the Tomfooleries, and it
moves with comparable speed. Shotover, an inventor, reputed to have sold
himself to the Devil in Zanzibar, insists on taking Ellie for the daughter
of his one-time boatswain, the pirate, Billie Dunn, despite her disclaimers,
denouncing the real father, the weak Mazzini Dunn, as an impostor. The
burglar, caught climbing on the roof, of course, proves to be the ex-pirate.

It is a strange, wild play with a wonderful collection of character parts
and there is no appropriate ending because there is no real plot. Shaw's
coup de théâtre brings the war suddenly on to the stage in a disconcerting
mixture of arbitrary event and poetic justice. Mangan and the Burglar are
blown up, even as they shelter; the clergyman's house, too, is destroyed
but, although Hesione and her household turn on all the lights and wildly
invite destruction from the skies, they survive. Capital, self-serving and
religion vanish together, leaving the inhabitants of Heartbreak House
rejoicing in the 'glorious experience' and the apocalyptic potential of
another zeppelin raid.

Shaw's plays declare with John Tanner that 'moral passion is the only
real passion' and that the theatre is a viable locus for its exploration. When
all is said, it is the lively intelligence reverberating through this body of
plays and the capacity to write social indignation into compelling theatrical
form that, despite the limitations, stakes Shaw's claim to recognition as a

major dramatist, a claim acknowledged by contemporaries as distinct as Brecht, Pirandello and O'Neill. The vitality of Shaw's plays drew a succession of writers to the drama of ideas but the fullest and most sustained recognition came from Sean O'Casey. As Shaw is different from Chekhov so O'Casey is different from Shaw, but the dialectic, the comic energy and the fundamental seriousness of Shaw recur in O'Casey's drama. Noting Shaw's abhorrence of poverty and the frequent assumption that it was inevitable, his rejection of sexual and social stereotyping, and his championing of education and freedom of belief, O'Casey declared: 'Shaw never wrote a tragedy, yet his comedy and his wit were a rushing mighty wind that swept through the theatre, tearing a mantle of false grandeur from the thousand trivialities that strutted on its stage.'[31]

Notes

1. Quoted, R. Williams, *Drama from Ibsen to Eliot* (1964), p. 155.
2. G. B. Shaw, Preface, *Three Plays for Puritans* (1901), p. xxxiv; Yeats's letter to Shaw (1904), reproduced in T. F. Evans, ed., *Shaw: The Critical Heritage* (1976), pp. 122–4.
3. Shaw to Archer in D. Lawrence, ed., *Collected Letters, 1874–97* (New York, 1965), p. 403. See, G. Bullough, 'Literary Relations of Shaw's Mrs Warren', *Philological Quarterly*, 41 (January 1962), pp. 339–58, and, for a full discussion of the theatrical context, M. Meisel, *Shaw and the Nineteenth Century Theatre* (Princeton, NJ, 1968).
4. *The Quintessence of Ibsenism* (revised edn., 1913), in Bernard Shaw, *The Major Critical Essays* (1986), p. 147.
5. Shaw (12.1.1895) in *Plays and Players* (1952), p. 2; Brecht, *Ovation für Shaw* (1926), in J. Willett, ed., *Brecht on Theatre* (1964), pp. 8–13.
6. *The Times* (2.11.1904).
7. See, for example, E. A. Baughan in the *Daily News* (2.11.1904) and a famous reproof from Tolstoi, 'you are not sufficiently serious', quoted, N. Grene, *Shaw, A. Critical View* (1984), p. 160. This was Archer's constant criticism and became Beatrice Webb's, for example, 'Diary' (2.12.1905), Evans, ed., *Shaw: Critical Heritage*, pp. 149–50.
8. Brecht, in Willett, *Brecht on Theatre*, p. 12; Shaw to Florence Farr, 28.1.1892, in C. Bax ed., *Florence Farr, Bernard Shaw, W. B. Yeats: Letters* (1946), p. 7.
9. W. Archer, *Theatrical World, 1894* (1895), p. 117.
10. Captain Shotover is frequently so made up, too (cf. Criterion Theatre production, London 1989), although Shaw directed 'Ibsen whiskers', for him.
11. Introduction, Brieux, *Three Plays*, trans. Charlotte Shaw (1911), p. xvii.
12. C. E. Montague, *Dramatic Values* (1911), p. 81.
13. W. D. Howells, *Harper's*, 131 (March 1916), pp. 634–7, in B. Murphy, ed., *A Realist in the American Theatre* (Athens OH, 1993), p. 181.
14. For outrage at blasphemy etc. see, for example, *Pall Mall Gazette, Morning Post* (29.11.1905); Grein, Beerbohm, in Evans, ed., *Shaw: Critical Heritage*, pp. 149, 157.
15. Shaw quoted Beatrice Webb, in Evans, ed., *Shaw: Critical Heritage*, p. 148.
16. Lillah McCarthy, quoted, J. Woodfield, *English Theatre in Transition, 1881–1914*

(Beckenham, 1984), p. 79; information on Shaw's theatre practice in the paragraph from B. Dukore, *Bernard Shaw Director* (1971), pp. 37–8.

17. Shaw, quoted Grene, *Shaw, A Critical View,* p. 153.
18. September, 1923; February, 1924, letters to Laurence Langner in J. Lyman, ed., *Perspectives on Plays* (1976), pp. 203, 204.
19. May 1923, quoted, A. Kennedy, *Six Dramatists in Search of a Language* (Cambridge, 1975), p. 40.
20. Shaw on rhetoric, *Spectator,* 26.2.1910, quoted, Denis Kennedy, *Granville Barker and the Dream of Theatre* (Cambridge, 1985) p. 71; on McCarthy, quoted, Jan Macdonald, *The New Drama* (1986), p. 29.
21. On operatic scoring and Shaw's conscious use of it see Meisel, *Shaw and the Nineteenth Century Theatre,* Chapter 4.
22. The story is told in M. Holroyd, *Bernard Shaw, II: 1898–1918 The Pursuit of Power,* 4 vols, pp. 332–3.
23. Shaw to Barker, 31.12.01, in C. B. Purdom, ed., *The Letters of George Bernard Shaw to Granville Barker* (New York, 1957), p. 10.
24. W. Archer, *Theatrical World, 1894,* p. 116.
25. The phrase is Williams's in *Ibsen to Eliot,* p. 169.
26. An aberration in the otherwise impressive Strand Theatre production with Imogen Stubbs as Joan, London 1994.
27. G. B. Shaw, *Our Theatres in the Nineties,* 3 vols. Vol. III, p. 127.
28. Shaw, 1927, quoted, Meisel, *Shaw and the Nineteenth Century Theatre,* p. 435.
29. Discussed perceptively by Grene, *Shaw: A Critical View,* pp. 115–17.
30. See Evans, ed., *Shaw: Critical Heritage,* p. 237.
31. S. O'Casey *The Green Crow* (1957), p. 65.

Chapter 7

Literary Drama: Henry James, W. B. Yeats and T. S. Eliot

What would you think of any other artist – the painter or the novelist – whose governing forces should be dinner and the suburban trains? (James, *The Tragic Muse*, Chapter 4)

T. S. Eliot's Harvard lecture on poetry and drama includes the enigmatic statement about Yeats that 'it was only in his last play *Purgatory* that he solved his problem of speech in verse, and laid all his successors under obligation to him'. Although this observation is not developed, the rest of the lecture, given over to analysis of the problems and failures of his own attempts at poetic drama, is suggestive. His recognition that verse 'must justify itself dramatically, and not be merely fine poetry shaped into dramatic form',[1] defined the task even while acknowledging previous failure – failure which included his own seemingly ground-breaking play *Murder in the Cathedral*.

Eliot's clear-sighted analysis of his own work reflected back on the attempts of the previous hundred or so years in which, one after another, major and minor poets had tried their hand at verse drama: Wordsworth (*The Borderers*), Keats (*Otho the Great*) and Shelley (the more considerable but still essentially unplayable *The Cenci*) early in the century, followed later by Arnold (*Merope*), Browning (*A Blot on the 'Scutcheon*), Tennyson (*Becket*) and Swinburne (*Locrine*). Although Eliot, unlike these forerunners, had consciously resisted literary pastiche – attempts to reproduce Shakespeare's verse form, images and turns of phrase – he pointed out, with devastating self-recognition, that *Murder in the Cathedral* still shared with them the special pleading of a mythological or remote historical setting:

> far enough away from the present for the characters not to need to be recognisable as human beings, and therefore for them to be licensed to talk in verse. Picturesque period costume renders verse much more acceptable. Furthermore, my play was to be produced for a rather special kind of audience – an audience of those serious people who go to 'festivals' and expect to have to put up with poetry.
>
> ('Poetry and Drama', 1950, p. 72)

To 'justify itself dramatically' a verse play must find an equivalent of the rich linguistic texture of Elizabethan drama, but must also offer a contemporary equivalent of Elizabethan immediacy of action if it is to quicken the attention of the audience not lull it, as the dramatic efforts of the nineteenth-century poets had done.

The years between 1890 and the outbreak of the Second World War are remarkable for the persistence with which established poets and novelists attempted to write plays. Henry James, Yeats and Eliot stand out. The third of the three great poets of the period, W. H. Auden, made a brief assault for political ends, first single-handed and then in collaboration with Christopher Isherwood. Lesser poets such as Stephen Phillips, James Elroy Flecker, John Drinkwater and Gordon Bottomley had their moments of acclaim with various versions of historical verse drama. D. H. Lawrence's experimentation with drama was of a rather different kind. While he was still finding his literary form, he demonstrated a notable openness to the possibilities of using language within the stage space. The plays completed once he had established himself as a novelist, *Touch and Go* or *David*, are much less interesting than those written when he was still searching for appropriate means of articulating his own experience. Observing the practice of other dramatists, he discovered something of what he wanted in Synge, whose *Riders to the Sea* he found in 1911 to be 'about the genuinest bit of dramatic tragedy, English, since Shakespeare'.[2]

Lawrence's recognition of Synge's achievement is, in itself, telling. The writers who are the subject of this chapter found little to admire in the contemporary avant-garde theatre. Indeed, most pitted their effort as much against Ibsen and his realist followers as against the commercial theatre. All saw themselves as reformers – bringing their evident and developed capacities as poets or novelists to a different and, perhaps to them, less necessary if potentially more popular medium. That mind and will dominated the effort is apparent not just in the plays written but in the theoretical writing about theatre that often accompanied the effort.

The inspiration, as well as the trap as Eliot perceived, was Shakespeare. Not only the greatest English dramatist, he was also the greatest poet, as demonstrated by the sonnets and narrative poems as well as the dramatic verse. But, which was equally challenging, this complex body of plays had commanded a popular audience in its own day and, self-evidently, continued to do so. Henry James was, perhaps, the most exercised by the *duty* of a serious writer to attempt to redeem such a past by trying his hand at drama and, by example, encouraging other creative literary minds to do so too.

Henry James and the idea of theatre

The notion that drama had once been and could be again an essential part of civilisation was the core of James's theatre criticism in the twenty years from 1872 and it was the impetus for his own dramatic activity in the 1890s. His sense of the decadence of English-speaking theatre, whose shallow acting reflected the poverty of its plays, was informed by the impression that by contrast:

> the theatre is an essential part of French civilization, in regard
> to which it keeps up a lively process of action and reaction.
> It is not a mere amusement, as it is in other countries; it is
> an interest, an institution, connected through a dozen open
> doors with literature, art and society.[3]

The disciplined acting of the Comédie française with its controlled inflections and studied gesture had impressed him deeply and a conversation with the actor Constant Coquelin in 1877 left him 'agitated with what it said to me that I might do – what I ought to attempt'.[4] That 'ought' with its implication of a willed rather than a necessary activity is significant.

While the public humiliation of the failure of James's play, *Guy Domville* in 1895 was surely terrible, the language in which James recorded the experience in his letters and notebooks: the 'ineffectual effort', 'the long vain study', 'long tribulation' – 'long tragic chapter', 'wasted piety and passion' – suggests that rather more had been at stake than the financial success he had hoped for when, after the failure of his novels *The Bostonians* and *The Princess Casamassima*, he agreed in 1890 to dramatise *The American*. With the play still in rehearsal he confided to Elizabeth Robins his consciousness of the split between the written text and its performance, writing, 'I may have been meant for the Drama – God Knows – but I certainly wasn't meant for the Theatre'.[5]

The theatre auditorium rather than the stage itself with its glaring footlights would seem to have been the ideal location for James. As a member of the audience, one is a legitimate observer and, because of the social function of theatre as a place for meeting and display, a legitimate observer of the audience as well as of the stage. Recurrently in nineteenth-century fiction, from Jane Austen through to the opening of Edith Wharton's *The Age of Innocence*, the opera glass is turned on the auditorium, glances or frank stares are exchanged between stalls and box or box and circle. The scrutiny of James's Hyacinth Robinson from the box of the Princess Casamassima at the performance of the melodrama, *The Pearl of Paraguay* is one of the more adroitly managed of such scenes. But, like

Eliot half a century later, he was both fascinated and repelled by the idea of performance.

The sensory appeal of theatre is registered in the statement in James's first article on theatre that:

> An acted play is a novel intensified; it realises what the novel
> suggests and by paying a liberal tribute to the senses,
> anticipates your possible complaint that your entertainment
> is of the meagre sort styled 'intellectual'. (1872)

The immediacy of performance offered to supply the very things his prose fiction lacked, but his Notebook discussion of 'the horrid theatre trade' (May, 1893) is characterised by images of battle and assault. 'Vulgar' is his recurrent adjective for the theatre, whereas fiction for all it is 'pale' is also 'sacred' and there is a constant sense of hostility to the production side of theatre and to his prospective public. He wrote of 'the practical odiousness of staging', his 'base theatrical errand', 'the huge foot of the public', 'the vulgarest of muses'. How far the despising of the audience was real and how far it stemmed from fearful anticipation of the public rejection he eventually faced, cannot be known, but the evident defensiveness before what he believed to be the demands of a public whose judgement he resented, is a felt weakness in the drama.

James's theory of the interactive nature of the Parisian stage, the process of 'action and reaction' between French drama and culture, deceived him into believing he could prevail by improving or perfecting the well-made play formula that had dominated the European stage for thirty years and more. Although as early as 1872 he criticised the 'meagreness of material' of the French drama, in 1875 the rigidity of form was 'a problem in ingenuity and a problem of the most interesting kind' and the highest ideal of success was to work 'beneath a few grave, rigid laws'.

As he settled to dramatise *Daisy Miller* in 1881, James declared that he had mastered the French stage and that this was 'the light by which one must work'. That the mastery was by no means liberating is evident from what he did when working by its light. Plot takes over. Developing the fleeting suggestion in the novella of a previous liaison for his narrator, Giles Winterbourne, James made the minor figure, the mysterious Russian widow, Madame de Katkoff, central to the plot of the play. The Millers' courier Eugenio, an out-and-out villain, is able because of a letter he possesses, to blackmail Katkoff into pretending affection for Winterbourne – a cold-blooded ploy to distract Winterbourne from Daisy who loves him, thus pushing her into marriage with Eugenio's partner in crime, the adventurer Giovanelli. Daisy, having ridden with Giovanelli to the Colosseum by moonlight because Winterbourne has cancelled an appointment, catches a fever and, rebuffed again by Winterbourne rushes out into the cold night. Overcome with remorse, Katkoff confesses all, Winter-bourne recognising the true state of his affections, rushes off in his turn and, having found Daisy as she is fainting away for probably the last time, carries her on stage and into the resuscitating warmth of a happy ending. The formulaic situation and characterisation subverts the suggestive force of the original story. The woman with a past, the villain, the fortunate recovery of the seemingly lost heroine; the mercenary motives, the heroic self-denial and all the mechanical turns of the plot would have been instantly recognisable by the contemporary audience. Similarly, when James adapted *The American*, he made the family's dark secret the core of the action; Newman became a comic hero whose catch phrase, 'that's what I want to see', punctuated the play which, with all difficulties fortunately resolved, culminated in the union of Newman and Madame de Cintré.

Although James was passionately concerend to re-establish the cultural centrality of theatre, the real struggle was being engaged simultaneously elsewhere by writers who realised that it was not a matter of discovering some prime material and style with which to invigorate the creaking French model, but of developing a new and necessary form for the ideas and experiences they pressingly wanted to explore. The real dramatic innovators who did (to the degree possible in such a complex and various period) reclaim the theatre as a serious art form – first Ibsen and Strindberg, then Shaw, Chekhov and Synge – trusted or challenged their audiences to catch up. They cut their losses so far as commercial theatre went and, where possible, worked with avant-garde production companies. While the initial hostility to their works was more extreme than anything met by *Guy Domville*, so was the enthusiasm. The sense of a new and telling thing, moreover, quickly came to outweigh the hostility as a new audience identified itself. James, by contrast, was working with a defunct model. In fiction, he would have recognised this.

James was driven to reappraisal of his assumptions by the failure of his play but also by his encounter with the work of Ibsen which coincided with it. From a position of initial hostility he found, as he returned fascinated, that Ibsen's plays threatened his certainty of the need for 'ingen-uity' and the 'few grave, rigid laws' of the contemporary French drama. After Elizabeth Robins' production of *Hedda Gabler* in 1891, he perceived that Ibsen had presented, 'that supposedly undramatic thing, the portrait not of an action but of a condition' with a central character who was 'various and sinuous . . . complicated and natural; she suffers, she struggles, she is human and by that fact exposed to a dozen interpretations'. In 1893, he was struck by 'the intensity and vividness' of the 'strangely inscrutable art' of *The Master Builder*; he persuaded Heinemann to let him see the translation of 'the ineffable play', *Little Eyolf*, at proof stage and, by 1897, when his own first venture into the theatre had been abandoned wrote,

'Ibsen strikes me as an extraordinary curiosity and every time he sounds his note the miracle of my perception is renewed'.

In 1908, thirteen years after the failure of *Guy Domville* and James's retreat from theatre, he wrote *The High Bid* in response to an appeal by the actor Johnston Forbes-Robertson. 'The perfidious Ellen Terry'[6] never had produced the one-act play, *Summersoft*, she asked James to write for her after the failure of *Guy Domville* but, having reworked it as the short story, *Covering End*, James now developed it into a three-act play which offers much sharper comedy than his earlier work and is an altogether more viable piece. While it is not exactly a neglected masterpiece – it being too late for James to work interactively with an avant-garde company – other models have evidently been absorbed and, in the changed circumstances resulting from the Court and Stage Society ventures, James, no longer attempting single-handed reform, demonstrates new confidence in both theatre and audience.

The principal characters of *The High Bid* are Captain Yule, one of Nature's gentlemen, a radical reformer who has just inherited a country house; Mrs Gracedew, a rich American connoisseur who is collecting English *objets d'art* to furnish the replica mansion she is building in the United States; and Prodmore, a vulgar capitalist to whom the estate is mortgaged, who proposes to release Yule from his debts on condition he marries Prodmore's daughter and, renouncing his radicalism, becomes a Tory MP. The force of this triangular confrontation is that the set of ideas and associated language of each are, while apparent to the audience, scarcely comprehensible between the characters. Their fundamental assumptions and world-views are so different that they recurrently talk past each other, find their expectations thwarted and are left staring in incomprehension while the action moves on. The audience is thereby brought into interesting dramatic relationship with the stage action as it was not in *Daisy Miller* where all was numbingly clearly spelt out.

The formulaic expository monologue by Chivers, the old retainer, that opened the one-act *Summersoft* is replaced in the later play by a more surprising conversation between the old retainer and an off-stage American voice. While the voice may gush, it is apparent once it is on-stage, that its owner, Mrs Gracedew, is knowledgeable and that, with a certain amount of self-parody, she can enjoy her own accuracy and enthusiasm to inform. She is, as she puts it, 'death on taste', which she teaches back at Missoura Top, but she also demonstrates an intensity of feeling for the potential loss of the great house to tasteless new money and evidently really is informed about the *objets* she admires. One game James plays with his audience is that it must come to respect the noisy American tourist and see her, for all her transatlantic wealth, as a repository of values the English characters have lost.

Character is evidently now of more interest than the machinations of plot. There is a Shavian willingness to allow the opposing side its say. In performance, to James's chagrin, the audience regularly applauded not Mrs Gracedew's argument for saving the old house but the social passion of Captain Yule's opposing view:

> I see something else in the world than the beauty of old show-houses and the glory of old show-families. There are thousands of people in England who can show no houses at all, and (*with the emphasis of sincerity.*) I don't feel it utterly shameful to share their fate.
>
> (Act III)

The lively dialectic freed the piece of didacticism.

James's repartee is less glittering than that of his 1890s rival, Wilde, but had learned from Wilde the comic power of subversive consciousness of the devices used. When, in Act II, Captain Yule having confided in Mrs Gracedew, the young *ingénue* proposes to do so too, her response is, 'you too? why it is good we came over', and while Chivers is a standard theatrical old retainer, the other characters disconcertingly recognise this in their response to him. Mrs Gracedew, delightedly tells him, 'you're the best I've struck yet, and I wish I could have you packed – put up in paper and bran – as I shall have my old pot there', while Yule's initial encounter with the family servant he has inherited is as surreal as anything in James's fiction:

YULE:
    I mean to whom do you beautifully belong?
CHIVERS (*who has really to think it over*):
    If you could really just tell me, sir! I seem quite to waste away – for someone to taken an order of.
YULE (*looking at him with compassion*):
    Who pays your wages?
CHIVERS (*very simply*):
    No one at all, sir.
YULE (*taking from his waistcoat pocket a gold coin, which he places with a little sharp click on a table near at hand*):
    Then there's a sovereign. (*Then having turned resignedly away*) And I haven't many.
CHIVERS (*Leaving the money on the table*):
    Ah then, shouldn't it stay in the family?
YULE (*wheeling round, struck by the figure he makes in this offer*):
    I think it does, I think it does.

(Act I)

James's gratified assessment that the play would 'remain and revive'[7] did not overstate the case. Although by no means as complex, the demand on audience attention to meaning and motive is now at least comparable with that of James's fiction. If not the work that would single-handedly redeem the past, it was arguably a more convincing play than any produced by the poets who subsequently tried their hands at drama.

The language of realism

Unlike James, W. B. Yeats began with a strongly held belief in the responsiveness of his Irish audience and a much fuller sense of European experiment and innovation in drama. He, too, wanted to restore the cultural centrality of the theatre but argued that this would only be achieved through the restoration of 'beautiful and vivid language'.[8] He despised the mechanical plots and glittering vacuity of the French as well as the English commercial theatre as much as ever Shaw did, and recognised the revolutionary impact of Ibsen but, though acknowledging that their enemies were the same, he resisted drama that seemed to attach itself insistently to middle-class life and to model its dialogue on everyday speech. After the Achurch-Charrington *Doll's House* he wrote that he could not 'admire dialogue so close to modern educated speech that music and style were impossible'.[9] Such works seemed to be draining away the power theatre once had.

Yeats's whole dramatic endeavour, sustained throughout his writing life, was given to exploring ways in which imagination might be restored to a theatre dominated by imitation. As he wrote:

> Our unimaginative arts are content to set a piece of the
> world as we know it in a place by itself, to put their
> photographs as it were in a plush or plain frame, but the arts
> which interest me, while seeming to separate from the world
> and use a group of figures, images, symbols, enable us to
> pass for a few moments into a deep of the mind that has
> hitherto been too subtle for our habitation.[10]

Not only did the imitation of everyday life limit the drama's expressive possibilities, it also meant the lamentable loss of its mythical dimension.

There is force in Yeats's observations. In their rejection of the linguistic artifice of melodrama and 1890s comedy the New Dramatists promoted the imitative fallacy. In the attempt to reflect behaviour and speech realistically and to make the linguistic medium seem transparent, they avoided song and gesture but also rhetorical devices: imagery, rhythm, evident repetition, stychomythia and all the other patterned possibilities of language that had helped create the complexity as well as the bravura effects of dramatic dialogue in the past. Although they developed some enabling strategies to allow them to vary and intensify the tone of their dialogue, if language did take off it was invariably qualified by the characters' own self-consciousness: 'Shall we finish this conversation in prose?' says Trebell in Barker's *Waste*, breaking into his own passionate flow, the soaring words undercut by the character before the audience can question their effusion. Or it was qualified by context: drunkenness, public speeches, drug addiction, nervous breakdown, madness or shock briefly eased a more rhythmic and highly charged language into realist plays.

Yeats argued that the impoverishment of dramatic dialogue was the logical effect of the attempt at a realistic imitation of life since 'in moments of great intensity, we gaze silently into the fireplace'. The emotion must 'be inferred from some commonplace sentence or gesture as we infer it in ordinary life'.[11] The final exchange of Barker's *The Voysey Inheritance* illustrates Yeats's point:

ALICE:
      I shall be foolishly proud of you.
EDWARD:
      It's good to be praised sometimes . . . by you.
ALICE:
      My heart praises you. Goodnight.
EDWARD:
        Goodnight.
      (*She kisses his forehead. But he puts up his face like a child,
      so she bends down and for the first time their lips meet. Then
      she steps back from him, adding happily, with perhaps a touch
      of shyness.*)
ALICE:
      Til tomorrow.
EDWARD (*echoing in gratitude the hope and promise in her voice*):
      Til tomorrow.
      (*She leaves him to sit there by the table for a few minutes
      longer, looking into his future, streaked as it will be with
      trouble, joy, etc.*)

                                                          (Act V)

While Barker clearly had an eye on the reader, these directions also ask the actor to convey what is not in the words. Subsequently the cinema would supplement realistic language with technical effect: the close-up of tearful or shining eyes; the fading or swelling of the musical score. Here, gesture, bearing, inflection must do the work.

The case needs qualifying. Shaw developed his own style, as did Synge and O'Casey, to particularly fruitful effect. While we may have the illusion that Ibsen's characters use everyday language, in fact, as recent critics have demonstrated, repetition, ironic echo and the use of key images, make their dialogue more evocative and more concentrated with meaning than a comparable stretch of real speech would be. The plays of the great realists have their own dramatic texture which leads audiences to encounter desire and frustration; to apprehend areas of feeling which otherwise defy definition, and to recognise universal experience within specific action. Silence, moreover, as Yeats didn't quite perceive, was used potently by writers as diverse as Synge and Lawrence, O'Casey and Corrie. But it is true that none of the other early twentieth-century English writers approached Ibsen's structured patterns of dramatic imagery, patterns that were, indeed, usually muffled in contemporary translations.[12]

W. B. Yeats and 'the deep of the mind'

Yeats's assault on theatre, unlike that of the other literary dramatists, involved years of practical experience. The driving force behind the founding of the Irish Players and, effectively, the policy director of the Abbey Theatre in its first two decades, he understood that performance made the fundamental difference between a dramatic script and other literary modes. He seized on new experiments in staging in his search for alternatives to the realist theatre which seemed to him a false growth. He argued for drama that would 'work by suggestion not by direct statement, a complexity of rhythm, colour, gesture'. It would not be 'space pervading like the intellect, but a memory and a prophecy'. Its energies would 'ally art to decoration and the dance'.[13] Where James saw that staging could compel audience attention and relied on the living presence of actors to intensify his finished text, Yeats conceived stage image and movement within the stage space at the same time as the words.

His idea of a holistic theatre, already quickened by the experience of French symbolist productions at the Théâtre de l'Oeuvre and by the text of Wilde's *Salomé* in the 1890s,[14] which, in turn, had drawn on the symbolism of Maeterlinck and the sensuousness of Paul Fort's short-lived Théâtre d'Art, gained further impetus with Gordon Craig's productions for the Purcell Operatic Society, in the first years of the new century. Craig, he found, had:

> discovered how to decorate a play with severe, beautiful, simple effects of colour, that leave the imagination free to follow all the suggestions of the play. Realistic scenery takes the imagination captive and is at best but landscape painting, but Mr Gordon Craig's scenery is a new and distinct art. It is something that can only exist in the theatre.[15]

Craig's work, revealing ways of escaping the traps of illusionism and stimulating audience imagination through the expressive use of draped curtains, lighting, swathes of richly coloured fabric, seemed to make the desired staging of suggestion, memory, prophecy, viable. Yeats's grateful acceptance of a set of screens and then, between 1909 and 1913, Craig's direct collaboration, led to his 1912 revisions of his early plays, *The Land of Heart's Desire* (1894), *The Countess Cathleen* (1899) and *The Hour Glass* (1903).

The Hour Glass was particularly ripe for such revision, since it already dealt directly with the discountenancing of rational thought by intuition, the proponent of the one being named simply 'Wise Man', of the other, 'Fool': an allegorising that was regularly practised by Yeats and had been stimulated by his encounter with *Everyman*, the newly rediscovered Medieval Morality play, that had been given its first modern production by Poel in 1901. The first version of Yeats's play, indeed, had been subtitled 'A Morality'. In the revised version, the allegorising remained clear-cut but language and form were developed and the characters wore costumes designed by Craig.[16]

The oppositions signified by Wise Man and Fool are simple in both versions: reason is opposed to belief, thought to intuition but, also, the rational speech of Wise Man is opposed to the lyric and gesture through which Fool communicates. Post-Craig, not only is some of the writing in verse but rhythm and imagery have a more evident shaping role in the mood and direction of the action. Word and gesture are more fully interactive: the opposition between the soulless reason of Wise Man and the joyful acceptance of being of Fool is emphasised by the subversive mime with which Fool parodies Wise Man's words and by Wise Man's insistence on translating into blunt language Fool's gnomic utterances and gesticulations.

Wise Man's shift in perception, which is the matter of the play, is signalled early when, recalling his dreams of a spirit world whose existence would abnegate all his thinking and teaching, he speaks with quickened rhythm and heavy use of personification:

Reason is growing dim;
A moment more and Frenzy will beat his drum
And laugh aloud and scream;
And I must dance in the dream.

(p. 303)

Having become truly wise in the final sequence, Wise Man is able to see with Fool's eyes and welcomes death as a joyful recovery of his whole being. Fool's final speech is lyric and gestural:

(*Angel enters holding a casket*)
FOOL:

> O, look what has come from his mouth! O, look what has come from his mouth – the white butterfly! He is dead, and I have taken his soul in my hands; but I know why you open the lid of that golden box. I must give it you. There then (*He puts butterfly in casket*), he has gone through his pains, and you will open the lid in the Garden of Paradise. (*He closes curtain and remains outside it*) He is gone, he is gone, he is gone, but come in, everybody in the world, and look at me.

> I hea⁻ the wind a-blow,
> I hear the grass a-grow,
> And all I know, I know.
> But I will not speak, I will run away.

(pp. 323–4)

The naiveté is appealing but I doubt whether even members of a coterie audience watch with more than passive interest.

Yeats's sense of the way a play might engage the audience's imagination was, in reality, very different from Craig's. Words were of small significance in Craig's theatre. Like the realists, he objected to the star system and the intrusion on to the stage of the personality of the actor but, whereas the realists wanted the actor to be absorbed into the role, to become the character represented for the duration of the play, Craig saw actors as cogs in the machine, impersonal projections on to the stage of the conception of director or designer: they should be masked to expunge personality and, if not actual marionettes, were to move in a formal and a-personal way. Yeats's words, by contrast, were to be potent and his players the core of the play, embodying the words. He was taken by the practical effects of Craig's stage design: not only was it aesthetically pleasing but removing 'the top hamper of the stage, all the hanging ropes and scenes' enabled 'the free play of light,' while decorative effects gave 'the actor a renewed importance' because they did not distract attention.[17]

What Yeats found in Nōh drama, to which he was introduced by Ezra Pound in 1915, was an ancient but, unlike the English Morality drama, a still living form and one remarkably concordant with his own idea of theatre in that its words were chanted, its gesture studied and conventional, its protagonists impersonal, its plots drawn from legend admitting an easy passage between the human and spirit world, and poetry, movement and costume were in complementary relationship. It was, moreover, particularly appealing to Yeats whose own drama had proved too esoteric for the Abbey audiences since, unlike the realist drama, it was an aristocratic form, having 'no need of mob or Press to pay its way'.[18]

Episodes from Irish legend, particularly the Cuchulain story, had been used from the outset by Yeats, the action of the heroic figures often reflected in those of commoners allegorised as fools, wise men, blind men or beggars. In *On Baile's Strand* (1904), Cuchulain slays his son unknowingly at the behest of High King Conchubar. The conflict between the two kings is echoed in that between Fool and Blind Man, and when the maddened Cuchulain vents his grief and fury in an off-stage fight with the waves, Fool recreates the terrifying contest in his description and mimic account of it:

> There, he is down! He is up again. He is going out in the
> deep water. There is a big wave. It has gone over him. I
> cannot see him now. He has killed kings and giants, but the
> waves have mastered him, the waves have mastered him!
>
> (p. 278)

Physical action is brought on to the stage but in the form of dance rather than imitation in Yeats's first four 'Plays for Dancers', written after his encounter with the Nōh. The very stage space is shown to be emphemeral, merely signified by the unfolding and folding of a cloth at the outset and at the conclusion. Properties are symbolic, costumes decorative, rather than realistic. Musicians, detached from the action, play on drum, zither and flute to accompany their singing at the opening and closing of each play and again as an interlude at the mid-point of the action, providing a series of evocative images, that, like images in T'ang poetry, are juxtaposed to rather than direct commentary on the action. Images of trees and wind, drought and flood characterise the first play of the series, *At the Hawk's Well* (1916), as do images of the sea and shore in *The Only Jealousy of Emer* (written, 1916); of clouds filling the valley and wine the cup in *The Dreaming of the Bones* (written, 1917), and of moonbeams and white birds in the last play, *Calvary* (written, 1920) that, disconcertingly, substitutes the Passion for Irish legend. Although Yeats derived this use of song from the Nōh, the effect is comparable to that of the songs in Shakespeare's comedies, most notably of Feste's 'When that I was and a little tiny boy' sung at the close of *Twelfth Night*. The difference lies in the much greater complexity, variety and immediacy of language and action to which the songs are in apposition in the Shakespeare play.

At the Hawk's Well is concerned with the matter of human mortality. It presents the moment when Cuchulain, about to seize on the water of immortality as it momentarily floods the usually dry well, is distracted from his quest by the wild compelling dance of the well's Guardian, and finally abandons the cheating quest for longevity in favour of the different immortality which will follow a lifetime's action and an heroic death. The desolate scene is peopled only by the Guardian of the Well and an Old Man who, watching for the past fifty years, has been lulled to sleep by the dancer on the rare occasions when the water flowed, is lulled again in the course of this play and is finally abandoned to his life-wasting vigil by Cuchulain.

The flow of dialogue into dance, and verbal image into scenic image integrates language and staging in these plays. At times, Yeats fails to trust the surrounding action to create a speaking silence and narrative slows the pace unduly, as when the Old Man, cheated yet again, provides a commentary on the dry well. Elsewhere, the complications of the spirit world, the motives and activities of the Sidhe and the Fand, are confusing. The audience is given little help in distinguishing the three versions of Cuchulain: deceiving simulacrum, spirit and man, in *The Only Jealousy of Emer*. The dance sequences have their own compulsion but otherwise the plays' quickening into life is at variance with Yeats's proclaimed desire for indirect, impersonal action. The sequence in which Emer, Cuchulain's queen, having surrendered her claim to his love to the Sidhe in order to win back his life, watches him wake and, oblivious to her presence and her sacrifice, call for his mistress, is one of the few fully dramatic moments of the play. The audience briefly becomes active: compelled by what has gone before to hear Eithne's triumph and watch the reunion of lovers while acutely conscious of the feelings of the discarded silent wife.

The method proves more problematic when historical figures are introduced into the action. Roman soldiers dancing in *Calvary* are more risible than spirits and legendary queens, and the intermingling of the immediately contemporary political situation in *The Dreaming of the Bones* demonstrates how little these plays really connect with their audiences. A republican fighter on the run in the wake of the Easter Rising, recognising the spirits who lead him to safety as the adulterous lovers Dervorgilla and Dairmuid, whose vengeance on her husband first brought the Normans to Ireland, refuses them the absolution they crave and for which they dance. The need to join the material and spirit worlds reveals Yeats's own uneasiness with the claims made for his chosen form: his insistence that the drama, although concerned with legends and heroes, is not esoteric. Cuchulain, recognising the futility of his desire for immortality; the Old

Man clinging desperately to it; Emer, contending with jealousy, are emblematic figures whose action can briefly quicken attention but whether they really allow the audience access to 'the deeps of the mind' or to a spirit world behind the world of the senses is more questionable.

What then of Yeats's *Purgatory* (1938) so highly praised by Eliot? Consonant with actual time, this late play uses neither music nor dance and has also abandoned the Nōh-derived folding and unfolding of the cloth to signify the stage space. The verse form, which has moved away from both blank verse and the ballad metre that recurs in such other late plays as *Full Moon in March* (1935) or *The Herne's Egg* (1938), is, as Eliot observed, remarkably flexible, credible as conversation although strongly rhythmical and suggestive through its imagery of meanings beyond those demanded by the plot.

Others of Yeats's late plays returned to earlier methods and *fin de siècle* themes. In *The Death of Cuchulain* (written, 1939) these are introduced by a spokesman whose tone veers between wry self-consciousness: 'I wanted a dance because where there are no words there is less to spoil. Emer must dance, there must be severed heads – I am old I belong to mythology – severed heads for her to dance before,' and splenetic attack on the potential audience: 'people who are educating themselves out of the Book Societies and the like, sciolists, pickpockets and opinionated bitches all,' and ends with furious spitting on 'the dancers painted by Degas', their 'short bodices, their stiff stays, their toes whereon they spin like peg-tops, above all upon that chambermaid face' (p. 694). This might be self-parody although the specificity of the commentary suggests that, if so, it is not wholly parody.

There is little of this in *Purgatory*. The action is brief. Two travellers, stop before a burnt-out house. The older tells the younger who, it emerges, is his son, the story of the house and his own part in the disasters that overtook it, including his murder of his debauched father, but interrupts himself to thwart the boy's attempt to steal his money bag which leaves the money scattered on the ground. An image of the dead man appears at a suddenly lighted window of the ruined house and, as the boy recoils in horror, the old man stabs him with the same knife he used to kill his father in the distant past. The light in the window dims; the old man cleans his knife and begins to pick up the money.

The very baldness creates echoes. A past action partly repeats itself but this time the younger generation does not supplant the older. The murder of a son specifically to prevent further begetting and the passing on of pollution carries a distorted echo of Greek tragedy. And while the audience may or may not register that the boy's birth appears to have coincided with the foundation of the Irish Free State, since he says he is sixteen and the play was written in 1938,[19] the kind of language employed and the generalising tendency of the Old Man's final speech, with its vision of recurring violence, does shadow the history of Ireland:

> Hoof beats! Dear God,
> How quickly it returns – beat – beat–!
>
> Her mind cannot hold up that dream.
> Twice a murderer and all for nothing,
> And she must animate that dead night
> Not once but many times!
>   O God,
> Release my mother's soul from its dream!
> Mankind can do no more. Appease
> The misery of the living and the remorse of the dead.
>   (p. 689)

While it is no more possible to claim this as a neglected major work than it is to make such a claim for *The High Bid*, the piece is compelling. The brevity, the compression of the action and the bare image of two tramps on a road work suggestively on audiences' imaginations. The image of down-trodden figures is taken most directly from Maeterlinck although used more robustly than in the work of the Belgian symbolist, but it reaches back to the Dover cliffs scene of *King Lear*, was used by Synge in *The Well of the Saints*, and prepares the way for the double acts of Beckett's Vladimir and Estragon, Hamm and Clov.

The verse drama movement

Like Yeats, T. S. Eliot chafed at the limitations the realist mode imposed and in a famous statement offered his equivalent of the 'deep of the mind', the scarcely articulable area of experience Yeats missed in prose drama:

> It seems to me that beyond the nameable, classifiable
> emotions and motives of our conscious life when directed
> towards action – the part of life which prose drama is wholly
> adequate to express – there is a fringe of indefinite extent,
> of feeling which we can only detect, so to speak, out of the
> corner of the eye and can never completely focus; of feeling
> of which we are only aware in a kind of temporary
> detachment from action.[20]

But although Eliot, who was present at the drawing-room performance of *At the Hawk's Well* in 1916, acknowledged that through Yeats 'the idea of a poetic drama had been kept alive when everywhere else it had been driven underground', he found that the 'very beautiful' Plays for Dancers did 'not solve any problem for the dramatist in verse'.[21]

Linguistic texture was the crucial issue for Eliot but the verse must be immediate not remote, must 'justify itself dramatically'. Early on, he perceived that 'the recognised forms of speech verse are not as efficient as they should be' and suggested that 'probably a new form will be devised out of colloquial speech'.[22] Although as suspicious of the theatre audience as James, he too was partly driven by consciousness that Shakespeare's drama had succeeded in the public theatre. He deplored the notion of writing for a coterie audience willing to 'put up with poetry' and 'enjoy the play and the language of the play as two separate things' and yet with a self-contradiction that runs through all his writing for the theatre, as early as 1933 he explained Shakespeare's success as deriving from just such a demarcation of response:

> In a play of Shakespeare you get several levels of significance. For the simplest auditor there is the plot, for the more thoughtful the character and conflict of character, for the more literary the words and phrasing, for the more musically sensitive the rhythm, and for the auditors of greater sensitiveness and understanding a meaning which reveals itself gradually.[23]

Yeats's attempt to establish a Poets' Theatre in October 1934 based on the Mercury Theatre quickly came to grief on the rocks of politics and performance style. While Yeats was suspicious of the motivations of Rupert Doone and the Group Theatre, Tyrone Guthrie, the chosen director, found visualisation of a likely staging for Yeats's *Player Queen* difficult,[24] but there was an intriguing brief congruence in the early 1930s of the theatrical activity of the Christian Conservative Eliot and the much younger quasi-Marxist, W. H. Auden. Where Yeats had looked to Craig and the aristocratic Nōh, they both learned from recent European drama – Eliot from Cocteau's theatrically self-conscious *Parade*, Auden from that and from Brecht's *Threepenny Opera* which he had seen in Berlin in 1928 – but also, despite markedly different political agendas, they learned from each other and from popular forms. Eliot's adaptation of the rhythms of jazz and popular song and the structure of the music hall programme in *Sweeney Agonistes* although, tellingly, not much liked by Yeats was judged 'by far the best thing in London' by Brecht[25] who was also in the audience for the Group Theatre's production in 1934. Auden, for his part, reviewing a book on poetic drama in the same year, concluded that:

The truth is that those who would write poetic drama refuse to start from the only place where they can start, from the dramatic forms actually in use. . . . These are the variety show, the pantomime, the musical comedy and revue.[26]

Auden's use of masks and dance in *The Dance of Death* (1934), had more in common with the syncopated rhythm of *Sweeney Agonistes*, than with Yeats's dance plays and, in 1935, the two works were performed as a Group Theatre double bill. Eliot, having accepted Auden's play for publication by Faber in 1933, then adapted elements of it for his contribution to *The Rock*, a pageant celebrating church building which he created with E. Martin Browne the next year, while the exploration of guilt beneath a calm surface and the covert psychoanalysing, that characterise Auden and Isherwood's *Ascent of F6*, recur in Eliot's later plays. From their very different perspectives, each relished the didactic possibilities of the public stage, seeing drama as, in Stephen Spender's description, 'a way out of isolation and obscurity',[27] although both were sceptical of finding many of those Eliot termed 'auditors of sensitivity and understanding' among the general public.

In synopsis, Auden's *danse macabre* seems a model of clarity: it begins with an Announcer's direct statement that what is to be presented is 'a picture of the decline of a class' – the middle class, whose members have 'death inside them' which death is to be represented by a dancer; episodes follow in which the chorus representing the middle class live hedonistically, don uniforms, are swayed by communism but overtaken by jingoistic patriotism, and the whole concludes with the collapse of the dancer, pronounced dead by Karl Marx. Developed at length, the action proves much more confused and confusing and Auden's light doggerel, while it races along, tends to glide over meaning. A surface liveliness is guaranteed by the eclectic method, which drew on vaudeville, Brechtian musical theatre and the agit-prop of the Workers' Theatre Movement with more than a nod to the Diaghilev dancers in bathing suits, tossing beach balls, in *Le Train Bleu* (1924). Eliot's incorporation of popular song into the dialogue of *Sweeney*, was extended into the parodic pastiche of dance tune, sea shanty, pious school anthem and popular song that punctuates Auden's play. Those acting the crowd sing, dance, mime, use their acrobatic skills to form an arch, to suggest a ship; their voices and bodies to suggest a storm, eventually representing drowning souls in a not quite coherent allegory of the sinking ship of England. The voices of communism crying for revolution come from figures placed in the audience. Rival groups vie with each other, conflicting opinions are exchanged and the Dancer, brilliantly performed by Rupert Doone in 1934, weaves through all this, appearing as Sun God who steals the clothes of the sea bathers, banging a drum to drown out protest, becoming a demagogue to divert the crowd from socialistic ideas, before whirling dervish-like into his final collapse. The action has meanwhile been diverted from one episode to another by metatheatrical sequences: the stage manager intervenes to insist the actors wear respectable clothes, a doctor intervenes from the audience to treat the collapsed Dancer, the female actors demand better roles.

The draping of the Union Jack over the dead body of the Dancer at the end is in witty contrast to its patriotic brandishing at the end of Coward's recent *Cavalcade*, but the abrupt appearance of Marx as *deus ex machina* is as unsatisfactory a resolution as the appearance at the end of *The Ascent of F6* of the spirit of the ambitious mother, in whose lap the hero, Ransom, dies as he reaches for the top of the mountain. The distorted version of Peer Gynt's return to Ase/Solveig far from resolving the play's obscurities, collapses them into simplistic Freudianism. To an audience struggling to make sense of the kaleidoscopic action, the solution in Marxism, here, is similarly anticlimactic. Auden alone or in collaboration with Isherwood never quite managed a play that could survive the bewildering excitement of its first performance.

The one scene in *The Rock* which Eliot claimed as his own is evidently derived from *The Dance of Death* and has a comparable scenic vigour. Red shirts, whose verse:

> Is free
> as the wind on the steppes
> as love in the heart of the factory worker
> (p. 43)

vie with the Black Shirts' precise couplets for supremacy but both kinds of totalitarianism are seen to fail when a plutocrat bears in the Golden Calf and they fall to greedy dismembering of it; their exeunt in noisy tumult leaves the stage free for the appearance of the Rock, 'brooding on the pinacle,' which ends Part I. Although its political analysis is crude, the scene shares the scenic and verbal vitality of Auden's play or the *Sweeney* fragments. Eliot's choruses which are, by comparison, surprisingly static, look forward to *Murder in the Cathedral*. The Chorus represents not a community of people but 'the voice of the church', probably the authorial voice, too, indicting 'miserable cities of designing men' who read 'but not the word of GOD', who build 'but not the house of GOD' (Part I). Somewhat contradictingly, the massed voices speak for the individual conscience and against the tendency to combine represented by the lesser choruses of Red Shirts and Black Shirts.

Neither of these two early works were completed by Eliot and neither was included by him in his *Collected Plays*. *The Rock* was shaped by E. Martin Browne with various contributions to the dialogue of the church-building scenes and historical flashbacks that alternate with the choruses.

Sweeney Agonistes is tantalisingly fragmentary. Only about a fifth of what Eliot had projected, it lacks the coherence of drama. Development of the action was to remain one of the severest problems in Eliot's subsequent plays although this is masked in *Murder in the Cathedral* by the cathedral setting and enabling framework of the liturgy. Removed from the church, with its assumptions of ceremony, choric responses and faithful congregation, into the theatre, the static nature of the action and Eliot's presumption of the audience's acquiescence in his religious statements, become more problematic. In the less spiritually potent stage space, the hollowness that results from failure to engage audience imagination fully is evident.

Murder in the Cathedral (1935)

Murder in the Cathedral was the archetypal occasional play, utilising the verse forms of *Everyman* as well as the shape of the liturgy, but also the very space and function of the cathedral Chapter House in which it was performed: pulpit for Thomas's sermon; clerestory as retreat for the frightened priests; great wooden door on which the murderous knights could pound and through which they could enter from the outside world, and, above all, the wonderful acoustic for the reverberations of the choric voices and the distant singing of the *Te Deum*. The building itself supplies the realistic context for all these elements.

Although the work is cast in dramatic form with parallel quartets of priests, tempters, murderous knights and a chorus who speak the fear and ignorance of the common people, the play is essentially a monodrama concerned with Thomas's willed consent to martyrdom and the distinction between this and heroism. The seeming dramatic climax of Part I when Thomas is caught off guard by the Fourth Tempter:

> The last temptation is the greatest treason:
> To do the right deed for the wrong reason.

dissolves. The audience is obliged to accept Thomas's declaration that he has come through on the strength of his negative perception, 'I shall no longer act or suffer to the sword's end', that brings Part I to its conclusion.

Thomas's speeches have a certain poetic power that is open to analysis in the study but, since they are rarely dramatic in the structure of their thought and feeling, these disquisitions hold the play up; they lack Shaw's 'audible intelligibility'. The soliloquies of Macbeth or Hamlet are dynamic even when meditative. Here, the struggle is presented to the audience, not experienced by them. Eliot's narrative verse is, like Browning's, remarkably dramatic, the glimpses of interacting and conflicting human activity frequent, but neither writer seems to have been able to create a stage drama, functioning in time and developing to a crescendo. That both fall short of convincing creation of stage character despite their skill in dramatic monologue is, I think, because dramatic monologue, for all its seeming impersonality, includes the strong shaping presence of the writer, using language with ironic detachment from the speaker. The creative tension in dramatic monologue is between what the character says and what the very construction allows us to perceive of the truth the character cannot identify. The dramatist uses dramatic irony. Audiences do perceive differently from characters but these are momentary not sustained distances, more powerful because at other times we do share the characters' sight. In Eliot's plays, the *raisonneur* is always present explaining action and motive to us.

The imagery of *Murder in the Cathedral*, drawn from the changing seasons, the creatures of the natural world and redemption through the shedding of blood, contributes as it does in Yeats's Plays for Dancers to the impression of inevitability, of Thomas's acceptance of his part in a natural process. Although the Chorus seem at times to resist, their reiteration of the word 'must' acknowledges the necessity of the events they are compelled to witness and helps to make the whole more pageant than play, although individual sequences such as the intercutting voices of the priests expressing their rising panic are striking. So are most of the choruses, taken as individual pieces, but there is little sense of development of image structure or of responses becoming more complex in the course of the work. As Denis Donoghue has pointed out, the Chorus's forboding of death in the speech, 'I have smelt them the death bringers', registers fear increasingly horrifically through the invasion of all the senses, the invocation of the death-tainted natural world and the spreading physical corruption:

> I have tasted
> The living lobster, the crab, the oyster, the whelk and the
> prawn; and they live and spawn in my bowels, and my bowels
> dissolve in the light of dawn. I have smelt
> Death in the rose, death in the hyacinth . . .
>
> (Part II)

But this is met by no matching language or range of reference in the final affirmatory chorus. Since the life heralded at the end of the play has little linguistic relationship with the earlier death, 'we miss', says Donoghue, 'the feeling that the new vision of faith has been won from the chorus of despair'.[28] The martyrdom is perceived by Eliot as cleansing and fertilising. The little people – both Chorus and congregation – must accept that they are redeemed by the sacrifice of the great spirit. The disgust with which the ordinary run of mankind is viewed is reiterated throughout the work although disguised by the onrush of the verse. The context makes us less ready to protest, since the small folk who live among small things, are the sure equivalent of the 'miserable sinners' of the Litany.

The comparison with Shaw's *Saint Joan*, indicated by Eliot himself, emphasises the problems of Eliot's piece. The influence of Shaw's treatment of history on *Murder in the Cathedral* is evident in the references to the modern world in the choruses. But the play is remote from the dialectic and certainly from the fun of Shaw's plays: the modern forensics of the knights' self-justification may be in part derived from *Saint Joan* but the evident speciousness of their arguments has more in common with the Announcer's rationalisations in *The Dance of Death* than with the eloquence of Shaw's Inquisitor. Moreover, the obvious dramatic features of the historical story: the personal emotion and rivalry of Henry II and Thomas, the political implications of Thomas's behaviour, even the struggle for power between church and state, are deliberately left out of the account by Eliot whose interest is entirely in the idea of martyrdom and the acquiescence in it of the prospective martyr.

That this is a monodrama tends to disguise the fact, glaringly apparent in his later plays, that for all his skill with the written word, Eliot is rarely alive to the movement of the spoken language, to the interaction of different ways of perceiving that is so essential a part of the dramatic imagination. His dialogue is only fleetingly convincing. Eliot himself subsequently gave a clear-sighted assessment of the problem when he said he had used the Chorus to bulk out the play, the matter of his argument being 'somewhat thin' and, being 'doubtful of [his] ability to handle dialogue', he had 'hoped to make up by choral effects what was lacking to the strictly dramatic action'.[29]

Verse and poetic speech is the accepted idiom of the church and the Anglican liturgy one of the repositories of traditional patterns, choric response and ordered ritualistic event and, as such, Eliot came to see the structure and method of *Murder in the Cathedral* as a tactic for avoiding the real problems of creating a poetic drama that could offer its audience access to experience beyond the 'nameable classifiable emotions'. The choral speeches do have a certain power, particularly in Part II when, Thomas's struggle resolved, the feeling of the play is centred in them. The voices move in successive speeches from self-abnegating fear, through despairing plea for intercession on their behalf, to the astonishing succession of cry, query, lament of the 'Clear the air! clean the sky! wash the wind!' chorus that coincides with the slaying of Thomas and then to the affirmatory selflessness and commitment to God of the final chorus.

The chorus offer accounts of their life and their emotions:

> We know of oppression and torture,
> We know of extortion and violence,
> Destitution, disease,
> The old without fire in winter,
> The child without milk in summer,
> Our labour taken away from us,
> Our sins made heavier upon us,
> We have seen the young man mutilated,
> The torn girl trembling by the mill-stream,
> And meanwhile we have gone on living,
> Living and partly living.
>
> (Part I)

But while such sequences tempt the *reader* of the work to let rip out loud, we never believe in them as living, breathing Women of Canterbury who know loss, experience fear or find redemption. The theatre audience is not implicated in what they have to say as happens, for example, with the much clumsier final speech of Juno in O'Casey's play or of Mrs Holroyd in Lawrence's *The Widowing of Mrs Holroyd*. For all their seeming poverty of expression on the page, the equivalence of these moments to the grief-stricken, silent gazing into the fire of real life compel attention to suppressed feeling and missed relationship when spoken in the context of the one woman's loss or as the accompaniment to the other's unexpectedly tender laying out of the dead body of her estranged husband. In these sequences the private and specific have also a universal significance as a commentary on human relationship that can speak powerfully to an audience. Both these dramatists have created words in action and given voice to otherwise scarcely articulable areas of feeling, while Eliot, despite his insistence on the need for verse to justify itself dramatically, has not.

Eliot's verse is (by contrast) a strait-jacket. The play remains a pageant. Its auditors are never overtaken by the Paradox of the Audience: that we can know ourselves in a theatre watching a performance that has been learned, rehearsed and will probably be repeated but, at the same time, can seem to lose ourselves in our imaginative engagement with the action, slip briefly out of self-consciousness. It is, I suspect, only in the non-verbal dance elements of Yeats's *Plays for Dancers* that such an engagement with the action occurs, if at all.

Beginning in 1939 and continuing spasmodically into the 1950s, in his attempt to move verse drama into the contemporary world, Eliot moved further from the sensuous elements of theatre. His idea, not unlike Drink-water's suggestion that the dialogue should be 'beautiful without letting anybody know about it',[30] was that there should be a scarcely apparent rhythm, 'preparing the ear of the audience for the moments of intensity' when actors would use 'the same rhythms, with the same vocabulary as before', but the change would be felt 'not in awareness of versification, but in awareness of the higher or lower charge of energy in the whole scene'.[31] Since such a charge is rarely experienced, the effect is that the power of poetry – economy, musicality and complexity – is all but drained from the dialogue. The resulting position is remarkably similar to that of the New Drama.

Acknowledging the failure of modern attempts to recreate a verse drama, in his Presidential address to the Poets' Theatre Guild in 1949, Eliot said:

> I do not believe that there is one poet in the theatre today, who can feel assured that he has found the right form, the right idiom, the right range of human emotions and experience to manipulate.[32]

His use of the word 'manipulate' reveals the same strained sense of audience as did the earlier notion of supplying different 'levels of significance' to keep the less sensitive members happy while communicating with the responsive few. Repeating James's mistake, in his effort to address the contemporary audience he took as his theatrical model not the music hall and jazz rhythms of the *Sweeney Agonistes* fragments nor the liturgical framework of *Murder in the Cathedral*, but the drawing-room settings and plots of commercial theatre, in this case predominantly murder mysteries. Plot elements and a choric structure derived from Greek Tragedy are imported into the modern setting but these too are disguised. The result, in 1939, was the dismal *Family Reunion* with its portentous action, disconcertingly class-ridden assumptions and wooden characterisation. Visual effect, music, dance, even movement and spatial relationship on the stage, are largely eliminated, leaving the didactic intent all too apparent despite the contortions of the plot. The realistic surface, melodramatic plots and verse dialogue of Eliot's post-Second World War plays sit just as awkwardly together.

Yeats's effort and insistence in the theatre were crucial in making a space for the works of genuine dramatic imagination of his earthier colleagues. As the scope and dramatic power of Synge's and O'Casey's plays were different in kind from his, so the hostility and enthusiasm accorded them were of a different order. Just as the outrage stimulated by early performances of *Ghosts* or *Mrs Warren's Profession* was different in kind from that provoked by *Guy Domville* and was matched by an enthusiasm at least as fervent, so the hostility to *The Playboy of the Western World* or *The Plough and the Stars* was different in kind from that met by the various verse dramas. Works by Ibsen and Shaw, by Synge and O'Casey, would before long be accepted as classics by precisely the people they had earlier appalled; would demonstrate again and again their capacity to absorb and disturb successive audiences. The plays discussed in this chapter have not been interactive with the culture of their time in this way. They remain interesting experiments.

Notes

1. T. S. Eliot, 'Poetry and Drama' (1950), in T. S. Eliot, *Selected Prose*, ed. John Haywood (1963), p. 71; p. 65.
2. Quoted, D. H. Lawrence, *Three Plays*, ed. R. Williams (1969), p. 10.
3. H. James, 'The Parisian Stage', *New York Tribune* (January 1876), reprinted in Allan Wade, ed., *Henry James: The Scenic Art* (1948; repr., 1957), p. 44. Subsequent quotations from James's essay on theatre can be identified in Wade from the dates noted in my text.
4. Quoted, L. Edel, ed., *The Complete Plays of Henry James* (1949), p. 44. Leon Edel's introduction and notes to this edition are an indispensable source of information about James's drama.
5. Elizabeth Robins, *Theatre and Friendship* (1932), other quotations in this paragraph are from the 1895 entries in, F. O. Matthiessen and K. B. Murdock, eds, *The Notebooks of Henry James* (1947).
6. Letter to William James, Quoted Edel, ed., *Complete Plays*, p. 549.
7. Quoted Edel, ed., *Complete Plays*, p. 553.
8. *Samhain* (October 1901), p. 68; see too, 'The Play, the Player and the Scene'. *Samhain* (December 1904); 'Literature and the Living Voice' *Samhain* (December 1906).
9. W. B. Yeats, *Autobiographies* (1955), p. 279.
10. W. B. Yeats, *Essays and Introductions* (1961), p. 224–5.
11. 'The Play of Modern Manners' in Yeats's *Essays and Introductions*, p 334.
12. On Ibsen's language see essays by I.-S. Ewbank and J. Northam in *Contemporary Approaches to Ibsen*, Vol. I (Oslo, 1966) (Proceedings of the International Ibsen Seminary); on translation, see Sara Jan, 'William Archer as a Translator of Ibsen', Chapter 2 of unpublished PhD dissertation, 'Ibsen in England, 1889–1914', (Cambridge, 1993).
13. Yeats, 1919, selected by Mrs W. B. Yeats in *Explorations* (1962), p. 255; p. 258.
14. The link with Wilde's play is suggested by Peter Raby, *Oscar Wilde* (Cambridge, 1988), p. 115.
15. Allan Wade, ed., *The Letters of W. B. Yeats* (1954), p. 366.
16. See T. R. Henn, *The Lonely Tower* (1965), p. 281 and K. Dorn, *Players and Painted Stage* (Brighton, 1984), pp. 25–32, for attention to and detailed discussion of the versions of this play. The editions I have used are *The Hour Glass* (1907) and the 1914 revision in *Collected Plays* (1952).
17. Letter to *Evening Telegraph* (9.1.1911), quoted Dorn, *Players*, p. 14.
18. 'Certain Noble Plays of Japan' (1919) in Yeats, *Essays and Introductions*, p. 23.
19. Suggestion in R. Taylor, *A Reader's Guide to the Plays of W. B. Yeats* (1984).
20. Eliot, 'Poetry and Drama', *Selected Prose*, p. 80.
21. Eliot, *Selected Prose*, p. 193; p. 71.

22. Eliot, 1926, quoted Carol Smith, *T. S. Eliot's Dramatic Theory and Practice* (1963), p. 52.
23. Eliot, *Selected Prose*, p. 66; *The Use of Poetry and the Use of Criticism* (1933), p. 153.
24. There is an excellent discussion of the abortive Poets' Theatre in M. Sidnell, *Dances of Death* (1989), pp. 266–9.
25. Sidnell, *Dances of Death*, p. 103.
26. Quoted E. Mendelson, *Early Auden* (1981), p. 262.
27. S. Spender, *New Left Review* (November 1936), p. 779.
28. D. Donoghue, *The Third Voice* (1959), p. 81.
29. T. S. Eliot, *The Aims of Poetic Drama* Presidential Address (Poets' Theatre Guild Pamphlet, 1949), p. 4.
30. Introduction to J. Drinkwater, *Collected Plays* (1925), p. viii.
31. Eliot, *The Aims of Poetic Drama*, p. 6.
32. Eliot, *The Aims of Poetic Drama*, p. 3.

Chapter 8

Dramatising Strife: The Working Classes on the British Stage

That's the spirit, my her'ties! sing! sing! tho' they hae ye
chained to the wheels and the darkness. Sing! tho' they hae
ye crushed in the mire. Keep up your he'rts, my laddies, you'll
win through yet, for there's nae power on earth can crush the
men that can sing on a day like this.

(Corrie, *In Time o' Strife*, Act III)

Among the few full-length plays produced by the Independent Theatre,
two from 1893 introduced working-class characters. George Moore's *The
Strike at Arlingford* was a Capital and Labour play. Although the other,
Elizabeth Robins' and Florence Bell's *Alan's Wife*, included a death from
an horrific industrial accident, it directed attention to maternal feeling
and the home rather than working conditions. Addressing aspects of
working-class life in markedly different ways, these two plays, introducing
themes that would resurface periodically, prefigured stage practice in the
next half-century.

Twentieth-century theatre has recurrently flared into life with plays
that, featuring industrial discord and strike action, count the physical and
emotional cost of Labour and its continuing conflict with, or exploitation
by, Capital. The characteristic method has been to present polarised political oratory and Factory-gate or Board-room debate. But there have also
been plays that attended to the experience of people affected by the strike
action or harsh working conditions and, doing so, have claimed a place
on the stage for a previously neglected sector of society. The strife,
centred in domestic life, is internalised. James Agate's recognition in 1925
that *Juno and the Paycock* 'is as much a tragedy as *Macbeth*, but it is a
tragedy taking place in the porter's family'[1] is suggestive beyond O'Casey's
play.

The two modes are already evident in the two mighty classics of the
new European realist theatre, of which *The Strike at Arlingford* and *Alan's
Wife* are local reverberations. Tolstoi's *Power of Darkness*, premièred at the
Théâtre Libre in Paris in 1888, is a bleak evocation of Russian peasant life
which explores the motivation of individuals involved in a callous infanti-

cide. Hauptmann's *The Weavers*, first produced in 1892 by the Freie Bühne in Berlin, uses some forty named characters to dramatise the discontent, combining for political action and eventual suppression by the military of the Silesian weavers, in a succession of increasingly powerful crowd scenes that, in early performances, had the audience on their feet with excitement.

Using similar material to Hauptmann's, Moore produced a remarkably old-fashioned play. Set entirely in the elegant drawing room of a mine-owner whose workers are on strike, its central concern is the dilemma of the 'great labour leader, John Reid'. His melodramatic reunion with the mine-owner, Lady Anne, who had rejected his love ten years previously when, as it emerges, he was her father's secretary, diverts him from his purpose. Like *The Weavers*, the play includes a dispute over wages, a strike and the eventual suppression of a riotous mob by the military, but it lacks Hauptmann's engagement with the lives and grievances of the workers and generates none of the dramatic excitement or intense emotion of that play. No irony seems intended when the employers watch the off-stage riot from their window through opera glasses. Their concern is to maintain the mine and with it – the claim is philanthropic – the jobs of the miners and to preserve civil order. The argument is that 'if the battle is lost here, we may expect strikes all over the North of England' (Act I). The members of the miners' delegation are demonstrably ignorant, with a forelock-touching admiration of the house and its lady and a comic propensity to be swayed by whoever spoke last. Reid's assistant is a bigotted schoolteacher whose mind is closed to rational argument and whose dialogue is peppered with parodic socialistic slogans. Reid's arguments, by comparison, turn on the pitiableness of the workers' conditions: 'that man, how miserable he seems – his slouching hungry gait. And those children who follow their mother. She has no bread to give them.' But circumstances force him to acknowledge the workers' in-bred monstrosity and ingratitude and his own fundamental class loyalties:

> The brutes. I still feel their foul breath on my face, and their
> foul hands. I abandoned my own class for their sakes, but
> I never could assimilate my life with theirs.
>
> (Act III)

The innovation of Robins' and Bell's *Alan's Wife*, by contrast with this, was its closely observed setting among northern working-class women whose gossip, flavoured with such dialect markers as 'Eh', 'nobbut', 'nowt', 'missis', is accompanied by ceaseless activity – knitting, preparation of food, housework. Unfortunately, although Grein borrowing the words of the French critic, Jean Julien, praised it as a 'slice of human life put on the stage with art',[2] the innovatory quality of the setting and the attribution to such people of a capacity for passion and thought was neglected by contemporaries in the furore provoked by its representation of purposeless suffering and the repudiation of Christian comfort, demonstrated in the young widow's smothering of her badly deformed child and her refusal to repent the deed.

Galsworthy's *Strife* (1909), rather than *The Strike at Arlingford*, provided the model for many of the subsequent strike plays. Its action is divided equally between the employers and the workers and, if by no means matching the crowd scenes of *The Weavers*, it at least includes a lively and vociferous strike meeting. The difference in political stance, though, is less than might at first appear: Galsworthy was notable among Edwardian dramatists for the number of working-class characters he included and for providing an impression of environment by setting individual scenes in their homes, but the almost uniform pathos of his presentation limits the effect. Where they are not brutally drunk or mouthing platitudes of loyalty and honest poverty echoed from nineteenth-century melodrama, his working-class characters are demonstrably feeble. Ford Maddox Ford, claiming the impact of Turgenev as the source of Galsworthy's approach, suggested that:

> The disease from which he suffered was pity . . . or not so much pity as an insupportable anger at the sufferings of the weak or the impoverished in a harsh world. It was as if some portion of his mind had been flayed and bled at every touch.[3]

Those, moreover, like the strike leader, David Roberts, in *Strife* who do stand up for their rights, are differentiated from the other workers. 'He was just as much a gentleman as my father', says Lady Anne of John Reid in Moore's play; and, 'I mean he's an engineer – a superior man', says Enid, in Galsworthy's. On the English stage, from *Coriolanus* to *Strife*, the common people have been roused or led astray by tribunes with superior ability and an axe to grind.

Much of the Edwardian New Drama's treatment of working-class as compared with middle-class women is notably soft: the indulgence patronises. Hackles rise when Enid's enlightened opinions are dismissed by her father with a 'read your books, play your music' in Act I of *Strife*, but the audience is embarrassed with and for her in Act II, in the face of the loyalty and suffering of the poor woman she had intended to succour who, knowing what her husband is about, intends to stand by him, literally, to the death. Similarly Flora, the seduced lady's maid in *The Eldest Son* (1913) is scarcely characterised beyond prettiness and a self-denying refusal to press her claims, whereas the genteel woman – her seducer's mother and sisters – are sharply drawn: one, fiery; another, a wry observer; a third, notably self-interested, and their differences are reflected in their dialogue. Whereas the middle classes are treated in a lively way, the working-class women are sentimentalised. The employers, however thoroughly castigated in the work of Galsworthy and like-minded contemporaries, are evidently 'we', the working classes remain 'they'. Harold Brighouse, who offered an attentive evocation of working-class environment in his short play *The Price of Coal* (1909), found it necessary to preface the published version with the hope that it would teach his readers to know the miner better and 'discover his simplicity of soul, his directness, his matter of fact self-sacrifice, the unconscious heroism of his life'.[4]

This judgement on the Edwardian Drama needs some qualification. Plays by Galsworthy's female and provincial contemporaries, Brighouse among them, did include some rather more robust working people. Often, under the influence of the growing feminist movement, these are young women. Fanny Hawthorn in *Hindle Wakes* (1912) roots her claim to determine her own lifestyle in her work when she declares, 'as long as there's weaving sheds in Lancashire I shall earn enough brass to keep me going', and, recognising the reality of social mobility, the mill-owner in that play reminds his wife that he 'wore clogs [him]self until [he] was past twenty'. The shopgirl, Maggie, in Elizabeth Baker's *Chains* (1909) and the ex-typist in Githa Sowerby's *Rutherford and Son* (1912) both demonstrate grit and firmness of purpose, as does the heroine of Cicely Hamilton's *Diana of Dobson's* (1908) when she resists the petty tyrannies of her employers, although Diana, like David Roberts, is superior in class terms to her work-mates – she is a doctor's daughter fallen on hard times.

Industrial disputes, injuries and injustices of employer to worker rumble in the background of many Edwardian plays even when they are not the central issue as they are in *Strife*. A miner in Moore's play has lost father and brother in a pit disaster, the mother in *The Price of Coal* was widowed in a pit fire. The constraint of the 'living-in' system which put shop workers at the beck of their employers in the brief respite from their long working hours is vividly reproduced in the first act of Cicely Hamilton's play and echoed in the shop scene of *The Madras House* (1910). We learn, in passing, in *Rutherford and Son*, that 'they're smashing things at Rayners', a neighbouring firm whose deliveries are delayed by a strike; the mill-owner in Hankin's *Return of the Prodigal* (1905) has extended working hours in his sheds by installing electric light, and, in *Chains*, a clerk has had an ultimatum to accept a cut in wages, or go.

Capital and Labour plays

In the 1920s, a number of plays deal directly with the conflict of Capital and Labour. Echoing the battle of wills between John Anthony and David

Roberts in *Strife*, they focus on the struggle between well-matched individuals with diametrically opposed opinions. Although the hardships the labourers endure evoke pity, the employers' position is sympathetically articulated. In Ernest Hutchinson's *The Right to Strike* (1920), which ran in the West End for eighty-two performances, a doctor whose colleagues have been killed in an attempt to bring food to a village, starving because of a railway strike, is struck off the register for refusing to operate on the wife of the strike leader. The situation is happily resolved, the complexities of the situation dissipated, when the doctor, despite having declared, 'for the right to strike I have sacrificed my livelihood and lost my dearest friend', renounces his determination not to operate because appealed to on the grounds of common humanity by his dead colleague's forgiving widow. Sentiment takes over. It is less the right to strike that is argued for than the futility and probable damage of exercising it which reiterates the comment that ended Galsworthy's play, 'D'you know, Sir, – these terms, they're the *very same* we drew up together, you and I, and put to both sides before the fight began? All this – all this – and – and what for?'. A similar line is followed in Eden Phillpotts's *Yellow Sands* (1926) and John Davidson's Yorkshire set, *Shadows of Strife* (1929), in both of which the strike is instigated not by well-meaning demagogues, as in Galsworthy, but by humourless Bolshevik agitators.[5]

The counter-polemic to the Bolshevik agitator play, offered by radical groups such as Workers' Theatre Movement and Unity, more readily acknowledged itself partisan. The issues remain remarkably similar to those of earlier years: as in *Strife* and, indeed, *The Strike at Arlingford*, there is fear on the bosses' part of strikes speading and anxiety among the strike leaders that privation will break the workers' spirits and lead to breakaway returns or that employers will bring in blackleg workers. But there is a novel specificity of information and the point of view is clearly that of the workers. Although oratory still plays a major part, the method is also new. In the wake of the General Strike and the realities of mass unemployment in the early 1930s, these groups, impatient with a realism that seemed to support the *status quo* and blur the clear-cut issues of the class struggle, used expressionistic and agit-prop techniques as a means of revealing the 'reality existing beneath the polite surface of capitalist society'.[6]

Bosses were caricatured, workers heroised. Statement, declaration and direct questioning of the audience were the favoured means of expression. Song was exploited as a dramatic device and choric speech, group action and stylised gesture emphasised the message. In one sequence of *The Rail Revolt* (1932), for example, the workers respond to news that the directors of the railways have imposed wage cuts:

> 4TH RAILMAN:
> They're driving us down – down – DOWN

ALL:
>AND ALL THIS TO KEEP UP PROFITS.

1ST RAILMAN:
>They cut down the size of the gangs – less men have to do more work.

2ND:
>They have introduced more and more powerful loco-motives – which pull double the load – and locomen are being degraded.

3RD:
>They build coal hoppers to sack hundreds of coalies.

4TH:
>They are introducing automatic carriage washers – and sacking cleaners.

. . .

5TH:
>This is what the Companies are doing – what are we to do?[7]

This is not dialectic; different figures speak contingent thoughts so that individual voices blend into communal utterance. The form reflects the ideology.

Expressive staging contributed. An episode in London Unity's *Busmen* (1938), dramatising the recent unofficial busmen's strike, begins with representative figures of the General Public discussing with varying degrees of sympathy the rights and inconveniencies of the strike. An impression is given of a huge march passing by when these figures respond with gestures of support and cries of wonder to the noise of tramping feet, shouted slogans, a band playing the 'Internationale' that come over the sound system, while shadows, as if of passing crowds and banners, are thrown on to the stage. In Montague Slater's *Stay Down Miner* (1936), which dramatises the occupation of pits in the Welsh coalfield, shafts of lantern light suggest the covert nature of a night scene and snatches of characteristic songs, whether 'Nearer my God to Thee' or 'The Red Flag' breaking out in the darkness are quickly suppressed. The urgent, responsible argument by Bronwen, an elderly miner's wife, that direct action – the derailing of a train bringing in non-Union workers – will give the scabs 'the shelter of men's pity' is counterpointed by the repeated chanting of 'Stop the ghost train' and 'Pick up your stones' from the anonymous voices.[8] Not only Bronwen but all the activists in these plays come, of course, from among the workers: any right to lead derives from oratorical skill and the knowledge that comes from self-motivated learning.

Many of these pieces have a documentary quality which quickens the assault on the audience. The occupation of pits in the Welsh coalfield to prevent the importation of non-union labour, enacted in *Stay Down Miner* was happening currently, and the final appeal of the play is directed out to the auditorium as in a political meeting:

BRONWEN:

    (*to audience*): You people of Cwyllynfach –

MAGISTRATE:

    No more speeches please.

BRONWEN:

    Tell the world

MAGISTRATE:

    Please –

BRONWEN:

    Tell England and Scotland.

MAGISTRATE:

    I said no speeches.

BRONWEN:

    Tell them to join Wales.

                                 (III. v)

In keeping with the claims of *Busmen* to be a Living Newspaper, facts and statistics about wages and working conditions had all been verified. With even greater specificity than the political figures and events in O'Casey's Dublin plays, actual Board members and Union officials, including Ernest Bevin, current President of the Transport and General Workers' Union, were portrayed in dialogue based on their own speeches. This texture of actuality is turned to powerful effect when the ordinary workers, Fred, Bob, Tim and Jack, who have functioned as representative busmen in individual episodes of the play, emerge when called by their full names at the culminating Union meeting, as well-known activists, suspended by the T&GWU for leading independent action. Although this play ends, like so many mainstream strike plays, with the protagonists disgusted by the Union's compromise with the Board, its final lines are positive. Fred gains a general answering 'Yes', to his closing appeal for support of the suspended members: 'Unity will secure reinstatements. Defeat the Board and end reaction in the Transport and General Workers' Union. Is it a go, boys?' They regroup ready to fight another day.[9]

    Industrial action and unemployment occur in another group of plays but as factors in the lives of their working-class participants. D. H. Lawrence *The Daughter-in-Law* (written, 1912), Joe Corrie *In Time o' Strife* (1927) and Ronald Gow's adaptation of Walter Greenwood's *Love on the Dole* (1934), although different in provenance and performance history, were written from inside the culture they depict and, like the earlier *Alan's Wife*, create an impression of intense realism. *The Daughter-in-Law*, which remained unproduced in Lawrence's lifetime, presents the tensions within a mining family while a strike brews in the background. *In Time o' Strife*, dramatising the experience of the 1926 strike in the Scottish coalfield and the pressure to return to work on men whose families are starving, was toured to institutes and music halls throughout Scotland. More conventionally successful, *Love on the Dole*, which introduces victimisation, unemployment and protest action rather than a strike as such, opened in Manchester in 1934 and played continuously until the summer of 1937.

Masters do not figure in the action of these plays, although each takes conflict between masters and men as axiomatic. The talk of the working-class characters might be ignorant or cogent, comic or desperately serious, according to the insights and attitudes of individual characters, but it is between them that lively debates about the rights and wrongs of political action, strike breaking and surrender take place. Leaders come from among the people: Anderson in Corrie's play, Larrie in Gow's, are thinking socialists who demonstrate a capacity for clear political analysis and make fiercely coherent speeches. The positions of others, for all they are strongly felt, may be much less soundly based, as the following exchange reveals:

TAM:
> It's the damned Bolshies that's keepin' us frae startin'.

JOCK:
> And here's luck to them, says I.

TAM:
> And it's them that dinna want to work that's on the pickets.

JOCK:
> D'ye mean that I dinna want to work?

TAM:
> I never mentioned you.

JOCK:
> I was on the picket, and I'm damned sure I'll work beside you ony day.

TAM:
> Did I say you couldna?

JOCK:
> No, and you better no'.
>
> (*In Time o' Strife*, Act II)

Juno, in *Juno and the Paycock*, greets her daughter's involvement in a strike with the more reactionary sarcasm of, 'wan victim wasn't enough. When the employers sacrifice wan victim, the Trades Unions go wan better by sacrificin' a hundred' (Act I).

The settings are domestic: the Lawrence and Corrie being set entirely indoors in the kitchens of miners' cottages, the Gow mainly so. Strike meetings, marches, pickets, take place off-stage, although discussed on it. The effects of the struggle impinge on the lives we see and, as in *The Weavers* and the antiphonal second act of O'Casey's *The Plough and the Stars*, that deeply impressed Corrie, the sounds of protest songs, workers marching and political speeches drift in as if from the street outside. Gow's two outdoor settings reveal two opposed aspects of working-class entertainment. First, in a Salford Back Alley, a row between drunken husband and angry wife gives way to a young couple's surreptitious court-ing, each pair retreating before a passing policeman. Excitement surges and a crowd gathers when news spreads that young Harry Hardcastle has won twenty-two pounds on a threepenny street bet from a unlicenced local spiv. Then, the scene having shifted to 'a high rock, against the sky' in the Peak District – this is two years after the mass ramble on Kinder Scout that claimed the right to walk the open moorland – Sally Hardcastle, introduced to the moors by her political activist sweetheart, Larry, expresses a momentary surge of hope, 'I've never found anything worth believing in Hanky Park. But it's different up here. Here you belong – you belong to something big – something grand.' (II. iii).

In both the Corrie and the Gow, as later in O'Casey's rather more expressionistic industrial action plays, *The Star Turns Red* and *Red Roses for Me*, there is a degree of heroising when the action culminates in disastrous news from off-stage brought to a waiting woman. Anderson, in Corrie's play, gets three years' imprisonment for joining the picket of blackleg workers, leaving Kate with a drunken father and small brothers and sisters to support; more melodramatically, Larrie, in Gow's, is killed attempting to divert a demonstration, leaving Sally dead to feeling. Although the action of *The Daughter-in-Law* is more private, even here, Act IV begins with mother and wife waiting up anxiously for their men to return from activity against blacklegs and although Mrs Gascoigne's fear ('when I heered that gun, I said: "Theer goes one o' my lads" ') proves unfounded, the sketching in of an anti-heroic version of what was to become a recurrent motif contributes to the tension of the scene, as well as to the reconciliation of Luther with his estranged wife.

In Time o' Strife, the most politically committed of these plays, opens with the off-stage singing of, 'We'll hang every blackleg to the sour apple tree', to the tune of 'John Brown's Body', but it soon becomes clear that, as the sequence quoted above indicates, the deprivations of a punishing strike are undermining unity: a breakaway of miners accepting the bosses shilling and returning to work is anticipated. The outcome, just as in *Strife*, is a return in defeat, as Jock says, 'we hae got knocked oot again'. But that 'we' is important: the structure of feeling of the play means that the audience participates in the collapse. The engagement with the lives por-trayed is felt as well as known and holds through the unexpectedly upbeat ending that Corrie appends. The mother, responding to distant singing of the 'Red Flag' with a sudden burst of prophetic fire, of the kind that informs the endings of the plays Clifford Odets wrote for the New York Group Theatre in the 1930s, cries:

> That's the spirit, my he'rties! sing! sing! tho' they hae ye
> chained to the wheels and the darkness. Sing! tho' they hae
> ye crushed in the mire. Keep up your he'rts, my laddies,
> you'll win through yet, for there's nae power on earth can
> crush the men that can sing on a day like this.
>
> (Act III)

In these plays the conflict of Capital and Labour, like that of the Irish Independence struggle and civil war in O'Casey's Dublin trilogy, is the context of an action remarkable for its close observation of character and place. Raymond Williams's suggestion that Lawrence's plays have 'an intense attachment' to experience which is at one and the same time 'both social and personal', and that they 'engage his audience, in a theatre of ordinary feeling raised to intensity and community by the writing of ordinary speech',[10] captures something of the truth of this writing. It not only breaks away from the usual class base of theatre, but is simultaneously alert to the individual and the general. Far from being the simple slice of life Williams's reiteration of 'ordinariness' might suggest, such realism is dense with implication, the effect of rigorous selection and organisation.

Domestic strife: D. H. Lawrence and others

A Collier's Friday Night (written, 1909), *The Daughter-in-Law* and *The Widowing of Mrs Holroyd* (1914), the three plays Lawrence wrote before his prime attention had settled on prose fiction, have a tantalising promise that, without a performing agency, was never developed. These plays, conceived under the influence of Synge's Irish peasant works, particularly *Riders to the Sea* which he deeply admired, and in opposition to the theatrical plotting and artificial dialogue of the 'bony, bloodless drama' of Shaw, Galsworthy and Barker,[11] gave Lawrence a means of exploring his experience of family relationship and mining community before he did so in prose fiction.

In each, a woman prepares the evening meal and a miner returns home after his working day in habitual heavy boots, moleskin trousers and pit dirt and goes through the routine of washing or being washed and changing into his home clothes and, in each, the tensions between husband and wife, child and possessive mother are charted. Contrived plotting is consciously resisted. There is, for example, no equivalent of the child murder in *Alan's Wife*, although the last of the three plays and, perhaps significantly, the only one of them to be produced in Lawrence's lifetime, *The Widowing of Mrs Holroyd*, does include a planned elopement and ends, in a grim parody of the daily return from work, with Holroyd's body, killed in an accident carried ceremoniously on stage like Alan's and like Bartley's in *Riders to the Sea*.

A Collier's Friday Night, much of which was subsequently rewritten into the novel *Sons and Lovers*, details events in a miner's home on pay night. Unspectacular but immensely interesting in the verisimilitude with which they are performed, these include, beside washing and eating, the baking (and inadvertant burning) of the week's bread, the departure for the pay-night market and the collier's careful counting out and division with others in his shift of the week's pay. In the course of this conscious reworking of Burns's genial celebration of Scottish working-class life, 'The Cottar's Friday Night', a devastating account emerges of marital hostility: the resentment of a woman with aspirations to a better life than the pit village offers and the anger of a man who feels himself despised. The two are locked into a cycle of bitter scorn and drunken abuse. *The Daughter-in-Law*, a lighter and more optimistic version of a similar relationship, ends with an acknowledgement of mutual defensiveness and affection, whereas the last play of the three brings a one-sided awareness as Mrs Holroyd, who had thought to leave her sullen and often-drunken husband, talks to him while laying out his body. The long speech Lawrence gives her, with its verbally inadequate exclamations and repetitions of her attempt to articulate her feelings ('my dear, my dear – oh, my dear. I can't bear it my dear – you shouldn't have done it . . .'), looks limp on the page. It is potent in performance where, accompanied by the careful washing of the dead man, it gains ironic force as the first non-confrontational encounter the two have had: a moment of too costly intimacy.

Lawrence, like O'Casey, Corrie, and Ena Lamont Stewart, writes about working-class people from the point of view of the characters, not that of a sympathetic middle-class observer. This is as apparent in those areas where they share ground with Galsworthy and company as in those where they differ markedly. Instead of stereotypical representations of stage poverty, the settings contrive to be typical but also distinctive, as they are in the Irish drama. A water pail and a tin mug for drinking from it, which is a feature of Corrie's set, helps to convey the extremity of deprivation but, for all that, a canary cage hangs in the window and the lad's cherished gramophone is the last item to be pawned. The box of coal, galvanised bath and curtained-off bedspace, denoters of poverty in Act I of O'Casey's Dublin tenement in *Juno and the Paycock*, are complimented by scattered books which attest to Mary's aspirations. That important contemporary status symbol, the gramophone, is featured here, too, as one of the showy signifiers of new-found affluence to which Juno's family treat themselves in Act II. There is an even fuller collection of books in *A Collier's Friday Night* as well as framed water colours and a glass jar of chrysanthemums. The miners' cottages in all the plays have blazing fires, a coal ration being part of their wages, but, although Mrs Gascoigne's kitchen is 'not poor', it exhibits none of the aspirations to gentility observable in that of her daughter-in-law. Gow makes the point in his stage directions for *Love on the Dole* that, 'it is important to remember that this is not slum property but the house of a respectable working man' (Act I). There are defining characteristics even in what and how individuals eat: while a hot *dinner* is prepared for Lawrence's collier after a day's labouring, his pupil-teacher daughter has buttered toast and – after a dispute – tinned apricots for her *tea*.

The concern of the women in *Strife* with the sources of survival, food and warmth, reappear in more closely observed form and function much more fully as signifiers of conflict and mutual dependency. Lawrence's angry collier is not hungry for his hostile wife's stew and complains about the pudding she offers him, whereas the submissive son Joe Gascoigne, in *The Daughter-in-Law*, readily eats the food his mother has prepared. Having rejected Juno's offer of food, O'Casey's Captain Boyle surreptitiously eats it, and the frightened son, Johnny, snaps at his mother's attempt at comfort with a, 'tay, tay, tay. You're always thinkin' o' tay. If a man was dyin', you'd thry to make him swally a cup o' tay' (Act I). Although the immediate model is Synge, the actions here are less symbolically interwrought than in *Riders to the Sea*, where the cake Cathleen kneads and bakes on the fire for Bartley's journey, forgotten by him and carried by Maurya in her premonition of his death, is later offered to the men who will make his coffin. They are closer to those of *Playboy*, whose village girls bring a brace of duck eggs, a pat of butter and 'a little cut of cake' as tribute to Christy Mahon. The rejections, manipulations and offers of food as comfort or conciliation, like the various stokings and dowsings of the household fire that occur, have a familiarity that, immediately recognisable by the audience, helps bind us to the action at a quite basic level.

The hard lot of working-class women which recurred as a theme in Edwardian drama is exemplified in a lament in Masefield's *Tragedy of Nan*:

> their cheeks all flaggin', and sunk. And dull as toad's bellies, the colour of 'em. And their eyes be 'eavy, like a foundered wold ewe's when 'er time be on 'er. And lips all bit. And there they do go with the backache on 'em. Pitiful I call

it. Draggin' their wold raggy skirts. And the baby crying.
And little Dick with 'is nose all bloody, fallen in the
grate. And little Sairey fell in the yard, and 'ad 'er 'air
mucked. Ah. Ugh. It go to my 'eart.

(Act II)

There are women worn by child care in the drama of domestic realism,
just as there are drunken and violent as well as feckless and work-shy
husbands. But characterisation in the later writing goes beyond the stereotypes. We are alerted to a range of possible ways of responding to circumstances. What goes to the heart here, besides recognition of social injustice,
is the likeness to ourselves of the men and women who encounter it, and
the complexities of the relationships in which they are locked.

Questions of language

How characters speak is crucial in establishing the impression of their
dramatic reality. Before radio and more extensive travel accustomed us to
hearing regional accents, dramatists could not assume that their audiences
would be familiar with a given accent or dialect form so, within the
theatre, conventions developed for signalling region or nation by certain
immediately identifiable and often crude or travestied speech markers for
what were usually comic or minor characters. In nineteenth-century
drama, the stage Irishman, the rustic, the loyal servant, are obvious cases
in point but the practice goes back at least to Shakespeare's Fluellen with
his repeated 'look you'. Lower-class speech was indicated by the inclusion
of occasional solecisms and the use of 'ye' for 'you' and 'ain't' for 'isn't'.
Dropped initial aspirates and final gs denoted a generalised urban vernacular; substitution of z for s and v for f, a generalised rural; the inclusion of
occasional familiar markers, such as a repeated 'sure' denoted Irish speech;
'bloomin' ' and 'Lor' bless you', London. The vernacular was indicated,
too, by an obsequiousness or chirpy brightness of manner. Although
readily recognisable, such conventionality blocked serious or individualised
treatment of character.

While the writers of the Manchester School were more attentive to
Northern speech and Masefield took care in his transcriptions of Devon
dialect words, Shaw made no such attempt. His unapologetic presentation
of stage cockneys sits happily enough beside his dogmatic dowagers and

outrageous capitalists, but seems contrived when used as a model by his New Drama contemporaries whose middle-class characters speak a more realistic standard-English. The malapropisms and dropped aitches Galsworthy gives to Bly, the working-class philosopher in *Windows* (1922), to suggest aspirations above his capacities, are embarrassing as is the idiolect of Hankin's Mrs Borridge in *The Cassilis Engagement* (1907) in, for instance, her whining lamentation about her daughter: 'I did so want 'er to be respectable. I 'aven't always been respectable myself, and I know the value of it.' The Shavian model spread still further, shaping the idiom of O'Neill's cockney socialist, Long, in *The Hairy Ape* and O'Casey's English soldiers in *Shadow of a Gunman* and *The Plough and the Stars*, for all the inwardness of the one dramatist with the possibilities of the Bronx vernacular and of the other with Dublin Irish.

With the exception of occasional vernacular expressions such as 'what's up?' or 'five bob', the dialogue of workers in Living Newspapers and other politically committed drama is cast in Standard English, although it was doubtless intended to be spoken with working-class and regional rather than Received Pronunciation accents. The dramatic reality of domestic realism, by contrast, is based on the impression the dialogue gives of being scrupulously faithful to the way people talk. Of course, none of these writers gives an exhaustive account of a dialect, any more than Synge did, for all his claimed reportage and listening through floorboards. Everyday speech cannot be simply transcribed for the stage. It would be far too slow and incoherent a process to permit meaning to emerge in the brief time-span of a play. Shaping, modification and the selection of markers to suggest a speech community, are all elements of even the most realistic-seeming dialogue, whether working-class or middle-class speakers are represented. The articulate characters of Galsworthy, Barker and company speak a prose form which, though derived from speech, is quite different from it in its syntax, its word-order and the load of significant information it carries. What is new in the representation of vernacular speech in the plays of Lawrence, Gow and Corrie, and later Ena Lamont Stewart, and gives such an impression of authenticity is that, like Synge and O'Casey, the writers work from a basis of experience and observation rather than from the generalised substandard in common use on the stage.

Specific vocabulary is an important element in establishing a credible speech mode. It occurs as characteristic pronunciation or forms of words ('canna'; 'dunna'; 'axin'); non-standard plurals or verb forms (Scots 'shoon' and 'gang awa'); vernacular expressions ('shilly-shallying'; 'get away'; 'don't talk daft'; 'looney'); trade jargon ('butty'; 'day-men'; 'hutches') and actual dialect words ('strap' [= 'credit']; 'nowt'; 'sluther'; 'slobber'; 'weans'; 'I ken that'). These, more or less strongly present according to character, create an impression of individual registers. Divergent syntax is also used to indicate colloquial usage but operates most crucially in the incorporation of syntactical patterns (repetition, irrelevancy, redundancy, hesitation, divergent word-order) commonly eliminated from written prose but characteristic of the flow of speech.

The action of these plays is as shaped as the voices that carry it. Mrs Hardcastle in *Love on the Dole* has her group of gossips whose easy intrusions not only add depth to the stage world with their variant voices and opinions, their tittle tattle, squabbling and tea-leaf reading, but also function as a kind of chorus, alert to the changes in fortune of the family as they reappear in successive acts. The dialogue often dictates activity which in turn extends the meanings in the words. In *The Widowing of Mrs Holroyd*, the dialogue between Mrs Holroyd and her admirer Blackmore runs simply:

MRS HOLROYD:
> Selvidge to selvidge. You'll be quite a domestic man, if you go on.

BLACKMORE:
> Ay. They are white, your sheets.

MRS H:
> But look at the smuts on them – look.

(I. i)

But the accompanying action which brings them progressively closer to each other, in the rhythmical folding of two sheets, functions as a kind of courtship dance before the words of courtship can be spoken.

Although none of these writers quite matches O'Casey in linguistic picturesqueness, there is colour and, frequently, a mordant humour lacking in contemporary representations of Standard speech. Unwanted pregnancy prompts: 'he'd seen th' blossom i' flower, if he hadna spotted the fruit a-comin' ' and 'a wench as goes sittin' in th' Ram wi' th' fellers mun expect what she gets, missis', and upward mobility: 'thinks I to myself, she's after a town johnny, a Bertie-Willie an' a yard o' cuffs' (all *The Daughter-in-Law*). There is also recourse to such folk sayings as 'thou'lt reap trouble by the peck and sorrow by the bushel', to jingles and to songs which increase the liveliness of linguistic texture.

An example of the modification of real working-class speech into dramatic language is apparent in the matter of swearing. W. S. Gilbert had parodied the objections to swearing in polite society and its censorship on the stage in *H.M.S. Pinafore* as long ago as 1878, when the full chorus reacts with horror to the Captain's 'damme, it's too bad' ('Oh, the monster overbearing/Did you hear him, he was swearing'). But although Eliza Doolittle's single utterance of the word 'bloody' in *Pygmalion* had passed the censor, its unaccustomed use still caused a sensation in 1914. When Tom Thomas, rather later, persuaded the Lord Chamberlain that linguistic

authenticity demanded some swearing in his adaptation of Robert Tressell's
Ragged Trousered Philanthropists (1927), they 'compromised on fifteen
"bloody's" '.[12] Joe Corrie, who usually avoided using such language, good
humouredly acknowledged its existence in a single exchange:

LIZ:
> I heard him swearin' the days, maw.

BOB:
> Wha heard me swearing'?

LIZ:
> Me

BOB:
> You're a flamin' wee liar. Where did you hear me
> swearin'?
>
> > (*In Time o' Strife*, Act II)

Miles Malleson, conscious of distortion in his brief First World War play,
'D' Company (1914), one of the few (with O'Casey's *Silver Tassie*) to be
set among common soldiers rather than officers, prefaced the play with
an acknowledgement that the dialogue had been modified from reality:

> It is impossible, even for the purposes of realism, to set down
> here in print the actual language of my barrack room. The
> three or four unpleasant words that occurred extraordinarily
> often and in the queerest series of combinations and
> connections, not only created a certain atmosphere of
> ugliness that would be necessary for any really true picture
> of life then, but also supplied a sort of lilt to the conversation
> that cannot be reproduced without them.
>
> > (p. 5)

Dramatists, nevertheless, contrived an impression of rough or abusive
language. By making language bare to the point of inanity, Malleson
achieved not only a remarkable amalgam of the brutalised and the touching
as his soldiers pass their time, complaining, pontificating, struggling to
write their letters or locked in futile argument, while anticipating transfer
to the front lines, but a credible rhythm despite the absence of those words
he identified as supplying 'a sort of lilt':

ALF:
> It's mine, then.

JIM:
> I know it ain't then.

ALF:
> I know it is.

JIM:
> I know it ain't.

ALF (*His face close to Jim's and an arm outstretched to drive home his accusation*):
> Didn't you sit at theat there table an' I saved mine an' you et all yourn?

JIM:
> I never.

ALF:
> I saw yer.

JIM:
> You never.

ALF:
> I tell you I saw yer.

JIM:
> I tell yer you never.

(p. 12)

Harsh language helps create the texture of a particular world as well as the register of a particular character. In *Love on the Dole*, Gow allows his midwife, Mrs Bull, the unusually strong: 'You bleedin' little gutter rat! Aye, and take your face inside. You're blocking the traffic in the street.' Superfluous to the plot this outburst, thrown over her shoulder as she enters, suggests the roughness of the Salford streets that lie beyond the Hardcastles' door. Similarly, in the very brief scene in the back alley between the drunk and his wife we find, 'great fat guzzling pig', 'shut your trap will you or I'll break your blasted jaw', 'lousy coward', 'your blasted snout' and 'soaking swine'. Although Mr Hardcastle's speech has a liberal sprinkling of mild oaths, such as 'blasted', Gow suggests his rhythm of belligerence less by this than by the use of negatives and restricted code declarations: 'I won't have no daughter o' mine . . .'; 'I'm shovin' no blasted mill-stone of weekly payments round my neck.' Malleson uses direct contradiction: to Alf's 'we're goin ter' Africa' Tilley replies mockingly, 'Africa. I don't fink.'

The casual verbalisation of physical violence in comments such as 'a cheeky bitch; 'er wants a good slap at th' side o' th' mouth', characterises the father's speech in *The Collier's Friday Night*. The expression, because stronger than the occasion warrants, conveys the frustrated rage of the man. The dislocation is more forcefully realised when Lawrence juxtaposes such words with startlingly irrelevant comment from another member of the family, whose distance is further registered because his words, although doubtless spoken with a regional accent, include no dialect markers. Following a sharp exchange with his wife which his son, absorbed in his newspaper, has ignored, the father watches his daughter shake the crumbs from the table cloth into the hearth:

> FATHER:
>> A lazy, idle, stinkin' trick! (*She whisks the tablecloth away without speaking.*) An' tha doesna come waftin' in again when I'm washin' me, tha remembers.
>
> ERNEST:
>> Fancy! Swinburne's dead.
>
> MOTHER:
>> Yes, so I saw. But he was getting on.
>
> (Act I)

The audience experiences the elimination of the father in such a moment.

Men Should Weep (1947)

Ena Lamont Stewart's *Men Should Weep* (Glasgow Unity) combines polemic and intense feeling with humour. Set in the 1930s, although written in the early 1940s, it represents the fulfilment of this tradition. It has the scale Lawrence's plays lack and offers a fresh encounter with the sexual as well as the domestic economics of women's role. The central character is the mother, Maggie, but while the representation of family interrelationship, dependency and hostility is extensively developed, she also exists in an extended family and a community of women whose daily lives continually impinge on each other. The Glasgow tenement comings and goings are reminiscent of O'Casey's presentation of Dublin tenement life but the texture of gossip here has its own vitality. These neighbours know each other's business: they bicker, malign each other, one accuses another of harbouring lice, but they also share services, borrow food and observe each other's unhappinesses.

While the illusion of authentic speech is beautifully realised, the exchanges have a rhythm and shape that is controlled. Characters engage in sharp disputes. Two ways of life are contrasted when Maggie and her sister Lily characterise each other's lifestyle; each woman, outspoken in defence of her own pitch, is scornful of the other's:

> MAGGIE:
>> Aye, I still love John. And what's more, he loves me.

LILY:

> Ye ought tae get yer photies took and send them tae
> the Sunday papers. 'Twenty five years marriet and I still
> love ma husband. Is this a record?'

MAGGIE:

> I'm sorry for you Lily. I'm right sorry for you.

LILY:

> We're quits then.

MAGGIE:

> Servin dirty hulkin brutes o men in a Coocaddens pub.

LILY:

> Livin in a slum and slavin after a useless man an his
> greetin weans.

MAGGIE:

> They're my weans. I'm workin for ma ain.

LILY:

> I'm paid for ma work.

(I. i)

As the dispute continues, the defences collapse. Maggie drops her guard
and, admitting the difficulties of her life, confesses her anxiety about her
daughter's threats to leave home. Opponents suddenly become collaborators:

MAGGIE:

> It hurts terrible tae hear her goin on and on aboot leavin
> hame. I'm sure it's no ma fault. I've din ma best. I've
> din ma best for every yin o them. (*She starts to cry. Lily
> stands and looks at her helplessly. She too sighs.*)

LILY:

> I ken ye've done yer best. Ye've done great. But – ye
> havenae had a life fit for a dog. I jist wish there wis
> something I could dae for ye.

MAGGIE:

> Oh Lily, ye dae plenty: ye've aye been good tae the lot
> o us.

LILY:

> I dae whit I can – but it's nae much.

(I. i)

The texture of human relationship is caught: a closely observed process of
hostility and warmth, irritation and support, defensiveness and impulsive
affection.

This texture is made more convincing by the ease with which the characters are sidetracked, particularly by attention-demanding children so that, while lines of action do persist, they are plaited with others. To take one example of a process that is difficult to demonstrate by brief quotation: the play opens with Maggie's sharp retort to the complaints of her live-in mother-in-law. Granny, Lear-like, has another daughter-in-law:

> I'll awa back to Lizzie's the morn.
>
> MAGGIE:
>> Ye're no due at Lizzie's till the end o the month and she'll no tak ye a day sooner.
>>
>> (I. i)

Unlike *King Lear*, but probably rather like reality, the mind of neither stays strictly on the argument. Maggie endorses Granny's observation about Lizzie's meanness but is cross again when her hymn-singing wakes the baby. The old lady is then all but forgotten under the pressure of other demands and intercutting voices until the sequence ends with:

> GRANNY:
>> It seems a lang while since I had onything. There wouldna be a wee drap left in the pot, Maggie?
>
> MAGGIE:
>> If ye'll go aff quiet tae yer bed, I'll mak a wee cup and bring it ben tae ye.
>
> GRANNIE:
>> Wull ye? A nice hot cup? Wi' sugar and condensed mulk? And a wee bit bread tae dip?
>
> MAGGIE:
>> Aye. Come on. (*Granny struggles out of her chair.*) That's the girl. Ups-a-daisy. Edie, put the kettle on and then come and help me get yer granny out o her stays.
>
> EDIE:
>> (*Wailing*): Aw ma. Must I?
>>
>> (I. i)

No rushing out into the storm here, instead a vivid account of the trivialities and necessities, resentments and momentary kindnesses of continuing daily existence. But the sheer pressure of housework and child-care, of tiredness and straightened circumstances, is realised as never before. Maggie, in no way a perfect mother, clouts her children; fearfully puts off taking her son for an X-ray; flies off the handle after coming home to a houseful of adults and the washing-up not done.

The play engages with the economic implications underlying male/

female power relationships. There is attention to the dilemma of the man, John, and recognition that he is as bound by convention and expectation as any woman and has internalised this. Unemployed, he is without power; with no substance to support the traditional role expected of him and by him. His sense of honour is genuine but it conflicts with the reality of his situation. He is destroyed by his failure to achieve the expectations society instils in him. Jobless, he cannot provide and becomes vulnerable to taunts.

MAGGIE:

> I've seen you'se men looking for work. Holding up the street corners; calling down the Government – tellin' the world what you'd do if you wis running the country.

JOHN:

> Shut yer mouth or I'll shut it for ye.

MAGGIE:

> John, what I meant was – ye should have tidied the place up afore ye went oot.

JOHN:

> To hell with this Jessie business every time I'm oot o a job. I'm no turnin' myself into a bloomin' skivvy. I'm a man.

ISA:

> Quite right. A woman disnae respect a man tha's nae man.

(II. i)

His sense of honour is genuine but it conflicts with the reality of his situation. Male and female pride; male violence; female dependency are exposed without evident strain or didacticism.

The complexity of the ending of the play stems from its demand on the audience to respond to a range of positions and to recognise their necessity for the individual characters. Daughter Jenny has escaped in the only way she knows given the condition into which she was born: she has been good to a man who would be good to her. Returning as a kept woman, she offers the family money. Where her father, John, like Mr Hardcastle in *Love on the Dole*, follows the dictates of contemporary morality, conventional stage practice and his own sense of honour, and angrily rejects this whore's money, the more practical Maggie sees that the money will help relieve their poverty and enable their son to come home to convalesce. She also recognises the affection in her daughter's offer and, with a flash of Shavian perception, turns John's morality against him, via his own sexuality: their having slept together before marriage and his evident sexual arousal by his daughter-in-law:

MAGGIE:
> Aw, I shouldna have said they things.

LILY:
> Why no? Ye wouldna hae said them if they wisna true?

MAGGIE:
> Naw. There's things atween husbands and wives shouldna be spoke aboot. I'm sorry. I lost ma heid.

JENNY (*Kneeling at her father's feet*):
> Daddy – Daddy – forget it. It disna matter. Daddy (*She tries to draw his hands from his face*) When I wis wee, you loved me, an I loved you. Why can we no get back? (*He does not answer, but he lets her take one of his hands from his face and hold it in both of hers.*)

MAGGIE:
> Dinna fret yersel, Jenny. I can manage him – I can aye manage him. (*She is still holding the roll of notes. . . . Very softly*) Four rooms, did ye say, Jenny? (*Pause*) Four rooms. Four rooms – and a park forbye! There'll be flowers come the spring!

> (Act III)

Social polemic underpins the emotion and the humour. The ending of the play, in which Maggie takes responsibility for herself and her family is not easy. Although there is hope in the amelioration Jenny's money brings, the personal cost to each of their social and gendered situation is not cancelled.

Notes

1. James Agate, *The Sunday Times* (16.11.1925).
2. J. T. Grein, preface to Anon, *Alan's Wife: A Dramatic Study in Three Scenes, Independent Theatre Series*, No. 2 (1893), p. vi. The play is reprinted in L. Fitzsimmons and V. Gardner, eds, *New Woman Plays* (1991).
3. Ford Maddox Ford, 1931, reprinted in *Memories and Impressions* (1979), p. 364.
4. *Repertory Plays no. 3* (Glasgow, 1911), p. 9.
5. For further information about these plays see Steve Nicholson, 'Bolshevism in Lancashire: British Strike Plays of the 1920s', *New Theatre Quarterly*, 30 (May 1992), pp. 159–66.
6. Statement, Workers' Theatre Movement Conference, 1932, quoted R. Samuel, E. MacColl and S. Cosgrove, eds, *Theatres of the Left* (1985), p. 101.
7. Text of *The Rail Revolt* is printed in Samuel, MacColl and Cosgrove, eds, *Theatres of the Left*, pp. 125–30, p. 129.

8. *Stay Down Miner*, II. v, produced by The Left Theatre (1936). Quotations here from its first published version under the title *New Way Wins* (1937), p. 45.

9. Quotations here from the script printed in J. Allen, ed., *Busmen* (Nottingham, 1985), scene 24, p. 23.

10. Quoted, Introduction, D. H. Lawrence, *Three Plays*, ed. R. Williams (1969), p. 14.

11. 1911; 1913, quoted, D. H. Lawrence, *Three Plays*, ed. R. Williams p. 10.

12. T. Thomas, 'A Propertyless Theatre for a Propertyless Class', in Samuel, MacColl and Cosgrove, eds, *Theatres of the Left*, p. 84.

Chapter 9

Variable Authenticities: Staging Shakespeare in the Early Modern Period

> It is the most ethical thing that Shakespeare ever wrote, and in this respect is to be classed with the productions of Zola and Ibsen, of Bernard Shaw and Granville Barker.
>
> (William Poel of *Troilus and Cressida*)

Shakespeare was the most performed English dramatist of the period between 1890 and 1940, rivalled only by Shaw. That *Troilus and Cressida* was rediscovered around 1912 as a play for performance and labelled a 'problem play', and that that other previously neglected work, *All's Well That Ends Well*, had eight different professional productions in the inter-war years, is no chance matter. As the New Drama came into its own, perceptions about the Shakespearean canon and methods of performance changed too. The shifts taking place within the contemporary theatre were reflected in the changes in Shakespearean production. And alongside the continuing debate about the function of drama ran lively, sometimes passionate, enquiry into the relationship of the dramatic classic to its subsequent audiences.

Startlingly different certainties about how a classic should be produced ran concurrently in the 1890s. On the one hand, Irving, followed by Beerbohm Tree, built on the archeological realism and scenic splendour introduced by Charles Kean at the Princesses in the 1850s. The detail, the order, the crowd scenes of the Saxe Meininger Company were exploited by Irving as was the potential for stimulating audience response to atmosphere, emotion and sheer visual beauty, made possible by technical innovations – gas lighting, smoke effects and ever more readily manipulable stage machinery, as well as the ability to darken the auditorium safely and quickly. Pitted against this was the more ascetic attempt by William Poel to rediscover the production principles of the Elizabethan Theatre and, by using a bare open stage, to recapture the speed and fluidity of Shakespearean narrative. In the next decade, Granville Barker's Shakespeare productions, complementing his work in the New Drama, confirmed him as a remarkable initiator. The first major Shakespearean director of the twentieth century, he introduced the eclecticism that has become a feature of sub-

sequent production of Shakespeare. Respectful of the language and structure of the text, he combined recent ideas about staging met in the work
of Diaghilev, Reinhardt and Gordon Craig with those elements of Poel's
theory which seemed most essential to representation of the movement
and meanings he found in close work on Shakespeare's text.

Historical authenticity: illusionist Shakespeare

At the beginning of the nineteenth century, when melodrama ruled, the
big theatres had a Proscenium Stage: perspective scenery behind the arch
and an apron out in front. While in no way an Elizabethan open stage,
there was an area of platform between the arch and the audience which
was the primary playing space. By mid-century, when Charles Kean in
particular had attended to the stage picture and made historical authenticity
one of the driving forces of his spectacular Shakespeare productions, this
had given way to the Proscenium Arch Stage with its acting area wholly
behind the arch and, often, an orchestra pit between the stage and the
audience. At the end of the century, the picture frame was actually completed in such new theatre buildings as the Haymarket (1880), Wyndham's
(1895) and the Aldwych (1905), by the extension of the arch into a gilded
rectangle that enclosed the stage opening.

Such an arrangement emphasises the fictive reality of the self-contained
stage event. The audience become passive onlookers on a separate world
and conventions such as direct address, which play on the interaction
between stage and audience, give way to those which emphasise the
illusion that the on-stage world is a real one. Bottom, Macbeth's Porter,
Edmund, can no longer talk to the audience in the way of the stand-up
comedian and such metatheatrical references as Fabian's surmising in
Twelfth Night, 'if this were played upon a stage now . . .' or Cleopatra's
rejection of some future squeaking actor 'boying' her greatness, are necessarily eliminated. The complex metaphorical relationship between the real
world and the world of the play is forfeited.

The structure of the late nineteenth-century well-made play was in
accord with the picture-frame stage and the curtain. It assumed the smooth
progression of events: scene and act building to a series of climaxes in a
succession of curtain lines. Time passed and place changed in the intervals
between the acts. Such a dramatic rhythm is quite different from that of
the Shakespeare text and, while nineteenth-century actor-managers could
often do the big scenes superbly, Shakespearean structure was severely

modified to match the needs of their theatres. Sets were magnificent, usually employing different designers, often members of the Royal Academy, for different kinds of scene. So, Telbin designed the state rooms for Tree's 1892 *Hamlet*; Walter Johnstone the more intimate rooms, such as Gertrude's closet, and W. Hann the outdoor scenes. To cope with the problems of changing elaborate sets, scene order had to be rearranged: the succession of brief scenes in shifting locations in the middle sequence of *Anthony and Cleopatra* is one of the most obvious victims, or the interchange between castle and heath in Act III of *King Lear*. Small, intimate scenes suffered and were often cut at the expense of the texture of the play and of subsequent events.

Unlike the well-made play, Shakespeare's drama shifts constantly between the public and the private; the large, many charactered scenes and the often brief, immediate exchanges between two or three characters. Large and small scenes give way to each other: King Lear's full Court flows in on the brief opening exchange between Kent and Gloucester and, having surged out after the division of the kingdom fiasco, leaves Cordelia facing her sisters on the bare stage, after which follows an exchange between Regan and Goneril culminating in, 'We must further think on't'/'We must do something and i' the heat', which immediately precedes the entrance of the embittered Edmund. Although the short final sequence between the sisters reveals emotion and drives the action forward it was invariably cut, since it offered no obvious climax and nothing for the leading actor.

Actor-managers shaped the Shakespearean text to contemporary expectations, enabling a clearer five-act structure to carry the play through the intervals essential for elaborate scene changes, providing strong curtain lines for the leading actor and endorsing the simplified morality of the nineteenth-century stage. The final Belmont scene of *The Merchant of Venice*, for example, was obviously redundant in a production that centred on Irving's tragic Shylock and was cut, as were sardonic jibes which might have undermined the romantic Hamlet offered by Irving or by Tree who, in his 1892 production, not only bent to kiss Ophelia's hair at the end of the nunnery scene but re-entered after the burial scene to strew her grave with flowers.[1] After seeing a performance of *Cymbeline*, Shaw commented that Irving, 'does not merely cut plays; he disembowels them. . . . The truth is that he has never in his life conceived or interpreted the characters of any author except himself' (*Saturday Review*, 26.9.1896). Although more respectful of the shape of Shakespeare's plays, Beerbohm Tree regularly cut as much as a third of the text to allow time for tableaux, dances and other special effects.

Irving emphasised the aesthetic quality of the stage picture. The least figure on his Royal Lyceum stage contributed to the mood and artistic unity of the production, although his own character was invariably placed centre stage, the rest of the company taking up their positions around him. His 1892 *King Lear*, was set in the post-Roman dark ages, in an atmospheric series of decaying palaces, after the retreat of the Romans – the ruins of a past civilisation offering a scenic counterpart for the ruin enacted on stage. Crowd scenes contributed to the mood: at the moment of Lear's death, for example, a stage full of silent, onlooking soldiers dropped their spear points to the ground in a tremendously moving visual image. That his interest in atmospheric effects was sometimes at odds with his claims to scenic realism is registered in William Archer's mockery of a scene in the 1889 *Macbeth*:

> The only visible source of illumination is a small hanging
> lamp but miraculous shafts of moonlight break in on every
> hand, and flashes of lightning make themselves visible (so far
> as one can understand) through walls of solid whinstone.[2]

Such effects were further heightened by the practice of introducing expressive extra-textual tableaux or holding a touching end of act image. Irving's *Macbeth*, opened with the witches dimly revealed on a rocky eminence at centre stage, after which the stage was plunged into darkness then lightened to show the three figures hovering in the air. Frank Benson introduced a pre-scene tableau of Hamlet composing his 'Murder of Gonzago' piece. Tree included a tableau of the signing of Magna Carta in his *King John* and, as Richard II, he rode on horseback through a stone-throwing mob after the deposition scene. His account of the end of his 1904 production of *The Tempest* is worth quoting at length because it so vividly recreates the method and the sentiment. After his 'And deeper than did ever plummet sound,/I'll drown my book':

> Prospero breaks his staff, at which there is lightning and
> thunder, followed by darkness. Through the darkness we
> gradually see once more a picture of the Yellow Sands
> enveloped in a purple haze. The nymphs are again singing,
> 'come unto these yellow sands' but their music is broken by
> the homing song of the sailors, and we see the ships sailing
> away. . . . For the last time Ariel appears singing the song of
> the bee. Taking flight at the words, 'Merrily, merrily shall
> I live now', the voice of the sprite rises higher and higher
> until it is merged into the note of the lark – Ariel is now
> free as a bird. Caliban listens for the last time to the sweet
> air, then turns sadly in the direction of the departing ship.
> The play is ended. *As the curtain rises again*, the ship is seen
> on the horizon, Caliban stretches out his arms towards it

in mute despair. The night falls, and Caliban is left on the
lonely rock. He is a king once more.[3]

(my italics)

If the visual image was shaped to nineteenth-century theatrical practice,
so was the use of sound. In Shakespeare's text, musical effects are always
signalled: noticed, demanded or suppressed by the characters – 'Whence
should this music be?'; 'If music be the food of love, play on. . . . Enough,
no more'. In the nineteenth-century theatre, by contrast, music operated
on audience emotions unnoticed by the characters, as with the sound
track of film today, and the practice was carried over into Shakespearean
production. As the spectacle became increasingly elaborate, so special
music was commissioned to support it. Lily Langtry's 1890 *Anthony and
Cleopatra* included, according to its programme, an 'Alexandrian Festival'
to console the defeated Anthony in Act III Scene ii and a 'Triumphant
Reception' of Anthony in Act IV Scene ii with 'Preludes, Ballets and
Incidental Music specially composed by Edward Jakobowski'. Beerbohm
Tree, who regularly commissioned appropriate music for his productions
and included an overture before each act, announced piously in publicity
for his 1899 *Midsummer Night's Dream*:

> There will be no ballet in the ordinary sense of the word,
> for that indeed, Mr Tree holds would be a desecration of
> Shakespeare but there will be certain gambols of the elves
> and fairies, just as long as Mendelsohn's music demands.

Although, in 1911, succumbing to desecration, he did include a ballet of
seventy-five children.[4]

Tree's, indeed, was the extreme version of spectacular realism. Where
Macready's 1847 *As You Like It* had included the off-stage sound of
birdsong at dawn and sheep bells, Tree famously put live rabbits into his
Midsummer Night's wood and used real horses for *Richard II*'s lists at
Coventry. A pugnacious defender of the technologically equipped, decorated stage, he declared illusion to be 'the alpha and omega of dramatic
art' and argued that Shakespeare's frustration with his primitive stage was
evident in the scenic developments in play such as *The Tempest*, written
after the move of the company to the Blackfriars indoor theatre. Producers
who used all the facilities of contemporary theatre to interpret the dramatic
imagination evident in the writing, were, therefore, truer to Shakespeare's
genius than those whose scholarly exhumations led to quaint but dull
shows.[5]

Scenic and spectacular Shakespeare delighted a general public that
relished 'frocks and frills' drama and drew large audiences. A. B. Walkley,
by no means an inconsiderable judge, wrote of Irving's contribution:

His series of Shakespearean land and sea scapes, Veronese
gardens open to the moonlight, a Venice unpolluted by
Cook's touristry, groves of cedar and cypress in Messina,
Illyrian shores, Scotch hillsides and grim castles, Bosworth
field – what a gorgeous panorama he has given us. The
sensuous, plastic, pictorial side of Shakespeare had never
been seen before as he showed it us.[6]

But other possibilities were being mooted from the very quarter responsible
for the attack on Society Drama, as Tree's defensive tone implies.

Victorian interest in history and scientific accumulation of evidence
prompted the use of settings and costumes authentic to the period in
which the action of the play took place, but then led on to further
questions of which authenticity? what origin? In his essay, 'The Truth of
Masks', Oscar Wilde noted that most *Hamlets* were 'placed far too early'
since Hamlet is self-evidently a Renaissance scholar, 'and if the allusion
to the recent invasion of England by the Danes puts it back into the ninth
century, the use of foils brings it down much later'.[7] The implication,
although Wilde did not pursue it, is that the period when the play was
written is at least as consequent as the period in which it is set.

At the same time, accuracy of the text was becoming increasingly
important to scholars interested in 'the progress and meaning of Shakspere's
mind'.[8] Such groups as the Malone Society, the Early English Text Society
and the New Shakspere Society, devoted themselves to the comparison of
early Quarto texts with the Folio, the establishment of an accurate chron-
ology of composition and, as the technology became available, the facsimile
reproduction of texts. Variant versions suggested to some scholars that
there might have been variations from the written text in performance,
or that Shakespeare may have rewritten in the light of performance. Such
suggestions increased recognition of Shakespeare as a practical man of the
theatre turning out scripts for performance under pressure.

Scholarly rediscovery of or new emphasis on other Elizabethan dramatists, similarly, served to put Shakespeare's work back into the context of
his own theatre. The plans for the Fortune Theatre were already known
but the discovery and publication of the de Witt Sketch of the open stage
of the Swan Theatre, in 1888, gave the first clear sense of what an
Elizabethan theatre may have looked like. The crucial figure in perceiving
the implications of such scholarship for theatre practice, and feeding back
into scholarship through his developing practice was William Poel. And
support came, perhaps unsurprisingly, from the Fabians, Ibsenites and
growing band of Shavians set on recapturing the theatre as a serious art
form.

A new authenticity: William Poel and Elizabethan staging

Poel argued that although Shakespeare had written for all time he had not written *out of time* but had seen the world through Elizabethan eyes.[9] Shakespeare's stagecraft, he believed, was concealed by adaptation to the nineteenth-century picture-frame stage, star system and illusionist scenery. 'Inducement to mutilation' came with 'the demand for carpentry'.[10] He argued that the 'limitations' under which Shakespeare worked would, if rightly understood, be seen as advantages. The bare platform, two rear doors and gallery space of the Elizabethan theatre allowed for speed of movement. Speed but also versatility because, besides utilising the various spaces and levels of the platform stage, the dialogue and the implications it carried for action and gesture utilised audience imagination, making the audience vitally interactive with the stage. He rejected the idea of intervals and act divisions, noting that Shakespeare worked by juxtaposing unlike scenes, every scene being opened by characters not present at the close of the preceding scene, which made for smooth flow of the action providing there were two entrances. While it was reasonable to cut lines, the common practice of cutting whole scenes interrupted the gradual cumulation of effects.

In 1881, Poel offered his 'authentic *Hamlet*': staged without act breaks on a bare, curtained platform in St George's Hall. The acting was evidently amateurish and the production still very much a transitional one, since Poel used the drop curtain for dramatic effect, actors being on stage when it came down and scenery being shifted behind it. But the stage was simple: curtains on either side formed a semicircular playing space and divisions in the curtains provided the arras behind which watchers could be concealed in the nunnery and closet scenes. The only additions were benches and chairs to denote indoor scenes and a green mound for the graveyard. Thus, the first court scene was played in the same space and setting as the battlements where the ghost had walked, the shift from one place to another being marked by the assumptions in the dialogue but also, by the formality and procession of the entrance of the Court.

Poel justified his use of the First Quarto on theatrical and polemical grounds. In a paper given to the New Shakspere Society in June 1881 he argued that if Q1 derived from what an actor remembered or someone saw in the theatre, then:

> in the arrangement of the scenes, the stage directions, the omissions, and the alterations, there is much to guide

[the director] and instruct him in the stage representation
of the play as it appeared in Shakespeare's time.

For all its flaws and garbled dialogue, Q1 represented an attempt to
reconstruct the performance as seen on Shakespeare's stage so that, if
cutting were called for, Q1 provided a guide while Q2, the good Quarto,
should provide the actual speeches. Use of this text, which outraged some,
was a direct challenge to the practice of adapting works from other times
or places to the style and expectations of contemporary theatre. As well
as cutting the text to emphasise the prince at the expense of other
characters, the current acting edition of the play eliminated Hamlet's
sardonic comments, directed that Gertrude be penitent and Hamlet tender
to her in the closet scene, lost Fortinbras and the dumb show and created
climactic curtain lines to tide the audience over each interval. Poel subsequently played the Folio text arranged in Q1 order (1900) and his own
version of the Second Quarto (1914). His claim was that choices should
be made about the text and made knowingly: textual scholarship being
relevant to the stage as well as the study.

The insights into Elizabethan staging offered by publication of the de
Witt Sketch were registered in Poel's production of *Measure for Measure* in
1893. He constructed a replica Elizabethan stage in the Royalty Theatre,
taking his measurements from the builder's plans for the Fortune Theatre
and including an apron which projected over the orchestra pit and a gallery
at the back of the stage which was decorated only with tapestry curtains.
To further the illusion of an Elizabethan theatre, he put extras on the stage
and in specially built side boxes to represent an Elizabethan audience. In
justification of his bare stage, he noted in a lecture eight days before the
production:

> Shakespeare himself considered it to be the business of the
> dramatist to describe the scene and to call the attention of
> the audience to each change in locality, and moreover he
> does this so skilfully as to make his scenic descriptions
> appear as part of the natural dialogue of the play.[11]

The interest roused by this production enabled Poel to found the Elizabethan Stage Society, sponsors of most of his subsequent productions.

Shaw welcomed Poel's initiatives from the outset and, when the Stage
Society came into being for the production of avant-garde plays, there was
a sizeable overlap of membership between the two groups, and, indeed
with the Fabian Society. For there was a political agenda here, too, that
went further than hostility to lavish display and the self-promotion of star
actors. An active socialist, Poel raised the question of where drama situated
itself. Promoting what he saw as Shakespeare's combination of 'the serious

and the ludicrous' (1889), he argued, as Robert Weimann would nearly a century later, that Elizabethan drama was based less in Court entertainments than in popular drama, hence the importance of intermingled comedy, the platform stage itself having developed from the medieval platform in the middle of the folk in the market square. A corollary of this, and of the direct address to the audience of the comic characters, is that the idea of theatrical artifice and playfulness is emphasised. Intriguingly, although increasingly characteristic of Shaw's writing, such artifice was as alien to the fourth-wall realism associated with Ibsen production and the avant-garde French theatre, admired by Poel's supporters, as it was to the proponents of Society Drama and spectacular Shakespeare. It was the shared opposition to the glamour and carpentry of the theatre of the actor-managers and the demand that theatre be re-instated as a serious art form which cast them as natural allies.

Poel's strong sense of historical context affected the way he read Shakespeare. He shared Wilde's perception that Hamlet was clearly a Renaissance figure, and he was the first to observe that Edmund in *King Lear* is an Elizabethan Machiavel. His argument is essentially that advanced later by Brecht: that acknowledging the similarities and differences accentuated by returning a work to its own period enabled better comprehension of both that other and one's own time. Equally, the rediscovery of other Elizabethan plays as possible scripts for performance helped him to put Shakespeare's work back into context. As well as his Shakespeare productions, this indefatigable man staged the first modern revivals of *The Duchess of Malfi* (1892); *Dr Faustus* (1896, followed by a nationwide tour); *Arden of Faversham* (1897); *The Broken Heart* (1898); *The Alchemist* (1899), and numerous others including the Medieval Morality play, *Everyman* (1901), newly discovered in the Lincoln Cathedral archives, which was to prove influential on the plays of both Eliot and Yeats.

In 1897, Poel produced *Twelfth Night* in the Middle Temple Hall, the very place where John Manningham recorded having seen it in 1601. The actors wore ornate Elizabethan costume, Olivia appearing in mourning and all her household in black. (A precedent rejected by actresses of the day who, used to appearing at their most glamorous on stage, regarded black as unbecoming but, like many of Poel's innovations, regularly followed since.) Certain now that the three- or five-act structure of contemporary drama was inimical to Shakespearean continuity, he introduced a single interval of ten minutes. Rejecting incidental music, he used the original setting of 'O Mistress Mine', played on an Italian virginal of 1550 and a Venetian lute of 1560.

Further experiments followed. All the actors in his 1900 production of *Hamlet* were male, a boy playing 'Ofelia'; a man, Gertrude. More sophisticated in theatrical artifice than when he had first attempted the play, he himself, playing Corambis (Polonius), directed the on-stage servants in their moving of the scenery. Extending his use of authentic music, he sat the Dolmetsch Ensemble, equipped with their early instruments, on the stage and dressed them in Elizabethan costume. More daring still but a logical conclusion of his sense of history, he used Elizabethan costume for productions of the Histories and Roman plays, notably for *Richard II* (1899) and *Troilus and Cressida* (1912), citing in support of this such lines as 'plucked me ope his doublet' and 'half their faces buried in their cloaks', from *Julius Caesar*.

Opposition was fierce. Replying to an attack on his 1898 *Julius Caesar*, Tree scorned:

> learned amateur societies who will present Shakespeare in
> such a way as to commend him to the few while boring
> the many . . . the business of the manager is to present
> Shakespeare in such a way as to commend him to the many,
> even at the risk of agitating the few.
>
> (*The Academy*, 5, 26.2.1898)

And William Archer parted company from his natural allies in his hostility to Poel's continuing experiments. He argued that the true end of Shakespeare production must be to make the plays 'really live for the modern playgoer' which could not happen with a production method that 'appeals only to the dilettante and enthusiast'.[12]

There were, indeed, problems with Poel's productions. Some parts of the experiment, such as the inclusion of quasi-Elizabethan audience members on stage, proved merely distracting. The literal-minded reproduction of a surface authenticity – wooden columns, quasi-stage boxes – tended to an antiquarian quaintness that could be as much of a barrier between stage action and audience as the picture-frame stage had been. Further, much of what Poel did was idiosyncratic. He seems to have had a tin ear for both iambic pentametre and metaphor and often cut the most startling and powerful sequences. A large part of Richard II's prison speech (lines 5–40) went, as did virtually all the best lines in *Coriolanus*, following Poel's intuition that they were written by Chapman. Particularly early on, there were often weak actors in the cast, as there were in Independent and Century Theatre productions which also relied on amateurs. The chief problem, though, was the purely practical and occasional one that arose from the kind of theatre spaces currently available. It was that of being obliged to attempt 'authentic' staging on non-authentic stages (to say nothing of the presence of a non-authentic audience).

The Proscenium Arch theatres in which Poel was obliged to construct his Elizabethan theatres made his claim to 'Elizabethan' staging problematic. In the 1900 *Hamlet*, he disguised the arch with curtains and used *trompe d'oeil* effects to suggest an open stage within the Proscenium Arch with, further back, a canopy, inner stage and balcony and a small on-stage audience. But the separation of stage and audience remained. The problem remained even when he moved into theatres accustomed to staging the New Drama. As C. E. Montague, who warmly welcomed Poel's initiative, wrote in response to his production for the Manchester Repertory Company at the Gaiety Theatre:

> Mr Poel did wonders but he could not get rid of the proscenium arch. What he gave us was not an Elizabethan stage as it was to Elizabethan playgoers, but a picture of an Elizabethan stage seen through the frame of the modern proscenium. So we gained a good visual idea of a Shakespearean stage but not the Elizabethan sensation of having an actor come forward to the edge of the platform in the midst of ourselves and deliver speeches from a position almost like that of a speaker from a pulpit or from a front bench in Parliament, with only the narrowest scope for theatrical illusion, with no incentive to naturalism and with every motive for putting his strength into sheer energy and beauty of declamation, giving his performance the special qualities of fine recitation as distinct from those of realistic acting.[13]

The realist stage and acting style were as much at odds with the anti-illusionist elements of Elizabethan theatre and the audience-stage interaction as were the stages and acting styles of West End theatre.

Open-stage theatre, as Poel and Montague perceived, privileged the actor, demonstrating that the human presence, alone and in relationship, is the vital element in drama. Voice and gesture interacting, contrasting, coordinating, create conflict, closeness, wonder or arousal and, working simultaneously with the power of the language used and the actions performed, engage the imaginative powers of the audience and draw in aspects of ourselves and of our fantasy lives. Poel could not entirely recreate this but, by urging audiences and theatre practitioners to challenge their assumptions about spaces and relationships in the theatre, was a significant enabler for twentieth-century theatre. The open stages available now all over the English-speaking world as well as more specific stage spaces, such as the Swan at Stratford-on-Avon and the Pit in the Barbican, owe their existence, in part, to his passionate experimentation. His theatrical children and grandchildren, moreover, have dominated Shakespeare production in the twentieth-century English theatre.

Among those who worked with Poel were the actors Edith Evans, discovered by Poel and revelatory as his Cressida, Lillah McCarthy, his Olivia, and Lewis Casson, who became one of the leading figures in performance of the New Drama. His influence went into the academies, too. Elsie Fogerty, Poel's 1897 Viola, subsequently became head of the Central School and Olivier's teacher, while the Cambridge Marlowe Society, subsequently the training ground of many classical actors, was influenced from the outset by the example of Poel whose nephew, Reginald, played Richard II in the Marlowe's 1910 production. Granville Barker, moreover, made his Shakespearean debut as Poel's Richard II in 1899. He always acknowledged his debt to Poel, and, either directly or via Barker, the leading directors of the 1920s and 1930s – Iden Payne, Harcourt Williams, Martin Harvey, Barry Jackson – also acknowledged his influence. Robert Atkins, director at the Old Vic for a decade, had acted and stage managed with Poel; Bridges Adams, director at Stratford for fifteen years from 1919, had acted with both Poel and Barker.

Some followers were literalists: Nugent Monck, probably Poel's strictest disciple, had a quasi-Elizabethan theatre built – the Maddermarket at Norwich – and from 1921, worked through the whole Shakespeare canon, very much on Poel principles. Lewis Casson, listing the necessities of Shakespearean production he derived from Poel, included the full text in its proper order, continuity between scenes without breaks between acts, a wide platform stage and Elizabethan dress.[14] Others, like Barker, were more eclectic, rejecting the surface Elizabethanism even while exploring different kinds of authenticity. He followed Poel in getting his actors to speak the verse swiftly with light, unpointed speech, as they did the New Drama. Instead of attempting to recreate a physical simulacrum of Shakespeare's theatre, though, he started from Poel's perceptions about the text: its speed, mobility, intercutting scenes and scenic form, and recognised the importance to its texture of the use of specific props, the locating power of words, and the ability to shift location when not bound by too fixed a set.

Like the founders of independent theatres towards the end of the nineteenth century, Poel offered an alternative vision to that of mainstream theatre. Although single-minded in his own approach, by demonstrating that there were choices to be made about production, he opened the way to the eclectisism that has been evident this century. As Robert Speaight wrote:

> There is nothing new today in *Hamlet* being performed in curtains; there is nothing sensational in the appearance of Fortinbras. No one will raise an eyebrow if you suggest that *Hamlet* is a play drenched in Renaissance thought, or that while Hamlet should never behave like an actor, there is every reason why he should, on occasion, behave like a cad. The romantic Hamlet is now the reactionary Hamlet and the sentimental one is obsolete. These changes might never

have come about if William Poel had not had the startlingly original idea of reading the play as if he had just borrowed the prompter's copy from the Globe theatre.[15]

Few would now claim there is one correct way to produce Shakespeare but any director is likely to be asked to justify his or her own practice.

Shakespeare's 'problem plays'

If Shakespeare production has, like English drama itself, responded to the needs of a changing culture, so has the nature of the canon. One form of Poel's proselytising lay in the conscious reintroduction of scarcely known Shakespeare works. *Measure for Measure, All's Well That Ends Well* and *Troilus and Cressida* were particularly privileged by him. The restoration to the national repertoire of what have come to be called 'the problem plays' is a notable feature of the period under discussion. He also shared with others a renewed interest in the English history plays.

Phelps's production of *All's Well That Ends Well* was the only notable one in the nineteenth-century. It had been played previously, but with the emphasis on Parolles and Helena's role much diminished. There had been a few Restoration and early eighteenth-century performances of Dryden's adaptation of *Troilus and Cressida* but it had not been played in any form since 1733. Similarly, although *Measure for Measure* provided subjects for paintings and the image of Mariana in her moated grange was evoked in Tennyson's renowned late Romantic poem, 'Mariana', the play itself was rarely performed. Poel, indeed, recalled having been advised by one of his teachers that the two Shakespeare plays he hoped he would never read were *Troilus* and *Measure*. In so far as that edict was an indicator of nineteenth-century fears and complacencies in matters of morality and the arts, defiance of his teacher was a motivating factor for Poel and his successors.

Only a small number of plays were performed regularly on the nineteenth-century stage: the romantic comedies, including *A Midsummer Night's Dream* and *The Merchant of Venice*, the big tragedies and, among the histories, *Richard III, Henry IV* and *Henry V.* Phelps, at Sadler's Wells between 1843 and 1862, was unusual in playing thirty-one of Shakespeare's plays, although not *Troilus and Cressida, Richard II, Henry VI* or *Titus Andronicus*, and Frank Benson produced all the Folio plays between 1892 and 1916, at the Stratford Festival or on tour, with the exception, again, of *Titus* and *Troilus and Cressida*.

That Phelps avoided *Richard II*, is a reminder that a remarkably successful production will inhibit or stimulate others. After Charles Kean's spectacular production in the 1850s, there was no performance of the play for forty years until Poel challenged the embargo in the 1899 production in which Barker made his debut, after which Beerbohm Tree, responding to the challenge of the up-start, adopted the role as his own. Tree's interpretation was, in turn, displaced by John Gielgud's beautiful, weak king which, seeming definitive, inhibited further productions until after the Second World War. Benson, for his part, created a context for the *Henry VI* plays. He staged these early works, with their brilliant flashes, longeurs and complicated twisting-and-turning story, as a cycle with *Richard II* and the other well-known English history plays. Although repeated since, this first experiment of the kind left Yeats for one 'moved as never before' in a theatre to encounter 'all the links that bind play to play unbroken'.[16]

Poel linked three obscure plays very firmly with one popular and, he felt, much misunderstood one when he wrote of *All's Well that Ends Well*:

> This comedy belongs to the transitional period of Shakespeare's dramatic art, the time, perhaps, when the poet showed the most creative power during his professional career. *Measure for Measure*, *Troilus and Cressida* and *Hamlet* are all characteristic plays of this period.[17]

He always associated *Hamlet*, a play that continually interested him, with these three neglected plays on the grounds of its supposed date of writing but, even more, on the basis of its sardonic tone. His insistence on working from the full Folio text and investigating the various Quarto versions of the play was part of his battle to retrieve the play and the 'corroding irony' of its protagonist from the romantic sentimentalising of the acting versions performed by the likes of Irving and Tree. He also promoted the other three works through his writing as well as through productions. *Measure for Measure* was the first play he produced for the Elizabethan Stage Society, in 1893. In 1912, he staged the first production since its own day, possibly the first production ever, of *Troilus and Cressida*.

These works gained the label 'problem plays' by which they are now commonly known, because they seemed to Edwardian audiences to share ground – sexual dilemmas, sardonic world-views, realisic portrayal of everyday life and notably independent-minded women – with the problem plays so characteristic of current avant-garde drama. Shortly before his production of *Troilus and Cressida*, Poel made the link firmly, claiming:

> It is the most ethical thing that Shakespeare ever wrote, and
> in this respect is to be classed with the productions of Zola,
> Ibsen, of Bernard Shaw and Granville Barker. [After the
> romantic comedies] he comes down from the clouds and
> says to his friends, 'Now I will tell you something about
> your fellow creatures as they are in Elizabethan London'.[18]

Certainly the spirit of the play chimed in with the strong anti-militarism
among the intelligentsia in the years immediately preceding the First World
War, a fact not lost on *The Times* which denounced it as decadent. After
Poel, it was produced successively by the Marlowe Society, in Cambridge;
after the First World War, at the Old Vic, and then at the Westminster
Theatre, in modern dress. There was renewed interest in *Measure for
Measure*, too, which was played with the Vienna street scenes intact and
there were eight separate professional productions in the inter-war years
of *All's Well* – Helena being widely regarded as a Shavian woman sharing
ground with the independent-minded Ann Tanner of *Man and Superman*.
While *Titus Andronicus* would have to wait a little longer before it roused
interest, the 'problem plays' came into their own in the first part of the
twentieth century.

Granville Barker and twentieth-century eclecticism

If, as Poel saw, scene is often evoked in Shakespeare's dialogue, the dialogue
also often evokes scenes that are not supposedly present on the stage. The
game of what should and what should not be imagined on the stage is
retrieved on the non-specific stage. The complex metaphorical relationship
between the play world and the real world becomes more available. Early
twentieth-century practitioners laid claim the modernity of Shakespeare's
problem plays on the basis of perceived similarities to the tone and subject
matter of the New Drama. Modernity, concerned with ideas and attitudes,
is, however, a different creature from modernism, which recognises and
delights in artifice. There is no real equivalent of literary modernism in
English *drama* of the period, except, perhaps, in Shaw's plays, and these
disguised their delight in artifice behind a façade of fourth-wall realism.
But there is an equivalent in English *theatre* and it centred itself, curiously
enough, in the Shakespeare productions of that most serious of New
Dramatists, Granville Barker.

Although his reputation as a director of Shakespeare is derived from just three productions – *The Winter's Tale* and *Twelfth Night* in 1912 and *A Midsummer Night's Dream*, in 1914 – and from his subsequent discussion of some of the plays, published as *Prefaces to Shakespeare*, Granville Barker the leading director of the New Drama was, arguably, with Peter Brook, the outstanding British Shakespeare director of the twentieth century. Like Brook in the 1960s, he was outstanding because of the combination of insight into the texts and excitement about them stimulated in audiences by his productions. He challenged the established traditions of illusionist/ realist Shakespeare production to more immediate effect than Poel because of his greater flexibility in recognising that there were different *kinds* of authenticity.

Barker was eclectic as Poel was not. He was alert to European innovations which allowed him to create a flexible stage without reproducing Elizabethan details and which had an immediacy or suggestiveness for the contemporary audiences that Poel's literalism lacked. Copeau's acknowledgement of theatrical artifice; Appia's use of a bare open stage, equipped only with lighting effects and blocks to allow a stage floor of variable height; Gordon Craig's screens; the sensuous movement and visual richness of Diaghilev's Russian Ballet, all fed into his productions.

For his 1912–13 season at the Savoy, Barker built an apron over the orchestra pit and raised the stage at the back but, rather than recreate a simulacrum of Shakespeare's theatre, he simplified his stage, relying primarily on the locating power of the dialogue to shift scenes but using lighting and semi-abstract settings to suggest particular places. Benches, white pilasters, and gold curtains suggested Leontes' palace, and a thatched cottage the sheep-shearing in *A Winter's Tale*. For *Twelfth Night* he used steps; six abstractly patterned drops at the back of the stage that could be flown quickly in with the changing scene, and representative pieces of stage furniture: a throne for Orsino, patterned like the backdrop; a tapestried table for the drinking scene; two brilliant-green toy-box trees above a pair of decorated benches at mid-stage to suggest Olivia's garden. The costumes, designed like the backdrops by Norman Wilkinson, were patterned and vividly coloured.

In a conscious acknowledgement of the artifice of theatre, Sir Toby, Maria and the other plotters hid between the benches and the audience to overhear Malvolio's response to their deceptions, their giggling reactions shared with the audience who look upstage with them to the strutting, gulled Malvolio. Malvolio in this production was a comic figure, not the sentimentalised near-tragic one Irving had presented, and the role of Feste was taken by Hayden Coffin, a musical comedy star who had not previously played in Shakespeare. As Barker declared in an interview before his first production:

> There is no Shakespearean tradition. We have the text to
> guide us, half a dozen stage directions, and that is all. I abide
> by the text and beyond that I claim freedom.[19]

Like Poel, he ran the play straight through with just two ten minute
intervals. The excitement resulting from that claim to freedom was such
that the simultaneously published editions, which included Barker's production notes as prefaces, sold out.

The denial of fourth-wall illusionism of the *Twelfth Night* production
was taken still further in *A Midsummer Night's Dream*, Barker's most celebrated production. The impact of Diaghilev's Russian Ballet, which had
first visited London in 1911, was felt in his investigation of ways of making
the action 'strange and admirable' for his generation. His *Dream*, virtually
contemporary with Beerbohm Tree's real rabbits and real tree trunks,
eschewed verisimilitude for expressive scenery created, again by Norman
Wilkinson, from draped fabrics in vivid colours. The palace was black and
silver, with white silk curtains. The wood was represented by a green
velvet mound with white flowers and by draped gauze curtains coloured
green, blue and purple, with lighting effects to reflect changing moods
and suggest the presence of glow-worms and fireflies. To make his fairies
really seem 'beings of another sort', he stylised their movements, gave them
metallic wigs and beards and, famously, painted them golden. Rejecting the
ingenious devices with which Tree and others made magic, Barker had
Oberon signal invisibility simply by stepping back and standing stock still
after his statement, 'I am invisible', while the lovers, tormented, ran wildly
between Puck, Oberon and other fairies, oblivious of their presence. As
a contemporary critic observed, 'it is without effort we believe these
quaintly gorgeous metallic creatures are invisible to human eyes'.[20]

The argument is that the wood, created in the language of *A Midsummer
Night's Dream*, is continually changing: it mirrors madness and has a
dangerous, erotic element. Lack of visual specificity in the setting enables
scale and mystery, whereas specificity confines. So, as Barker pointed out
in his Preface to *As You Like It*, suggestive scenery for the forest of Arden
can allow snakes and lions, olives, as well as copses with shepherds and
sheep; can admit the blowing winter wind and the summertime of the
courtship and weddings. In Tree's production, the fairies were all feminised
and even Oberon was played by a woman. Here, for the first time for
generations, the supernatural figures were dangerous: not just Oberon but
Puck and most of the fairies were played by men.

Barker was alert to the comedy in a play that had customarily been
considered primarily lyrical. Puck was recognisable as the 'knavish sprite',
Robin Goodfellow, dressed as he was in scarlet with bushy black eyebrows
and red berries in his hair and round his ankles, while Bottom and his

fellows seemed real and earthy; the individuality apparent in their dialogue realised in the acting. According to Desmond MacCarthy:

> Everyone praised Bottom and his friends. . . . The fussy,
> nervous, accommodating Quince, the exuberant Bottom,
> poor, timid old Starveling, Snout with his yokel's grin, and
> Flute with the meek blankness which marks him out for
> the lady's part, the laconic and cautious Snug – they were
> perfect.[21]

Although Barker withdrew from the theatre after the First World War, he continued to ponder the performance possibilities implicit in the Shakespeare text. His *Prefaces to Shakespeare* were not only used by theatre directors but helped with the slow shift in Shakespeare studies towards recognition of the plays as theatre scripts. Post-Barker, the quest for originality, the need to 'make it new', characterised Shakespeare production. Barry Jackson made a claim for the immediacy of Shakespeare's writing and a different return to Shakespeare's practice in his modern dress productions of *Cymbeline* (1923), *Hamlet* (1925), *Macbeth* (1928) and *The Taming of the Shrew* (1930) at the Birmingham Repertory Theatre. Initially startling, evening dress for Court scenes and modern artillery and rifles for battle scenes became the vogue, but certain correspondences still had the capacity to move and surprise their audiences. A contemporary commentator wrote of Tyrone Guthrie's Old Vic full-text or 'entirety' *Hamlet* (1938) with Alec Guinness as the lead, that 'for the first time one realised how a modern dress production may give new life and reality to Shakespeare's characters without losing intellectual excitement or beauty', and registered not just the visual impact of Ophelia's funeral 'with its dreamy vista of wet umbrellas and dripping mackintoshes' but the startling way in which playing the gravediggers as modern British workmen emphasised the sharpness of observation and the dry humour of the scene.[22] The problem is that the effect of such correspondences depends on their originality. While the first *Julius Caesar* to put Anthony's faction into Fascist uniforms, a modern-dress version at the Embassy Theatre during the Second World War, suggested a frightening relevance, the sharpness goes as successive directors repeat the analogy.

Shakespeare had been played in modern dress through the eighteenth century with, as was the practice in the Elizabethan theatre, additional signifiers of time, place, trade or race – blackface for Othello; a red wig for Shylock; exotic headdresses for strangers; helmets and breast plates for soldiers with short leather skirts and cloaks fastened over one shoulder, to denote the classical world. The world of the play in such staging is conceived as contiguous with the real world, an extension of it, but not it. The difference of these twentieth-century modern-dress productions from the practice of the eighteenth century and earlier again lies with the eclecticism. What was done once as a matter of course is now one possibility among many. The way in which a play is dressed – authentic Elizabethan; authentic to the period of fictional time; period merely suggested; a-historical decorative – signals attitudes and allegiances to the audience.

Once such eclecticism is acknowledged, the next stage is to find analogies in historical periods distinct from the time either of the play's setting or its writing, as George Rylands did when he set his 1932 *Hamlet* for the Marlowe Society, in the Napoleonic period. Wilder still, eclecticism could be brought into a single production, styles and periods mixed, the historical with the a-historical. Intriguingly, Poel, who had relaxed his strict Elizabethanism for his 1914 *Hamlet*, led the way in this in his 1931 *Coriolanus*, when he was nearly eighty: Volumnia was dressed as a Gainsborough in hat and plumes; Vergilia, as a pre-Raphaelite; Coriolanus as a Hussar in full dress uniform but donning the helmet and breastplate of a Roman general when dressed for battle; the Tribunes were in academic cap and gown and the citizens were garbed like French railway porters.

All this performance practice was, in one way or another although increasingly loosely, a development from Poel's insistence on returning to Shakespeare's script, but Terence Gray, between 1926 and 1933, returned to something much closer to the philosophy of Irving or Tree, although wearing a distinctly modern dress. His Festival Theatre at Cambridge became famous as a centre of experimentation and European ideas. He produced over 100 plays, putting into practice the ideas derived from Craig, Appia and Meyerhold. He used platforms, ramps and steps but, more importantly than this, he insisted that the play must serve the director's idea; that the script was merely one element contributing to the theatrical moment. Writers' Theatre gives way to Directors' Theatre; post-modernism, already in the late 1920s, threatens to displace modernism. His *Cymbeline* was played on a chequer board, like a game of chess; characters in *Twelfth Night* sped around on roller skates; in *The Merchant of Venice*, Shylock and Tubal fished lobsters (pink ones) out of the Grand Canal; the Duke played with a yoyo during the trial scene, and the onstage audience yawned through Portia's rather bored drawling of the 'quality of mercy' speech. Gray's credo was that:

> The producer's business, his sole artistic justification in fact,
> is to create an independent work of theatre-art, using the
> playwright's contribution as material towards that end.[23]

At its best the freshness and originality of such an approach engages the audience's intellect and emotion and a quasi-independent work is created, albeit an essentially ephemeral one. At its worst, the play becomes a vehicle for directorial showmanship: ingenuity and sensation are all.

Although there was no single director of Barker's stature in the inter-war years, Poel's experimentation and the revelatory nature of the work at the Savoy had evidently revived the challenge of Shakespeare for a succession of twentieth-century directors. That the first broadcast drama on radio (in February 1923) consisted of extracts from Shakespeare is hardly surprising, nor that the Shakespearean actor, John Gielgud, and the director, Tyrone Guthrie, were among those most concerned with the possibilities of the new broadcast medium. Not only was Shakespeare the national dramatist and this the new national medium but, being also a sound-only medium, it represented the triumph of word over visual image; the ultimate rejection of the cluttered stage and spectacular scenery of nineteenth-century theatre.

Notes

1. H. Pearson, *Beerbohm Tree* (1956), p. 63.
2. W. Archer, *The Scottish Art Review* (1889), pp. 249–55, p. 251.
3. B. Tree, *The Tempest*, 50th performance souvenir programme, 1904.
4. See Pearson, *Beerbohm Tree*, p. 128.
5. B. Tree, *Thoughts and Afterthoughts* (1913), pp. 42, 62, 305; especially 'The Living Shakespeare', pp. 39–72 and 'The Tempest in a Teacup', pp. 211–24.
6. A. B. Walkley, 'Henry Irving', *Black and White* (23.5.1891).
7. Oscar Wilde, *The Artist as Critic*, ed. R. Ellmann (1970), p. 421.
8. *Proceedings of the New Shakspere Society* (1874).
9. See, Robert Speaight, *William Poel and the Elizabethan Revival* (1954), p. 43. One of Poel's actors, Speaight is an essential source for Poel's activity.
10. April 1889, reprinted W. Poel, *Shakespeare in the Theatre* (1913), p. 155. My information on Poel is drawn from this volume; from Speaight; from *Transactions of the New Shakspere Society* (1894); *Notes on William Poel's Stage Productions* (Elizabethan Reading Society, 1933), and Poel's promptbooks which are in the Theatre Musuem, London.
11. Poel, *Shakespeare in the Theatre*, p. 6. Poel's use of the apron is discussed in A. J. Harris, 'William Poel's Elizabethan Stage: The First Experiment', *Theatre Notebook*, 4 (Summer 1963), pp. 111–14.
12. W. Archer, reviewing Poel's *Shakespeare in the Theatre*, *The Nation* (5.7.1913).
13. C. E. Montague, *Dramatic Values* (1911), p. 244.
14. Quoted, R. F. Lundstrom, *William Poel's Hamlets* (1985), p. 4.
15. Speaight, *William Poel*, p. 57.
16. W. B. Yeats, *Essays and Introductions* (1961), p. 97.
17. 'Elizabethan Reading Society Notes' (British Library 11757. 85), n.p.
18. Poel, Speech, 1912, quoted, Speaight, *William Poel*, p. 193.
19. Letter to *Daily Mail* (26.9.1912), quoted, Dennis Kennedy, *Granville Barker and the*

Dream of Theatre (Cambridge, 1985), p. 123. I am indebted to this work for my understanding of Barker's productions.

20. Desmond MacCarthy, quoted, Kennedy, *Granville Barker*, p. 165.
21. D. MacCarthy, *Drama* (1940), p. 12.
22. A. Williamson, *Old Vic Drama* (1948), p. 106.
23. 'Producer v. Playwright', *Festival Review* (Cambridge, 7.11.1931).

Chapter 10

The Blindfold Medium: Early Radio Drama

MARY (*sharply*):
 Hello. What's happened?
JACK:
 The lights have gone out.
MARY:
 Where are you?
JACK:
 Here.
 (*Pause. Steps stumbling*).

(Richard Hughes, *Danger*)

The opening words of *Danger* the first play written specifically for radio (Broadcast January 1924), acknowledge the peculiarity of the new dramatic medium with its strict limitation on the senses. The characters, like their audience, are robbed of sight from the beginning. The play, set in a Welsh coal mine, takes place in darkness the light breaking through only in the final moments. Experience for the characters, as for the audience, is therefore determined by what is heard. The published version of the play, labelled 'a listening play', advises that, 'for direct presentation, it should be acted in pitch darkness, and is thus better suited for performance in a room, without a stage at all, than in even a little theatre'.[1] And the dialogue reinforces the recognition that sight is absent:

MARY:
 I didn't know there could be such utter blackness as this,
 ever. It's so dark, it's as if there never was such a thing
 as light anywhere. Oh, Jack, it's like being blind.

(p. 176)

Subsequent radio dramatists, including several of the most adept, while rarely imitating the predicament of their listeners as thoroughly as Hughes did, have nevertheless recurrently afflicted their characters with non-sight, often with literal blindness as, for example, with the blind seer in Louis

Macneice's *The Dark Tower*; Captain Cat, narrator of Dylan Thomas's *Under Milkwood*, and Michael Rooney, the central male figure of Beckett's *All That Fall*.

The question of how an audience would cope with a sound-only medium was a pressing issue among writers and producers. In 1925, to hear drama in one's own home was a novel experience. Advice in *Radio Times* suggested that dimmed lights and a comfortable armchair were basic necessities for effective listening but, by 1931, Val Gielgud could observe that, 'this turning out of lights is only a trick, for once you become familiar with the medium, it is as easy to listen to a play in a lighted room as in the dark'.[2]

The characters in *Danger* are sharply, if simply, delineated and the plot line very clear, features assisted by the tersity of Hughes's dialogue and the brevity of the play – just fourteen pages of printed text. Using the highly charged event of English visitors trapped in a Welsh mine, Hughes created a model for subsequent radio writing as he traced emotional shifts from levity to panic, resignation and then relief. The dialogue has a realistic edge. It includes not only unheroic bickering and self-interest but marked clashes of age and culture. If the sudden last-minute vying between the two men for the most self-denying position, as all struggle to get to safety, seems an unconvincing assertion of the social assumptions of their own period, a final twist saves the play from the facility into which it had seemed to be about to collapse. The action moves very quickly to its end as the flood water rises and the rescuers break through:

JACK:

> After you. You're an older man than I am. Quick sir or there won't be time.

BAX:

> You've got Mary to think of – now, Jack – Haul away above there.

JACK:

> No, no. Lower me. It's me you're hauling up, and it ought to be Bax.

VOICES:

> We'll have you up first; there's no time to waste. Right?

JACK:

> I'm alright. Lower away again. Below there, Bax. Catch hold, have you got it? (*Pause*) Hi. (*Pause*) Bax. Bax – Good God, he's gone.

> (p. 191)

The admirable control of this, the abrupt ending, the speed of the final action, the refusal to waste words in exposition or epitaph, compels the audience to share the recognition of the young couple, saved in the nick of time, that the gruff, elderly man with whom they have been at odds has drowned while they have been rescued.

Hughes solves the problem of scene setting, one that recurs in early radio drama, very simply. Before the action begins, an announcer tells the audience that the scene is a coal mine, but all subsequent indications of place and event come through the dialogue and sound effects which consist of an explosion, a rush of water, footsteps, the sound of voices singing, the noise of a pick. An echo indicates that the characters are in a tunnel. Gradation of sound helps signify depth and spatial relationship: footsteps, the sound of the pick, growing louder, imply that they are coming nearer as does the increasing volume of the water rush, while the faintness of the singing voices implies distance. The Welsh words sung to a hymn tune reinforce the sense of location and suggest that the miners are showing courage in adversity. The listener is trusted to join the characters in interpreting sounds. Dramatic conventions appropriate to the sound medium are being established.

The bare stage and centrality of the word enabled Elizabethan dramatists to range in space and time. Radio dramatists found a like freedom. Whereas William Poel and Granville Barker had had to struggle through argument and example to free Shakespearean production from the constraints of act and scene division and realistic staging, and television drama has tended to stay within the bounds of theatrical realism, radio dramatists quickly realised that their unseen images need not be confined by the unwritten rules of the realistic stage. The closeness to thought or daydream of what is heard in sound-broadcasting, encouraged fluidity of form.

The White Chateau (1925)

In the first full-length radio play, *The White Chateau*, Reginald Berkeley did not use an announcer as such. Instead, he alternated sequences of choric verse spoken by a Chronicler with acted scenes in colloquial prose, to chart the process of European war through the changing fortunes and shifting occupations of a chateau in Flanders. While retaining the musical overture and division into scenes of contemporary theatre and the verse currently in vogue for chronicle plays, Berkeley offers an episodic rather than a continuous action. War overwhelms the chateau, the family is driven away and different armies take possession, loot, use it as a hospital or barracks, abandon it in retreat before, finally in scene 6, Diane the daughter of the family who has reappeared in scene 5 as a nurse, returns to the ruined chateau resolved to rebuild it.

Plot and structure are again very simple. Whereas Hughes's three characters in *Danger* had voices differentiated by sex or by age, in a more complex piece such as Berkeley's, voice quality and linguistic mode play a more important part in creating distinctions, and extensive *realistic evocative* sound effects are used to supply what the eye cannot see. The opening sequence is characteristic:

> CHRONICLER:
> > This story of the White Chateau,
> > That in the thriving Flanders plain,
> > Was builded centuries ago,
> > Burned down and builded up again,
> > And ever, through succeeding years,
> > Destroyed and built up once more,
> > Shall come familiarly to ears
> > Attuned to the din of war.
> > (*The cheerful sounds of the breakfast table. A bell is struck.*)
> A MAID'S VOICE:
> > Madame rang?
> MME VAN EYSEN:
> > Bring in a fresh pot of coffee.
>
> > > > > > > > > > (scene 1)

The Chronicler, who introduces each scene in verse has a tendency to archaism and linguistic quaintness which with his very title, 'Chronicler', suggests a mythic overview of events. The phraseology, too, 'succeeding years', 'din of war' and, later, 'Grand Attack', 'fought another day' has a general rather than a specific quality of reference making the shift to everyday speech of the dialogue that follows the sound effect particularly striking.

Exposition is reduced as the play progresses. In scene 3, the Chronicler's verse, become onomatopoeic and with a comic edge gained from its shift into couplets, introduces the experience of the fighting soldier. While trusting to the listeners' growing capacity to interpret sound signals, Berkeley follows this with a montage of song, voices and non-verbal sound:

> CHRONICLER:
> > An army in prolonged retreat,
> > Trudge, trudge of tired feet,
> > Trudge, trudge, through rain and sludge,
> > Trudge – trudge – trudge – trudge . . .
> > Heavy heart and drooping head,

> Scanty rations, scantier bed.
> Failing strength and dizzy brain,
> Trudge, trudge . . . on again.
> (*The nondescript sound of a quiet day in the trenches.*)
> A VOICE (*dolefully humming*):
> If you want ter find the Sergeant, I know where 'e is,
> I know where 'e is, I know where 'e is
> (*The muffled thump of a shell overhead.*)
> A VOICE (*plaintively*):
> I wish they wouldn't. It puts the candle out every time.
> ANOTHER:
> To say nothing of waking up weary Company Com-
> manders.
> (*A prodigious yawn.*)
>
> (scene 3)

The voices, intercutting, stoical, wryly humorous, excited, create a power-ful effect of individuals within the mass, momentarily heard, then lost. It is a sequence remarkably attuned to the possibilities of radio.

The sound effects required in this short scene seem now, by comparison, excessive, over-anxious. Following the 'muffled thump of a shell' and the 'prodigious yawn', come in the course of a very short scene:

> *scramble of someone descending the dug-out stairs*
> *clatter of enamel plates*
> *sound of rending envelopes*
> *da-da, da-da on the buzzer 'phone*
> *crack of a rifle*
> *heard walking off down the trench*
> *Tut-tut-tut-tut-tut on the machine gun*
> *Crack. Sound of a shambling fall*
> *The telephone buzz buzz buzz buzz*
> *Far-away BOOM . . . noise like a runaway train . . .*
> *CRANG, and the thud of falling debris*
>
> (scene 3)

It is evidently an attempt to supply an equivalent of stage set and visual action.

A forerunner of Sherriff's *Journey's End* and O'Casey's *Silver Tassie*, Berkeley's play made such a strong impression that, written for the seventh Armistice Day anniversary, it was repeated on Armistice Day the following year. Its evocation of the horror and futility of war carries a strongly pacifist message:

CHRONICLER:

> You know about the Grand Attack,
> And how we drove our enemies back,
> And how they threw their arms away
> And fled – and fought another day.
> You know the cost . . . a bagatelle,
> A mere ten million souls or so,
> The land a holocaust or shell
> On which no blade of grass could grow

(scene 6)

The ending has some complexity: hope for the future is qualified and a sudden demand is made on the listeners. Although the setting is Flanders and occasion of performance clearly indicates the 1914–18 war, the Chronicler's verse and the absence of specific dates, nationalities, battles, has given the play an abstract quality. When the Chateau catechises Diane in the closing moments as to the point of the war and she replies that not only was it 'the war to end wars' but that 'we have made the League of Nations', the familiar phrase and topical reference brings the action sharply into the present. The Chateau's warning that one war has frequently paved the way for another and that the League may prove to be a picturesque idea rather than a reality gives the play immediacy and qualifies the optimism of Diane's concluding expression of faith. The address is direct to each listener as the Chateau appeals for courage and observes that, 'it is so small a step to the Dawn'.

Familiarity with the medium

In 1930, the *BBC Yearbook*, recorded that 'technical production reached what is probably its highest level in the history of broadcast drama, and an author was found with an almost uncanny sense of the appropriate balance of writing for the microphone'.[3] The author in question, L. du Garde Peach, was a prolific writer and one who revelled in the broadcast medium. His full-length action dramas, allegorising current events through comic fantasies or improvising on them, utilised radio's capacity to range in time and space even more boldly than Berkeley had done in *The White Chateau*.

In *Ingredient X*, the work referred to in the *Yearbook*, a Board-room discussion of the Synthetic Rubber Company was intercut with exciting but brief scenes at sea, in the laboratory and in the heart-of-darkness African forest. The listener is led to understand that the Board's complacent account of events is at odds with the perilous search for and attempt to identify the mysterious ingredient of the synthetic rubber that the men in the field have experienced. *Marie Celeste* offered Peach's version of the reasons behind the strangely empty ship found drifting on the ocean, while *The Path of Glory* recounted the hostilities between two imaginary Balkan states – the Republic of Thalia and the Kingdom of Sardonia. But, successful as these plays were when first broadcast, the short pieces Peach also wrote, mostly for two voices and many lasting for little more than five minutes of broadcasting time, are more interesting now and offer the greatest potential for revival. Often witty, sometimes zany, these quintessential early radio pieces make play with the audience's role as listeners-in.[4]

The literalism of Hughes setting that first radio play in darkness is parodied in *Switched* which begins with the announcement, 'The scene is a flat in complete darkness'. A couple heard stumbling about looking for the light switch, believe they must have been robbed, only to discover when they finally locate it that they are in the wrong flat. *The Séance*, even more pointedly, begins:

HE:

Switch off the lights.

SHE:

But must you have the lights off?

HE:

Yes. Much better chance of something getting through in the dark.

Strange moanings and wailings, her fear of the dark, his insistence on listening and concentration, distant sound of a violin growing gradually louder, all create an expectation of a supernatural visitation but at the end of the piece an American voice breaks in with 'Hello folks. New York calling'. The joke is on the gullible listener as He turns out to have been a radio hack searching for a station and the eerie violin, a broadcast concert.

In other pieces, Peach parodies radio's use of conventional sound signifiers and the ubiquitous announcer. In *The Wedding*, the same action is played twice: the first time as written by the enthusiastic playwright with sound effects which, in four pages of text, include a storm, waves, a door opening and closing, a foghorn, church bells, seagulls, hailstones, a knock, a muffled explosion and an aeroplane. The replay which is quite without effects is offered as the jaundiced producer's version and includes lines such as:

GRACE:
> Can you hear the church bells?

OLD JOHN:
> Church bells?

GRACE:
> Yes, of course. They're ringing for my wedding.

OLD JOHN:
> No, I can't hear them.

GRACE:
> Neither can I. The wind must be wrong.

The interpolation of such parodies of radio practice among serious items implies an intimacy with the audience that is evident, too, in the very direct and often informal address of some of Peach's announcers. In *Taps*, for example:

ANNOUNCER:
> It is a quiet country road, an unspecified number of miles from anywhere, and probably further than that to anywhere else.
>
> One moment. Yes. A nice little new two-seater is humming down the road towards us. Do you hear it?
>
> (*The sound of a car approaching.*)
>
> Do you recognise the radiator? It is one of those with a – but here it is.

In some respects, the listener to radio drama has more in common with the reader of a novel than the audience of a stage play. The listener is not only likely to be solitary but is also required to process language directly, without interpretative visual prompts. Live voices and sounds differentiate the medium from the purely narrative form, giving it a greater immediacy. Lance Sieveking, one of the early practitioners, observed that, 'elaborate, wordy, descriptions of landscapes and houses, of people's faces and clothes more often than not defeat their own ends'. Narration needed only to be sufficient to enable listeners to bring their own experience into play.[5] While the use of an announcer to set the scene and mark scene or time changes quickly became standard practice, the more experimental writers often eschewed narration altogether, relying on intercutting, fade-in and -out and cross-fade to indicate changed mood or location.

The Squirrel's Cage (1929) and The Flowers Are Not For You To Pick (1930)

No narrator sets the scene of Tyrone Guthrie's *The Squirrel's Cage* in which the humdrum life of Henry from birth to maturity is charted through a succession of low-key scenes as the child's initiative and spirit of adventure are drawn into conformity with middle England, family responsibilities and respectable work. Instead, the end of each episode is marked by the stroke of a bell, the scream of a siren and a *melée* of voices. Choric interludes are used to convey the process of Henry's socialisation as voices give orders, offer information, speak the language of daily commuting or of office routine, but do so in staccato, non-interactive phrases that are usually restrictive and often repetitive. Each choric interlude rises to a thunderous crescendo, suggesting the pressure behind the surface, the soul-destroying constriction of Henry's existence. The director at the mixing panel, using four separate studios, faded the actors, the chorus, the sound effects and the orchestra in or out as appropriate.

The Squirrel's Cage is a small neat play. Its bleak perception is voiced specifically through the title image. The squirrel, eternally running round in its cage believing it is getting somewhere, appals a visitor at Henry's birth in the opening scene before anonymous voices cut in with, 'Don't baby ... Baby you're not to ... Stop it baby ... Baby you're very naughty ...' As the action proceeds, Henry tries and fails to break out of his increasingly routine existence characterised by further sequences of patterned voices:

> Up in the morning
> Down at night
> Suburban trains.
> Do you mind if we have this window open?
> Up and down Up and Down
> Rhythm of train, 'tickets please'.
> (Interlude III)

and repetitions of 'What will people think?', 'What will the neighbours think?' until, as the wheel of the play and of Henry's life comes full circle in scene 6, the title image is evoked again by Henry himself:

> HENRY:
>> It's the monotony that gets irksome – the same old routine day after day – round and round – like a squirrel in a cage.

IVY:

> Round and round. (*Pause*) Cheer up, Henry, good times are coming.

HENRY:

> That's it – that's just what makes it worthwhile – the feeling that we're *progressing*, not just running round and round – and the feeling that all the time one's building up something solid – something sound.

(scene 6)

The irony is compounded when he turns on his son with, 'haven't I told you before that you're not to touch my things. How many times have I got to tell you that you're *not to, not to, not to*', and the voices from the beginning of the piece cut in echoing him loudly and only finally fading out as the play ends.

Soliloquy and its modern form, stream of consciousness, which had proved a problem in the realistic theatre, found a place in radio drama, disembarrassed of the solid visual presence of actors pretending not to overhear or freezing awkwardly while a character expresses his or her inmost thoughts. Shifts from external reality to interior perception, from actuality to dream or fantasy are more readily made, signalled by alteration of voice tone, musical accompaniment, a slight echo effect. Citing *The Squirrel's Cage*, Raymond Postgate argued in *The Listener* that expressionism was far more appropriate to radio where 'space and spatial relations do not exist' than the stage since:

> a wireless listener will imagine for you without any demur a complete railway journey – a change in space. But he will also accept a series of more or less confused and repetitive noises as a fair representation of a whole series of railway journeys, of years and years of railway journeys – a change in time. This he does because the wireless gives his imagination freedom to visualise whatever memories are suggested by a repetition of phrases such as, 'It simply means I shall have to travel by the eight fifteen'. A series of such phrases, repeated, varied slightly, and plastered one upon the other, is accepted by the mind as a fair record of a life-time of railway journeys, for the reason that the mind, looking back on such a perspective of real journeys recalls just such a plaster and repetition of little-varying phrases and sounds run together by the passage of time.[6]

Certainly, a 1956 recording of the play bears out Postgate's claim that the expressionist interludes have a dramatic force the realist episodes lack.[7]

The action of Guthrie's *Matrimonial News* (written, 1931) takes place in the mind of a woman who sits alone in a cheap restaurant in the Strand waiting to meet a man from the lonely hearts column, and the whole of *The Flowers Are Not For You To Pick*, Guthrie's most notable radio play, broadcast in 1930 with Flora Robson and Harold Scott in the leading roles, is a form of interior monologue. Like William Golding's much later novel, *Pincher Martin*, the action takes place as if in the mind of a drowning man but, unlike Golding's novel, this is made apparent throughout by the recurring sound effects of the waves and by the announcer's introduction:

> It is said that their past lives float before the eyes of drowning men. From a ship, bound for China, a young clergyman has fallen overboard . . . even now he is struggling for life in the water . . .
> (*The sound of waves fades in*)
> His name is Edward. And before his eyes float pictures . . . voices sound in his ears . . . voices . . . voices . . . his past life.
> (*The waves fade as the first scene begins*)
>
> (scene 1)

In a series of flashbacks, *The Flowers Are Not For You To Pick* reveals the thwarted life but tenacious spirit of the central character, enacted in a series of scenes from childhood, when he refused to give up the rose he had disobediently picked, through his youthful determination to be ordained despite the hostility of his family, to his mature disappointments in the evident tediousness of his sermons and rejection by the woman he loved, to his imminent drowning. Linguistic disruption and patterning in stichomythic form is employed to suggest emotional extremity. When, for example, Edward reels at the news that Vanessa is to marry a man in Birmingham, the impact is conveyed through the alternating voices and interweaving meanings of two bystanders:

FANNY:
> Loosen his collar, quick.

MRS DOLAN:
> Something he must have eaten.

FANNY:
> Loosen his collar, quick.

MRS DOLAN:
> Something he must have eaten.

FANNY:
> Loosen his collar, quick.

MRS DOLAN:
　　Something he must, Vanessa . . .
FANNY:
　　Loosen his Birmingham, quick.
MRS DOLAN:
　　Birmingham married, Vanessa.
FANNY:
　　Loosen his Birmingham, quick.
MRS DOLAN:
　　Edward can't marry Vanessa.
FANNY:
　　Birmingham, Birmingham, quick.
MRS DOLAN:
　　Edward can't marry Vanessa, Edward can't marry
　　Vanessa.

(scene 14)

Like *The Squirrel's Cage*, *The Flowers* is cyclical and, again, the title words provide a suggestive undercurrent to the action. Used in the first scene, they recur when the opening sequence is repeated in the final one but with a density and poignancy gathered from the intervening action and verbal texture.

Guthrie's plays are among the most achieved of the radio drama written in this period. The main action here, as in his other pieces is mundane. But, interested in audio-suggestion and believing radio to be 'less substantial but more real'[8] than theatre, Guthrie uses not sound effects so much as voice and voices to explore the experience behind the commonplace mask. That he was conscious of doing so is clear from a plea he issued to radio dramatists in 1931 that they should:

> make more use of rhythm in the writing and speaking; more
> deliberate use of contrasting vocal colour, changing tempo,
> varying pitch. One feels that only by attacking the subject
> from a symphonic angle is it possible to rid the mind of
> unwanted literary and artistic conventions.[9]

The stripping to essentials, the emphasis on the fluidity permitted by the spoken word, the faith in the interpretative capacities of the audience are recognisably of the same kind as Guthrie's inventive work as a theatre director, for which he is now better remembered. For all the bleakness of theme, his radio plays have linguistic vigour and a significant perception of the possibilities of the medium. As Mary Crozier observed of *The Flowers* in 1933:

Something about the play began to strike me; this was no blindfold theatre; it was a play which meant something in terms of sound; it used sound to take the imagination, and produce a sequence of images and a state of mind.[10]

Although Guthrie's withdrawal as director of Yeats's *The Player Queen* was one reason for the collapse of the projected Poets' Theatre, his radio work, with its exploration of rhythm and suggestion, its expressive use of abstraction was a truer inheritor of Yeats's attempt to create a literary drama than the subsequent plays of either Eliot or Auden. It prepared the way for Louis Macneice's *The Dark Tower* and the dramatic achievements of post-Second World War radio from *Under Milk Wood* to *A Slight Ache* and *All That Fall*.

Notes

1. Introduction to Richard Hughes, *Plays* (1928), p. 171.
2. Val Gielgud, 'The Play from the Armchair', *The Listener* (14.1.1931), p. 62.
3. *BBC Yearbook* (1930), p. 77.
4. Several can be found in L. du Garde Peach, *Broadcast Sketches* (1927).
5. Lance Sieveking, *The Stuff of Radio* (1934), p. 76.
6. R. Postgate, 'Expressionism and Radio Drama', *The Listener* (23.9.1929), p. 405. Guthrie's radio plays can be found in *The Squirrel's Cage and Two Other Microphone Plays* (1931).
7. LP23862c BBC Sound Archives. Full recordings of first broadcasts of the plays discussed here do not exist but brief snippets of many of them are collected on a record in the sound archive. They appear to have been used to illustrate a talk on the Broadcast Play delivered by Val Gielgud to accompany the Festival of Radio Theatre, 1933.
8. T. Guthrie, *The Squirrel's Cage* (1929), p. 9.
9. T. Guthrie, *BBC Yearbook* (1931), p. 189.
10. Mary Crozier, 'Taking Stock of the Drama', *The Listener* (16.8.1933), p. 253.

Chronology

Note: Dates of plays refer to first British production except where circumstances delayed this unduly. In such cases, date of composition is given, signalled by **wr**. Place of production is London unless otherwise noted.

Other abbreviations used are as follows: **D** Dublin; **M** Manchester; **E** Edinburgh; **G** Glasgow; **B** Birmingham; **N** Newcastle; **NYk** New York; **P** Paris; **B** Berlin; **MI** Malvern Festival; **U** Unity Theatre; **MAT** Moscow Art Theatre; **CI** closed-house productions by the Independent Theatre, Stage Society or Arts Theatre Club of banned plays; **wr** play written, not yet produced; **n** novel, subsequently dramatised; **d** died; **f** founded; **tr** English translation published; **pub** published; **r** radio; **fm** film.

DATE	PLAYS	FOREIGN PLAYS AND OTHER WORKS	CULTURAL AND HISTORICAL EVENTS
1890	Henley and Stevenson *Beau Austin* Jerome *New Lamps for Old* Pinero *The Profligate*	Ibsen *Hedda Gabler* Shaw *The Quintessence of Ibsenism* Maeterlinck *Les Aveugles* Fraser *The Golden Bough* (to 1915) General Booth *In Darkest England* James *The Tragic Muse*	*Ghosts* **P** Théâtre d'Art **P f** Freie Volks Bühne **B f** Saxe-Meininger final tour Boucicault **d** Van Gogh **d**

DATE	PLAYS	FOREIGN PLAYS AND OTHER WORKS	CULTURAL AND HISTORICAL EVENTS
1891	Jones *The Dancing Girl* Gilbert *Rosencrantz and Guildenstern* Ibsen *Ghosts* **CI** *Hedda Gabler* Wilde *Salomé* **wr**	Wilde *Picture of Dorian Grey* Wedekind *Spring Awakening* Hardy *Tess of the Durbervilles* Morris *News from Nowhere* Gissing *New Grub Street*	Independent Theatre **f** Kelmscott Press Actors Association (Equity) **f** Parnell **d** Melville **d**
1892	Wilde *Lady Windermere's Fan* Shaw, *Widowers' Houses* Thomas *Charley's Aunt* Yeats *The Countess Cathleen* **wr**	Hauptmann *The Weavers* Ibsen *The Master Builder* Conan Doyle *Sherlock Holmes* Booth *Life and Labour of the People in London* Zangwill *Children of the Ghetto*	Parliamentary Select Committee on Censorship Keir Hardy elected Tennyson **d**
1893	Pinero *The Second Mrs Tanqueray* Wilde *A Woman of No Importance* Moore *The Strike at Arlingford* Robins and Bell *Alan's Wife* Ibsen *The Master Builder* Shaw *Mrs Warren's Profession* **wr**	Gissing *The Odd Women* Maeterlinck *Pelléas et Mélisande* Egerton *Keynotes*	Théâtre d'Oeuvre **P f** Duse's English début Gaelic League **f** Second Home Rule Bill fails Independent Labour Party **f**

DATE	PLAYS	FOREIGN PLAYS AND OTHER WORKS	CULTURAL AND HISTORICAL EVENTS
1894	Shaw *Arms and the Man* Yeats *The Land of Heart's Desire* Jones *The Masqueraders* *The Case of Rebellious Susan* Grundy *The New Woman* Ibsen *The Wild Duck*	du Maurier *Trilby* **n** Moore *Esther Waters* Webbs *History of Trade Unionism I* Beardsley illustrates *Salomé* Hope *The Prisoner of Zenda* **n**	Elizabethan Stage Society **f** Gladstone resigns Dreyfus case, France Farr manages Avenue *The Yellow Book*
1895	Wilde *An Ideal Husband* *The Importance of Being Earnest* James *Guy Domville* Pinero *The Notorious Mrs Ebbsmith* Shaw *Candida*	Wells *The Time Machine* Hardy *Jude the Obscure* Conrad *Ayalmer's Folly* Appia *La mise en scène du drame Wagnerienne* Nordau *Degeneration* **tr**	Shaw at the *Saturday Review* Irving knighted Théâtre d'Oeuvre in London First films made Oscar Wilde trial National Trust **f** Institute of Women Journalists **f**
1896	Barrett *The Sign of the Cross* Hope *The Prisoner of Zenda* Jones *Michael and his Lost Angel* Ibsen *Little Eyolf*	Jarry *Ubu roi* Housman *A Shropshire Lad* *Kelmscott Chaucer* Chekhov *The Seagull* Puccini *La Bohème*	*Salomé* **P** *Dr Faustus* revived (Poel) Arts and Crafts Exhibition First modern Olympics Disc gramophone patented William Morris **d**

DATE	PLAYS	FOREIGN PLAYS AND OTHER WORKS	CULTURAL AND HISTORICAL EVENTS
1897	Jones *The Liars* Pinero *Trelawny of 'The Wells'* Ibsen *John Gabriel Borkmann*	Rostand *Cyrano de Bergerac* Stoker *Dracula* James *The Spoils of Poynton* Kipling *Recessional* Ellis *Studies in the Psychology of Sex*	Moscow Art Theatre **f** Tate Gallery opens National Union of Women's Suffrage Societies **f** Royal Jubilee
1898	Jerome *Miss Hobbs*	Shaw *Plays Pleasant and Unpleasant* **pub** Strindberg *To Damascus* Hardy *Wessex Poems* Zola *J'Accuse*	*The Seagull* **MAT** Irish Literary Theatre **D** Curies discover radium Beardsley **d**
1899	Yeats *Countess Cathleen* **D** Martyn *The Heather Field* **D** Pinero *The Gay Lord Quex* Maugham *Marriages Are Made in Heaven* Shaw *Caesar and Cleopatra* **N**	Chekhov *Uncle Vanya* Ibsen *When We Dead Awaken* James *The Awkward Age* Wells *The War of the Worlds* Baum *The Wizard of Oz* Tolstoi *Resurrection*	Stage Society **f** Poel's *Richard II* BOER WAR Magnetic recording of sound Dreyfus pardoned Becque **d**

DATE	PLAYS	FOREIGN PLAYS AND OTHER WORKS	CULTURAL AND HISTORICAL EVENTS
1900	Jones *Mrs Dane's Defence* Shaw *Captain Brassbound's Conversion* Phillips *Herod*	Puccini *Tosca* Conrad *Lord Jim* Dreiser *Sister Carrie*	Isadora in Paris British Labour Party **f** Relief of Mafeking Oscar Wilde **d** Nietzsche **d**
1901	Barrie *Quality Street*	Shaw *Three Plays for Puritans* **pub** Chekhov *Three Sisters* Kipling *Kim* Freud *Interpretation of Dreams*	*Everyman* revived (Poel) Wireless and telegraph at sea Nobel Peace Prize Queen Victoria **d** Accession Edward VII
1902	Barker *The Marrying of Ann Leete* Barrie *The Admirable Crichton* Shaw *Mrs Warren's Profession* **CI** Housman *Bethlehem* **CI** Yeats *Cathleen ni Houlihan* **D**	Strindberg *A Dream Play* Gorki *The Lower Depths* James *The Wings of the Dove* Kipling *Just So Stories* Bennett *Anna of the Five Towns* Conan Doyle *The Hound of the Baskervilles*	Local Education Authorities established Lords defeat Divorce Bill BOER WAR ENDS Transatlantic radio Zola **d**

DATE	PLAYS	FOREIGN PLAYS AND OTHER WORKS	CULTURAL AND HISTORICAL EVENTS
1903	Maugham *A Man of Honour* Yeats *The Hour Glass* **D** Synge *In the Shadow of the Glen* **D**	Chekhov *The Cherry Orchard* Yeats *The Celtic Twilight* James *The Ambassadors* Butler *The Way of All Flesh* Moore *Principia Ethica*	Censorship ended, France Women's Social and Political Union **f** Wright Brothers' flight Ford Motor Co **f**
1904	Shaw *John Bull's Other Island* Barrie *Peter Pan* Yeats *On Baile's Strand* **D** *The Shadowy Waters* **D** Gregory *Spreading the News* Synge *Riders to the Sea* **D**	Chekhov *The Cherry Orchard* Puccini *Madame Butterfly* Hardy *The Dynasts* James *The Golden Bowl* Conrad *Nostromo*	Abbey Theatre **D** Barker-Vedrenne at Court Theatre Tree's Acting School **f** RUSSO–JAPANESE WAR ENTENTE CORDIALE National Gallery refuses a Degas Chekhov **d**
1905	Barker *The Voysey Inheritance* Shaw *Man and Superman* *Major Barbara* Hankin *The Return of the Prodigal* Synge *The Well of the Saints* **D**	Craig *On the Art of the Theatre* Wilde *De Profundis* Wells *Kipps* Forster *Where Angels Fear to Tread*	Reinhardt at Deutsches Theatre **B** Meyerhold **MAT** Studio Tree Shakespeare Festival **f** Einstein Theory of Relativity Potemkin Mutiny Russia Irving **d**

DATE	PLAYS	FOREIGN PLAYS AND OTHER WORKS	CULTURAL AND HISTORICAL EVENTS
1906	Shaw *The Doctor's Dilemma* Galsworthy *The Silver Box* Pinero *His House in Order* Bantock *The Girl Behind the Counter*	Ibsen *Collected Works* **tr** Archer Claudel *Partage du midi* Galsworthy *The Man of Property* Kipling *Puck of Pook's Hill*	Abbey Theatre's first English tour The Royal Academy Dramatic Art **f** Ellen Terry Jubilee 53 Labour MPs elected San Francisco earthquake Ibsen **d**
1907	Galsworthy *Joy* Barker *Waste* **CI** Robins *Votes for Women* Hankin *The Last of the De Mullins* Synge *The Playboy of the Western World*	Barker and Archer *The National Theatre* Strindberg *The Dream Play* Conrad *The Secret Agent* Gosse *Father and Son* Belloc *Cautionary Tales*	Manchester Repertory Co **f** *Playboy* riots **D** Intimate Theatre Stockholm **f** Kipling wins Nobel Prize Defeat of Female Enfranchisement Bill
1908	Shaw *Getting Married* Masefield *The Tragedy of Nan* Barrie *What Every Woman Knows* Hamilton *Diana of Dobson's* James *The High Bid*	Strindberg *The Ghost Sonata* Maeterlinck *The Blue Bird* **MAT** Forster *A Room with a View* Grahame *The Wind in the Willows* Davies *The Autobiography of a Super Tramp*	Actresses' Franchise League **f** Gaiety Theatre **M** opened Old Age Pensions introduced First Model T Ford cars Suffragette Rally Hyde Park International Art Show London

DATE	PLAYS	FOREIGN PLAYS AND OTHER WORKS	CULTURAL AND HISTORICAL EVENTS
1909	Galsworthy *Strife* Pinero *Mid Channel* Baker *Chains* Shaw *The Shewing Up of Blanco Posnet* **D** Chekhov *The Seagull* **G** Lawrence *A Collier's Friday Night* **wr**	Craig *The Mask* (to 1929) Wells *Ann Veronica* *Tono Bungay* Stein *Three Lives* Webbs *Minority Report of Poor Law Commission*	Ballets Russes **P** Glasgow Repertory Theatre **f** Committee on Censorship Commission on Divorce Lords veto 'People's Budget' Blériot flies Channel Synge **d**
1910	Shaw *Misalliance* Galsworthy *Justice* Barker *The Madras House* Synge *Deirdre of the Sorrows* **D** Baker *Miss Tassey* Housman *Pains and Penalties* **CI**	Yeats *The Tragic Theatre* Wells *The History of Mr Polly* Forster *Howard's End* Bennett *Clayhanger* Russell and Whitehouse *Principia Mathematica* Stravinski *The Firebird*	Russian Ballet in London Post-Impressionist Exhibition Pioneer Players **f** Miners' strike South Wales Tolstoi **d** Edward VII **d** Accession George V
1911	Shaw *Fanny's First Play* Hamilton *Just to Get Married* Chekhov *The Cherry Orchard* Knoblock *Kismet*	Reinhardt *Sumurun*, Savoy *The Miracle*, Olympia Conrad *Under Western Eyes* Mansfield *In a German Pension* Stravinski *Petrushka*	*Playboy* riots **NYk** Futurist Manifesto Maeterlinck wins Nobel Prize Prison Reform Act National Health Insurance Bill Activist suffrage campaign

DATE	PLAYS	FOREIGN PLAYS AND OTHER WORKS	CULTURAL AND HISTORICAL EVENTS
1912	Houghton *Hindle Wakes* Sowerby *Rutherford and Son* Lawrence *The Daughter-in-Law* **wr**	Conrad *Twixt Land and Sea* Claudel *L'Annonce faite à Marie* Craig's *Hamlet* **MAT** Nijinski's *L'Apres midi d'un faune*	First Royal Command Music Hall Second Post-Impressionist Exhibition *Titanic* sinks Chinese Republic proclaimed Strindberg **d**
1913	Maugham *The Promised Land* Shaw *Androcles and the Lion* Galsworthy *The Fugitive*	Shaw *Quintessence of Ibsenism* (2nd edn) Lawrence *Sons and Lovers* Proust *Du côté de chez Swann* Freud *Interpretation of Dreams* **tr** Mann *Death in Venice*	Birmingham Repertory Co **f** Copeau Vieux Colombier **P f** Bensusan Womens' Season *Rite of Spring*, furore **P** Suffrage Bill fails Armory Show **NYk**
1914	Shaw *Pygmalion* Hardy *The Dynasts* Lawrence *The Widowing of Mrs Holroyd* **wr**	Yeats *Responsibilities* Joyce *Dubliners* Marinetti *Futurist Manifesto* Tressell *The Ragged Trousered Philanthropists* **n**	Poel 2nd Quarto *Hamlet* Barker's *MSND*, Savoy Old Vic Co **f** FIRST WORLD WAR Panama Canal opened
1915	Drinkwater *The Storm* **B** Robinson *The Dreamers* **D**	Ford *The Good Soldier* Brooke *1914 and Other Poems* Lawrence *The Rainbow* Griffith *The Birth of a Nation* **fm**	Provincetown Players **NYk f** Zeppelin raids YPRES Einstein General Theory of Relativity

DATE	PLAYS	FOREIGN PLAYS AND OTHER WORKS	CULTURAL AND HISTORICAL EVENTS
1916	Brighouse *Hobson's Choice* Phillpotts *The Farmer's Wife* **B** Yeats *At the Hawk's Well* Ashe and Norton *Chu Chin Chow*	Theatre Arts Magazine **NYk** Kaiser *From Morn to Midnight* Joyce *Portrait of the Artist* Kafka *Metamorphoses* Douglas *South Wind*	Dada Exhibition Zurich Easter Rising **D** VERDUN THE SOMME Henry James **d**
1917	Barrie *Dear Brutus* Maugham *Our Betters* Lonsdale *The Maid of the Mountains*	Kaiser *Gas* Apollinaire *Les Mamelles de Tiresias* Eliot *Lovesong of J Alfred Prufrock* Jung *Psychology of the Unconscious* **tr**	PASSCHENDALE RUSSIAN REVOLUTION America enters War
1918	Drinkwater *Abraham Lincoln* **B** Joyce *Exiles* **wr**	Brecht *Baal* Lewis *Tarr* Sassoon *Counter Attack* Hopkins *Poems*	Ulster Literary Theatre **f** Dada Manifesto FIRST WORLD WAR ENDS Partial female suffrage Wedekind **d**

DATE	PLAYS	FOREIGN PLAYS AND OTHER WORKS	CULTURAL AND HISTORICAL EVENTS
1919	Yeats *The Player Queen* Milne *Mr Pimm Passes By*	O'Neill *Beyond the Horizon* Lang *The Cabinet of Dr Caligari* **fm** Sassoon *The War Poems* Yeats *The Wild Swans at Coole* Woolf *Night and Day*	TREATY OF VERSAILLES Theatre Guild **NYk f** Bauhaus Weimar **f** Amritsar shootings First woman MP ANGLO–IRISH WAR Flight across Atlantic
1920	Barrie *Mary Rose*	O'Neill *The Emperor Jones* Owen *Poems* Eliot *Poems* Pound *Hugh Selwyn Mauberley* Mansfield *Bliss*	2000th performance *Chu Chin Chow* Theatre National Populaire **f** Marconi Co begins broadcasts LEAGUE OF NATIONS Joan of Arc canonised Prohibition in US
1921	Masefield *Esther* Maugham *The Circle* Dane *Bill of Divorcement* Shaw *Heartbreak House*	Yeats *Four Plays for Dancers* **pub** Toller *Masses and Man* Capek *The Insect Play* Pirandello *Six Characters in Search of an Author* Lawrence *Women in Love* Chaplin *The Kid* **fm**	*Waste* licenced IRISH FREE STATE First birth control clinics Sun Yat Sen leads China Civil disobedience in India

DATE	PLAYS	FOREIGN PLAYS AND OTHER WORKS	CULTURAL AND HISTORICAL EVENTS
1922	Galsworthy *Loyalties* Maugham *East of Suez* Yeats *The Only Jealousy of Emer* Coward *The Young Idea*	O'Neill *The Hairy Ape* Pirandello *Henry IV* Eliot *The Waste Land* Joyce *Ulysses* Galsworthy *The Forsyte Saga*	**MAT** tours Europe and US BBC established Lord Reith Director BBC Mussolini in power Italy IRISH CIVIL WAR
1923	O'Casey *The Shadow of a Gunman* **D** Maugham *Our Betters* Shaw *Back to Methuselah* Flecker *Hassan*	Rice *The Adding Machine* Lawrence *Kangaroo* Keynes *Tract on Monetary Reform* Wodehouse *The Inimitable Jeeves* Keaton *Our Hospitality* **fm**	Gray at Festival Theatre Cambridge Yeats wins Nobel Prize *Radio Times* launched Sarah Bernhardt **d**
1924	Shaw *Saint Joan* Coward *The Vortex* O'Casey *Juno and the Paycock* **D** Hughes *Danger* **r**	O'Neill *Desire Under the Elms* Stanislavski *My Life in Art* Hemingway *In Our Time* Forster *A Passage to India* Mann *The Magic Mountain* Ford *Some Do Not*	Piscator at Volksbühne First Surrealist Manifesto Lenin **d**; Stalin in power First (brief, minority) Labour Government Conrad **d** Kafka **d**

DATE	PLAYS	FOREIGN PLAYS AND OTHER WORKS	CULTURAL AND HISTORICAL EVENTS
1925	Coward *Fallen Angels* *On with the Dance* *Hay Fever* Travers *A Cuckoo in the Nest* Berkeley *The White Chateau* **r** Kaiser *From Morn to Midnight* Chekhov *The Cherry Orchard*	Woolf *Mrs Dalloway* Ford *No More Parades* Kafka *The Trial* Dos Passos *Manhattan Transfer* Eisenstein *Battleship Potemkin* **fm** Chaplin *The Gold Rush* **fm**	State subsidy for Abbey Theatre Pirandello Teatro d'Arte Rome **f** Hitler writes *Mein Kampf* *Mrs Warren's Profession* licensed 'Monkey Trial' Tennessee
1926	Coward *Easy Virtue* Lawrence *The Widowing of Mrs Holroyd* Travers *Rookery Nook* Dane *Granite* O'Casey *The Plough and the Stars* **D**	Brecht *Man is Man* Webb *My Apprenticeship* Ford *A Man Could Stand Up* Hemingway *The Sun Also Rises* Keynes *End of Laissez Faire* Lang *Metropolis* **fm**	Workers' Theatre Movement **f** Stratford Memorial Theatre burns Baird demonstrates television GENERAL STRIKE
1927	Corrie *In Time o' Strife* **G** Maugham *The Constant Wife* Travers *Thark*	Toller *Hoppla, Wir Leben* Woolf *To the Lighthouse* Kern and Hamerstein *Showboat* Cocteau *Orphée* Gance *Napoléon* **fm**	Cinematograph Films Bill Transatlantic telephone Directors' Cartel **P** First 'Talkies' Lindbergh flies Atlantic solo Isadora Duncan **d**

DATE	PLAYS	FOREIGN PLAYS AND OTHER WORKS	CULTURAL AND HISTORICAL EVENTS
1928	Sherriff *Journey's End* Druten *Young Woodley*	Brecht *The Threepenny Opera* Sassoon *Memoirs of a Fox Hunting Man* Woolf *A Room of One's Own* Huxley *Point Counter Point*	Abbey Theatre rejects *Silver Tassie* Full female suffrage Fleming discovers penicillin Hardy **d**
1929	O'Casey *The Silver Tassie* Shaw *The Apple Cart* **MI** Coward *Bitter Sweet* Johnston *The Old Lady Says 'No'* **D** Griffith *Red Sunday* **CI**	Priestley *The Good Companions* **n** Rice *Street Scene* Giradoux *Amphitryon 38* Faulkner *The Sound and the Fury* Graves *Goodbye to All That* Hemingway *A Farewell to Arms* Grierson *Drifters* **fm**	First Malvern Festival Group Theatre **NYk f** Actors' Equity **f** Wall Street Crash Great Depression begins Minority Labour Government
1930	Coward *Private Lives* Guthrie *The Flowers Are Not For You To Pick* **r** Yeats *The Words Upon the Window Pane* **D**	Brecht *The Rise and Fall of the City of Mahagonny* Eliot *Ash Wednesday* Auden *Poems* Crossman *The God that Failed*	Gate Theatre **D f** Lawrence **d** 2 million unemployed in UK

DATE	PLAYS	FOREIGN PLAYS AND OTHER WORKS	CULTURAL AND HISTORICAL EVENTS
1931	Priestley *The Good Companions* Coward *Cavalcade* Johansson *Brigade Exchange* **r** Johnston *The Moon in the Yellow River* **D** Yeats *The Dreaming of the Bones* **D**	O'Neill *Mourning Becomes Electra* Woolf *The Waves* Chaplin *City Lights* **fm** Fritz Lang *M* **fm**	Compagnie des Quinze **P f** National Government formed Britian abandons Gold Standard IRA banned Ireland
1932	Daviot *Richard of Bordeaux* Priestley *Dangerous Corner* Maugham *For Services Rendered* Shaw *Too True to be Good* **MI** Bridie *Tobias and the Angel*	Huxley *Brave New World* Faulkner *Light in August* *New Signatures* poetry anthology Brecht *Saint Joan of the Stockyards*	Theatre of Action **f** New Theatre Stratford on Avon Jarrow hunger march Kinder Scout mass trespass Gandhi arrested India Roosevelt elected President USA *Scrutiny* **f**
1933	Shaw *On the Rocks* Travers *A Bit of a Test* O'Casey *Within the Gates* **wr** Coward *Design for Living* **wr**	Orwell *Down and Out in London and Paris* Lorca *Blood Wedding* Greenwood *Love on the Dole* Yeats *The Winding Stair* Spender *Poems*	Pitoëff tours to London Hitler Chancellor Germany Reichstag fire Germany quits League of Nations Galsworthy **d**

DATE	PLAYS	FOREIGN PLAYS AND OTHER WORKS	CULTURAL AND HISTORICAL EVENTS
1934	Auden *The Dance of Death* Eliot *The Rock* *Sweeney Agonistes* Gow *Love on the Dole* **M** *1066 and All That* **B**	Hellman *The Children's Hour* Lorca *Yerma* Priestley *English Journey* Flaherty *Man of Aran* **fm** Hitchcock *The Man Who Knew Too Much* **fm**	Anti-fascist demonstration Hyde Park *Queen Mary* launched Long March China First Stalinist purges USSR Pinero **d**
1935	Eliot *Murder in the* *Cathedral* Housman *Victoria Regina* Priestley *Cornelius* Coward *Tonight at 8.30* Auden and Isherwood *The Dog Beneath the* *Skin* Williams *Night Must Fall*	Odets *Waiting for Lefty* Gershwin *Porgy and Bess* Giradoux *The Trojan War Will Not* *Take Place* MacNeice *Poems* Empson *Some Versions of Pastoral* Hitchcock *The Thirty-Nine Steps* **fm**	Theatre Union **f** Federal Theatre Project in US Artaud Theatre of Cruelty **P f** Italy invades Abyssinia Radar invented Penguin 6d paperbacks

DATE	PLAYS	FOREIGN PLAYS AND OTHER WORKS	CULTURAL AND HISTORICAL EVENTS
1936	Slater *Stay Down Miner* Rattigan *French Without Tears*	Lorca *House of Bernada Alba* Stanislavski *An Actor Prepares* **tr** Auden *Look Stranger* Faulkner *Absalom Absalom!* Dos Passos *USA* Wright *Night Mail* **fm** Chaplin *Modern Times* **fm**	First television broadcasts Left Book Club **f** SPANISH CIVIL WAR Germany occupies Rhineland George V **d** Edward VII abdication crisis Accession George VI Lorca **d**
1937	Priestley *I Have Been Here Before* *Time and the Conways* Auden *The Ascent of F6* *English Family Robinson* **r** first radio serial	Orwell *The Road to Wigan Pier* Jones *In Parenthesis* Rosenberg *Collected Works* Tolkien *The Hobbit* Harrison and Spender *Work Town*	Unity Theatre opened Guthrie Director Old Vic Writers' Congress Madrid Japan invades China Germans bomb Guernica Lilian Bayliss **d**

DATE	PLAYS	FOREIGN PLAYS AND OTHER WORKS	CULTURAL AND HISTORICAL EVENTS
1938	Priestley *When We Are Married*	Wilder *Our Town*	House UnAmerican Activities Committee US
	Spender *Trial of a Judge*	Artaud *Theatre and Its Double*	Hitler annexes Austria and Czechoslovakia
	Busmen **U**	Beckett *Murphy*	Munich Agreement Germany annexes Austria
	Babes in the Wood **U**	Isherwood *Goodbye to Berlin*	Stanislavski **d**
	Yeats *Purgatory* **D**	Richardson *Pilgrimage*	
		Eisenstein *Alexander Nevsky* **fm**	
		Hitchcock *The Lady Vanishes* **fm**	
1939	Eliot *The Family Reunion*	Hellman *The Little Foxes*	National Theatre site acquired
	Priestley *Johnson over Jordan*	O'Neill *The Iceman Cometh*	Franco in power Spain German-Soviet non-Aggression Pact
	Coward *This Happy Breed* *Design for Living*	Brecht *Mother Courage* *Galileo*	SECOND WORLD WAR Nuclear fission Yeats **d**
		Joyce *Finnegan's Wake*	
		Steinbeck *Grapes of Wrath*	
		Ford *Stagecoach* **fm**	
1940	O'Casey *The Star Turns Red*	Brecht *Good Person of Setzuan*	OCCUPATION OF PARIS Churchill forms National Government
	Williams *The Corn is Green*	O'Neill *Long Day's Journey Into Night* **wr**	BATTLE OF BRITAIN Final Stage Society Production
		Koestler *Darkness at Noon*	
		Greene *The Power and the Glory*	

General Bibliographies

Note: Each section is arranged alphabetically. The place of publication is London unless otherwise stated.

As well as the daily press, the following journals are particularly good sources of information about contemporary social, cultural and theatrical life:

Black and White
The Era
The English Review
The Fortnightly Review
The Mask
The Monthly Review
The New Review
The New Age
The Nineteenth Century
The Pall Mall Gazette
The Saturday Review
The Yellow Book
The Weekly Comedy

The William Archer Collection in the London Theatre Museum is an essential source for work in this period as is the Lord Chamberlain's Collection of plays in the British Library.

Constable, Heinemann, Macmillan, Sidgwick and Jackson, then Gollancz and Faber were notable publishers of play texts in this period.

(i) Historical and cultural context

A. General background 1890–1940

Briggs, A. *The History of Broadcasting in the United Kingdom*, 5 vols (1995) (Creation, administration and structure of the BBC, with passing comments on drama.)

Booth, C. *Life and Labour of the People of London* (1889–1903). (Ground-breaking study that opened the eyes of many to social and economic conditions of their contemporaries.)

Cole, M. *The Story of Fabian Socialism* (1961). (Shaw and colleagues in their political context.)

Frazer, J. G. *The Golden Bough* (1890–1915). (The work that changed a generation's view of culture.)

Hynes, S. *The Edwardian Turn of Mind* (1968). (Exploration of currents of thought which give rich insight into social and cultural life of the period.)

Jackson, H. *The 1890s* (1913). (Early study still has much to offer: argues *fin de siècle* 'a pose as well as a fact'.)

Nicholson, S. 'Censoring Revolution: the Lord Chamberlain and the Soviet Union', *New Theatre Quarterly*, 32, VIII (November 1992). (Revelatory discussion of censorship in inter-war years.)

Pankhurst, C. *Unshackled: The Story of How We Won the Vote* (1959). (Participant's account of suffrage campaign.)

Pelling, H. *History of British Trade Unionism* (1963).

Priestley, J. B. *English Journey, 1933* (1934). (Valuable insights both into period and Priestley's own part in it.)

Robertson, J. W. *The Life and Death of a Newspaper* (1952). (Discussion of *Pall Mall Gazette*, with insights into contemporary political life.)

Rubinstein, D. *Before the Suffragettes* (Brighton, 1986). (Discussion of female emancipation and opposition to it in the 1890s.)

Shaw, G. B. *The Intelligent Woman's Guide to Socialism* (1928). (Shaw's runaway success that may have affected the election result in 1929.)

Showalter, E. *Sexual Anarchy: Gender and Culture in the fin de siècle* (1991). (Stimulating, well-researched account; reference points mainly in prose fiction.)

Stokes, J. *In the Nineties* (Hemel Hempstead, 1989). (Particularly telling discussion of press, music hall and popular entertainments.)

Webb, B. *My Apprenticeship* (1926). (Vivid account of the development of a political consciousness.)

Williams, R. *Culture and Society 1780–1950* (1958). (Innovative history of ideas in its time; still telling discussion.)

Wilson, E.   *The Triple Thinkers* (1952). (Essays on literature and ideas, including discussions of James and of Shaw.)

B. Literary background

Clark, J., M. Heinemann, D. Margolies and C. Snee, eds   *Culture and Crisis in Britain in the Thirties* (1979). (Exploration of often ignored areas.)

Conolly, C.   *The Modern Movement 1880–1920* (1965).

Dowling, L.   *Language and Decadence in the Victorian fin de siècle* (Princeton, NJ, 1986). (Invigorating modern study.)

Ellmann, R., ed.   *Edwardians and Late Victorians* (New York, 1960).

Fletcher, I. and M. Bradbury, eds   *Decadence and the 1890s* (1979).

Lehmann, J.   *New Writing in Europe* (1940). (Terse, lucid account by one much involved as a writer in the 1930s.)

Lodge, D.   *The Modes of Modern Writing* (1977). (Includes discussion of new journalism.)

Upward, E.   *In the Thirties* (1962). (A view from the left.)

C. Diaries, collections of letters

Bax, C., ed.   *Florence Farr, Bernard Shaw and W. B. Yeats* (Dublin, 1941). (Correspondence between three dominating figures of alternative theatre.)

Burkhart, C., ed.   *The Letters of George Moore to Edmund Gosse, W. B. Yeats, R. I. Best, Miss Nancy Cunard and Mrs Mary Hutchinson* (Michigan, 1958). (Not much on drama but does evoke their world.)

Webb, B.   *Diaries, 1912–14*, ed. M. Cole (1952). (Sharp observations including on theatre.)

(ii) General dramatic criticism

Archer, W.   *The Old Drama and the New* (1923). (Sometimes dogmatic and grinds axes but opinions are grounded in experience.)

Arden, J.   *To Present the Pretence* (1977). (Dramatist's meditations on theatre, including strong defence of O'Casey.)

Craig, G.   *On the Art of the Theatre* (1911). (Inspired, idiosyncratic, still rather neglected credo.)

Fergusson, F.   *The Idea of a Theatre* (Princeton, NJ, 1949).

Styan, J. L.   *The Dark Comedy* (1968). (Stimulating discussion of Shaw and Eliot among other examples.)

Modern Drama in Theory and Practice 3 vols (Cambridge, 1981). (Necessarily quick but well-informed survey of European drama with copious illustration.)

Williams, R.   *Drama from Ibsen to Eliot* (1952). (Some penetrating observations; mainly European drama but includes strong mid-century valuation of Eliot's drama and too ready dismissal O'Casey.)

(iii) English drama 1890–1940

A. Bibliographies, indices and theatre collection catalogues

Davenport Adams, W.   *A Dictionary of the Drama* (1904). (Who's who of dramatists and listings of plays.)

Howard D.   *London Theatres and Music Halls, 1850–1950* (1970). (Includes numerous theatrical records.)

Ireland, N.   *Index to Full-Length Plays 1895–1964* (1965).

Mikhail, E. H.   *A Bibliography of Modern Irish Drama 1899–1970* (1972).

The Player's Library   *The Catalogue of the British Drama League* (1950). (Play texts then available for loan.)

The Stage   *The Stage Year Book* (1908–28). (Good source of information on productions.)

Wearing, J. P.   *The London Stage 1890–1899* (Minneapolis, MN, 1976). (Listing, with dates of plays and players.)

Who's Who in the Theatre (1912 and subsequent revisions).

B. Anthologies of play texts

Donohue and J. Ellis   *English Drama of the Nineteenth Century* (New Canaan, 1965). (Microfiche collection of Plays.)

Everyman   *Modern Plays* (1956). (Includes work by Sherriff, Milne, Maugham).

Faber   *My Best Play* (annually from 1934). (Plays chosen at publisher's request by their authors.)

Fitzsimmons, L. and V. Gardner, eds   *New Woman Plays* (1991). (Includes plays by Bell and Robins, Sowerby and Baker.)

Gardner V., ed.	*Sketches from the Actresses' Franchise League* (Nottingham, 1985). (Pioneering collection of suffrage plays.)
Goorney, H. and E. MacColl, eds	*Agit-Prop to Theatre Workshop* (Manchester, 1986). (Otherwise unavailable Unity and Theatre of Action play texts.)
Marriott, J. W., ed.	*Best One-Act Plays of 1931* (1932, and annually to 1946).
Rowell, G., ed.	*Nineteenth-Century Plays* (1953). (One play by Grundy otherwise range of pre-1890 plays.)
	Late Victorian Plays 1890–1914 (1972). (Includes works by Barker, Jones, Galsworthy, Hankin, Houghton, Pinero.)
Sidgwick and Jackson	*Plays of Today* 2 vols, Vol. I (1925). (Includes work by Drinkwater, Houghton, Baker, St. John Ervine and Barker.)
	Plays of Today, Vol. II (1925). (Includes work by Masefield, Monkhouse and Sowerby.)
Spender D. and C. Hayman, eds	*How the Vote Was Won and Other Suffragette Plays* (1985). (Includes work by Hamilton and Robins.)

C. Contemporary reviews and accounts of theatre

Agate, J.	*Playgoing* (1927). (Leading theatre reviewer of inter-war years.)
	Those Were the Nights (1946). (Account of turn of the century actors and productions.)
Archer, W.	*The Theatrical World of 1893; 1894* etc. (1894; 1895, to 1898). (Reviews, synopsis of playbills, tabulation of productions, providing invaluable source of information on theatrical scene of 1890s.)
Beerbohm, M.	*Around Theatres 1898–1910* (rev. edn 1953). (Shaw's successor at *Saturday Review* almost matches him in wit and penetration.)
Darlington, W. A.	*Six Thousand and One Nights: Forty Years a Critic* (1960). (Perceptions of inter-war theatre.)
Goldman, E.	*The Social Significance of Modern Drama* (1914; repr. New York, 1987). (Polemical reading of wide selection of pre-1914 plays, particularly praises Galsworthy.)
Grein, J. T.	*Dramatic Criticism* (1899). (Oddly straight-laced reviews by founder of the Independent Theatre.)
MacCarthy, D.	*Drama* (1940). (Cogent, wide-ranging observation of Edwardian drama.)
	The Court Theatre 1904–7 (1907). (Account by observer sympathetic to aims.)
Montague, C. E.	*Dramatic Values* (1911). (Penetrating dramatic criticism by *Manchester Guardian* reviewer.)

Moore, G.   *Impressions and Opinions* (1891). (Founding of independent theatre movement, excitement of new writing and shifts in social status of actors.)

O'Casey, S.   *The Green Crow* (1957). (Partisan and often acerbic accounts of theatre of 1920s and 1930s.)

Scott, C.   *The Drama of Yesterday and Today* 2 vols (1899). (Writings of leading conservative critic.)

Shaw, G. B.   *Dramatic Opinions and Essays* (New York, 1906).

                 Our Theatres in the Nineties (1932). (Shaw's brilliant *Saturday Review* articles are essential reading.)

Symons, A.   *Plays, Acting and Music* (1909). (Sensitive contemporary observations.)

Walkley, A. B.   *Playhouse Impressions* (1892). (Collection of early reviews, including several of first English Ibsen productions by leading critic of 1890s new wave.)

D. Aspects of theatre, staging, actors' memoirs

Ashwell, L.   *Myself a Player* (1936). (Memoirs of feminist theatre director and actress.)

Campbell, Mrs P. *My Life and Some Letters* (1922).

Gielgud, J.   *Early Stages* (1939; repr., 1990). (Good-tempered memoirs of one of significant players of inter-war years.)

Gielgud, K. T.   *A Victorian Playgoer*, ed. M. St C. Byrne (1980). (Acute observations by retired leading actress.)

Grein, J. T.   *The New World of Theatre* (1924). (Memoirs of initiator of new movement.)

Jerome, J. K.   *Stageland: Curious Habits and Customs of its Inhabitants* (1893). (Humorous observations of mainstream theatre world.)

Moussinac, L.   *The New Movement in the Theatre* (1931). (Magnificent collection of illustrations of 1920s work in stage design: mainly European.)

Neilson, J.   *This for Remembrance* (1940). (Actress recalls turn of century theatre.)

Robins, E.   *Ibsen and the Actress* (1928). (Animated account of impact of encounter with Ibsen's drama by leading exponent.)

                 Theatre and Friendship (1932). (Correspondence with James includes much discussion of contemporary theatre.)

                 Both Sides of the Curtain (1940). (Account of 'learning and growth' beginning from arrival in London, 1888.)

E. Theatrical context and history of drama in the period

Chothia, J.	*André Antoine* (Cambridge, 1991). (Theatrical practice of the founder of the Théâtre Libre.)
Donaldson, I., ed.	*Transformations of Modern European Drama* (1983). (Essays on translating plays from one culture or language to another includes fine account by I. Britain of *A Doll's House* in England.)
Elsom, J. and N. Tomalin	*The History of the National Theatre* (1978). (Clear account of the battle for a subsidised theatre.)
Foulkes, R., ed.	*British Theatre in the 1890s* (Cambridge, 1992). (Essays on less familiar areas, Toole, toga drama, etc.)
Hobson, H.	*Theatre in Britain: A Personal View* (Oxford, 1984). (Strong expression of independent taste, often partisan but sharp observations of an astute critic.)
Kaplan, J. and S. Stowell	*Theatre and Fashion* (Cambridge, 1994). (Delightful study of complex interactions between the two worlds.)
Miller, A.	*The Independent Theatre in Europe* (New York, 1931). (Work-a-day account of new movements in the theatre from 1880s.)
Nicoll, A.	*A History of late Nineteenth-Century Drama* (Cambridge, 1949).
	English Drama, 1900–1930 (Cambridge, 1973). (Rather dry but indispensable background information about what was played and where.)
Richards, K. and P. Thomson, eds	*Nineteenth-Century British Theatre* (1971). (Includes interesting essay by J. Donoghue on first production of *The Importance of Being Earnest*.)
Trewin, J.	*The Theatre Since 1900* (1951). (Lucid, straight-forward account.)
Woodfield, J.	*English Theatre in Transition, 1881–1914* (Beckenham, 1984). (Substantial study with generous quotation from original sources, includes full list of Stage Society productions.)

F. Dramatic criticism

Clarke, I.	*Edwardian Drama* (1989). (Lively sense of context and implications, succinct but convincing discussion of individual dramatists.)
Innes, C.	*Modern British Drama 1890–1990* (Cambridge, 1992). (Grand study; convincingly demonstrates extent to which later British theatre was founded in earlier period.)
MacDonald, J.	*The 'New Drama'* (1986). (Particularly interesting on Hankin.)
Meisel, M.	*Shaw and Nineteenth-Century Theatre* (Princeton, NJ, 1963). (Very useful account of nineteenth-century dramatic kinds; numerous plays described.)

Powell, K. *Oscar Wilde and the Theatre of the 1890s* (Cambridge, 1990). (Packed with information about plethora of Victorian plays.)

Stokes, J. *Resistible Theatres* (1972). (Excellent discussion of alternative theatres of 1890s, and of work of Wilde.)

G. The repertory movement, independent theatres and individual companies

Archer, W. *The Vedrenne-Barker Season, 1904–5* (1905). (A record and commentary by close observer.)

Chisholm, C. *Repertory: An Outline of the Modern Theatre Movement* (1934). (Useful statistics help chart development.)

Goodie, S. *Annie Horniman, A Pioneer in the Theatre* (1990). (Partisan biography, little in the way of dramatic criticism.)

Hamilton, C. and Lilian Baylis *The Old Vic* (1926). (Disappointingly general account by playwright and director.)

Howe, P. P. *The Repertory Theatre: A Record and a Criticism* (1910). (Analysis of Barker's Duke of York's season.)

Incorporated Stage Society *Ten Years 1899–1909* (1909). (Indispensable record.)

Kemp, T. C. *The Birmingham Repertory Theatre: The Playhouse and the Man* (1943). (Full account informed by evident admiration of Barry Jackson.)

McCarthy, D. *The Court Theatre, 1904–7* (1907). (Eye-witness account.)

Pogson, R. *Miss Horniman and the Gaiety Theatre Manchester* (1952). (Useful account.)

Rowell, G. and A. Jackson *The Repertory Movement: A History of Regional Theatre in Britain* (Cambridge, 1984). (Informative account of growth and development.)

Trewin, J. C. *Birmingham Repertory Theatre, 1913–63* (1963). (Enthusiastic and substantial account. Appendix lists all productions and performers since foundation.)

Trewin J. C. and W. Trewin *The Arts Theatre, London 1927–81* (1986). (Interest is mainly post-1945 but single succinct chapter on 1927–40 period.)

H. Radical and feminist drama and the woman question

Case, S. E. *Feminism and the Theatre* (1988). (Discussion of pre-nineteenth-century theatre but useful background and some methodology.)

Davis, T. C. *Actresses as Working Women* (1991). (Account of Victorian actress's lot as 'low paid, low status, casualised and sexualised'.)

Dowling, L. 'The Decadent and the New Woman in the 1890s', *Nineteenth Century Fiction* 33 (March 1979), pp. 434–53. (Important

essay arguing that aesthetes and emancipated women
identified together as threats to society.)

Finney, G. *Women in Modern Drama* (Ithaca, NY, 1989). (Freudian
readings of European modern classics; includes discussion of
Salomé and *Candida*.)

Gardner, V. and S. *The New Woman and Her Sisters, 1850–1914* (1992). (Mixed
Rutherford, eds collection of essays on representation of women and
women's role in the theatre, well worth looking out.)

Goorney, H. *The Theatre Workshop Story* (1981). (1930s theatre in first two
chapters; Theatre Union documents and extracts from
Living Newspapers.)

Holledge, J. *Innocent Flowers* (1981). (Women in the Edwardian theatre.)

MacColl, E. 'The Grass Roots of Theatre Workshop', *Theatre Quarterly*,
III (9) (March 1973), pp. 58–68.

Samuel, R., E. *Theatres of the Left, 1880–1935* (1985). (Important
MacColl and S. supplement to usual histories; describes recurrent upsurge
Cosgrave, eds of radical drama.)

Sidnell, M. *Dances of Death: The Group Theatre of London in the Thirties*
(1984). (Authoritative history of the company with attention
to plays of Auden and Eliot.)

Stowell, S. *A Stage of Their Own: Feminist Playwrights of the Suffrage Era*
(Manchester, 1992).

Thomas, T. 'A Propertyless Theatre for a Propertyless Class', *History
Workshop*, 4 (Autumn 1977), pp. 113–42.

I. The Irish theatre

Fay, F. *Towards a National Theatre* (Dublin, 1970).

Fay, W. G. and C. *The Fays of the Abbey Theatre* (1935). (Accounts of policy
Carswell debates and staging practice.)

Flannery, J. W. *W. B. Yeats and the Idea of a Theatre: The Early Abbey Theatre
in Theory and Practice* (Toronto, 1976). (Includes good
discussion of Yeats's work with Craig.)

Gregory, A. *Our Irish Theatre* (1914). (Memoirs and important
documents.)

Kilroy, J. *The 'Playboy Riots'* (Dublin, 1951).

Maxwell, D. E. S. *Modern Irish Drama* (Cambridge, 1984). (Survey of great
insight and common sense; sceptical of Yeats, perceptive
about Synge and O'Casey.)

Hunt, H. *The Abbey, Ireland's National Theatre* (Dublin, 1979). (Full
account of politics and the *Playboy* riots.)

Robinson, L. *Ireland's Abbey Theatre, 1899–1951* (1951). (Account by
writer and sometime director.)

Worth, K.   *The Irish Drama of Europe from Yeats to Beckett* (1978). (Challenging argument for line of descent from late nineteenth-century Symbolism.)

J. Verse drama and dramatic language

Donoghue, D.   *The Third Voice: Modern British and American Verse Drama* (1959). (Still the most penetrating discussion of the subject.)

Eliot, T. S.   *The Aims of Poetic Drama* (1949). (Analysis of disappointments to date, hopes for the future.)

Kennedy, A.   *Six Dramatists in Search of a Language* (Cambridge, 1975). (Critically alert study with telling observation about work of Shaw and Eliot.)

Kermode, F.   *Romantic Image* (1971). (Includes discussion of *Salomé* and of Yeats's drama in the light of late nineteenth-century Symbolism.)

Peacock, R.   *The Poet in the Theatre* (1946, repr., 1960). (Post-Second World War developments date this but meditation ranges wide; enthusiasm for Eliot and strong defence of Yeats.)

K. Shakespeare production

Cave, R.   *Terence Gray and the Cambridge Festival Theatre*, Theatre in Focus (Cambridge, 1980). (Copious illustrations help recreate Gray's work.)

David, R.   *Shakespeare in the Theatre* (Cambridge, 1978). (Critically alert account of ways of seeing and playing Shakespeare.)

Gray, T.   *Dance Drama, Experiments in the Art of Theatre* (Cambridge, 1925). (The director discusses his practice.)

Hughes, A.   *Henry Irving, Shakespearean* (Cambridge, 1981). (Perceptive account of Irving's practice with well-chosen illustrations.)

Poel, W.   *Shakespeare in the Theatre* (1913). (Guiding ideas and some account of practice.)

Speaight, R.   *William Poel and the Elizabethan Revival* (1954). (Well-documented study of the Elizabethan authenticity movement.)

Sprague, A. C.   'Shakespeare and William Poel', *University of Toronto Quarterly*, XVII (1) (October 1947), pp. 29–37. (Includes account of attacks on Poel's ideas.)

Wilde, O.   *The Artist as Critic* ed. R. Ellmann (1970). (Astute observations about historical setting.)

L. Radio drama and film

Drakakis, J., ed.   *Radio Drama* (Cambridge, 1981). (Essays on post-Second World War drama but includes useful introductory essay by the editor on pre-war period.)

Gielgud, V.   *British Radio Drama 1922–56* (1957). (Brief, rather dry history but important for insider's view and detailed account of process of producing a radio play.)

Lewis, P., ed.   *Papers of the Radio Literature Conference* (Durham, 1977). (Mixed collection of essays but some attention to radio drama.)

Lloyd, A. ed.   *Movies of the Thirties* (1983). (Brief but authoritative essays; lavish illustration.)

Robinson, D.   *A History of the Cinema* (New York, 1973). (Includes an excellent chapter on the documentary movement.)

Rodger, I.   *Radio Drama* (1982). (Unreliable dates but valuable thinking about implications of sound-only medium from 1930s listener and practitioner.)

Sieveking, L.   *The Stuff of Radio* (1934). (From the horse's mouth. Extract from *Kaleidoscope* in appendix – its only published form.)

Warren, P.   *Elstree, The British Hollywood* (1983). (Information about problems and achievements of early years of British film industry.)

Individual Authors

Notes on biography, works and criticism

Each entry is divided into three sections:
(a) *Outline of author's life and literary career.* Dates of plays refer to first performance except where otherwise noted. Authors included are primarily known as playwrights, unless signified.
(b) *Selected works, letters, autobiographies and biographies.* Modern reprints of otherwise obscure texts are noted as are the publishers of standard editions of major authors. Place of publication here and in (c) is London unless otherwise noted.
(c) *Selected critical studies etc., of author's plays (not other genres).* Works of history and criticism in the General Bibliography should also be consulted, as should appropriate volumes in the Casebook, Critical Heritage and Twayne Authors (Boston, Mass.) series.

The following abbreviations are used:
b. = born; m. = married; d. = died; educ. = educated; perf(s). = performance(s); prod. = produced; dir. = directed; Th. = Theatre; wr. = written; pub. = published; f. = founded; trans. = translated by; adapt. = adapted by/adaptation; incl. = including, ed[s]. = editor[s]; repr. = reprinted; NYk. = New York.

ACHURCH, Janet (1864–1916), actress, th. manager, producer of Ibsen, minor play-wright; m. Charles Charrington, actor and co-manager with her of Novelty Th. 1886; collaborated with Charrington on adaptation from the French of *Frou Frou.* After acting in various melodramas became first English Nora in co-prod. with Charrington (Torvald) of Ibsen's *A Doll's House* (1889); subsequently toured the play in England and abroad. Mother-daughter relationship, suspect business and seedy background of her *Mrs Daintree's Daughter* (licensed 1894) reworked by Shaw in *Mrs Warren's Profession.* Became alcoholic and performances suffered.

> with C. Charrington, 'A Confession of their Crimes' (1893).

ACKERLEY, J[oseph] R[andolph] (1896–1967), b. London; educ. Rossall School and

Cambridge; fought in First World War. Father, it later emerged, lived double life with a second family. *The Prisoners of War*, concerning homosexual passion among First World War Officer-prisoners of war, prod. by the 300 Club to huge applause; denied licence for public perf. Following stretch in India as private secretary and tutor in a maharajah's family, wrote *Hindoo Holiday* (1932). Literary editor of *The Listener* 1935–59.

> *My Father and Myself* (1968).

ACKLAND, Rodney (1908–91), b. Norman Ackland Bernstein; father, a businessman; mother, musical comedy star, Ada Rodney. Initially an actor; first role, in *The Lower Depths* (1924); others included the title role in John van Druten's *Young Woodley*. Also worked in cinema as writer and director. Somewhat dark plays: characters dispossessed, struggling misfits. Wrote *Improper Pride* (1929) under influence of Komisarjevski production of *The Three Sisters*. West End writing debut, *Strange Orchestra* (1932), first modern play directed by Gielgud – critical success but modest box office. *The Old Ladies*, adapt. from Walpole's novel with Edith Evans, dir. by Gielgud who acted in his adapt. of *Crime and Punishment* (1946). Other plays include: *Birthday* (1934); *After October* (1936); and *The Dark River* (1943). *The Pink Room*, rejected as a moral outrage by H. M. Tennant, was staged in 1951. In 1952 m. Mab Lonsdale, daughter of playwright, Frederick Lonsdale. Last West End play, *Dead Secret*, staged 1956.

ANTHONY, C. L. (1896–1990), b. Doris Gladys [Dodie] Smith, Whitefield, Lancashire. Father Ernest d. in her infancy. Lived with grandparents in Old Trafford; 1910 moved to London on mother, Ellen's, remarriage; educ. St Paul's Girls' School (Gustav Holst as music teacher) and RADA. Unsuccessful actress; buyer for Heal's Art and Toy Departments. Friend of Christopher Isherwood. 1939 m. Alec Beesley. *Dear Octopus* (1938) best known work – 376 perfs; nine other plays incl. *Autumn Crocus* (1931) – 371 perfs at Lyric – about spinster's love affair in Tyrolean Hotel populated by eccentric guests; *Service* (1932), set among loyal staff in big store hit by recession; *Lovers and Friends* (1942) and *I Capture the Castle* (1952), all light works with glittering casts. Fifteen years in US writing screen plays for Paramount. Romantic novelist under the pseudonym Dodie Smith: *One Hundred and One Dalmations* (1956) sold over two million copies; filmed by Walt Disney (1961).

> *Look Back With Love* (autobiography, 1974).
> *Look Back with Mixed Feelings* (1978).

ARCHER, William (1856–1924), critic, translator of Ibsen, minor playwright; b. Perth; grew up in grandparents' house, Larvik, Norway; educ. various English and Scots schools and, 1872, Edinburgh University. Read Ibsen in 1870s, saw *Peer Gynt* in Christiana (1876) and *A Doll's House* and *Ghosts* (1884). In 1877, with R. W. Lowe, wrote attack on Irving, *The Fashionable Tragedian*, but offered more judicious commentary in *Henry Irving, Actor and Manager* (1883). Gained notice with *English Dramatists of Today* (1882), which hailed Pinero as regenerator; theatre reviewer for *The World* (1884–96); became, with Clement Scott, the leading critic of the 1890s; unlike Scott, strong proponent of Ibsen, meeting him first in 1881. Ibsen's foremost translator into English, providing acting texts for most early Ibsen prods incl. *A Doll's House* (1889), and *Ghosts* (1891), leading to eleven vol. *Collected Edition* (completed, 1908), with collaboration from Edmund Gosse; his wife, Frances; his brother, Charles; and Eleanor Marx-

Aveling. Met the then unknown Shaw, who became a life-long friend, while both working in British Library in 1880s, helping him to reviewing work and collaborating on abortive play, later reworked by Shaw into *Widowers' Houses*. Founded New Century Th. Hostile to Poel's Shakespearean experiments. Campaigned against censorship and for a National Theatre, publishing detailed proposals with Granville Barker, 1907. His plays, unsuccessful romantic fantasies, but *The Green Goddess* was prod. 1921. Among critical works: 'Masks or Faces?' (1898); *Playmaking* (1912); *The Old Drama and the New* (1923). Son, Tom, died in a German hospital of war wounds, 1918. D. following operation for cancer. His collection of articles, playtexts, programmes and cuttings, now in the Theatre Museum, is leading resource for theatre research.

> 'A Plan for an Endowed Theatre', *Fortnightly Review*, 269 (May 1889), pp. 610–26.
> *The Theatrical World of 1893; 1894*, etc. (1894; 1895 etc.). (Invaluable and exhaustive coverage of London Th. scene.)
> *Three Plays*, foreword, G. B. Shaw (1927).
> *A National Theatre: Schemes and Estimates* (1907; privately, 1904).
> Archer, C., *William Archer: Life, Work and Friendships* (1931).
> Postlewait, T., ed., *William Archer on Ibsen: The Major Essays, 1889–1919* (Westport, Conn., 1986).

> See: Postlewait, T., *Prophet of the New Drama: William Archer and the Ibsen Campaign* (1984).

AUDEN, W[ystan] H[ugh] (1907–73), poet who also experimented with politically radical verse drama; b. York; father, a doctor; a youngest son with close relationship with mother; educ. Gresham's School and Oxford; worked as schoolmaster and later with GPO film unit. Friend of Christopher Isherwood from schooldays, and of Benjamin Britten and other artists on the Left. Met Brecht in Berlin, 1928–29. First book printed by university friend, Stephen Spender (1928); recognition with publication of *Poems* (1930). Member of Group Th. which prod. his plays: *The Dance of Death* (1934), strongly influenced by Cocteau and German Expressionism – the Dancer, as bourgeois death wish (mask by Henry Moore) deceives chorus and audience; with Isherwood, ambitious but finally unconvincing, *The Dog Beneath the Skin* (1936); *The Ascent of F6* (1937; revived Old Vic, with Alec Guinness, 1939), and *On the Frontier* (1938). Provided film script for *The Coal Face* (1935), dir. Cavalcanti, music by Britten; best known GPO film: *Night Mail* (1936). Also wrote opera libretti for: Britten, *Paul Bunyan* (1941); Stravinski, *The Rake's Progress* (1951). Intriguing later play: *The Age of Anxiety: a Baroque Eclogue* (1948), whose four characters voice their thoughts in a New York bar: interweaving private monologues (forerunner of Robert Patrick's *Kennedy's Children*). Served in ambulance unit in Spain, 1937; emigrated to US with Isherwood, 1938; American citizen, 1946. M. Erika Mann, 1935, to aid her escape from Nazi Germany but main relationships with men; Chester Kallman his partner from 1939. Professor of Poetry at Oxford, 1956, living in Christchurch; d. in Vienna.

> Mendelson, E., ed. *Plays and Other Dramatic Writing by W. H. Auden 1928–38* (1989). (incl. otherwise unavailable fragments and number of related essays by Auden.)
> *Letters from Iceland*, with Louis MacNeice (1937).
> *The Dyer's Hand* (1963) – criticism.
> Carpenter, H., *W. H. Auden, a Biography* (1981).

See: Everett, B., *Auden* (1964).
      Bloomfield, B. C., *W. H. Auden: A Bibliography* (1965).
      Mendelson, E., *Early Auden* (1981).

BAKER, Elizabeth (1876–1962), first came to notice with single perf. of *Chains* at the
     Court (1909); revived following year at Duke of York's, with Sybil Thorndike
     and Lewis Casson, and in 1924 by Birmingham Rep, becoming popular reper-
     tory theatre play. *Miss Tassey* (Royal Court, 1910) is set among shop girls in
     their living-in dormitory; her one-act, *Edith*, prod. Women's Suffrage League,
     1912; member of Pioneer Players, 1918–20. Number of plays written for Bir-
     mingham Rep: *Over the Garden Wall* (1915); *Partnership* (1917); *Mrs Robinson*
     (1918) and *Bert's Girl* (1925), concerned with social distinctions among lower
     middle classes.

        Chains repr. in Fitzsimmons, L. and V. Gardner, eds, *New Woman Plays*
        (1991).

BARKER, Harley Granville (1877–1946), b. Kensington; mother, reciter and bird
     mimic; father, architect who managed her tours. Very scanty educ. included
     Sarah Thorne's Theatrical School, Margate, for six months in 1891. First play,
     with fellow student Berte Thomas, 'A Comedy of Fools' (1895) (destroyed),
     and three more in next three years: 'The Family of the Oldroyds', *The Weather
     Hen* (prod. 1899) and 'Our Visitor to Work-Day'. London acting debut, 1892,
     in play by future censor, Charles Brookfield, *The Poet and the Puppet*; 1894,
     general understudy with Florence Farr's Avenue Company; various touring
     companies including Ben Greet's, whose leading lady, Lillah McCarthy, he
     married, 1906 (no children). In 1899, his year of arrival, played Richard in
     Poel's Elizabethan Stage Society *Richard II*; joined Fabians and Stage Society,
     becoming member of Council of Management, and wrote, *The Marrying of Ann
     Leete*, with its regenerator heroine. The following year, acted in Stage Society
     League of Youth and *Candida* (Marchbanks) and made directing debut. Friendship
     with Archer and Shaw. Supported by professional acting engagements with
     Marie Tempest, Ben Webster, Marion Terry. Became leading actor and director
     for Stage Society: 1902, Frank in closed-house perf. *Mrs Warren's Profession*; dir.
     own *Marrying of Ann Leete* and moved into Adelphi, near Shaw. 1904, dir. *Two
     Gentlemen of Verona* on condition allowed six matinées of *Candida* whose success
     led to 1904–7 Barker-Vedrenne management of Royal Court Th. with responsi-
     bility for choosing, casting, directing, all plays except Shaw's. Often regarded as
     first English director, introducing faithfulness to text, long, careful rehearsals,
     ensemble playing, inner truth through low-key acting style, unity of whole
     production, repertory system. Court seasons gave Shaw and numerous new
     playwrights a stage. Prod. own, *Prunella* (1904), wr. with Laurence Housman
     and *The Voysey Inheritance* (1905), which sustained a four-week run. Ambitious
     1907–8 season at Savoy Th., a financial failure; own *Waste* banned but given
     closed-house perf. Continued to direct short seasons of advanced plays and,
     1910, Frohman sponsored season at Duke of York's where own best play, *The
     Madras House*, premièred as well as Galsworthy's *Justice*. 1907–12, on executive
     of Fabians; leader in battle against censorship and for National Th.; visited
     Reinhardt in Berlin. With Lillah McCarthy, managed Little Th., 1911 season,
     and Kingsway for next three years. Epoch-making Shakespeare productions at
     Savoy, *A Winter's Tale* and *Twelfth Night* (1912) and *A Midsummer Night's Dream*
     (1914), followed by final venture as director in London, Hardy, *The Dynasts*.
     First World War, turning point in his life. 1915, toured US with McCarthy;

some service with Red Cross; relationship with Helen Huntington, wife of US millionnaire, and acrimonious divorce. After remarriage, 1919, moved to Netherton Hall, Jacobean mansion in Devon; hyphenated his name; rejected former socialism; severed old theatre ties, and scarcely saw Shaw again. Became first Chairman of British Drama League and devoted himself to writing and scholarship including important *Prefaces to Shakespeare*. Two unperformed plays, *The Secret Life* (1922) and *His Majesty* (1922–28) both concerned with abandonment of power, wordy and dramatically unconvincing. Revised earlier plays for reissue, and translated Spanish plays of Gregorio Sierra and Joaquin Quintero, with Helen Barker. Assisted on revival of *Waste*, 1936, and consultant to Guthrie and Casson for 1940 *King Lear* at Old Vic, with Gielgud. Occasional lectures including *On Dramatic Method*, the Clark Lectures for 1930. Lived partly in Paris, where died.

> Publisher: Sidgwick and Jackson.
> *A National Theatre: Schemes and Estimates*, with William Archer (1907).
> *Farewell to the Theatre* (1917).
> *The Exemplary Theatre* (1922). (Fullest expression of ideas based on directing experience.)
> *Prefaces to Shakespeare* five series (1927–47). (Innovatory discussions of plays as scripts for performance.)
> Purdom, C. B., *Harley Granville Barker: Man of the Theatre, Dramatist and Scholar* (1955). (Useful inclusion of information from Lillah McCarthy but quotations and references not always reliable.)
> Purdom, C. B., ed., *Bernard Shaw's Letters to Granville Barker* (1956).
> Salmon, E., *Granville Barker: A Secret Life* (1983). (Critical biography, incl. much new information.)

> See: Morgan, M., *A Drama of Political Man* (1961). (Stresses role of political ideas; insights into Barker's stage work and plays.)
> Kennedy, D., *Granville Barker and the Dream of Theatre* (Cambridge, 1985). (Often revisionary reading of Barker's career; essential reading for skills as director and theatre reformer.)

BARRETT, Wilson (1846–1904), actor-manager producing mainly melodramas and toga plays, incl. G. R. Sims', *The Lights o' London* (1881); *The Last Days of Pompeii* (1885). Collaborations incl. with H. A. Jones, *The Silver King* (1882); with Sidney Grundy, *Clito* (1886). E. W. Godwin designed sets for him (until d. in 1886). His Christian melodrama, *The Sign of the Cross*, one of three most popular of late nineteenth century, 348 perfs at Lyric, 1896–97 – the hero, Marcus Superbus, played by Barrett, falls in love with and is converted by the virtuous Christian maiden (played on tour by Lillah McCarthy).

> See: Thomas, J., *The Art of the Actor Manager: Wilson Barrett and the Victorian Theatre* (1984).
> Mayer, D., 'The Romans in Britain: Pain's *The Last Days of Pompeii* 1886–1910', *Theatrephile* (1984).
> Mayer, D., 'Toga Plays', in Foulkes, R., ed., *British Theatre in the 1890s* (Cambridge, 1992).

BARRIE, J[ames] M. (1860–1937), also novelist and journalist. Ninth of ten children; educ. Edinburgh University; close attachment to mother, subsequent difficulty forming close relationships and dismally failed marriage. Made mark 1891, with burlesque, *Ibsen's Ghost, or Toole Up to Date*; the following year, *Walker, London,* with 497 perfs, also at Toole's, one of most popular plays of 1890s; prolific, thereafter, including: *Becky Sharp* (1893); *The Professor's Love Story* (1894); *The Admirable Crichton* and *Quality Street* (1902), and *Peter Pan* (1904). Various light comedies, responding to feminist movement, give women the initiative: *What Every Woman Knows* (1908); *The Twelve Pound Look* (1910, prod. Barker, Duke of York's), in which divorced first wife revealed as happy with independence and typewriter; romances: *Dear Brutus* (1917), and *Mary Rose* (1920), a sentimental ghost play. Recurrent pattern of his plays has characters returning to opening condition older and wiser after fantastic events. Plays printed with jocular, novelistic commentary. Instrumental in persuading Frohman to finance Barker's Duke of York's season, 1910; made a Baronet, 1913; lost godson, George Llewellyn Davies, in First World War; sponsor of RADA.

> Publisher: Hodder and Stoughton.
> Mackail, D., *The Story of J. M. Barrie* (1941).
> Dunbar, J., *J. M. Barrie: The Man Behind the Image* (1970).

See: Cutler, D. B., *Sir James M. Barrie: a Bibliography* (1931).
Darlington, W. A. C., *J. M. Barrie* (1938).
Griffin, P., 'The First Performance of *Ibsen's Ghost*', *Theatre Notebook*, XXXIII, 1 (1979), pp. 30–7). (Lively account of Barrie's first success.)

BELL, Florence (1852–1930), known as Mrs Hugh, later Lady Bell. Interested in Ibsen's drama; her translation from Swedish of Alfhild Agrell's *Karin*, staged at the Vaudeville, 1892. Correspondent and friend of Henry James in 1890s. Studies of working-class life in Middlesborough informed *Alan's Wife*, written with Elizabeth Robins. The infant murder and unrepentant heroine caused a sensation when staged anonymously by the Independent Th., 1893 (authorship revealed only in 1925). One-act play, *Between the Posts*, ran for 119 perfs at the Comedy Th. the same year. Praised for her witty dialogue. Among her other plays: *Chamber Comedies* (1890); *An Underground Journey* was a collaboration with Brookfield (1893); Ibsen parody, *Jerry Builder Solness* given single prod. by Grein (1893); *The Way the Money Goes* (Stage Society, 1910), a light comedy of working-class life, and *The Heart of Yorkshire* (1923), a pageant play.

> *Alan's Wife*, repr. in Fitzsimmons L. and V. Gardner, eds, *New Woman Plays* (1991).
> *At the Works: A Study of a Manufacturing Town* (1907). (Account of her Middlesborough investigations.)

BENNETT, Arnold (1867–1931), novelist and journalist; b. Hanley, Staffs; father, solicitor; initially in father's office, worked as solicitor's clerk after move to London; became assistant editor of *Woman*, 1893. Realist novels set in the potteries including: *Anna of the Five Towns* (1902), dramatised as *Cupid and Commonsense* (1909); *The Old Wives' Tale* (1908); *Clayhanger* (1910). M. Mary Soulie 1907, separated, 1921 (no children); daughter by subsequent relationship with Dorothy Chester. Play, *Milestones* was a collaboration with Edward Knoblock (1912), chronicling different phases of a man's life. In 1920s active in managing Lyric Hammersmith.

> *Journal* (1929; 1930).
> Drabble, M., *Arnold Bennett: A Biography* (1974).

See: Hepburn, J., *The Art of Arnold Bennett* (1965).

BERKELEY, Reginald (1890–1935), Author of first full-length play especially for radio, *The White Chateau*, produced Armistice Day, 1925. Another chronicle play, *The Lady with the Lamp*, with Edith Evans as Florence Nightingale, transferred from Arts Theatre Club to run at Garrick, 1929.

> *The White Chateau* incl. in J. W. Marriott, ed., *Great Modern British Plays* (1932).

BOTTOMLEY, Gordon (1874–1948), b. Keighley, Yorks; parents, Alfred and Maria; grammar school educ.; delicate health; lived mainly Silverdale, near Morecambe; 1905 m. Emily Burton of Arnside. Initially a poet; first play, *Crier by Night* (wr. 1901, prod. 1916), Irish supernatural theme. Best plays: two Shakespearean prequels, *King Lear's Wife* (Birmingham Rep, 1915), and *Gruach*, dramatising girlhood of Lady Macbeth (1923), with Sybil Thorndike as Gruach. Wrote some 30 plays, mostly historical or legendary themes, most one-act; after *Gruach*, mainly verse dramas strongly influenced by Yeats, for choric recital or reading rather than th. perf. but Scottish National Players prod. *Britain's Daughter*, about resistance to Roman invasion, in 1927 and *Ardvorlich's Wife* in 1931. Last play, *Deirdre*, four acts in rhythmic prose, combining song, dance and verse, published simultaneously in English and Gaelic in 1944. Fellow Royal Society of Literature, 1925.

> *A Stage for Poetry: My Purposes with My Plays* (Kendal, 1948).

> See: Farmer, A. J., 'Gordon Bottomley', *Etudes Anglaises*, 9 (1956), pp. 323–7.
> Spanos, W. V., *The Christian Tradition in Modern British Verse Drama* (Rutgers, 1967).

BRIDIE, James (1888–1951), b. Osborne Henry Mavor (first pseudonym, Mary Henderson), son of a Glasgow doctor. Influenced by Shaw. Wrote over 50 plays, often humorous and poignant, many for Birmingham Rep and for Scottish National Players incl.: *What It Is To Be Young* (1929); *The Anatomist*, a Burke and Hare play (1931); *Tobias and the Angel*, attacking fundamentalism (1931); *Jonah and the Whale* (1932); *A Sleeping Clergyman* (1933). F. Glasgow Citizens' (1943) whose first perf. his *Holy Isle*, with mission to encourage 'a national drama through the production of plays of Scottish life and character'. Later plays include: *Mr Bolfry* (1943); *The Forrigan Reel* (1945); *The Queen's Comedy* (1950); and *Gog and Magog* (1951).

> See: Bannister, W., *James Bridie and his Theatre* (1955).

BRIGHOUSE, Harold (1882–1958), b. Eccles, Manchester; educ. Manchester Grammar School; left to join family textile business. In London office for early Vedrenne-Barker Court Th. seasons. Journalist on *Manchester Guardian*; spell in airforce, 1914. Wrote in pungent, lively style about stoic Lancashire people for Manchester Repertory Company, also played by other Northern Reps. Comedies, attentive to characterisation. Three one-act plays, the *Strife*-like, 'Dealing in Futures'; a tense potential pit disaster, 'The Price of Coal', and 'Lonesome Like', produced by Glasgow Repertory Company, 1909, and published 1911. Outstanding play, *Hobson's Choice*, a comic *King Lear*, first performed in New York, dir. Iden Payne, 1915; London 1916 (filmed 1953, with Charles Laughton). Wrote some 70 plays mainly one acts, among them: *Safe Among the Pigs* (1929); *A Bit of a War* (1933), a League of Nations play. *Hobson's Choice*, revived in opening repertory of National Theatre, 1964.

Plays for the Meadow and Plays for the Town (1921).
What I Have Had (1953). (Autobiography).

BROOKFIELD, Charles (1857–1913), prolific author of farces and adapt. from French over career of some 30 years. Collaborations incl. comedy with F. Bell, *An Underground Journey* (1893). His long-running *Dear Old Charlie*, cited in censorship discussion (1910) as example of vulgar, obscene works regularly granted licence when serious plays banned. Article, 'On Plays and Playwriting', shortly afterwards, describing 1865–85 as golden age of British drama probably led to his appointment as Chief Examiner of Plays on resignation of G. A. Redford (1911); protests in House of Commons followed.

'On Plays and Playwriting', *National Review*, 345 (November 1911), p. 249.

BUCHANEN, Robert (1841–1901), one of many prolific late nineteenth-century dramatists, reworker of popular themes, accepted moral standards; some 50 plays, mainly farces for Adelphi and Vaudeville, mostly averaging six-week runs; a number of his plays prod. Three in first years at Haymarket, incl. *Partners* (1888); *A Man's Shadow* (1888); and *The Charlatan* (1894). Collaborations incl. with Henry Murray, *A Society Butterfly* (1894), acted by Lily Langtry, which, according to Archer, *Theatre World, 1894*, 'somehow suggested a revue in which all the plays, not only of the season but of the age, were stirred up together in a monster medley' (p. 147).

CARTON, R. C. (1853–1928), b. Richard Claude Critchett. Initially an actor and author of light problem plays and Society Dramas, prominent in late 1880s and 1890s. First play, collaboration with Cecil Raleigh, *The Great Pink Pearl* (1885); among others: *Liberty Hall* (1892), *The Squire of Dames*, *The Home Secretary*, a 'perfect man' play (1895); *A White Elephant* (1896); *Lord and Lady Algy* (1899) – his greatest success with 304 perfs.

COLUM, Padraic (1881–1972), b. Longford, Ireland; father, workhouse master; educ. National School; worked as clerk until 1903; member, Irish National Th. Association. *Broken Soil* included in Irish Players' first London tour (1903; revised 1907 as *The Fiddler's House*). Became one of most popular Abbey dramatists with plays notable for clear, simple language; realistic texture and convincing characters. Broke with Yeats and Synge, 1906, becoming founder member of Th. of Ireland, with some use of Abbey stage. Among plays: *The Land* (1905), concerns oppression of peasants and escape through emigration; the hero of *Thomas Muskerry* (1910), set in a workhouse, has been cheated of his land. Left Ireland 1914, settling in US.

See: Bowen, Z., *Padraic Colum* (S. Illinois, 1970).

CORRIE, Joe (1894–1968), b. Slamannan, moved to Cardenden, West Fife, as young child; father, a grocer then colliery surface man at Bow Hill pit, suffered ill health and died 1915; mother, a farm labourer; two brothers, one sister. Began work as a miner in 1908 after scanty education, often out of school to help with family income; attended W. E. A. classes and Miners' Welfare Institute Library. During First World War worked at Mossblown Colliery, Ayrshire, returning to Cardenden after the War. Involved in 1920 Bow Hill Strike and subsequent national lockout of miners and 1926 General Strike and six-month lockout. Sketches and poems published in *The Miner*, then published *The Image o' God and other poems* (1928); *The Road the Fiddler Went and other poems* (1930), preface by Ramsay MacDonald. Sketches and one-act plays perf. 1926 by amateur Bow Hill Players culminated in *Hogmanay,* a miner's New Year. *In Time o' Strife,* realistically portraying a mining community and the effect of strike on it, perf. North Camberwell Progressive Club, 1927, and toured Scottish coalfields Sept.–Dec. 1928, by Bow Hill Players who became Fife Miner Players for Scottish tour, Feb.–Dec. 1929. Work values humanity and commonsense. Visited Soviet Union, 1929, in part payment of royalties on Russian translation of *The Last Day and Other Stories;* travelled to Leipzig, 1930, to see Collective of Proletarian Actors in *In Time o' Strife.* 1930, m. Mary McGlynn; one daughter, Morag, b. Jan 1932. Broadcast for Scottish Home Service after War. Among many songs wrote, 'It's fine to keep in with the Gaffer'; among numerous plays, mainly performed by amateur working-class groups, the one-act: *Martha* (1935); *And So To War* (1936), and a pit disaster play, *Hewers of Coal,* all won Scottish Community Drama Association awards; *Dawn,* an anti-war play, banned 1943; *A Master of Men* (1944) and *The Roving Boy* (1958), performed Glasgow Citizens. 7:84 Company staged successful revival of *In Time o' Strife,* 1982.

> *Black Earth,* 1939. (Novel.)
> 'What is this Scots Drama?', *The Scottish Stage,* April, 1931.

See: Mackenney, L., ed., *Joe Corrie: Plays, Poems and Theatre Writings* (Edinburgh, 1985). (Important source with useful introduction.)

COWARD, Noel (1899–1973), b. Teddington; family of genteel poverty; grandfather, Crystal Palace organist; father, piano-tuner turned salesman. First stage appearance, 1911, when mother answered advertisement; toured with fellow juvenile, Gertrude Lawrence; among roles, Slightly in *Peter Pan.* 1917, in D. W. Griffith's film, *Hearts of the World,* with the Gish sisters. Began writing in 1914, one-acts, revues, the Shaw-influenced, *The Young Idea* (1922), success coming, 1923, with revue, *London Calling. The Vortex* (1924) at Hampstead Everyman, gained a West End transfer and notoriety for staging of sex and drugs; followed, 1925, by West End productions of *Fallen Angels, On With the Dance* (revue) and *Hay Fever.* Suffered minor nervous breakdown (1926). Performed in revues and many of own plays of which completed over 40, usually written very quickly; many popular successes, most with near simultaneous American openings. Plays often conceived for stars: *The Marquise* (1927) for Marie Tempest; *Private Lives* (1931) for self and Gertrude Lawrence; *Design for Living* (wr. 1932) for self and Lunts. These two last, with *Hay Fever, Present Laughter* (wr. 1939, prod. 1942) and his poltergeist play, *Blithe Spirit* (1941), enduring; less so, romantic nostalgia of *Bitter Sweet* (1929) or patriotic emotional fervour of *Cavalcade* (1931). Frequent world cruises: wrote *Private Lives* in Shanghai and polemical First World War play, *Post Mortem* (wr. 1930; amateur perf. 1944, German POW camp), after brief stint acting in *Journey's End* in Singapore. *Semi-Monde* banned (wr. 1926, prod. 1977) and *Design for Living* delayed (prod. America, 1933; England, 1939). Wrote many well-known songs incl.: 'Mad Dogs and Englishmen', 'The Stately Homes of England'. Brief army service in First World War; in Second, co-director with David Lean and star of film, *In Which We Serve* (1941) and screenplay for *Brief Encounter* (1944), from 'Still Life', one-act play from *Tonight at 8.30* (1935). Other plays including, *Easy Virtue; The Vortex; Private Lives* and *Cavalcade,* filmed. Post-Second World War plays marked by reactionary political stance and sentimentality: including, *Peace in Our Time* (1947); *Nude with a Violin* (1956). Symbol of past for new dramatists. Famed for his urbanity and style, began cabaret work in 1951. Wit again in evidence in *Waiting in the Wings* (1960), set among elderly actresses in retirement home. Lived to see renewed success of his work, incl. own production of *Hay Fever*, with Edith Evans, Maggie Smith, Robert Stephens and Derek Jacobi for opening of National Theatre (1964); evident impact on work of Pinter and Joe Orton. Knighted in 1970; d. in Jamaica of heart attack; memorial in Westminster Abbey.

> Publisher: Heinemann; paperback, Methuen.
> *Present Indicative* (1937); *Future Indicative* (1954); *Middle East Diary* (1944). (Autobiography).
> *To Step Aside* (1939); *Star Quality* (1951). (Short stories.)
> *Not Yet the Dodo and Other Verses* (1967).
> *The Lyrics of Noel Coward* (1983).
> Morley, S., *A Talent to Amuse* (1969).
> Lesley, C., *The Life of Noel Coward* (1976).

See: Mander, R. and J. Mitchenson, *Theatrical Companion to Coward* (Rockliff, 1957).
> Lahr, J., *Coward the Playwright*, (1982).
> Gray, F., *Noel Coward* (1987). (Brief but perceptive study.)
> Holland, P. D., 'Noel Coward and Comic Geometry', in Cordner, M., P. Holland and J. Kerrigan, eds, *English Comedy* (Cambridge, 1994), pp. 267–87.

DANE, Clemence, (1887–1965), b. Winifred Ashton, Blackheath; educ. France and Slade School; taught in Geneva; first play, *A Bill of Divorcement* (1921), considerable success. Further plays, notable for strong emotion and modern heroines but never quite achieving potential suggested by first play, incl.: *Granite* (1926), a melodrama set on Lundy Island; *Wild Decembers* (1933), a chronicle play about the Brontës, and *Moonlight is Silver* (1934), a drawing-room drama about marital mistakings. During Second World War, *The Saviours* (1941), broadcast by BBC, a series of seven verse plays centring on the recurrence of the Merlin/Arthur theme in British legend, working through Alfred, Robin Hood, Elizabeth and Essex, and Nelson, to the Unknown Warrior. Post-war: historical dramas developed from these, broadcast in 1958: the Lady Godiva story, *Scandal at Coventry* (1958), and *Till Time Shall End*, concerned with the Queen's refusal to marry, for the quatercentenary of the accession of Elizabeth I. Novels incl.: *Regiment of Women* (1917) and *The Moon is Feminine* (1938).

> Publisher: Heinemann

DAVIOT, Gordon (1896–1952), b. Elizabeth Mackintosh, Inverness; historical novelist under name, Josephine Tey; parents, Colin and Josephine; educ. Royal Academy, Inverness, and Anstey Physical Training College, Birmingham; worked as PE teacher; 1929 publ. mystery novel, *The Man in the Queue* about a murder in a theatre queue. First and most famous play, *Richard of Bordeaux*, a modern *Richard II*, prod. John Gielgud at the Arts Th. Club in 1932, played West End throughout the following year, extensively revised (with much imput from Gielgud), designed by Motleys. One of favourite roles of Gielgud who had been a memorable Richard in Shakespeare's play in 1929. Several other plays with historical settings including, *Queen of Scots* (1934), for Gwen Ffrangcon Davies, with Olivier as Bothwell, and *Dickon* (1935) about Richard III: similar theme but less successful than her novel, *The Daughter of Time* (1951). She died of cancer.

See: Gielgud, J., *Early Stages* (1938).
        'Richard of Bordeaux: An Illustrated Supplement', *Theatre World*, 19, 98 (March, 1933).

DAVISON, John (active inter-war years), Yorkshire engineer; strike play, *Shadows of Strife*, prod. Sheffield, 1928, Birmingham Rep, 1929, and then Arts Th. Club. Nurtured by Barry Jackson, wrote *The Brontes of Haworth Parsonage* (1933) and dramatised *Wuthering Heights* (1940), both for Birmingham Rep.

DRINKWATER, John (1886–1937), b. Mosely, Birmingham; wrote lyric poetry and promoted verse drama; worked as insurance clerk initially, acting with amateur Pilgrim Players for whom wrote one-act plays, *Fifinello* (1910); *Cophetua* (1911). Manager of theatre Barry Jackson built for the Players, reformed as Birmingham Repertory Company (1913); Malvolio in opening prod. Wrote and dir. own verse plays including, *Rebellion* and *The Christmas Party* (1914); *The Storm* (1915); *X=O: A Night of the Trojan War* (1917); before huge success of first full-length play, *Abraham Lincoln* (1918) brought it to Lyric Hammersmith (466–night run) and him from Birmingham. A series of historical plays followed, *Mary Stuart* (Hampstead, 1922); *Oliver Cromwell* (His Majesty's, 1923); *Robert E. Lee* (1923). Birmingham again with one-act, *A Bird in Hand* (1927), with Olivier and Peggy Ashcroft.

> Publisher: Sidgwick and Jackson.
> *The Gentle Art of Theatregoing* (1927).
> *Discovery: Being the Second Book of an Autobiography, 1897–1913* (1932).

DRUTEN, John Van (1901–57), b. London; fame with *Young Woodley*, about a public school boy infatuated with housemaster's wife, banned 1925, perf. 1928, at the Arts Th. Club and, following lifting of ban, long run at the Savoy. *After All*, an exercise in 'restrained naturalism', also at the Arts, 1930. American citizen, 1944.

> *The Way to the Present* (1938). (Reminiscences.)
> *The Playwright at Work* (NYk., 1953).

DUNSANY, Lord (1875–1957), b. Edward John Drax Moreton Plunkett; short story writer: *The Time of the Gods* (1906). First plays prod. Dublin, at Abbey Th. incl. *The Glittering Gate* (1909); briefly celebrated for part in rejection of realism in plays incl. invented mythology and stylised language; London staging for *The Gods of the Mountains* (1911); *The Golden Doom* (1912); most subsequent work prod. Dublin but *If* had London run, 1921.

ELIOT, T[homas] S[tearns] (1888–1965), poet and essayist; b. St Louis, America; educ. Harvard (1906–10, 1911–14), Sorbonne (1910), Oxford (1915); supported self as teacher, bank-manager, then dir. of Faber and Faber. M. 1. Vivien Haigh-Wood, 1915, settled London; separated, 1933; she in mental hospital, 1938 till death in 1947; m. 2. Valerie. British citizenship, 1927. Associate of Ezra Pound; poems and articles in *The Little Review* and *Poetry*; became leading modernist poet with publ. of *The Love Song of J. Alfred Prufrock* (1917); *Poems* (1919) and *The Waste Land* (1922). Criticism incl. *The Sacred Wood* (1920). Founded *The Criterion* (1923) and editor for seventeen years. Much impressed by Pound's work on Nōh drama and interested in Yeats's ideas of theatre; verse drama absorbed his attention in later years. Dramatic fragment, *Sweeney Agonistes*, regarded by many as most interesting attempt, wr. 1926, prod. Group Th. 1934, in double bill with Auden's *Dance of Death*; followed, by most enduring, *Murder in the Cathedral*, written for the Canterbury Festival, 1935. Subsequent plays, all drawing-room format with verse dialogue. Incorporated Greek-style chorus in *The Family Reunion* (1939); didactic symbolism in *The Cocktail Party* (1949). *The Confidential Clerk* (1953) and *The Elder Statesman* (1958) followed. Received into Anglican church, 1928; Nobel Prize, 1948 and awarded OM.

> *The Aims of Poetic Drama* (Poets' Theatre Guild Pamphlet, 1949).
> 'Poetry and Drama' (1950) in Hayward, J., ed., *Selected Prose* (1953).
> 'The Three Voices of Poetry' (1953).
> Gordon, L., *Eliot's New Life* (1988).

See: Jones, D. E., *The Plays of T. S. Eliot* (1960).
  Smith, C. H., *Eliot's Dramatic Theory and Practice* (Princeton, NJ, 1963).
  Browne, E. M., *The Making of T. S. Eliot's Plays* (1969).
  Chiari, J., *T. S. Eliot, Poet and Dramatist* (1973).

ERVINE, St John (1883–1971), b. Belfast; moved to London, 1900; met Shaw and developed interest in Fabianism; returned to Ireland before First World War becoming manager of Abbey Th. 1915; having fired whole Company after disagreement, own resignation followed, 1916; hostile to Easter Rising; wound in First World War resulted in leg amputation. Used vernacular dialogue for realistic social problem plays about Irish political bigotry or new woman questions: *Mixed Marriage* (1911) and *The Magnanimous Lover* (1912), prod. Abbey; *Jane Clegg* (1913), with strong, sympathetic heroine, prod. Manchester Repertory Company. Other plays include: *The Orangeman* (1914); *John Fergusson* (1915); *The First Mrs Frazer* (1929). Plays with N. Irish setting prod. at Abbey, following return to Ireland: *Boyd's Shop* (1936); *William John Mawhinney* (1940); *Friends and Relations* (1941).

> *John Fergusson* (NYk., 1920). (Useful introduction by Ervine.)
> *The Organised Theatre: A Plea in Civics* (1924).

FIELD, Michael, pseudonym of Katherine Bradley (1846–1914) and Edith Cooper (1862–1913); several unperformed verse plays incl. 'Callirhoe', still-born work in quasi-Elizabethan style. Prose play, *A Question of Memory* prod. Independent Th. 1893.

FLECKER, James Elroy (1884–1915), lyric poet; b. South London, father a clergyman and Head of Dean Close School, Cheltenham; educ. Dean Close and Uppingham, Classics at Trinity, Oxford, 3rd class degree, 1902; Graduate Student in Oriental Studies, Caius Cambridge, 1908, and two years later Interpreter with Levant Consular Service; friend of T. E. Lawrence, Rupert Brooke; wrote novel, 1914; contracted tuberculosis in Constantinople, exacerbated by swimming Hellespont; d. in Swiss Sanatorium. Posthumous fame with poetic drama, *Hassan* (wr. 1914, prod. 1923), company of 100, incidental music by Delius, ballet by Fokine, 281 perfs; *Don Juan* (300 Club, 1926) less successful.

> Sherwood, J., *No Golden Journey* (1973).

See: Lawrence, T. E., *An Essay of Flecker* (1937).
  Kidd, T., '*Hassan*: the road to the Haymarket', *Theatre Research International*, 4 (May 1979), pp. 198–213.

GALSWORTHY, John (1867–1933), novelist and playwright; b. Kingston Hill, Surrey; father, solicitor, property and land speculator; educ. governess, prep school, Harrow, Oxford; called to Bar, 1890; m. Ada, cousin's wife, having been cited in acrimonious divorce. Under pseudonym, Sin John, pub. short stories, *From the Four Winds* (1897) at own expense, followed by several unsuccessful novels until, *The Island Pharisees* (1904), pub. under own name. Recognition with *The Man of Property* (1906), first of Forsyte Saga and first play, *The Silver Box*, with powerful trial scene, prod. Barker at Court Th. same year. Contributed to all Barker's subsequent seasons and plays popular with repertory theatres. Friend of Conrad, Edward Garnett and Ford Maddox Ford, admired Turgenev and Zola. Plays have realistic settings and address issues: of divorce, *Joy* (1908), *The Fugitive* (1913), *The Skin Game* (1920); and class struggle, *Strife* (1909), *The Eldest Son* (1913). Prison scene of *Justice* (1910, filmed 1917) led directly to prison reform proposals. Constant theme: 'haves' imposing on 'have-nots'; heroes: idealists, middle-class professionals (lawyers, writers, politicians) with advanced ideas. Post-First World War: *Loyalties* (1922) detective format; *Escape* (1926), prisoner on-the-run play, but attention mainly to prose fiction and developing Forsyte Saga. Refused knighthood; awarded OM; Nobel Prize, 1932.

> Publisher: Duckworth.
> Garnett, E., ed., *Letters from John Galsworthy* (1934).
> Marrot, H. V., *The Life and Letters of John Galsworthy* (1935).
> Grindin, J., *John Galsworthy* (1987).

> See: Fréchet, A., *John Galsworthy: A Reassessment* (1982).

GIELGUD, Val[entine Henry] (1900–81), Head of BBC drama; theatrical family background; older brother of John; unsuccessful actor; joined BBC, 1928: six months as assistant editor *Radio Times*; a studio manager on Sieveking's *Kaleidoscope*, then sudden elevation to Head of Drama on resignation of R. E. Jeffrey, 1929. Worked with Sieveking and Lawrence Gillam in drama and features department; insisted repertory company of actors formed for radio drama; essentially created National Theatre via radio, with productions from Aeschylus and Shakespeare to Rostand and Shaw; sponsored new radio plays. Own radio play: *Red Tabs* (1930), war-set duologue, intercut with gunfire. As radio producer, ambitious projects incl.: Sayers, *Man Born to Be King* (1941); *War and Peace* adaptation (1942). Initially promoting new work, came to be regarded by many as conservative force in Radio drama, initiative passing to Features. Seconded to Alexandra Palace, 1939, to learn about television broadcasting; reserve occupation during the War. Produced own *Ending It* (TV, 1939); *Party Manners* (radio then TV, 1950), light comedy that caused outcry for perceived hostility to socialist government. Number of radio handbooks and many thrillers and crime novels including, *Death at Broadcasting House* (1934).

> *How to Write Broadcast Plays* (1932).
> *British Radio Drama* (1957). (Radio history and detailed account of job of radio producer.)

GILBERT, W[illiam] S[chwenck] (1836–1911), eldest child of naval surgeon; kidnapped aged three and ransomed for £25; educ. King's College, London; clerk in educ. department of Privy Council, 1857–62; called to the Bar, 1863; and worked as journalist; m. Lucy Blois Turner, 1867 (no children); published *Bab Ballads* (1869), illustrated with own sketches. Astonishing virtuosity in use of language and adroit rhyming and punning. Best known for collaboration with Arthur

Sullivan on satirical comic operas that began with *Trial by Jury* (1875); incl. *H.M.S. Pinafore* (1878); *Patience* (1881) caricaturing Wilde and aesthetic movement; *The Mikado* (1885); *Utopia Limited* (1893); and concluded with *The Grand Duke* (1896). Libretti for comic operas with other composers incl. *His Excellency* (1894), with Dr. Carr. Prolific dramatist and meticulous director of own plays setting new standard for stage management. Insistent that nonsense be played earnestly. First play *Dulcamara*, a burlesque (1866), sponsored by Tom Robertson, followed by series of farces and extravaganzas in the manner of Planché but characterised by own brand of absurdity or 'topsy-turvy', recognised by epithet 'Gilbertian': *The Palace of Truth* (1870) a blank verse ironic comedy, set in a fantastical royal court, mocks contemporary social mores; *Topsy Turvydom* (1874), set in a land of reversal; hero of *Engaged* (1877) makes 'an honest living' poaching, running illegal whisky still and offering hospitality to the passengers of trains he has derailed. Something of this developed by Shaw. One of the few nineteenth-century dramatists to see work into print: *Original Plays* (1876). Among works with more serious tone: *Pygmalion and Galatea* (1871), *The Wicked World* (1873) and *Broken Hearts* (1875). Owner, Garrick Theatre, 1889. Shakespeare burlesque, *Rozenkrantz and Guildenstern* prod. 1891. As theatre's Grand Old Man: played Associate in *Trial By Jury* revival for Ellen Terry Jubilee, 1906; first dramatist to be knighted, 1907; evidence to Select Committee on Censorship, 1909. Savoy operas recaptured audience with restaging, 1919, thereafter performed continually by D'Oyly Carte Company.

Pearson, H., *W. S. Gilbert: His Life and Strife* (1957).
Bailey, L., *The Gilbert and Sullivan Book* (1956).

See: Barker, H. G., 'Exit Planché – Enter Gilbert', *The London Mercury*, XXV (March and April 1932) pp. 457–66, 558–73.
Hamilton, E., 'W. S. Gilbert', *Theatre Arts Monthly*, XI (October 1927), pp. 781–90.
Smith, G., *The Savoy Operas* (1963).
Steadman, J. W., *Gilbert before Sullivan: Six Comic Plays* (1967).
Hibbert, C., *Gilbert and Sullivan and their Victorian World* (NYk., 1976).

GOW, Lawrence (1899–1993), b. Heaton Moor; educ. Manchester University; research chemist, then schoolteacher in Manchester; engaged in amateur theatre and wrote plays for his pupils. *Gallows Glorious*, performed Croydon Rep. 1933 and, following year, dramatisation with Walter Greenwood of Greenwood's novel, *Love on the Dole*, prod. Manchester Repertory Company. M. Wendy Hillier who made name as heroine, Sally Hardcastle. Play toured continuously, at times with two companies, until August 1937 (London 1935; NYk., 1936, Paris 1937 as *Rêves Sans Provisions*). Subsequent work included adaptations of *Ann Veronica* and *Tess of the d'Urbervilles*. In later life lived in Buckinghamshire.

GREENWOOD, Walter (1903–74), educ. Longworthy Road Council School, Salford, left aged 13; range of jobs incl. milkman, clerk, pawnbroker, cab-driver, warehouseman. His novel *Love on the Dole* (1933), dramatised with Gow (see above), prod. Manchester, 1934, London 1935 with 391 perfs; wrote screenplay with B. Emery and R. Gamble for 1941 film. Only two other plays made much mark: *A Rod of Iron* (later called *A Cure for Love*) prod. Robert Donat (Westminster Th. 1945) and *Saturday Night at the Crown* (Morecambe, 1954; Garrick Th., 1957). Among other plays gaining London prods: *Give Us the Day* (1940) and *So Brief the Spring* (1946). Hon D.Litt. from Salford University, 1971. Autobiography, *There Was a Time*, dramatised as *Hanky Park*, prod. Mermaid Th. 1971.

There Was a Time (1967). (Autobiography).

GREGORY, [Isabella Augusta], Lady (1852–1932), daughter of landed Irish Protestant Persse family; m. 1880 Lord Gregory, retired Governor of Ceylon, d. 1892; one son, William Robert, b. 1881; lived at Coole Park, Co. Galway. A Nationalist collected Irish folklore, edited husband's autobiography and met W. B. Yeats 1896, with whom drafted manifesto of Irish Literary Th. and organised fund from social contacts. Director of Abbey Th. 1904 to her death. Generous hostess to writers at Coole (Yeats spent summers there for twenty years) and prolific output of own: seventeen plays prod. Abbey Th., mostly one-act comedies of Irish peasant life, including *Spreading the News*, chosen for Abbey opening (1904) and *The Workhouse Ward* (1908), but also full-length plays of ordinary folk caught up in incidents in Irish legend or history: *The White Cockade* (1905), James II after Battle of Boyne, or *Dervorgilla* (1907), about the arrival of the English romantic tragedies of Irish patriotism: *The Gaol Gate* (1906) and *The Rising of the Moon* (1907), and trans. into Kiltartan dialect of Goldoni and Molière. Trans from Irish of Douglas Hyde. Collaborations with Yeats, incl. *A Pot of Broth* Son's death in First World War recorded in Yeats's poems, 'An Irish Airman Foresees his Death' and 'In Memory of Major Robert Gregory'.

> Publisher: Colin Smythe.
> *Our Irish Theatre* (1913). (History of Abbey with lengthy extracts and quotation from numerous documents.)
> *Visions and Beliefs in the West of Ireland*, 2 vols (1920).
> Robinson, L., ed., *Lady Gregory's Journals, 1916–30* (1946).

See: Saddlemeyer, A., *In Defence of Lady Gregory, Playwright* (Dublin, 1966).
       Saddlemeyer, A., *Lady Gregory, Fifty Years After* (Gerrard's Cross, 1987).

GREIN, Jacob T. (1862–1935), theatre manager and critic; b. Amsterdam of German and Anglo-Dutch parentage; worked in uncle's bank in Amsterdam until collapse in 1885 then London offices of Dutch trading company; theatre reports for Dutch papers, and agent in Holland for Pinero, Jones and Jerome, ensuring plays known and royalties paid. In Paris, 1887, coinciding with opening of Antoine's Th. Libre; argued for a British Th. Libre in *The Weekly Comedy*, ed. with C. W. Jarvis until it folded in 1889. F. Independent Th. in London, 1891, as home for new uncommercial drama. First prod., Ibsen's *Ghosts*, caused outrage; other incl. Shaw's debut, *Widowers' Houses* (1892), and the anonymous [Robins and Bell], *Alan's Wife* (1893). Invited Lugné Poe's Th. d'Oeuvre, 1895. Conservative in many ways, refused Shaw's: *The Philanderer* and *Mrs Warren's Profession* Resigned Independent Th. to Charrington, 1895, on promotion to managing dir. of his firm. Own plays of little interest, include, with C. W. Jarvis, *A Man's Love* (wr. 1889); *Reparation* (wr. 1892). Critic for *Sunday Times* among others supported ban on *Waste* and judged *The Madras House* a sexless abstract dissertation. 1900–7 ran season of German plays in London and promoted Beerbohm Tree's tour to Germany. Given dinner at Criterion, 1907, to honour twenty-five years as drama critic. Founder member, Critics' Circle, 1913. Advocate of womens' suffrage, gaining licence for first public perf. *Ghosts* as Suffrage Benefit 1914.

> *Dramatic Criticism* (1899).
> *The New World of Theatre* (1924).
> Orme, Michael [Mrs J. T. Grein], *J. T. Grein, The Story of a Pioneer* (1936).

See: Schoonderwoerd, N. H. G., *J. T. Grein, Ambassador of the Theatre* (Assen, 1963).

GRIFFITH, Hubert [Freeling] (1896–1953), critic on *The Observer*; his three-act play, *Red Sunday*, prod. Komisarjevski at Arts Th. Club, 1929, with Gielgud as Trotsky, Athene Seylor as Czarina; attracted complaints from *émigré* Russians and denied transfer; published 1929, with preface on censorship. Other plays include *Tunnel Trench; The Tragic Muse*.

> *Red Sunday*, publ. in W. G. Fay, ed., *Five Three Act Plays* (1933).
> *Iconoclastes, or, the Future of Shakespeare* (1928).

GRUNDY, Sidney (1848–1914), b. Manchester, where father was Lord Mayor; initially a barrister, first play, *A Little Change*, prod. Haymarket, 1872. Prolific journeyman playwright, G. R. Sims and F. C. Phillips among collaborators; popular in late nineteenth century; many adapts. of French plays, incl. *Mammon* (1877) from Octave Feuillet, *Montjoye*, rewritten for Tree as *A Bunch of Violets* (1894) and *The Musketeers* (1898), after Dumas, also for Tree; capable of lively fluent dialogue; plays set in society or suburbia with sexually titillating themes. Accused Wilde of plagiarising his *Glass of Fashion* (1883) in *Lady Windermere's Fan* but one of few to protest at removal of Wilde's name from playbills, following trial. Among more interesting plays: *White Lie* (1889), a light comedy; *A Pair of Spectacles* (1890), a farce; *A Fool's Paradise* (1892); *Sowing the Wind* (1893). Conservative attitudes evident in the satirical, *The New Woman* (1894) and *The Degenerates* (1899). Society plays continued into new century with, for example, *Frocks and Frills* (1902). Growing hostility to Ibsen and the New Drama voiced in *The Play of the Future, by a Playwright of the Past* (1914) which included an embittered attack on plays of Wilde and Shaw.

> *A Pair of Spectacles* in Rowell, G., ed., *Nineteenth Century Plays* (1953). (One of few modern reprints.)

GUTHRIE, Tyrone (1900–71), great-grandfather, the Irish character actor, Tyrone Power, which adopted as pseudonym; acted with J. B. Fagan's Oxford Rep with John Gielgud; joined 2LO radio station, 1923; posted to Belfast following year as 'Uncle William' on Childrens' Hour; 1926–27, dir. Scottish National Players, and prod. own play, *Victorian Nights*. Author of experimental radio plays, concerned with constraints people accept on lives: *Squirrel's Cage* (BBC, 1929) and *The Flowers Are Not For You To Pick*, with Flora Robson (BBC, 1930), but stopped writing for radio when production of third play, *Matrimonial News* (wr. 1930), delayed. Distinguished director with stints at Festival Th., Cambridge, 1929–30, Group Th., 1932–33, and Old Vic, 1933–34; 1936–38, taking charge of Vic-Wells company in 1937, on death of Lilian Bayliss. Pioneer of open stage; moved to Stratford Ontario, 1952, to establish Shakespeare Festival Th.; then Guthrie Th., Mineaplis, 1956.

> *A Life in the Theatre* (1960).

See: Forsyth, J., 'Tyrone Guthrie: Pioneer in the Field of Radio Drama', in P. Lewis, ed., *Papers of the Radio Literature Conference* (Durham, 1977), pp. 121–35.

HAMILTON, Cicely (1872–1952), b. Cicely Hammill; one of four children of army commander, farmed out while parents abroad; father died when she was eighteen

year old; educ. private schools, England and Germany; briefly, pupil teacher
never married. Dramatist, actress, translator, novelist; wrote for *Time and Tide*
Active feminist: member Women's Social and Political Union; Actresses' Franchise League; founder member, Women Writers' Suffrage League; 1909, wrote
words for Ethel Smythe's 'The March of the Women' and, for Actresses' Franchise League, with Christopher St John, a farce, *How the Vote Was Won;* /
Pageant of Great Women (prod. Edy Craig, 1910). Most influential work a play
Diana of Dobson's, adapted from her novel of same name, which, in 1908, ran
for 171 perfs at Kingsway and, in 1920s, became favourite with S. London
Cooperative drama groups. Recurrent theme: importance of employment fo
female self-respect developed in prose study, *Marriage as a Trade* (1909), continue
in play, *Just To Get Married* (Little Th., 1911, revived Birmingham Rep, 1918)
Ran Rep company in Abbeville, 1917; and, post-First World War, wrote numerous articles on such issues as birth control and abortion, and a large number o
short plays produced by Birmingham Rep including, *The Old Adam* (1924) and
The Human Factor (1925). Wrote *The Old Vic* (1926), with Lilian Baylis
and *Modern Germanies: As Seen By an Englishwoman* (1931). Awarded civil lis
pension for services to literature, 1938.

> Modern reprints in *Plays of the Actresses' Franchise League*, (Nottingham
> 1985) and in Fitzsimmons, L. and V. Gardner, eds, *New Woman Play*
> (1991).

HAMILTON, Patrick (1904–62), b. Sussex; educ. Westminster School; acting debut
aged seventeen; sister, Lalla m. playwright Sutton Vane who supported Hamilton
in becoming full-time writer. By 1928 three novels published, third, *Tuppenc*
Coloured, being about theatre. West End success with *The Rope*, 1928, presenting
the motiveless murder of a contemporary by two callous undergraduates (radio
adaptation, 1932; revived Wyndham's, 1994; filmed Hitchcock, 1948). Heavy
drinker; m. Lois Martin, 1930; became marxist. Number of dramatic thriller
incl. *Gaslight* (1939), Victorian thriller in which fading gas jet reveals murdere
lurking in room above, long run in NYk. under title *Angel Street* (1941); radio
thrillers incl. *Money with Menaces* (1937) and *To the Public Danger* (1939). Among
novels, *The Midnight Bell* (1929) and *Hangover Square: A Story of Darkest Earl*
Court (1941). Less successful in later life, became alcoholic; d. kidney failure.

> Hamilton, B., *The Light Went Out* (1972).

HANKIN, St John (1869–1909), b. Southampton; educ. Malvern School and Oxford
m. Florence Routledge (no children); brief stretch as journalist in India contracted malaria and returned to London, 1895. Followed distinguished line of dram.
critics on *Saturday Review*, also wrote for *The Times*. Made mark with series o
comic sequels of famous plays as *Caste* and *A Doll's House* for *Punch*, published
as *Mr Punch's Dramatic Sequels* (1901) and *Lost Masterpieces* (1904). On counci
of Stage Society, which staged first full-length play, *The Two Mr Wetherbys* (1903)
Subsequent plays produced by Society or at Court Th. with no West End
transfers but subsequently much performed by Birmingham Rep. Highly
regarded by Shaw and Barker. Satirical, sometimes jaundiced, tone for quasi-
Society Drama, best plays being *The Return of the Prodigal* (1905), a satirical
version of the Bible parable, and a feminist play, *The Last of the de Mullins* (1908)
Also wrote, *The Charity that Began at Home* (1906), *The Cassilis Engagemen*
(1907); two short plays and, 1905, trans. Brieux' *Les trois filles de M Dupont*

Conscious of having contracted the deteriorating disease that had crippled his father, committed suicide by drowning in 1909.

Publisher: Secker.

'Puritanism and the English Stage', *The Fortnightly Review* 480 (December, 1906), pp. 1055–64.

See: Phillips, W. H., *St John Hankin: Edwardian Mephistophiles* (1979).

HOUGHTON, Stanley (1881–1913), b. Ashton upon Mersey; educ. Manchester Grammar School, leaving aged sixteen to enter father's textile business. Amateur actor with more than 70 roles, 1901–12; occasional contributor, 1905–06, then critic on *Manchester Guardian*. Beginning, 1908, with *The Dear Departed* as curtain raiser for prod. Shaw's *Widowers' Houses* and, full-length *Independent Means* (1909) for Manchester Repertory Company, became leading member of Manchester School: plays with middle- and working-class Lancashire characters and vernacular dialogue. Plays include: *The Master of the House* and *The Younger Generation* (1910), a response to Shaw's *Misalliance*; *The Perfect Cure* and *Trust the People* (1913) as well as hugely successful comedy, *Hindle Wakes* (1912), which, wr. for Stage Society prod. at Aldwych, London, by Manchester cast, toured extensively, being declared out of bounds for Oxford students by Vice-Chancellor on grounds of immorality of strong-minded heroine. After this, wrote for Garrick Th. incl. *Phipps*, a London farce (1912). Travelled to Paris and Venice; began novel about Lancashire life shortly before death, aged 32, following lung operation.

HOPE, Anthony (1863–1933), novelist and playwright; b. Anthony Hope Hawkins; best known for Ruritanian, *The Prisoner of Zenda*, (novel 1894; play, 1896); associated with New Drama when *Helena's Path*, wr. with Cosmo Gordon Lennox, given two perfs in Barker's 1910–11, Duke of York's season.

HOUSMAN, Laurence (1865–1959), b. Bromsgrove, Worcestershire, sixth of seven children; oldest brother, Alfred, poet of *The Shropshire Lad* (1896). Educ. Bromsgrove School and National Art Training School, South Kensington, training as black and white illustrator; book designer for Kegan Paul. Wr. two books of fairy tales (1894, 1895) and, by 1899 three of poems. *An English Woman's Love Letters*, pub. anonymously, 1900, was a sensational best-seller; art critic, *Manchester Guardian*, 1907. *Prunella*, Pierrot play with music, wr. with Barker, failed (Court Th., Christmas 1904), but successfully revived subsequently; *The Chinese Lantern*, fairy tale in curious quasi-Chinese dialect, contributed to verse drama revival (prod. Barker, 1908). Reputation as most banned British dramatist began with *Bethlehem*, banned for depiction of Holy Family, closed-house prod. dir. Gordon Craig, great hall of Imperial Institute ran three weeks, 1902; eventually licensed (1921) on condition Virgin remained mute and Jesus did not appear; *Pains and Penalties*, banned (1910) for defamation of Queen Caroline: indignation meeting held in interval of Edy Craig's closed-house production following appointment of Charles Brookfield as new Examiner of Plays (1912, ban lifted 1921). *Little Plays of St Francis*, begun 1916 with *Good as Gold*, *St Francis Poverello* (1918), published 1922 with preface by Barker, much performed by amateur companies; few more added every year, 1925–51. *Victoria Regina* (NYk., 1935; London, 1937, on 100th anniversary of Victoria's accession), hugely successful.

The Unexpected Years (Indianapolis, IN, 1936). (Autobiography with useful insights into collaboration with Barker.)

HUGHES, Richard (1900–76), best known for novels, *A High Wind in Jamaica* (1929) and *The Fox in the Attic*, first part of unfinished trilogy; father and only two siblings dead by the time he was aged five; educ. Charterhouse and Oxford; settled in Wales; wife, Frances, a painter. Chamber plays performed closed house, initially: *The Sister's Tragedy* (1922) in Masefield's house, then Little Th.; *A Comedy of Good and Evil* (1924) 300 Club Th., Portmadoc, then Oxford Playhouse; *The Man Born to be Hanged*, Portmadoc, then Lyric Hammersmith (1924), in which three tramps murder a woman but, shocking audience, escape by pinning it on a drunk. *Danger*, first British play wr. for broadcasting, prod. 15 January 1925; revived, Home Service, 1956.

Publisher: Chatto.
R. P. Graves, *Richard Hughes* (1994).

HUTCHINSON, Ernest (d. 1921), impact with *The Right to Strike* (1920), personal ethics play with leading character, Ben Ormorod, doctor pitted against striking railway men; d. following year.

ISHERWOOD, Christopher (1904–86), see, W. H. AUDEN.

JAMES, Henry (1843–1916), novelist; b. NYk.; childhood in Albany and Europe, with frequent visits to theatre; educ. schools in Geneva, London, Paris and private tutor, art studies at Newport (1860), Harvard (1862–63); first serious stories accepted by *Atlantic Monthly* (1865). First visit to Th. Français, 1870; travelled in Europe; long stay in Paris, 1875–76, meeting Turgenev, Zola, Flaubert, Goncourts, admired Coquelin and Th. Français acting. Settled London, 1876, wr. th. criticism, essays, novels, short stories. Recognition with *Daisy Miller* (1878), adapt. invited by Madison Square Th. while in America, 1881–82 (rejected). Novel about theatre, *The Tragic Muse* (1890), after which five years' attention to drama: scenarios, readings to managers, discovering Ibsen's plays. Adapt. of *The American*, prod. Compton, 1890, with Elizabeth Robins, 70 perfs, London. Publ. *Theatricals* (1892); negotiations with Augustin Daly for prod. of *Disengaged*, 1893, foundered. *Guy Domville*, prod. George Alexander (1895), to hostile furore: ran four weeks with extensive critical discussion but James withdrew from theatre. One-act 'Summersoft' for Ellen Terry, not prod. Thereafter, used scenario in planning fiction and notable scenic and narrative economy; *The Awkward Age* (1899), entirely in dialogue. Further attempt on th.: *The High Bid*, prod. Forbes Robertson (Edinburgh, 1908; London, 1909); *The Saloon*, prod. Gertrude Kingston (1908); *The Outcry*, prod. Stage Society (1917). Parents d. 1882; sister Alice, 1894; brother William, 1910; moved to Lamb House, Rye, 1897; revisited America, 1905; British subject, 1915; OM, 1916.

Publisher: Hart-Davis.
Guy Domville, ed. L. Edel (1961). (Reprints reviews of play by Shaw, Wells, Bennett.)
Wade, A., ed., *The Scenic Art* (1949). (Collection of James theatre criticism.)
A Small Boy and Others (1913). (Memoirs.)
Matthiessen, F. O., and K. B. Murdock, eds, *The Notebooks of Henry James* (1947).

Robins, E., *Theatre and Friendship* (James's letters to the actress.)
Edel, L., *Henry James*, 5 vols (1953–57).
Edel, L., ed., *Letters*, 3 vols (1981).

See: Egan, M., *Henry James The Ibsen Years* (Cambridge, 1972).

JEROME, Jerome K[lapka] (1859–1927), b. Walsall, Staffs. to non-conformist family; father, failed ironmonger; orphaned aged fourteen; three years on stage as touring actor; best known for novel, *Three Men in a Boat* (1889). Worked briefly as actor. Some 25 plays incl. first play *Barbara*, one act (1886); full-length farce, *New Lamps for Old* (1890), 160 perfs; with Eden Phillpotts, *The Prude's Progress* (1895); *Miss Hobbs*, a New Woman play (1899), 210 perfs. Great success with benign *Lower Depths* play, *The Passing of the Third Floor Back* (St James's, 1908), set among seedy characters in London boarding house with Forbes Robertson as the mysterious stranger.

> *On Stage and Off* (1885); *Stageland* (1889). (Insider's accounts of contemporary theatre.)

JOHNSTON, Denis (1901–84), prosperous Irish family; father, a supreme court judge; read law at Cambridge and, 1924, Harvard, where interested in Boston independent th.; called to English, Irish, N. Irish Bars, 1925; practised as barrister, Dublin. Saw Kaiser, *From Morn to Midnight* with O'Casey at London, Gate Th.; acted and directed, Pirandello, O'Neill, Strindberg, Toller, for Drama League. Wrote nine plays: Irish subjects, irreverently treated. Expressionist 'Shadow-dance' produced by Gate Th., Dublin, as *The Old Lady Says 'No'* following, 1929, rejection by Abbey Th. More realist *The Moon in the Yellow River* accepted Abbey Th., 1931. Popular success with *Blindman's Bluff* (1936). *The Scythe and the Sunset* (1958) a farcical treatment of 1916 Rising reworks *The Plough and the Stars*. BBC scriptwriter, 1936; radio play, *Weep for Polyphemus*, 1938, then, 1942–45, war correspondent, publishing experiences as *Nine Rivers from Jordan* (1953). Divorced 1945; second wife, actress, Betty Chancellor; two sons; moved to NYk., 1947, worked on NBC Theatre Guild of the Air; 1950–60, lecturer, Mount Holyoak; 1967–68 Iowa; returned to Ireland, 1973; Hon DLitt, Coleraine, 1979.

> Publishers: Colin Smythe.

See: Ferrar, H., *Denis Johnston's Irish Theatre* (Dublin, 1959; 1973).
Ronsley, J., ed., *Denis Johnston, A Retrospective* (Gerrard's Cross, 1981).

JONES, Henry Arthur (1851–1929), b. Buckinghamshire to family of non-conformist tenant farmers; left school, aged twelve; autodidact, admiring Matthew Arnold and reading classics, Darwin, Huxley, Spencer; worked in uncle's draper's shop in Ramsgate; moved to London, aged eighteen; theatre-going and amateur theatricals; 1870–79, commercial traveller in drapery; m. Doris, 1875, settling Exeter. Melodrama, *Hearts of Oak*, brought him to attention in 1879, after which full-time playwright with series of short pieces: *Harmony Restored*; *It's Only Round the Corner*; *A Clerical Error*. Archer's faith in his capacities was vindicated with *The Silver King* (1882), melodrama with social-problem touches, and *Saints and Sinners* (1884), addressing religious hypocrisy. *Breaking a Butterfly* with Henry Herman (1884), notorious adapt. of *A Doll's House*, ending with reconciliation. With Pinero, leading 1890s playwright; important less for individual plays, of which wrote some 47, than for attempt to reclaim th. for more serious ideas and observant comedy. Regarded himself as a major English dramatist; hostile to Ibsen but supported Independent Theatre and Stage Society; developed social-problem play with unhappy ending, used also by Pinero. Previous records broken, 1891, with *The Dancing Girl*, over 300 perfs: Quaker girl becomes dancer then mistress to a lord, eventually dying in misery. *The Tempter*, verse drama (1893), unsuccessful attempt at recreating poetic drama after which he returned to sentimental realism with *The Case of Rebellious Susan* and *The Masqueraders* (1894), and to comedy with *The Triumph of the Philistines* (1895). Other comedies include *The Rogue's Comedy* (1896) and *The Liars* (1897). *Michael and his Lost Angel* (1896), with clergyman hero, and *Mrs Dane's Defence* (1900) are ambitious woman-with-a-past plays that end sadly. Lectured at Harvard, 1906; awarded honorary MA, following year. Fall from popularity after 1910; several later plays premièred in US: *The Lie* (1914); *Cock o' the Walk* (1915). Numerous books and pamphlets on drama. Later years miserable: physical and nervous breakdown, 1912; operation for cancer left him semi-invalid; hostile to contemporary theatre; quarrelled with friends, including Shaw, 1915. Last play, *The Pacifists* (1917), vitriolic attack on opposition to the First World War.

> Publishers: Macmillan; Little Brown & Co, NYk.
> *The Renascence of the English Drama* (1895). (Collection of letters and articles on theatre.)
> *The Foundations of a National Drama* (1913). (Argument for state-supported theatre.)
> Jones, Doris A., *Life and Letters of Henry Arthur Jones* (1930).

See: Cordell, R. A., *Henry Arthur Jones and the Modern Drama* (1932, repr., 1968).

KENNEDY, Margaret (1896–1967), father a barrister; educ. Cheltenham and Oxford; m. 1925, David Davies, later promoted QC by Lloyd George. *The Constant Nymph* (1926), adapt. Kennedy and Basil Dean from her novel; Noel Coward then Gielgud took the lead, hugely successful, ran for a year. *Escape Me Never* (1933), comic drama that darkens. Numerous other West End plays, incl. *The Midas Touch* (1938).

LAWRENCE, D. H. (1885–1930), novelist and poet; b. Eastwood, Notts; one of four children of miner father and more genteel mother who d. 1910; educ. Nottingham High, Ilkeston Pupil-Teacher Centre; coming top in country-wide King's Scholarship Examination; University College, Nottingham, 1906; teacher in Croydon, 1908–11. Writing poems from 1903; novel, *The White Peacock*, begun 1905 (publ. 1911). Impressed by Synge's naturalism and hostile to 'rule and measure' New Drama. First extended attempt to find form for experience of Nottingham working people and family relationships in plays: *A Collier's Friday Night* (wr. 1909); *The Daughter-in-Law* (wr. 1911) and *The Widowing of Mrs Holroyd* (wr. 1910; publ. 1914; prod. Altrincham, 1920; Kingsway, London, 1926). Published novel, *The Trespasser* (1912) and began work on *Sons and Lovers* (1913); *The Rainbow* (1915). Met Frieda Weekly (von Richthoven), April 1912, in May left for Germany with her and lived abroad until her divorce enabled marriage (no children). Wrote three dramatic 'impromptus', *The Fight for Barbara*, *The Merry Go Round* and *The Married Man*, in 1913. Rejected by army (unfit), hounded by locals as spy when living in Cornwall. Left England permanently, 1918. *Touch and Go* (publ. People's Plays series, 1920); last play, *David* prod. 1927. First three plays impressive as television productions, 1967–68; later plays are more conventional.

Cambridge edition of Works begun 1980.

Moore, T. H., ed., *Collected Letters*, 2 vols (1962).

Sagar, K., *The Life of D. H. Lawrence* (1980).

Worthen, J., *D. H. Lawrence, The Early Years, 1885–1912* (Cambridge, 1992).

See: Brown, I., 'Love – And the Other Thing', *The Saturday Review* (18 December 1926), p. 767. (Review of prod. of *The Widowing of Mrs Holroyd*.)

Sklar, S., *The Plays of D. H. Lawrence* (1975).

LONSDALE, [Lionel] Frederick (1881–1954), b. Jersey, son of John Leonard, a tobacconist; army, then ran away to Canada; worked on Southampton docks; returned to Jersey, 1903; m. Lesley Hoggan, taking name Lonsdale by deed poll, 1908; moved to Weymouth then, in 1923, to London. Three daughters incl. biographer, Frances Donaldson. Made name in 1908 with *King of Cadonia*, with music by Sidney Jones: 330 perfs at Prince of Wales Th.; among libretti, *The Maid of the Mountains*, 1917, 1,352 perfs; some 28 plays, mainly comedies, among them *The Last of Mrs Cheyney*, with Gerald du Maurier and Gladys Cooper (1925); *On Approval* and *The High Road* (1927); *Canaries Sometimes Sing* (1929), brought social and theatrical celebrity. Friend of Noel Coward; daughter, Mab, m. Rodney Ackland; early 1930s screen writing in Hollywood; exiled himself to US during Second World War. Two reasonably successful plays post-war, *But for the Grace of God* (1946) and *The Way Things Go* (1950), thereafter lived in France.

Donaldson, F., *Freddy Lonsdale* (1957).

MacCOLL, Ewan (1915–91), folksinger, b. Jimmy Miller; father, iron founder; mother, cleaner; lived Salford; educ. Grecian St Elementary School; voracious reader; worked in wire factory, then unemployed; various short-term jobs; member of Cheetham Young Communists' League; wrote for Party journals and sold them at factory gates; joined Clarion Players, 1929; formed agit-prop group, Red Megaphones; wr. five-minute sketches for factory gate performance and other pieces for Workers' Theatre Movement; 1933, directed by Toller in Rusholme Rep prod. Toller's, *Draw the Fires*. F. Theatre of Action with Joan Littlewood; prod. *Waiting for Lefty*; became Theatre Union, 1935, performing radical European plays and sketches in aid of Spain. Songs include, 'The Manchester Rambler', 'Dirty Old Town'. Helped organise Kinder Scout Mass Trespass. After Second World War, f. Theatre Workshop with Joan Littlewood. M. 1. Joan Littlewood; m. 2. the folk singer, Peggy Seeger.

MALLESON, Miles (1888–1969), before First World War wr. one-act lyric, fairy plays; *Paddly Pools*; *The Little White Thought*; joined army at outbreak of war; private in Territorials in Malta; invalided out with foot trouble, January 1915. Two war plays, *'D' Company* and *Black 'Ell*, seized by police on publication, 1916, as 'deliberate calumny on the British soldier'. After war, prolific dramatist, mainly for left-wing groups and wrote account of Independent Labour Party (ILP) Arts Guild; director Masses Stage and Film Guild in 1920s – ILP group supporting film and amateur theatre; *Conflict* cross-party love affair and conversion (1926), prod 'Q' Theatre; with Harry Brooks, *Six men of Dorset*; member Unity Theatre. Adapts. of Molière, *Le Misanthrope*, *Le Malade Imaginaire* and *Sganarelle* for Birmingham Rep, 1957.

MARTYN, Edward (1859–1923), Irish Catholic land-owning family; founder, with Yeats and Lady Gregory of Irish Literary Th., 1898; *The Heather Field* in first prod., 1899, in Dublin; five plays staged at Gaiety, Dublin, 1900, included his *Maeve*; Ibsenesque writing; urged realist theatre on lines of European avant-garde; left off Board of Irish Theatre Company, 1905, instead became President of rival Irish National Th. Company, 1906, with some use of Abbey stage.

See: Gwynn, D., *Edward Martyn and the Irish Revival* (1930).

MASEFIELD, John [Edward] (1878–1967), poet, b. Hertfordshire; orphaned early; 1891, trainee seaman. Collections of ballads of sea, open road, beginning with *Salt Water Ballads* (1902); subsequently, long narrative poems, *Dauber* (1913) and *Reynard the Fox* (1919). *The Campden Wonder* (1907), prod. Court Th., highly regarded by Shaw. Best-known play, *The Tragedy of Nan* (dir. Barker, Haymarket, 1908), a rural tragedy that attempts to join verse dialogue with realistic setting, frequently revived on pre-First World War stage. *The Witch* (1910), dir. Barker for Glasgow Rep; thereafter, historical spectaculars: *The Tragedy of Pompey the Great* (1910); *Philip the King* (1914); *Esther* (1921). Among novels, *Sard Harker* (1924); *The Box of Delights* (1935). Became Poet Laureate, 1930.

> Babington Smith, C., *John Masefield, A Life* (1978).
> Lamont, C. and L., eds, *Letters of John Masefield to Florence Lamont* (Columbia, 1979).

See: Spark, M., *John Masefield* (1953; rev. edn, 1992).

MAUGHAM, [William] Somerset (1874–1965), novelist, short story writer and drama-tist; b. Paris where he lived until aged ten; educ. King's School, Canterbury and Heidelberg University; trained as doctor; realist novel *Liza of Lambeth* pub. 1897, then literary career. Among novels, *Of Human Bondage* (1915); *The Moon and Sixpence* (1919); *Cakes and Ale* (1930). Thirty-two plays staged 1899–1933, mainly comedies, some quite dark, many about adultery and misalliance; very popular *c.* 1908–mid 1920s; later work more cynical. First full-length play, *A Man of Honour*, prod. by Barker for Stage Society (1903); lighter version of same situation in *Smith* (1909). Among plays: *Caesar's Wife* (1919); *Our Betters* (wr. 1915, prod. 1923); *The Constant Wife* (1927). Serious, even didactic tone of last two plays, *For Services Rendered* (1932) and *Sheppey* (1933), resulted in failure after which abandoned stage. Lived on French Riviera; Companion of Honour, 1954.

> *The Summing Up* (1938).
> *A Writer's Notebook* (1949).
> Cordell, R. A., *W. Somerset Maugham* (1937).
> Raphael, F. W., *Somerset Maugham and his World* (NYk., 1976).
> Morgan, T., *Somerset Maugham* (1980).

See: Mander, R. and J. Mitchenson, *Theatrical Companion to Maugham* (1955).
       Barnes, R. E., *The Dramatic Comedy of Somerset Maugham* (The Hague, 1968).
       Curtis, A., *The Pattern of Maugham* (1974).

MAURIER, George du (1834–96), with English mother and French father, brought up first Paris, then London; educ. Birkbeck College, then studied art in Paris; lost sight of one eye; magazine illustrator in London from 1860; staff cartoonist on *Punch*, 1864–94; friend of Henry James. Oversaw adapt. of his novel, *Trilby*, by Paul M. Potter for Tree, who played the mesmerist, Svengali – ran many months at Haymarket, 1895; costumes and stage images closely modelled on du Maurier's own illustrations; filmed with Tree as Svengali, 1914.

> Ormond, L., *George du Maurier* (1969).

See: Kelly, R., *George du Maurier* (Boston, MA, 1983).

MILNE, A[lan] A[lexander] (1882–1956), children's writer; father, John Vine Milne, a teacher; educ. Wistern School; read mathematics, Trinity College, Cambridge; 1905, novel, *Lovers in London*; on staff of *Punch*, 1906–14 then joined army; m. Dorothy de Selincourt, 1913. Friend of J. M. Barrie, who sponsored prod. of first play, *Wurzel Flummery*, 1917; some two dozen plays, only real successes, *Mr Pimm Passes By*, 1919, revived Birmingham Rep, 1931; and *Toad of Toad Hall* adapt. from *Wind in the Willows*, 1929. Among others, *The Dover Road*, a light comedy (1922) and *Miss Elizabeth Bennett* (1936), an adaptation of *Pride and Prejudice*. Best-known for verses, *When We Were Very Young* (1924) and Christopher Robin stories, *The House at Pooh Corner* (1928).

MONKHOUSE, Alan (1858–1936) b. Barnard Castle; educ. private schools; joined Manchester cotton trade; m. 1. Lucie Dowie, 1893, d. 1894; m. 2. Elizabeth Pearson; two sons, two daughters; joined *Manchester Guardian*, 1902, and reviewed for *New Statesman*; wr. for Manchester and other Northern Repertory Companies, twenty plays, mostly one-act and farces, incl. *Reaping the Whirlwind* (1908); *Mary Broome*, in which man has affair with a housemaid who rejects his offer (1911, and London transfer). Annie Horniman played herself in a one-act comedy, *Nothing Like Leather* (Manchester, 1913). *The Great Chaim's Diamond* in which a stolen diamond is kept by a housewife through whose window it is thrown, prod. 1918; broadcast, 1927, became amateur th. staple. *The Conquering Hero* (1924) a First World War play concerned with heroism and disillusion. Other plays incl. *The Hayling Family* (1924) and *First Blood* (1925).

MOORE, George (1852–1933), novelist and journalist; Irish Catholic absentee landlord family with lands in Mayo; *The Mummer's Wife* (1885), Zolaesque novel set in a squalid touring company; saw *Ghosts* at Théâtre Libre in Paris, 1891; wrote articles for *The Hawk*, edited by brother, Augustus; advocate of English Théâtre Libre and of French realist novel; supporter of Independent Th. which prod. his *The Strike at Arlingford*, 1893; 1897, joined Yeats, Martyn and Lady Gregory in Irish Literary Th, plans; 1901, moved to Dublin and wr. *Diarmid and Grania* with Yeats, incidental music by Elgar; social realist play, *The Bending of the Bough* prod. 1903. Disagreed with colleagues over wish for more European plays and not on reconstituted Abbey Board in 1903. Returned to London, 1911, for Stage Society adapt. of his successful 1894 novel, *Esther Waters*. Among other plays *The Making of an Immortal*, a one-act comedy with Shakespeare, Jonson and Burbage among the characters (Arts Theatre Club, 1928); *The Passing of the Essenes*, debating the divinity of Christ (1930).

> *Impressions and Opinions* (1891). (*Hawk* articles; theatre criticism.)
> *Hail and Farewell*, 3 vols (1911–14). (Autobiography.)
> Burkhart, C., *The Letters of George Moore*, ed. Burkhart (Maryland, 1958).
> Hone, J., *The Life of George Moore* (NYk., 1936).

See: Brown, M., *George Moore: A Reconsideration* (Seattle, WA, 1955).

Jeffares, A. N., *George Moore* (1965).
Dunleavy, J. E., *George Moore* (Lewisburg, 1973).

MURRAY, T. C. (1873–1959), among second band of Abbey playwrights; *The Wheel of Fortune*, produced Cork Dramatic Society, 1909. First Abbey play, *The Birthright*, 1910, included in New York tour: its harsh farm setting and plot, one son emigrates, the other stays, and conclusion in one displacing the other is basis for O'Neill's first full-length play, *Beyond the Horizon*. *Michaelmas Eve* (1932), returns the compliment, being a version of *Desire Under the Elms*. Other plays include, *Aftermath* (1922) and *Autumn Fire* (1924).

O'CASEY, Sean (1880–1964), b. Dublin, youngest of thirteen children, eight of whom d. in childhood; lower middle-class Protestant family; father d. 1883; scanty educ.; very poor eyesight but voracious reader, incl. Shakespeare and Shaw. Began work as a clerk, aged fourteen; gaelicised name to Sean from John, 1906, on joining Gaelic League. Various jobs incl. docker and stoker; labourer, Great Northern Railway of Ireland, 1902 until 1911 strike, after which dismissed for refusal to resign union membership; Secretary, Women's and Children's Relief Fund during seven-month lock-out of Dublin union members, 1913. Same year, resigned Irish Republican Brotherhood after seven years membership, because of nationalists' lack of interest in poverty. Secretary, 1914, of reorganised Irish Citizen Army, protecting union members from police brutality, resigned in protest at increasing links with anti-Labour nationalists; publ. *The Story of the Irish Citzen Army*, 1919. Ballads, including anti-war, 'The Grand Oul Dame Britannia', popular, 1916; observed Easter Rising. Sister, then mother, d. 1918. Two-act play rejected by Abbey; 'On the Run', set in Irish Independence fight, produced Abbey, 1923, as *The Shadow of a Gunman*, followed by the theatre's greatest success, *Juno and the Paycock*, 1924; with English première, 1925, and Hawthornden prize, he became full-time writer. Riots during first week of third Dublin play, *The Plough and the Stars*, 1926; thereafter embattled relationship with Eire and clergy. M. Eileen Carey Reynolds, 1927; two sons, Brian (b. 1928), Niall (b. 1935, d. 1957 of leukemia), one daughter, Shivaun (b. 1939). Settled in England, living in Devon from 1929, following Abbey rejection of First World War play, *The Silver Tassie*, 1928 (prod. London, 1929 with Charles Laughton), after which he offered the company no further plays and refused invitations from Yeats and Shaw to become founding member of Irish Academy of Letters; subsequent reconciliation with Yeats but hostility to and from Irish institutions continued, incl. banning of first volume of autobiography, *I Knock at the Door* (1939). Visited US for NYk prod. of Expressionist *Within the Gates* (1934). Notable among subsequent plays, the politically radical, *The Star Turns Red* (Unity Theatre, 1940) and *Red Roses For Me* (1946); *Cock a Doodle Dandy*, satirical attack on life-denying aspects of Catholicism and Irish society (People's Th., Newcastle, 1949; English Stage Company, 1959; Abbey, 1978). Return to Dublin with Tyrone Guthrie's prod. *The Bishop's Bonfire* (1955), stimulated press attacks and demonstrations outside theatre; withdrew *The Drums of Father Ned* from Dublin Festival (1957) following Archbishop of Dublin's objection to this and work by Joyce, at which, Beckett having withdrawn his own work in protest, Festival collapsed; refused to permit further prods. of work in Eire until shortly before death in 1964. Later work largely ignored by English-speaking theatre but 1962 O'Casey Festival at Mermaid Theatre incl. choric *Purple Dust*, also perf. by Berliner Ensemble, 1966. O'Casey's energy, fun and fierce satire, strong influence on work of John Arden, John MacGrath.

Publisher: Macmillan.

The Silver Tassie rev. edn, *Collected Plays* (1949). (Incorporates rewritten last act and O'Casey's notes for 1929 London production.)

The Flying Wasp (1937); *The Green Crow* (1957). (O'Casey's own, often ascerbic, criticism of contemporary drama.)

Autobiographies (1963).

Ayling, R., ed., *Blasts and Benedictions* (1967).

O'Casey, Eileen, *Sean* (1971).

Krause, D., ed., *The Letters of Sean O'Casey* (1975).

See: Hogan, R., *The Experiments of Sean O'Casey* (NYk., 1960). (Includes documentation of *Silver Tassie* dispute.)

Ayling, R., ed., *Sean O'Casey* (1969). (Includes reviews of early productions.)

Deane, S., 'Irish Politics and O'Casey's Theatre', *Threshold*, 24 (Spring 1973), pp. 5–16.

Kilroy, T., ed., *Sean O'Casey: A Collection of Critical Essays* (New Jersey, 1975). (Including essay by John Arden.)

Krause, D., *Sean O'Casey, the Man and his Work* (NYk., 1975).

Ayling, R., *Continuity and Innovation in Sean O'Casey's Drama* (Salzburg, 1976).

Ayling, R. and M. J. Durkin, eds, *Sean O'Casey: A Bibliography* (1978).

Krause, D. and R. Lowery, eds, *Sean O'Casey, Centenary Essays* (Gerrard's Cross, 1980).

O'Riordan, J., *A Guide to O'Casey's Plays* (1984).

PEACH L[awrence] du Garde (1890–1974), father a vicar; educ. Manchester Grammar School and Manchester University; lecturer Gottingen University, 1912–14; m. 1915; war work, army and intelligence, 1914–19; lecturer in English literature, 1922–26, when he joined BBC; producer and prolific writer; contested Derby constituency unsuccessfully in the general election of 1929. First radio play, *Light and Shade* (1924); numerous short works, mostly for two or three voices, published as *Broadcast Sketches*, 1927; also wr. historical ballad operas, incl. *Up the River*, on life and times of Shakespeare, and *The True History of Henry VIII* (1928). Notable among full-length radio plays utilising technical resources of Savoy Hill studios: *Ingredient X* (1929); *The Path of Glory* (1931); *The Marie Celeste* (1931); by 1931 had written more radio plays than anyone else in England – some 400 in all. Strong social conscience evident in *Bread* (1932), saga of family and poverty from 1840 emigration to 1930 Depression. *Gold* (1933), on inflation and the gold market, subject to internal BBC censorship and six-month postponement, after which abandoned contemporary subjects for history plays for children. Post-war, author of numerous history stories for Ladybird Books.

Broadcast Sketches (1927)
Radio Plays (1931).

PHILLIPS, Stephen (1867–1915), b. Summertown, Oxford; father, a parson, became Precenter of Peterborough Cathedral; mother, Agatha Dockray, a descendant of Wordsworth; educ. Stratford and Peterborough Grammar Schools; began career in Civil Service but joined his cousin Benson's acting company. Brief acclaim for blank verse dramas in West End: *Paolo and Francesca*, prod. George Alexander, 1899, highly praised; *Herod*, play of fierce passions, based on Josephus, commissioned by Tree for Her Majesty's Th., 1900 – huge success; thereafter, series of plays in grandiose, rhetorical verse set in spectacular ancient world sets with large crowd scenes, incl. *Ulysses* (1902); *Nero* (1906); *Faust* collaborated with Comins Carr, all ran for more than 100 perfs. Frittered money and became alcoholic. Collapse of interest in his work by 1915 and last play, *Armageddon*, had only 14 perfs.

PHILLPOTTS, Eden (1862–1960), b. Rajputana, India; father, political agent in India; educ. Monnamead School, Plymouth; clerk in Sun Fire Insurance Co, London; began writing 1880s, by 1890 earning enough to give up other work; moved to Devon, where he settled; m. 1. Emily Topham, d. 1928; one daughter; m. 2. Lucy Robins Webb; Wrote eighteen Dartmoor novels. First produced play, a farce, *The Policeman*, wr. with Walter Helmore (1887); *The Prude's Progress* (1895) with Jerome K. Jerome. Adapt. own novel, *The Secret Woman* (1905), at Barker's suggestion, attacked by censorship, prod. Stage Society, uncut, 1912. First real dramatic success *The Farmer's Wife*, prod. Birmingham Rep, 1916, led to long association and virtually annual play written for Barry Jackson, often with London transfer, incl. *Devonshire Cream* (1924); *Yellow Sands* (1926), a comedy set in Devonshire village disrupted by a humourless Bolshevik, 610 perfs, Haymarket; *The Runaways* (1928); *The Good Old Days* (1930), set in the Widdecombe of 1870.

One Thing and Another (1954).

See: Girvan, W., ed., *Eden Phillpotts: An Assessment and a Tribute* (1953).

PINERO, Arthur Wing (1855–1934), b. Islington; family of Portuguese Jewish origin; educ. Clerkenwell; elocution evenings at Birkbeck College and member of College Dramatic Society; father, rather unsuccessful lawyer, in whose office worked from aged ten; solicitor's clerk in Lincoln's Inn Fields 1870 to death of father, 1874, when he became 'General Utility' at Theatre Royal Edinburgh, then ten years in minor acting roles in various London companies incl. Guildernstern with Irving at Lyceum, 1876, and engagement with Bancrofts, 1881. M. Myra Holme, a widow with two children, 1883. Most prolific and successful of late nineteenth-century dramatists, with 55 performed plays and many impressive runs; hailed by William Archer as reformer, attacked by Shaw. Began with a number of short pieces incl. *The Money Spinner* (Manchester, 1880; London; 1881) and *The Squire* (1881). First successes with full-length farcical comedies, deriving tone from Tom Robertson and plotting from the French well-made play. Deftly handled crises and polished dialogue notable in *The Magistrate*, 1885, with 363 perfs and *Dandy Dick* two years later with 262 perfs; New Woman comedy with *The Weaker Sex*, 1889, and *The Amazons*, 1893; sentimental comedies incl. *Sweet Lavender*, 1888, with record breaking 683 perfs and *Trelawny of the 'Wells'*, 1898, a tribute to, and pastiche of, Robertson. Virtually a play a year throughout 1890s. Like Jones, he turned to social-problem melodrama. Brilliant success with *The Second Mrs Tanqueray* (1893), less so with *The Notorious Mrs Ebbsmith* (1895), the action of both centring on a woman with a past, played by Stella Campbell. Last outstanding success, *His House in Order*, 1906, 430 perfs, but interest still with *Mid Channel* (1909), also prod. in Moscow by Meyerhold: heroine, an updated Paula Tanqueray, commits suicide following affair, and *The Mind the Paint Girl* (1912), a backstage play comparable with *Trelawny*. A great craftsman; like Gilbert before and Shaw after, directed own plays with assiduity. Chairman, Ellen Terry Jubilee Committee, 1906; knighted, 1909; first President of Dramatists' Club; Fellow Royal Society of Literature, 1910; continued writing but little success post-First World War; wife d. 1919.

Publisher: Heinemann.

Dunkel, W. D., *Sir Arthur Pinero* (Chicago, 1941). (Enthusiastic biography with letters.)

Wearing, J. P., *The Collected Letters of Sir Arthur Wing Pinero* (Minneapolis, 1974).

Weaver, J. W. and E. J. Wilson, 'A. W. Pinero: An Annotated Bibliography', in *English Literature in Transition*, 23 (1981), pp. 231–9.

See: Fyte, H., *Sir Arthur Pinero's Plays and Players* (1930).

Davies, C. W., 'Pinero: The Drama of Reputation', *English*, 14 (1962).

Dawick, J., 'The First Night of *The Second Mrs Tanqueray*', *Theatre Quarterly*, 9(35) (1979).

Quigley, A. E., *The Modern Stage and Other Worlds* (1985). (Includes challenging reading of *Mrs Tanqueray*.)

Rowell, G., ed., *Selected Plays of Arthur Wing Pinero* (Cambridge, 1986). (Incisive introduction.)

POEL, William (1852–1934), theatre director; initiator, Elizabethan staging movement; b. Westminster; fourth child of Matilda and William Pole, practising civil engineer and professor at University College and Examiner for musical degrees, London, an FRS and Vice-President Royal College Organists. Used as a child model by family friend, Holman Hunt, for Jesus in 'The Discovery of Christ in the Temple' and by Frederick Burton for 'The Knight's Esquire'; formal educ. scanty; delicate, having fallen on railway line, aged twelve; voracious reader and museum visitor; apprenticed, aged seventeen, to craftsman builder, Lucas Bros; worked on window frames of Albert Hall; impressed by acting of Charles Matthews and by Got and Salvini tours; left Lucas, 1876, to join Matthews' Co, Bristol, as 'General Utility'; various minor theatrical jobs; acting lessons, 1878. Meanwhile Shakespearean theories developing: toured provinces with recitals from Shakespeare, demonstrating scene painting in dialogue and distortions of commercial theatre. With small company, The Elizabethans, 1879, toured costumed Shakespeare recitals; 1881, lecture attacks on current acting editions of Shakespeare, finding ideas endorsed by Grigg's publication of 1st and 2nd *Hamlet* Quartos, then own prod. of 1st Quarto, St George's Hall, the same year, to widespread ridicule. Manager Royal Victoria Temperance Hall (subsequently Old Vic), 1881–83; stage manager with Benson's Co; instructed Shakespeare Reading Society, University College, London, 1887, initiating platform perfs of whole texts without act divisions. Created Elizabethan staging movement: converted Royalty to resemble ancient Fortune Th. for first 'authentic' prod. *Measure for Measure*; revived *Duchess of Malfi*, 1892, for Independent Th. and the rarely played *Two Gentlemen of Verona*; *Twelfth Night* on bare stage, 1893; f. Elizabethan Stage Society, 1894; *Dr Faustus*, 1896. Some 90 prods 1880–1932, of Shakespeare and neglected works incl. *The Tempest*, with no interval, 1897; *Richard II*, giving Barker first Shakespearean role, 1899; Swinburne, *Locrine*, 1899; *Hamlet*, with all-male cast, 1900; first of rediscovered *Everyman*, 1900; Euripides, *The Bacchae*, 1908; first modern revival of *Troilus and Cressida*, 1912; 2nd Quarto *Hamlet*, 1914; Morris, *Love is Enough*, 1920; an eclectic *Coriolanus*, 1931. Trained actors, incl. Edith Evans. Elizabethan th. behind Proscenium Arch for many prods but, in 1927, used platform stage with 30–foot thrust in Holborn Empire. Wrote six plays – adaptations from literary or historical sources incl: *Lady Jane Grey* (1885); *Equality Jack* (1891), a musical adapted from Captain Marryat; *The Redemption of Agnes* (1907), none very successful. Eccentric and obsessive; indefatigable in prods and proselytising; lifelong socialist; frequent lectures and essays on Shakespeare; active campaigner for National Theatre; refused knighthood, 1929.

> *Shakespear in the Theatre* (1913) – collected essays.
> *What is Wrong With the Stage?* (1920).
> *Notes on Some of William Poel's Stage Productions* (Shakespear Reading Society, 1933). (Includes some early prod. photographs.)
> Speaight, R., *William Poel and the Elizabethan Revival* (1954). (Indispensable critical biography.)

See: William Poel Portrait Committee, *William Poel and his Stage Productions, 1880–1932* (1933). (Checklist of prods.)
Sprague, A. C., 'Shakespeare and William Poel', *University of Toronto Quarterly*, XVII, 1 (October 1947), pp. 29–37. (Some account of attacks on and much quotation from Poel.)
Casson, L., 'William Poel and the Modern Theatre', *Listener* (10.1.1952), pp. 56–8.
Glick, C., 'William Poel: His Theories and Influence', *Shakespeare Quarterly*, 15 (Winter 1964), pp. 15–25.
Lundstrom, R. F., *William Poel's Hamlets* (1985).

PRIESTLEY, J[ohn] B[oynton] (1894–1984), novelist, essayist, broadcaster; b. Bradford; mother d. when was an infant; father, schoolmaster; educ. Belle Vue High School; clerk in wool office; Front-line army command, 1914–19; m. 1. Pat Tempest; read history and political science on officer's grant, Trinity Hall, Cambridge, after which a free-lance writer. Two daughters born, 1923 and 1924; wife d. of cancer, 1925; m. 2. Jane Wyndham Lewis, 1926: three children. Fame with novels *The Good Companions* (1929; dramatised, 1931) and *Angel Pavement* (1930). Impressed by J. W. Dunne *Experiment with Time* and Ouspensky *New Model of the Universe*, he incorporated shifting time sequences, often of a mystical kind, into his own plays incl.: *Dangerous Corner* (1932); *Time and the Conways* and *I have Been Here Before* (1937), and, perhaps most famously, *An Inspector Calls* (Moscow, 1945; London, 1946). Formed his own production company, 1933, continuing as theatre manager for seven years. Plays very successful in England and in translation in 1930s and 1940s, among them, *Laburnum Grove* (1933); *Cornelius*, with Ralph Richardson in lead (1935); *When We Are Married* (1939); *Johnson Over Jordan* (1939), with music by Britten. Serious treatment of northern life; evident humanitarianism and left-wing politics inform prolific writing. Renowned broadcaster, especially in Second World War with notable ten-minute talk after evacuation of Dunkirk. Among later prose works, *Victoria's Heyday* (1972); *The English* (1973). After divorce, 1953, m. 3. archaeologist, Jacquetta Hawkes, both became founder members of Campaign for Nuclear Disarmament; refused peerage, accepted place on Board of National Theatre, 1965; received OM, 1977.

> *Theatre Outlook* (1947).
> *Instead of the Trees* (1977).

See: Lindsay, J., 'J. B. Priestley', in D. Baker, ed., *Writers of Today* (1946).
Brown, I., *J. B. Priestley* (1957).
Evans, G. L., *J. B. Priestley – the Dramatist* (1964).
Cooper, S., *J. B. Priestley; Portrait of an Author* (1970).

ROBINS, Elizabeth (1862–1952), b. Louisville, Kentucky; brought up, Ohio; while still a child, mother committed to insane asylum; briefly studied medicine at Vassar; 1880s, toured with James O'Neill's Company, playing Mercedes in *The Count of Monte Cristo* then in Shakespeare with Edwin Booth, supporting mother and medicine studies of younger brother by acting and writing. Husband, actor G. R. Parkes, committed suicide bizarrely shortly after marriage, 1888. Visited friends in Norway, travelling via Liverpool, after which, encouraged by Tree and Wilde, found acting work in London; friendship with Henry James after role of Madame de Cintré in *The American*; resisted Shaw's propositioning; co-founded New Century Th. with Archer, with whom probably had affair. Became leading exponent of Ibsen: acted in *Pillars of Society*, 1889; with Marion Lea, prod. *Hedda Gabler*, 1891, playing Hedda and working with Archer to make English text speakable; Rebekka in *Rosmersholm*, Agnes in *Brand* and Hedwig in *The Master Builder*, all 1893, also *Little Eyolf* (1895). With Florence Bell wrote *Alan's Wife* and acted lead role in anonymous Independent Th., prod. 1893; abandoned acting for writing incl.: acting version of Jose Echegaray's *Mariana* assisted by James (prod. 1897); *Benvenuta Cellini* (prod. Tree, 1900); and most significantly, *Votes for Women* (prod. Barker, 1907; publ., 1909), subsequently rewritten as novel, *The Convert*; among novels, under pseudonym C. E. Raimond: *George Mandeville's Husband* (1894) and *The New Moon* (1895). Travelled to Alaska to search for lost brother, Raymond, 1900; with Octavia Wilberforce adopted a child; member of Women's Social and Political Union from 1903; founder member of Actresses' Franchise League; articles for suffrage journal, *Votes for Women* and *Ancilla's Share: An Inditement of Sex Antagonism* (1924).

> *Ibsen and the Actress* (1928).
> *Theatre and Friendship* (1932). (Correspondence with Henry James.)
> *Both Sides of the Curtain* (1940). (Memoir of early years.)

See: Gates, J. E., *Elizabeth Robins, Actress, Novelist, Feminist* (Alabama, 1994).

ROBINSON, Lennox (1886–1958), manager Abbey Th., 1910–15; encouraged rural domestic drama; responsible for opening Abbey Th. on Edward VII's death leading to break with Annie Horniman; resigned after disagreements with Lady Gregory; manager again, 1919–35 and on Board of Directors from 1923 until death; policies and slant of own plays led to dominance of realism at Abbey. Wr. problem plays, often with bitter comic tone, incl.: *The Harvest* (1910); *The Dreamers*, an account of abortive uprising of Robert Emmet (1915); *The Lost Leader* in which psychiatrist and journalist investigate possibility that Lucius Lenihan is Parnell survived and living in Western Ireland (1918); *The Big House*, episodic presentation of effect of First World War on Anglo-Irish family (1926). Later work more experimental, incl. Pirandellian, *Church Street* (1934) and *The Lucky Finger* (1948).

> *Curtain Up: An Autobiography* (1942).
> *Towards an Appreciation of the Theatre* (Dublin, 1945).
> *Ireland's Abbey Theatre: A History* (1951).

See: O'Neill, M. J., *Lennox Robinson* (NYk., 1964).

SCOTT, Clement (1841–1904), leading theatre critic through 1870s and 1880s; increasingly embattled in 1890s with such newcomers as Archer, Walkley and Shaw. Drama critic for *The Daily Telegraph*, 1871–98, and *The Illustrated London News*; from 1879, editor *The Theatre*. Fierce opponent of Ibsen and, indeed, of Pinero's *Second Mrs Tanqueray*. Adapted numerous plays from French incl.: *Off The Line* (1871), a farce; *Diplomacy*, from Sardou's *Dora* (1878, revived 1893); *Odette*, from Sardou (1894); various collaborations incl. with Arthur Matthison, *The Great*

Divorce Case, a marriage farce (1876), and *The Swordsman's Daughter*, with Brandon Thomas (Adelphi, 1895).

SHAW, George Bernard (1856–1950), b. Dublin; two sisters; emotionally deprived childhood; father, George Carr Shaw, unsuccessful mill-owner and alcoholic from otherwise respectable Dublin family; haphazard educ. incl. briefly, Wesleyan School but music via maverick musician and teacher, Vandaleur Lee (model for Svengali in du Maurier's *Trilby*) who lived with family; mother, Lucinda Elizabeth Gurley, amateur singer, followed Lee to London, 1873. Left school aged fourteen, minor clerk until, aged 20, joined mother and sister Lucy in London, 1876; piano accompanied but largely supported by mother and sister; free-lance writer with little success initially although contributed unsigned articles to *Pall Mall Gazette* and four of his five novels, written before 1883, serialised in socialist magazines, incl. *Cashel Byron's Profession* (wr. 1882), noticed by Archer and Stevenson. Admired William Morris; became committed socialist, vegetarian and proponent of rational dress; voracious reading and daily study in British Library impressed William Archer who found him job as music critic for *The Star* (pseudonym, Corno di Basseto), then, 1890–94, for *The World*. Brilliant reviews here and, 1895–98, as drama critic for *The Saturday Review*, made his name and had shaping influence on subsequent perception of period. With Sidney Webb, moving spirit of Fabian Society, which he joined in 1884; as executive member, series of Fabian tracts and policy documents; edited *Fabian Essays on Socialism*, 1889, and wrote, among others, *Fabianism and the Fiscal Question*, 1904. Curious relationships with women: admired May Morris, lived briefly with her and her husband; avoided marriage with various young Fabians; number of affairs incl. with Florence Farr; passionate correspondence with Ellen Terry; m. Charlotte Payne Townsend, 1898, (no children) – *mariage blanc* but close relationship; fell in love with Mrs Patrick Campbell. Strong proponent of Ibsen after seeing *A Doll's House*, 1889; Ibsen lecture for Fabian Society series, developed into *The Quintessence of Ibsenism*, 1891. Th. debut at invitation of Grein with *Widowers' Houses*, prod. Independent Th., 1892, followed by defiant speech to audience. *Mrs Warren's Profession* banned, 1893 (private Stage Society prod., 1902). Wrote plays throughout 1890s including *Candida*, prod. 1897 with Janet Achurch, Aberdeen, and *You Never Can Tell* (wr. 1896); several out-of-town productions and copyright readings but disappointments in attempts on West End; *Arms and the Man*, 1894, ran 50 perfs in Farr's Avenue Season and *The Devil's Disciple* in NYk., 1897, made £200 which, with publ. of *Plays Pleasant and Unpleasant*, 1898, enabled him to give up *Saturday Review* job (to Max Beerbohm), followed with *Three Plays for Puritans*, publ. 1901, incl. *Caesar and Cleopatra*, prod. London, 1907. Growing interest in Germany with prods at Deutsches Völkstheater and in Vienna. Breakthrough with Stage Society and Court Th. productions where staged own work in collaboration with Barker. First big success with *John Bull's Other Island*, wr. for Abbey at Yeats's invitation, staged London, 1904; Royal Command Perf., 1905; Abbey, 1916. Other Court Th. successes: *Major Barbara* (1905), *Man and Superman* (1905), *The Doctor's Dilemma* (1906). Subsidised Vedrenne-Barker Savoy season heavily. During next ten years became most performed British dramatist with revivals and new plays incl.: *Getting Married* (1908); *Misalliance* (Duke of York's, 1910); *Fanny's First Play* (1911); *Androcles and the Lion* (1913) and immense international reputation. Tree staged *Pygmalion*, 1914, with Mrs Patrick Campbell, after which only short plays and tomfooleries until *Hearbreak House*, written during the War, prod. 1921. 1918–20 writing mammoth pentateuch of plays, *Back to Methuselah*, staged Th. Guild, NYk., 1922; Birmingham Rep, 1923. Renewed acclaim with *Saint*

Joan, Th. Guild, 1923; London, 1924, with Sybil Thorndike in leading role. Central figure of Barry Jackson's Malvern Festival which premièred last significant play, *The Apple Cart*, in its opening year, 1929. Intellectual energy and sense of absurd mark public and theatrical life. Councillor for St Pancras as Progressive, 1897–1903, speaking for women and poorer constituents. 1907 onwards regular attender of Fabian summer schools; resigned from Fabian executive, 1911, but remained active supporter. Frequent traveller; enthusiastic cyclist then motorist. Frequent passionate letters to press for women's suffrage; socialised health service; Irish Home rule; National Theatre; against corporal punishment; censorship. Long testimony to Select Committee on Censorship published with *The Shewing Up of Blanco Posnet* (Abbey, 1909 following English ban) as *The Rejected Statement on Censorship*. Opposition to First World War although contributed £20,000 to British War Loan; *Common Sense About the War* (1914) caused outrage, with papers refusing subsequent articles and letters from him. 90,000 print-run of *The Intelligent Women's Guide to Socialism* sold out immediately, 1928, fifth reprint by May following year. Friends included Archer, Barker, Elgar and, from 1922, T. E. Lawrence who became frequent visitor and took the name Private Shaw; 70th birthday celebration dinner hosted by Ramsay MacDonald. Refused knighthood and other public honours but accepted Nobel Prize, 1926, putting all prize money into Trust Fund for translations of Swedish writing. Growing dislike of democracy; late in life increasing support for totalitarian regimes; scarcely critical in admiration of Soviet Russia; of Mussolini and of Oswald Mosley. Long proponent of cremation, willed ashes to be scattered with those of his wife over garden at Ayot St Lawrence, which resolved rival demands of St Patrick's, Dublin and Westminster Abbey. Fortune shared between British Library, RADA and movement for rational spelling.

Publisher: Constable.

Dramatic Opinions and Essays (NYk., 1906).

Our Theatres in the Nineties (1932) (3 vols of *Saturday Review* articles).

Wisenthal, J. L., ed., *Shaw and Ibsen: Bernard Shaw's Quintessence of Ibsenism and related writings* (Toronto, 1979).

St John, C., ed. *Ellen Terry and Bernard Shaw: A Correspondence* (1931).

Bax, C., ed., *Letters: Florence Farr, Bernard Shaw, W. B. Yeats* (1946).

Dent, A., ed., *Bernard Shaw and Mrs Patrick Campbell: their Correspondence* (1952).

Purdom, C. B., *Bernard Shaw's Letters to Granville Barker* (1956).

Lawrence, D., ed., *Collected Letters*, vol. 1 (1965); vol. 2 (1972).

Weintraub, S., *Shaw: An Autobiography, 1856–98, Selected from his Writings 1856–98: 1898–1950* (NYk., 1969; 1970).

Jackson, H., *Shaw* (1907).

Henderson, A., *Shaw: His Life and Works* (1911). (Authorised biography much shaped by Shaw.)

—— *G. B. Shaw: Man of the Century* (NYk., 1956). (Useful documents.)

Weintraub, S., *Private Shaw and Public Shaw* (1963).

Holroyd, M., *Bernard Shaw*, 3 vols (1988–91).

See: West, A., *A Good Man Fallen Among Fabians* (1950). (Concerned with Shaw's political ideas.)

MacCarthy, D., *Shaw* (1951).

Meisel, M., *Shaw and Nineteenth Century Theatre* (1963). (Discussion of transformation of contemporary conventions.)

Dukore, B., *Bernard Shaw Director* (1971). (Copious evidence demonstrating Shaw's supervision of every aspect of production.)

Morgan, M. M., *The Shavian Playground* (1972).

Grene, N., *Bernard Shaw, A Critical View* (1984). (Measured account; appreciative of Shaw's achievements, clear-sighted recognition of defects.)

SHERRIFF, R[obert] C[edric] (1896–1975), b. Kingston; educ. Kingston Grammar and New College, Oxford; joined father, Herbert, in insurance business until outbreak of First World War; captain in East Surrey Regiment, wounded Ypres, six months in hospital; ten years as claims adjuster with Sun Insurance Co; joined in amateur theatricals and wrote plays for company. After rejection by numerous theatres, *Journey's End* prod. by Stage Society with Laurence Olivier as Stanhope (December 1928) and, with Shaw's help, at Savoy (1929). Huge success, after which became full-time writer. Other plays, none as successful, incl.: *Badger's Green* (1930); *Windfall* (1933); *St Helena*, in collaboration with Jeanne de Casalis (1935); *Miss Mable* (1948); *Home at Seven* (1950) and *The Long Sunset*, about Britain during collapse of Roman Empire, performed on radio and at Birmingham Rep (1955). Well-received novel, *A Fortnight in September* (1931). Registered as a mature student at Oxford but left to write film scripts for Universal, incl. some of most distinguished of time: *The Invisible Man* (1933); *Goodbye Mr Chips* (1933); *No Highway* (1951) and *The Dam Busters* (1955). Fellow of Royal Society of Antiquarians.

No Leading Lady (1968). (Autobiography.)

SIEVEKING, Lance[lot de Giberne] (1896–1972), b. Harrow; educ. Switzerland and Cambridge; mother a suffragist and he became active in suffrage movement; pilot in First World War, gained DSO; prisoner of war. Wrote novels and some verse, incl. nonsense verse. Began broadcasting, 1926, responsible for feature, *The Wheel of Time* with the Sitwells, among others. Appointed to Research Section of BBC, 1928, a small experimental group with interest in creative possibilities of radio; absorbed into Drama, 1929. Numerous radio plays and features incl. much discussed *The First Kaleidoscope* (1928). Produced Pirandello, *The Man with a Flower in his Mouth* as first televised play in Britain, 1930. Adaptation of *The Strange Case of Dr Jeckyll and Mr Hyde* (1956).

The Stuff of Radio (1934). (Autobiography and discussion of radio medium with selection of own short plays.)

SHIRLEY, Arthur (1853–1925), jobbing actor and writer, wrote over 120 plays, mostly melodramas, many in collaboration with such as G. R. Sims, incl. with Sutton Vane, *Saved; or a Wife's Peril* (1885), one of the source plays of Wilde's *Lady Windermere's Fan*. Among the more notable of his many plays: *The Cross of Honour* (1890); *Straight for the Heart*, with Benjamin Landeck (1896); *The Sight of St Paul's* with Sutton Vane (1896) and, the farce, *Mrs Othello* (1893), for Toole.

SIMS, G[eorge] R[obert] (1847–1922), columnist for *The Referee* and prolific melodramatist; house writer of farces for the Adelphi. *The Lights o' London* (1881) was a great success, revived 1891; *The Black Domino* (1893). Many collaborations incl., with Grundy, *The Glass of Fashion* (1883); with Robert Buchanen, *The Trumpet Call* (1891); with Shirley, *The Star of India* (1898). Dramatist of old school but supported Independent Theatre and provided £100 to fund production of George Moore, *The Strike at Arlingford* in 1893.

SLATER, Montague (1902–56), wrote for *The Observer* and *The Telegraph*; joined Communist Party (1930); chief editor *New Left Review*. *Stay Down Miner* (1936), originally a novel, then a play, produced by Left Theatre with music by Benjamin Britten. Instigator and collaborator on numerous left-wing theatrical events including, in 1938, writing the words for Pageant of the Co-operative Movement, Wembley Stadium, and collaborating on Living Newspaper, *Busmen*, under the 'editorship' of John Allen, and, in 1939, words and production of *Pageant of South Wales*, in celebration of 100th anniversary of Chartist Movement, performed simultaneously on May Day in Abertillery, Pontypool and Ystradgynlais with 6,000 participants, music by Bamford Griffiths. Fought in International Brigade in Spanish Civil War. Head of scripts in film division of Ministry of Information during Second World War. F. quarterly, *Theatre Today* (1947). Wrote libretto for Britten's *Peter Grimes* (1946); novels include *Once a Jolly Swagman* (1944) and *The Inhabitants* (1948).

SOWERBY, Githa (1876–1970), b. North-east England; wrote eleven children's books, many illustrated by her sister, Millicent. Her play, *Rutherford and Son*, prod. Court Th., 1912, transferring to Little, then Vaudeville, ran for 133 perfs and was well received in New York – central character a woman, ex-office worker who stands up to snobbish bullying father-in-law; only woman dramatist mentioned in Emma Goldman, *The Social Significance of Modern Drama* (1914), where warmly praised. Other plays include one-act, *Before Breakfast* (1912); the rather sentimental *Sheila* (1917); and *The Stepmother* (1924).

> Publisher: Sidgwick and Jackson.
> *Rutherford and Son* reissued in Fitzsimmons L. and V. Gardner, eds, *New Woman Plays* (1991). (Production by the National Theatre, 1994.)

SUTRO, Alfred (1863–1933), b. London; father, naturalised immigrant from Germany; great-grandfather, a rabbi; educ. City of London School; employed in family wholesale business but, after marrying artist Susan Isaacs, 1894, moved to Paris where he became English translator of Maeterlinck, including essays, *The Treasure of the Humble* (1897) and the play, *Aglavaine and Selysette*, included in Barker's first Court season in 1904. Also trans. Renard, *Poil de Carrotte* as *Carrots* (1900). Founder member with Archer and Robins of New Century Th. Tendency in own plays to pick up and rework current ideas so moves from H. A. Jones style Society Drama to New Drama themes, usually light tone, often aristocratic setting. First success, comedy with Arthur Bourchier, *The Chili Widow* (1895); first non-collaborative success, *The Walls of Jericho* which ran for fifteen months (1904); 40 plays in all.

SYNGE, John Millington (1871–1909), b. Wicklow to respectable, clerical branch of Anglo-Irish protestant land-owning family, only one of whom (a cousin) ever saw his plays on the stage; mother, a fundamentalist Christian. Moved to Germany to study in 1893 and then Paris, where he wrote symbolist poetry. Yeats, whom he met in 1896, was instrumental in persuading him to return to Ireland and visit Aran Islands and the West. Lived in Aran Islands, 1898; kept detailed notebook and recorded lives in photographs. Became the outstanding dramatist of the first phase of the Abbey Th. and played leading part in its administration as one of three directors with Yeats and Lady Gregory from 1905 to early death from Hodgkin's Disease. One-act comedy, *In the Shadow of the Glen* (1903), attacked in *United Irishman* for slight on Irish womanhood; next play, the stark one-act, *Riders to the Sea*, well received (subsequently set as an opera by Vaughan

Williams). Full-length play, *The Tinker's Wedding*, not performed until much later (Abbey première, 1971) but two other comedies, *The Well of the Saints* (1905) and *The Playboy of the Western World* were. Productions of the latter at Abbey (1907) and in New York (1911) notoriously sparking Nationalist riots. Last play, *Deirdre of the Sorrows*, a tragedy, unfinished at his death, performed posthumously, 1910. Loved Abbey actress, Maire O'Neill (Molly Allgood), to whom he became engaged.

> Publisher: Oxford University Press.
> *The Aran Islands* (Dublin, 1907). (Notebooks of experiences in West.)
> Saddlemyer, A., ed., *Some Letters of J. M. Synge to Lady Gregory and W. B. Yeats* (Dublin, 1971).
> Yeats, W. B., *J. M. Synge and the Ireland of his Time* (1910, repr. in *Essays and Introductions*, 1961).
> Kilroy, J., *The 'Playboy' Riots* (Dublin, 1971).
> Grene, N., ed., *The Synge Manuscripts in the Library of Trinity College, Dublin* (Dublin, 1971).

See: Skelton, R., *The Writings of J. M. Synge* (1971).
> Harman, M., ed., *J. M. Synge: Centenary Papers* (1972).
> Grene, N., *Synge: A Critical Study of the Plays* (1975). (Outstanding among commentaries on the plays.)
> Kiberd, D., *Synge and the Irish Language* (1979).
> King, M., *The Drama of J. M. Synge* (1985).

THOMAS, Brandon (1856–1914), actor and playwright. *Charley's Aunt* (1892) a farce, most popular single play of 1890s, ran for four years with 1,469 perfs and persists in the English repertoire when others equally regarded at the time have vanished. Thomas played title role (undergraduate disguised as elderly aunt) in many revivals. Among other plays, none as successful, *Comrades*, with B. C. Stephenson (1882); *Marriage* (1894); *The Swordsman's Daughter*, a melodrama, with Clement Scott (1895). Adapted foreign plays, incl. *Clever Alice* from Willbrant's *Die Maler*, acted by Janet Achurch in 1889.

THOMAS, Tom (1902–77), b. Dalston; father, a basket maker and Liberal trade unionist; left school aged fourteen, becoming stockbroker's clerk. Thrilled by Russian Revolution and finding Robert Tressell's *The Ragged Trousered Philanthropists* revelatory, became a socialist. Member of Queen's Players, performing in Shakespeare and Shaw; joined Philharmonic Choir, 1919; started Hackney Labour Dramatic Group, 1926, which became Hackney People's Players and branch of Workers' Theatre Movement, 1928, playing Shaw, Sutro, Capek, *RUR*, Rice, *The Adding Machine*, and active in nationwide development of Workers' Theatre Movement. Adapted *Ragged Trousered Philanthropists* for stage, performed mainly in local clubs but licensed for public perf. in Edmonton Town Hall, 1929. Other writing for stage included two 1928 one-act plays: *Women of Kirbinsk*, set in Russian Village at time of Revolution and *The Fight Goes On*, set in English mining village during General Strike, includes marching and singing of large demonstration, modelled on Hauptmann's *The Weavers*; also, in 1929, a revue, *Strike Up*. In 1940s became Treasurer of People's Theatre, Newcastle-Upon-Tyne. Left Labour Party in 1926 for Communist Party because of policies over General Strike; rejoined after Second World War.

> 'A Propertyless Theatre for the Propertyless Class' (1977), included in

Samuel, R., E. MacColl and S. Cosgrove, eds, *Theatres of the Left* (1985). (An account of Workers' Theatre Movement by Thomas.)

TRAVERS, Ben (1886–1980), father, a company director with interests in tea and dried fruit; educ. Charterhouse where appalled by bullying; joined father's business, various posts abroad; impressed by reading Pinero's plays; back in London he became reader for the Bodley Head; joined RAF in First World War. His novel, *The Dippers*, dramatised by Sidney Blow for Charles Hawtrey (1922). His own farce, *A Cuckoo in the Nest* (1925), taken by Tom Walls and Ralph Lynon at Aldwych, followed by nine hit farces for Walls incl. *Rookery Nook* (1926), *Thark* (1927), *Plunder* (1928). Retirement for many years in Rye and then service flat in Victoria. Following abolition of censorship returned to theatre after twenty-three years silence with *The Bed Before Yesterday* (1975) and then *Plunder* (1976) and *Barnaby Ridge* (1938) revived.

WILDE, Oscar (1854–1900), b. Dublin; 2nd son of Sir William (an eye surgeon, d. 1876) and Jane Francesca (Nationalist writer under pseudonym Speranza and great niece of Charles Maturin, author of *Melmoth, The Wanderer*); educ. Portora Royal School, Enniskillen and Trinity College Dublin, where won medal for Greek and scholarship to Magdalene, Oxford; brilliant if outrageous student, obtained first-class degree and, in 1878, Newdigate Prize for poem 'Ravenna'. Travelled to Greece and to Italy where flirted with Catholic conversion; heroes included Morris, Pater, Ruskin and, initially, Whistler; already notorious as aesthete and self-publicist. Renown as raconteur and wit, proved on lecture tour of America, 1882–83, paid for by D'Oyly Carte as preparation for Gilbert and Sullivan's *Patience* in which aestheticism satirised. Term 'oscarism' current in late 1880s to define epigrammatic witticism. Substance given to fame with publication of *Poems* (1881); two early plays, *Vera or the Nihilists* (1880) and *The Duchess of Padua* (1883; prod NYk., 1891), and *The Happy Prince and Other Tales* (1888). M. Constance Lloyd, 1884; two sons: Cyril (b. 1885) and Vyvyan (b. 1886). Earned living by journalism: editor *Woman's World*, 1887–89. Befriended Elizabeth Robins, Lily Langtry. As frequent visitor to Paris, *au fait* with current theatre, friends incl. Gide, Mendès. Sensational publication of *The Picture of Dorian Grey* (1890) and, following year, wrote *Salomé* for Bernhardt, in French, but banned while in rehearsal (trans. Wilde and Afred Douglas, publ. 1894; prod. Théâtre d'Oeuvre, 1896; Stage Society, 1906; ban lifted, 1927). Obsessed with Douglas, whom he met in 1891, the year he published, *The Soul of Man Under Socialism*; *Lord Arthur Savile's Crime and Other Stories* and a collection of essays, *Intentions*. Commissioned by Alexander for St James's, *Lady Windermere's Fan* (1892) – earned Wilde £7,000; followed, in quick succession, by *A Woman of No Importance* (prod. Tree, 1893); *An Ideal Husband* (January, 1895), culminating in *The Importance of Being Earnest* (February, 1895). Sued Marquess of Queensbury (father of Douglas) for calling him 'sodomite'. When libel action failed, following testimony from male prostitutes, Wilde arrested on charges of indecency, Section 11 of Criminal Law Amendment Act; found guilty after retrial, first jury having failed to agree. Sentence of two years' hard labour served mainly in Reading jail. While in prison, declared bankrupt; mother died; names of Constance and children changed to Holland; Wilde forbidden to see children again. Wrote *De Profundis* as open letter to Douglas: intense account of suffering caused by lover and search for self-knowledge; trusted to Robert Ross, who became literary executor and deposited it in British Museum, 1909 (selections pub., 1905; complete edn, 1960). Moved to France on release, assuming name Sebastian Melmoth; Constance died, 1898; wrote *The Ballad of Reading Gaol,* pub. under prison number, C33 (1898), but projected plays never completed. Lived briefly with Douglas again but quarrelled. Travelled in Italy, Switzerland, France, settling in Paris, where died in poverty at Hôtel d'Alsace; remains transferred to Père Lachaise cemetery, 1909.

> Hart Davis, R., ed., *The Letters of Oscar Wilde* (1962).
> —— ed., *More Letters of Oscar Wilde* (Oxford, 1987).
> Ransome, A., *Oscar Wilde* (1912).
> Pearson, H., *The Life of Oscar Wilde* (1946).
> Montgomery Hyde, H., *The Trials of Oscar Wilde* (1948). (Includes transcript of proceedings of trials.)
> Ellmann, R., *Oscar Wilde* (1987).

See: Ross, R., ed., *Wilde: Complete Works* (1908). (Valuable prefaces and notes.)
> Gide, A., *Oscar Wilde, A Study* (1905; 1949).
> Montague, C. E., 'Oscar Wilde's Comedies', *Dramatic Values* (1911).
> Tydeman, W., ed., *Wilde, Comedies: A Selection of Critical Essays* (1982).
> Worth, K., *Oscar Wilde* (1983). (Excellent short study, demonstrating modernity of Wilde's comedies.)
> Gagnier, R., *Idylls of the Marketplace: Oscar Wilde and the Victorian Public* (Stanford, 1986). (Very useful contextual material.)
> Raby, P., *Oscar Wilde* (Cambridge, 1988). (Concise with telling discussion of individual plays.)
> Powell, K., *Oscar Wilde and the Theatre of the 1890s* (Cambridge, 1990). (Wilde in context, demonstrates remarkable extent of his absorption of contemporary drama.)
> Small, I., *Oscar Wilde Revalued: An Essay on New Materials and Methods of Research* (Queensboro', NC, 1993). (Discusses shift in valuation of Wilde in last fifteen years.)

WILLIAMS, Emlyn (1905–87), b. Mostyn, N. Wales; father, a miner then greengrocer, then iron-works foreman; mother, strict Calvinist; Welsh speaker till aged ten; encouraged by local teacher, scholarship to St Julien's, Switzerland then Christchurch, Oxford; one-act play, *Vigil*, prod. Oxford. First full-length play, *Full Moon* (1927), prod. Oxford Playhouse and London (1929); *Spring 1600* (set in Burbage's company) prod. Gielgud. Thrillers, including *A Murder has Been Arranged* (1930); *The Late Christopher Bean* (1934), toured by Scottish National Players. Regularly acted in own plays including lead in best-known work, *Night Must Fall* (1935). Story of own education in *The Corn is Green* (1938), with Sybil Thorndike as teacher. Later in life one-man shows incl. on Dickens and Dylan Thomas.

> *Emlyn: An Early Autobiography 1927–1935* (1973).

See: Hope-Wallace, P., 'Emlyn Williams, Playwright, Actor, Producer', *Theatre Arts*, 32 (January 1948), pp. 16–19.

YEATS, William Butler (1865–1939), poet, essayist and dramatist. Anglo-Irish Sligo family; brother Jack, a painter; at age twenty-one met and much influenced by Nationalist, John O'Leary; following year, left Ireland, spending time in Paris as well as London. Admirer of William Morris; early poetry notably pre-Raphaelite. Conceived unrequited passion for Republican, Maud Gonne, 1889, for whom wrote most nationalistic play, *Cathleen ni Houlihan* (1902). First performed play, *The Land of Heart's Desire* (1894), staged with Shaw's *Arms and the Man* by

Florence Farr, financed by Annie Horniman. Impressed by Maeterlinck's *Pelléas et Mélisande*. Main force behind establishment of Irish Literary Th. f. 1898 with Augusta Gregory and Edward Martyn: manifesto stressed oratory and imagination; Dublin-based from 1900; joined by Fay brothers and gained financial security when Annie Horniman bought Abbey Th., 1904, and leased it rent free; same year, Abbey tour to London included Yeats's *The King's Threshold* and *The Pot of Broth* (written with Augusta Gregory). Closely involved in running of th., editing its magazine, *Beltaine* (1900) and *Samhain* (1901–5, 1908), planning its programmes and general administrative responsibilities, largely to exclusion of poetry, 1904–10; difficult colleague, partly because committed to own idea of poetic and specifically Irish th., separating from Colum and Martyn (who founded Theatre of Ireland), 1906; Fays, 1908, and Horniman, 1910. Tri-partite directorship with Synge and Gregory from 1908. Defended Synge during *Playboy* attacks and O'Casey during *The Plough and the Stars* but rejected Synge, *The Tinker's Wedding*, Shaw, *John Bull's Other Island* and, disastrously, O'Casey, *The Silver Tassie*. 1898–1912 wrote plays for the public th. mainly with Irish heroic themes, notably: *The Countess Cathleen* (1899), *On Baile's Strand* (1904), *Dierdre* (1907). Correspondence with Gordon Craig, who designed costumes for Abbey and sent set of screens and model theatre, used 1911 for revised *The Hour Glass* (1st version, 1903). Friend of Ezra Pound; worked with him on Japanese Nōh drama, 1913–15, leading to *At the Hawk's Well* (London, 1916), first of four Plays for Dancers, others being, *The Only Jealousy of Emer* (1922), *Calvary* (wr. 1920, prod. 1960) and *The Dreaming of the Bones* (wr. 1917, prod. 1932). M. 1917; one daughter; awarded Nobel Prize, 1923. Frequent guest at Coole Park, where later chamber plays performed. Persuaded Ninette de Valois to set up Abbey School of Ballet, 1927; attempt to establish poets' th. with Eliot and Auden collapsed. Versions of Sophocles' Oedipus plays (Abbey Th., 1926, 1927) enjoyed great success, followed by the dance play, *Fighting the Waves* (1929) and the séance play, *The Words Upon the Window Pane* (1930) in which spirit of Swift called up. Last plays: the short *Purgatory* (1938), much admired by T. S. Eliot and *The Death of Cuchulain* (wr. 1938, prod. 1945). Prolific poet: notable editions at different stages of his development: *In the Seven Woods* (1903); *The Wild Swans at Coole* (1919); his major poetic achievement, *The Tower* (1928) and *Last Poems* (1939).

Publisher: Macmillan.
Autobiographies (1927; 1955).
Essays and Introductions (1961).
Bax, C., ed., *Florence Farr, Bernard Shaw, W. B. Yeats: Letters* (1946).
Wade, A., ed., *The Letters of W. B. Yeats* (1954).
Ellman, R., *Yeats: The Man and the Masks* (1978).

See: Henn, T. R., *The Harvest of Tragedy* (1954).
       Wilson, F. A. C., *Yeats's Iconography* (1960).
       Ure, P., *Yeats the Playwright* (1963). (Makes high claims for the plays.)
       Vendler, H. H., *Yeats 'Vision' and the Later Plays* (1963). (Dismissive of plays as drama.)
       Moore, J. R., *Masks of Love and Death: Yeats as Dramatist* (Ithaca, NY, 1971.)
       Donoghue, D., *Yeats* (1971). (Measured account of the plays.)
       Jeffares, A. N., *A Commentary on the Collected Plays of W. B. Yeats* (1975).
       Flannery, J. W., *W. B. Yeats and the Idea of a Theatre* (Toronto, 1976). (Good on Yeats and Craig.)
       Parkin, A., *The Dramatic Imagination of W. B. Yeats* (Dublin, 1978).

Dorn, K., *Players and Painted Stage* (Brighton, 1884). (Insights into original staging of Yeats's plays.)

Taylor, R., *A Reader's Guide to the Plays of W. B. Yeats* (1984).

ZANGWILL, Israel (1864–1926), novelist and playwright; b. Whitechapel, of Jewish immigrant parents: father, Moses, from Latvia, mother, Ellen, from Poland; early life in Bristol then returned Whitechapel 1872 where educ. Jews' Free School and became pupil-teacher, leaving 1888 when wrote novel with fellow teacher, Louis Cowen, *The Premier and the Painter*, followed by one-act play, *The Great Demonstration* (1892). BA London University, 1884. Became Zionist, 1895, following meeting with Theodore Herzl but growing belief after turn of century in need for tolerance and assimilation; m. Edith Ayrton, 1903, feminist and novelist. Plays incl.: *Six Persons*, farce with Cicely Cardew-style *ingénue* and ran for 92 perfs at Haymarket (1893); *The Revolted Daughter*, dir. Granville Barker (1901); *Merely Mary Ann* (NYk., 1903; London, 1904), sentimental love story of poor people who make good. Fascination with American immigrant society registered in dramatisation of own novel, *Children of the Ghetto* (1899) and *The Melting Pot* (NYk., 1909; London, 1914).

See: Jackson, H., 'Israel Zangwill', *The Bookman*, 46 (May 1914), pp. 67–73.

Wohlgelernter, G., *Israel Zangwill: A Study* (1964).

Index

(Note: bracketed page numbers refer to bibliographical entries. Plays, novels, theatres and individuals mentioned only in passing are not included in this index.)